GABRIEL MIRÓ:

His private library and
his literary background

IAN R. MACDONALD

GABRIEL MIRÓ:

His private library and his literary background

TAMESIS BOOKS LIMITED

LONDON

Colección Támesis

SERIE A - MONOGRAFÍAS, XLI

Depósito Legal: M. 10.855-1975

Printed in Spain by Talleres Gráficos de EDICIONES CASTILLA, S. A.
Maestro Alonso, 23 - Madrid

for

TAMESIS BOOKS LIMITED
LONDON

TO MY WIFE
    FAY

CONTENTS

CONTENTS

PREFACE

The library of Gabriel Miró, preserved with affection and concern by his daughters, is the starting-point for the major part of this study. The sad death in 1972 of Doña Olympia Miró, who had looked after it following the death of her sister Clemencia, makes it impossible for me to thank her for all her kindnesses and for her hospitality, but I wish to record at the outset my debt to her generosity in allowing me to spend as much time as I needed in the library and in making that time pleasant and fruitful.

I also wish to thank Professor Edmund King for his advice and help when I was starting research on Gabriel Miró's work. In Alicante I should like to thank Mrs. Doris Haselden, and Don Vicente Ramos, librarian of the Biblioteca Gabriel Miró, and in Valencia, Professor Sánchez-Castañer. Professor L. J. Woodward and Mr. Terence May supervised my research work: I am grateful to them both for their advice and encouragement throughout, as I am to my colleagues Anthony Clarke and John Cummins. I have also been fortunate in my typists: first my wife and then Margaret Garvie have coped skilfully with the complications of drafts and manuscript.

Finally I wish to thank the Carnegie Trust for the Universities of Scotland, and Aberdeen University for their generous financial help.

ABBREVIATIONS

WORKS OF GABRIEL MIRÓ

EC	*Obras completas, Edición conmemorativa,* 12 vols., Barcelona, 1932-1949
OC	*Obras completas,* fourth ed., one vol., Madrid, 1961
Glosas	*Glosas de Sigüenza,* Buenos Aires, 1952
Mujer	*La mujer de Ojeda,* Alicante, 1901
Hilván	*Hilván de escenas,* Alicante, 1903
DVi	*Del vivir,* Alicante, 1904
Amigos	*Los amigos, los amantes y la muerte,* Barcelona [1915]
'San Vicente'	'Estudio histórico del templo de San Vicente de Ávila', *Clavileño,* No. 16 (July-Aug. 1952), 65-72
'Santo Tomás'	'Estudio histórico de la iglesia y convento de Santo Tomás de Ávila', *Clavileño,* No. 17 (Sept.-Oct. 1952), 66-71
Huerto	*Del huerto provinciano, Nómada,* Barcelona, 1930

OTHER WORKS

BAE	*Biblioteca de autores españoles*
King, *Humo*	Gabriel Miró, *El humo dormido,* ed. E. L. King, New York, 1967
Ramos, *Literatura*	Vicente Ramos, *Literatura alicantina,* Barcelona, 1966
Ramos, *Mundo*	Vicente Ramos, *El mundo de Gabriel Miró,* second edition, Madrid, 1970
Ramos, *Vida*	Vicente Ramos, *Vida y obra de Gabriel Miró,* Madrid, 1955

Note on quotations

Since Miró uses suspension periods thus ... with great frequency, confusion would arise between these and periods indicating ellipsis. Therefore, in quotations from Miró (and not other writers), ellipsis is indicated thus (...).

INTRODUCTION

*La palabra es la misma idea hecha carne, es la idea
viva transparentándose gozosa, palpitante, porque
ha sido poseída.*

GABRIEL MIRÓ.

Gabriel Miró died in 1930 at the age of fifty. His art had matured
slowly and it was not until the nineteen-twenties that he had published
his masterpiece, the novels *Nuestro padre San Daniel* and *El obispo
leproso,* novels that are more properly seen as one single novel in two
parts. Peritonitis robbed Spain of a writer from whom major work
could still be expected, and by truncating his career made it harder to
perceive its overall meaning.

Born and brought up in Alicante, Miró's early years as a writer
were broadly linked with *modernismo,* but almost at once, though for a
time in parallel with the admiration for *modernismo,* there began a process of overcoming the *modernista* refusal to look the world in the face.
This double drive, towards *modernista* fashion, and towards transcend-
ing it, is expressed clearly in *Las cerezas del cementerio,* the novel published in 1910, where the hero, though viewed with deep sympathy, is
seen as falling victim to the illusions of the symbolist artist-hero.
Around 1912 Miró began to be seriously interested in the study of the
origins of Christianity, and of the social and cultural context of its
birth. Books on the Bible and the Middle East begin to appear in
quantity in his library. The *Figuras de la pasión del Señor* of 1916 and
1917 were the result of these studies. The problem of the nature of
fiction had arisen before in Miró's work (*Del vivir,* for example, com-
bines an account of a journey made by Miró with the narrative techniques of fiction); now in the *Figuras* Miró apparently moves away from
fiction by basing his prose work on an intimately known set of historical episodes. Yet the crucial development is not any abandonment of

1

fiction, but the introduction of the use of documentation from scholarly sources as opposed to the use of personal experience and traditional literary models. The documentation, as with all Miró's materials, was not used directly to provide an air of realism, but as raw material on which the writer's imagination could work.

After the publication of the *Figuras* Miró continued to plan and work on further sets of *Figuras,* but the major step forward now was to fuse documentation, personal experience and literary models in the two novels of Oleza, *Nuestro padre San Daniel* and *El obispo leproso.* Oleza is Orihuela, where Miró was at the Jesuit school that figures in the novels. He searched his own memories and researched the social and historical background to create his study of Oleza. With these novels and the other work of the twenties Miró emerged almost as a contemporary of the young poets whose work had flowered after the new start at the end of the Great War.

But though the Oleza novels share the concern for verbal density and precision of the young poets as well as their love of imagery, the rich and complex writing also serves more traditional purposes, though these were further disguised by an overall structure that was based more on the thematic linking of scenes than on plot in the conventional sense. Miró gives us magnificent studies of his major characters, of their relationships, and of the conflicts within and between them : sexuality and repression, generosity and inhibition, open-hearted and restrictive views of life. Repression leads to subtle cruelties or occasionally breaks out into savage action, while generosity can all too easily crumble to sentimentality. Few characters can walk the tight-rope that involves love for others and self-discipline as well as penetrating imagination.

All this is set in a social and political context : new and old are in conflict, Carlism and Liberalism fight it out, class conflict is evident, and the Church is split between conservatives and liberals, between legalists and those who place charity above all. But the achievement that makes these novels especially rewarding is the way in which Miró forces social and individual studies to illumine each other. Social conflicts are seen to be expressions of conflict between psychological types, while attitudes are seen to spring in part from social environment. In this way Miró contrives to see the Spanish social conflict of his time in terms of its psychological roots without losing sight of the rôle of social structures. If this account of the Oleza novels seems to relate Miró to the concern of his contemporaries for the problem of Spain, this is only one level of the novels. At a lower level these are also novels of a region and a moment, but at other levels they have the universal validity of every great novel : the power of Miró's language and imagery

2

enables us to see, with a shudder of recognition, deep into human motivation, as he uncovers the layers of self-mystification through which we work savagery on each other and on ourselves. Only the love that emerges from the disciplined imagination of a Don Magín can offer an escape.

This emphasis on the individual is of course a part of Miró's liberal outlook: it is in this sense that the novels are traditional, for many of their themes stem from the nineteenth-century novel, while others, together with the use of thematic structures, stand in line of descent from the major Spanish tradition, and especially from Cervantes. Miró's contribution lies in the richness of insight that his language enabled him to capture, and in his widening of the scope of individual motivation to bring in the unconscious and to take account of our unacknowledged urges to cruelty and destruction while still asserting the traditional answer of love.

We have seen Miró's links with his near contemporaries of 1898 and *modernismo,* but the differences are clear and more important. Miró's life reflects this separateness. He did not follow his contemporaries in going to Madrid, but continued to work from the coast until the age of forty-one. Even then he disliked Madrid literary life and in the summers fled to Alicante. It is perhaps this difference from other writers that has led to perplexities in evaluating his work and to a misunderstanding of his aims. In spite of his popularity with the younger writers of 1927 his reputation since then has been a curiously ambivalent one, and it is this problem that needs tackling.

Gabriel Miró is commonly thought of as a writer the riches of whose language conceal a lack of depth and large-scale cohesion. This majority view is documented in detail in the first part of this book: Miró is mostly seen as an 'estilista', a writer who specialises in fine writing but who has little to say. But there is a significant number of critics, writing from a wide variety of points of view, who have strongly contested the commonplace assessment. L. J. Woodward, Joaquín Casalduero, Alfred W. Becker, Edmund L. King, Joaquín de Entrambasaguas, Ricardo Gullón, and, most recently, G. G. Brown, [1] all have different attitudes to Miró, but all are emphatic that conventional criticism has misunderstood Miró. Sharing this dissatisfaction I have looked at Miró's literary background and his work in relation to it to see if the evidence supports a different view.

Since the overthrow or at least the profound modification of the traditional view requires some explanation of how so many in the past

---

[1] Woodward, p. 110; Casalduero, p. 220; Becker, p. 189; King, *Humo,* p. 16; Entrambasaguas, p. 597; Gullón, p. 125; Brown, pp. 45-53 (full references will be found in the bibliography).

could be so wrong, or at least so partial, I start by examining how the critical consensus was reached. I shall argue that Miró suffered at first from the inappropriate criteria of contemporary critics, who saw form and content as almost entirely separable (the word 'estilista' presupposes such a separation), while Miró himself saw the idea and the word as one flesh. Later, in the twenties, his work was admired on much more appropriate grounds, yet it was still partially admired, because the young poets and critics were especially preoccupied with language and small-scale forms and saw their own interests reflected in Miró's work. The case for Miró as a writer of extended prose forms was allowed to go by default. Miró's death allowed this situation to crystallise, and the 'estilista' argument has persisted since then, with condemnatory overtones of 'dehumanisation'.

The second part of the book describes Miró's private library and the third his references to and quotations from other writers while the final part attempts to show how the view of Miró developed in these chapters is borne out by the text of *Del vivir*.

The book is a revised version of a doctoral thesis presented at Aberdeen University in 1970 entitled 'The literary background of Gabriel Miró'. I hope that I have avoided the worst defects of the species, but, as Miró writes in *Años y leguas,* '¡Levante! Levante era más poderoso que la sabiduría británica'.

I

MIRÓ AND HIS CRITICS

At the beginning of 1901, the year in which his work first appeared in print, Gabriel Miró was twenty-one. He was engaged in a thorough study of the Spanish and ancient classics. He had recently graduated from Granada University with the customary law degree. He was about to write his first novel, later excluded from his Complete Works, *La mujer de Ojeda,* an obvious transposition of Valera's *Pepita Jiménez.* And on 16 November he was to marry Clemencia Maignon. In this year that so clearly marks his entry into adulthood, Miró contributed to a volume entitled *De mi barrio,*[1] a collection of articles on persons and places in the Alicante suburb of Benalúa. Miró's parents had moved to Benalúa from the centre of town in 1883 and in *De mi barrio* we read how the new suburb had been modelled on 'British ideas', with straight streets, modern sewage, and hygiene very much in mind. The men and families described, whom Miró knew as the society of which he was a part at this time, breathe the same sturdy bourgeois liberalism that comes through in their housing ideas. Benalúa is now a declining district but the novelty of its terraced houses with gardens is still obvious. Miró's father, Juan Miró Moltó, was a typical enough member of this society. *Ingeniero Jefe de primera clase,* he was the senior official in the provincial *Jefatura de Obras Públicas.* Alicante was a traditionally liberal province (in the 1901 elections to the *Cortes* eight liberals and two conservatives were returned) and the town's establishment was largely liberal, one into which the Miró family fitted comfortably. The issue of *El Ibero,* a magazine edited by a close friend of Miró, for 1 January 1902 lists the officials of the province and town — again and again one comes across names associated with Miró. But this was of course property-owning, middle-class, liberalism: Juan Miró Moltó was a member of the *Liga de contribu-*

[1] Ed. Mendaro del Alcázar.

yentes de Alicante y su provincia,[2] an association for the protection of property against excessive taxation.

This society in which Miró was brought up was one in which the arts were respected. *De mi barrio* tells us that Juan Miró Ferrer, Miró's elder brother, was a good pianist and amateur composer and fond of Verdi. Gabriel Miró himself and his fiancée and her family all enjoyed music. Oscar Esplá, the composer, has described how he met Miró at a chamber concert given in a private studio in Alicante in the early years of the century: 'Miró tenía afición y cultura musicales, contra lo habitual en escritores españoles.'[3]

As a child Miró had evidently been brought up with an affection and concern that were reflected in his personality. In 1887, at the age of eight, Miró was sent to the Jesuit *Colegio de Santo Domingo* in Orihuela, an experience whose harshness found expression in 'El señor Cuenca y su sucesor' in *Libro de Sigüenza*. His father completed a questionnaire for the school that has recently been discovered. In answer to '¿Cuál es su carácter?', Juan Miró writes: 'Bondadoso en alto grado.' And to '¿Por qué medios se consigue de él la aplicación y la enmienda de sus defectos?', he replies: 'Con muchísimo cariño y afabilidad hasta exagerada' — advice that can hardly have appeared sound doctrine to the teachers of Orihuela. Juan Miró also requests that Miró attend special classes in music.[4]

The main features of these years preceding the crucial ones of 1901 to 1903 have been well summed up by E. L. King. He brings out the lasting effect on Miró's imagination of the Ignatian Spiritual Exercises used at the Orihuela school, an influence more profound than the severity of the college. He points also to the influence of Miró's uncle Lorenzo Casanova who taught painting in Alicante until his death in 1900. King rejects Miró's own reason (the death of his uncle) for not becoming a painter and suggests instead that Miró was at least as much influenced by his uncle in his reading as in his interest in painting. For Lorenzo Casanova was an avid reader of the latest French and Spanish books. King sums up: 'But the expansion of his intellectual horizons, the sharpening of his vision, and the beginnings of an aesthetic doctrine were not Miró's only acquisitions from his uncle's studio. He also learned to share the attitude of painters as artists.' Finally King suggests that Miró's practice of reading aloud to his friend Figueras Pacheco, who became blind at eighteen, helped to refine his awareness of language.[5]

[2] Ripoll, *Memoria.*
[3] *Evocación de Gabriel Miró*, p. 9.
[4] Roig, 'Diálogo con el padre de Gabriel Miró'.
[5] King, *Humo*, pp. 23-9.

In Miró's own contribution to *De mi barrio,* on 'Domingo Carratalá', and his first published work (full of exaggerated inversions: 'Es mi paleta en colores pobre'), Miró exalts art: 'Soy yo de los que creen que el arte no se define, como todo sentimiento, como el cariño, la pasión... Todo esto es subjetivo y grandioso.' He denies the notion that art is a body of rules: without 'inspiración' Wagner, Verdi, and Gounod could not have succeeded. If only all men were artists, crime, selfishness, and evil would disappear 'porque no comprendo que exista el arte que lo sublima todo en un corazón ruin'. [6] The beautiful and the good: the Platonic fusion of ethics and aesthetics is Miró's starting-point as a young writer, though he soon lost his faith in the immaculacy of the individual artist. The important point is that the ethical is from the beginning present in Miró. Only because it is disguised by being fused with the aesthetic have so many critics for so long dismissed (or praised) Miró as an ivory-tower aesthete, an artist devoid of moral insight. Such a judgement would surely have seemed a contradiction in terms to Miró.

In another article in *De mi barrio* the editor of *El Ibero,* Miró's friend Francisco Figueras Pacheco, writes on 'Don Gabriel Miró Ferrer': 'Gabriel Miró reúne, entre muchas buenas cualidades, todas las condiciones que pueden exigirse a un orador.' And again: 'Miró está llamado a ser un hombre de los que moldean opiniones y dirigen voluntades a su capricho' (p. 44). He imagines the future Miró in parliament, a prophecy curiously remote both from the retiring, private writer that Miró was to become and from the sensitive child that he had been. Also interestingly, Figueras makes no mention of his friend as a writer. Evidently Miró had not yet begun to devote himself to literature above all else: in *De mi barrio* he draws his examples from the art of music; as we have seen, he had also spent time studying painting with his uncle Lorenzo Casanova; now, early in 1901, Figueras sees him as an orator, not a writer. But if Miró's vocation was still uncertain it did not remain so for long. By the time that he started *Del vivir* (late 1902), Miró had, as has often been remarked, found himself as a writer.

Probably this discovery of a personal way of writing corresponds to psychological self-discovery. Esplá writes: 'La timidez de Miró no provenía de ese complejo corriente que apoca el ánimo y suspende la acción, sino de otro, en cuyo entresijo se amalgaman curiosamente la humildad y el orgullo.' [7] Miró was aware of the two poles of self-doubt and self-assertion within himself. Jiménez, the shy-agressive hero of 'Del natural', published early in 1902, hates himself and, at

[6] *De mi barrio,* pp. 46-9.
[7] *Evocación de Gabriel Miró,* p. 15.

7

the same time, feels superior to the crowd. The narrator tells us that if he had only accepted himself he would have been a success instead of a failure as an artist.[8] Pedro, in *Hilván de escenas,* a little later in 1902, but still before *Del vivir,* is trying to find a new way outside society, religion, and morality. But very soon, in *Del vivir,* just as Miró discovers a style, so too he discovers in Sigüenza a literary personality who is shy, innocent, well-intentioned, quite the opposite of aggressive or oratorical, and ironically treated. At about the same time Miró is starting on a novel, *Las cerezas del cementerio,* that will reject the notion of the artist as a necessarily superior being who has no duty to the moral code that is good for the masses. The same point of view is confirmed in *Dentro del cercado* where Luis is an example of an artist who toys with the idea of his own superiority as an excuse 'pareciéndole que si fuese excelso entre todos los hombres, podía merecer lo vedado sin sumisión a la disciplina de la ética de los medianos corazones...' (*OC,* p. 295). The context makes it clear that for Miró this is mere rationalisation. It looks as if the process of self-discovery revealed in these characters, in showing Miró his true vocation as a writer, brought the two poles of doubt and assertion closer together, so that the extreme exaltation of art and the artist became moderated as the years passed. From these formative years emerge the main characteristics that we recognise in Miró's mature work: a fundamental goodness, a striving to capture experience with total honesty, subtle ethical and psychological insight, and irony, an essential technique for the expression of that insight.

In the year 1901 Miró published *La mujer de Ojeda.* How did critics receive the work of this new worshipper at the shrine of Art? How, indeed, was Miró's work received throughout his life? The accepted textbook view of his work sees his claim on our attention as that of a great stylist, a great craftsman of the Castilian language, or even a poet who, rather oddly, chose to write in extended prose forms. How did this view, as a result of which the final evaluation of Miró's work depends on one's taste for fine writing, become established? The process is worth looking at in some detail if we wish to understand Miró aright.

The first critic *La mujer de Ojeda* had was the writer of its preface, Luis Pérez Bueno, friend, Conservative *concejal,* official of the *Sociedad Orfeón de Alicante,* and author of a book dealing with Lorenzo Casanova and his school, in which he defends the principle of art for art's sake. 'Marcar tendencia es defecto corriente en algunos grandes novelistas' (*Mujer,* p. vii), he writes, clearly sharing Miró's own outlook

[8] *El Ibero,* 16 March-16 May 1902.

8

and the rejection of the realist writers. Miró 'tiene condiciones para llegar, porque es observador y sabe ver' (p. x).

Another friend, Figueras Pacheco, reviews the book in *El Ibero* (16 November 1901). The chief object of the book is 'el rendir culto ferviente a la belleza y hacer experimentar al lector, sensaciones que estén por encima de la mortificante rusticidad del vulgo'. More than a review this is a reflection of Miró's own views. Figueras adds that the book includes many 'reflexiones filosóficas muy atinadas', the inclusion of which was a characteristic of all Miró's early work. And as a measure of the eclecticism of the reading of Miró and Figueras at this time, Figueras praises Miró for including, as Hermosilla required, excellent descriptive passages.

A final review seen is that by J. Mingot in an unknown Alicante newspaper. 'Es Gabriel Miró un poeta ante todo', gives to Mingot the honour of being probably the first to use what became a critical cliché. For Mingot, Miró's virtue is that 'nos recrea y extasía al dejarnos percibir las bellas perspectivas que ofrece el estudio del alma humana que, como imagen divina, ofrece un campo extenso, sin límites, a la observación del artista'. But, adds Mingot sternly, Miró should not think his novel is as good as Sienkiewicz's *Sin dogma.* [9]

With Miró's second novel, *Hilván de escenas* (published in 1903), there appear for the first time reviews in national journals. Two of these seem to be known [10] and the contrast with the Alicante reviews is remarkable. Instead of the enthusiastic adherence to the latest ideas of the Alicante writers, the Madrid reviewers seem to write from an older standpoint, even though one is published in *Helios,* the *modernista* review. In fact almost all the standard criticisms of Miró conspicuously missing from the reviews of *La mujer de Ojeda* appear here. Ganivet's friend Francisco Navarro y Ledesma writes in *Lectura* (3 [1903], 363-4), that Miró does not know 'lo que son las proporciones, los contrastes, los clarobscuros, toda la parte de composición pictórica y de distribución arquitectónica de una novela'. He compares Miró to 'su maestro Blasco Ibáñez' and to 'su paisano Martínez Ruiz, a quien imita con insistencia'. The first comparison is superficially justified insofar as Miró deals with themes such as the evicted peasant, and uses italicised local expressions. As for Azorín, it is suggested that the poor construction of *Hilván de escenas* is due to an attempt to copy the 'buscada incoherencia' of Martínez Ruiz. Apparently this works well

[9] Cutting seen at Biblioteca Gabriel Miró, Alicante.
[10] Inevitably this chapter does not cover every review. Occasionally periodicals have been unobtainable; in other cases, mention of a particular article has been omitted as offering nothing new.

for Azorín since his strong personality comes across through it, whereas Miró lacks this personality.

In *Helios* (10 [1903], 372), José Ruiz-Castillo, much later to become Miró's publisher, writes: 'Se trata de un libro *tendencioso.*' In spite of Miró's and Pérez Bueno's opposition to 'tendencias', this is obviously true, for Miró attacks caciquism, sexual hypocrisy, exploitation of peasants, and the stigma of illegitimacy, while in the epilogue Pedro is said to be trying to find a new way outside society: 'Sí, precisa rasgar, despreciar ese patrón de *uso* (...) que implacablemente impone la sociedad. (...) El, se apartará del ordinario camino' (*Hilván,* p. 233). His intentions turn out, as so often in Miró, to be illusions: '«¡La vida es diversa,» se dice con alientos primero, y después con quejido y deliquio de víctima, añade: ¡Pero la sociedad es una!' (p. 243).

Ruiz-Castillo offers what were to become the standard objections: 'La acción, a menudo desatendida por el autor, y a veces olvidada, no es más que un pretexto para la copia de paisajes y figuras.' And 'muy frecuentemente tan excesivo es el ímpetu con que acomete al idioma, que quedan al descubierto hasta las entrañas de las palabras, y el espectáculo, que es sangriento y humeante, sorprende al lector y le distrae del deleite estético, cuando no mata por completo la emoción'. These are precisely two of the major criticisms that would be made by Ortega in 1927 in his celebrated review of *El obispo leproso*: that the plot is a pretext to bring together otherwise unrelated passages and that the language distracts. Yet these critics praise Miró. For Navarro y Ledesma he is an 'artista ... bastante más que discreto'. For Ruiz-Castillo he is an 'hábil estilista'. Here the essential problem begins to emerge: for these writers Miró is an excellent stylist, but not much of a novelist. In a word, his writing is decorative. This criticism of Miró (and here we are not singling out these two reviewers, but considering a point of view that became commonplace) depends of course on an extreme separation of form and content; it depends on the critic believing that style is a matter of the plaster embellishments on a brick structure, of externally applied ornaments on a text that would still mean the same without its 'style', though it might be less of a pleasure to the reader. There was thus a fundamental gap between Miró's practice and his critics' working notions. Even if a decorative theory of style had been useful, say, for Galdós, it was fatal for Miró (although even in the case of Galdós the commonplace about him being a great novelist but a bad writer is very close to an absurdity). The notion of language as the dress of thought is, of course, at its most pervasive in Europe in the eighteenth century rather than the nineteenth, but in Spain it clearly remained influential much later. For example, in *De mi barrio* Miró refers to Mudarra as a theoretician of literature whom he has obviously read. Prudencio Mudarra y Párraga was the author of *Lecciones de literatura general y literatura española*. The fourth edition (Seville, 1895) is 'arreglada al plan vigente de enseñanza', so that its ideas were current in contemporary Spanish education; Miró probably used it as a text-book. The opening definition of 'literatura general' is: 'La ciencia que estudia la bella expresión del pensamiento humano por medio de la palabra hablada o escrita' (p. 9). One of the neo-scholastic Mudarra's first distinctions is between form and content, and he affirms specifically that ideas can be studied quite independently of form. Such notions were quite inadequate for writing such as Miró's. Indeed they became increasingly discredited among young writers. The very word 'estilo' became deeply suspect, as any of Baroja's remarks on the subject shows. But the old idea of style as dress did not simply die away. In an article in 1911 Miró quotes Azorín as saying: 'El estilo supremo es no tenerlo.' Azorín writes also that Flaubert, at the end of a life 'preocupado en *hacer estilo*' saw 'la inanidad de su ilusión y escribió «Bouvard y Pecuchet» sin estilo' (*Glosas,* p. 120). For Azorín 'estilo' meant not the characteristic manner of a writer, but ornamentation. For Baroja and Azorín such ornamentation was anathema; the word 'estilista' became an insult. Yet the underlying separation of style and matter was retained: the aim was to write 'sin estilo', as if style was icing, an optional extra. Miró's own view was in total contrast. When he writes that 'la palabra es la misma idea hecha carne' (*Glosas,* p. 118), he does not reject ornament in favour of no ornament, but in favour of the indissolubility of form and content. Perhaps it was because Miró's friends in Alicante understood his intentions that their reviews of his work do not criticise it in the more old-fashioned terms of the Madrid reviewers.

Along with the failure to penetrate Miró's use of language goes a failure to understand the structure of *Hilván de escenas,* and the criticism that Miró could not construct a plot. Of course the novel is in many ways a weak one, yet it foreshadows the structural method of Miró's great novels — a series of episodes thematically linked, a method that goes back to Cervantes and the picaresque novels. Critics have always insisted on the word 'escenas' in the title, forgetting that it is an 'hilván', a linked series that together makes up a whole. The stumbling-point for critics was that they brought to Miró nineteenth-century notions of plot as the sole possible method of articulating a novel.

Miró's next book was *Del vivir,* reviewed at length in *La república de las letras* (8 July 1905, pp. 7-8), by one Luis de Vargas, evidently a pseudonym of Andrés González-Blanco, since the review reappears a few years later, almost unaltered, as a chapter on Gabriel Miró in

González-Blanco's *Los contemporáneos* (I, ii, 276-90). González-Blanco takes as his starting-point that Flaubert and Zola are the founders of the modern novel, from whom contemporary modes of writing derive: 'Queremos eliminar todo virus naturalista; pero conservamos de estos grandes maestros el afán de la exactitud de la observación.' Miró fits into this pattern: 'Y aquí tenemos un nuevo novelista que se ha afirmado como estilista robusto y como experimentador y observador.' González-Blanco deals at length with Miró's language, distinguishing it from the 'uso de palabras rancias y arcaísmos afectados por vano lucir de novedades'. Miró's language derives from 'un acendrado estudio del genio de la lengua'. 'Pasma verdaderamente el estudio que este hombre ha debido hacer de nuestro idioma y de las lenguas madres y afines.' It was a fashionable notion that a knowledge of the classical languages was essential for a writer, [11] but there is little to suggest that Miró did much study of 'las lenguas madres y afines'. González-Blanco points out that Miró must have studied 'los grandes autores' and picks out 'la influencia directa de los novelistas picarescos, entre los del siglo de oro, y, entre los de este siglo de hierro y de electricidad la de Martínez Ruiz'. He ends his review with a summary that finds in Miró a much wider range of virtues than most contemporary critics discover: 'Tiene, pues, Miró ... excelsas cualidades artísticas: descripción rica y matizada del paisaje, que a veces se hace demasiado fatigosa, y desluce un poco sus obras; conocimiento del idioma como muy pocos de sus contemporáneos; fuerza patética usada con discernimiento y mesura; espíritu filosófico, reflexivo y moralista ... y sobre todo, para remate de su ya afirmada personalidad, una penetrante visión de las cosas del mundo exterior complicadas con las del alma, agudas *visiones de vida,* expresadas en un estilo muy rancio y a la vez muy moderno.'

González-Blanco's review, compared with others, is a careful and intelligent description of one reader's reactions. But it is significant that even his critical preconceptions, mixed as they are with fervent support for what is modern (Miró uses 'sintaxis verdaderamente moderna y postflaubertiana'), are essentially late nineteenth-century. He defends Miró's language, but only on the grounds that it forms a homogeneous style, and is not 'esmaltado de voces poco oídas'. He mentions 'un deseo de eliminar todo nudo o trama novelesca ... y de dejar la obra reducida a sensaciones fragmentarias, desanudadas y sin cohesión'. Indeed, in attempting to fit Miró to his own notions he makes

---

[11] E.g.: 'En ... el tiempo del modernismo ... había quienes afirmaban que para escribir bien el castellano había que conocer el sentido de las palabras, no sólo en el lenguaje propio, sino también en el latín y en el griego.' Baroja, *La intuición y el estilo,* p. 285.

the incorrect supposition that Miró was a copious note-taker: 'Se ve
... que Miró trabaja, como he indicado al principio, por el método naturalista, y que laboriosamente toma apuntes que convierte después
en bosquejos ampliados.'

Also in 1905, Azorín wrote his first article on Miró:

> El autor es, ante todo, un paisajista; mas un paisajista origi-
> nalísimo, que se ha creado en la lectura de los clásicos —es-
> pecialmente de Santa Teresa, la gran desarticuladora del idio-
> ma— un estilo conciso, descarnado, lapidario, reseco, que nota
> los detalles más exactos con una rigidez inaudita y que llega,
> en ocasiones, a producir en el lector una sensación extraordi-
> naria de morbosidad y de inquietud...
>
> Yo envío mi saludo a este intérprete del gran pueblo: un
> hálito de la divina Grecia flota sobre sus campos y sobre sus
> poblados exultantes y claros. [12]

This is very much Miró seen through Azorín's own preoccupations.
The emphasis on 'paisajismo' and an original style is natural coming
from Azorín, though it was unfortunate that his influence should be
used to reinforce the growing stereotype. He also starts here the comparison that he was to continue to draw between St. Teresa and Miró,
and one wonders whether the link, that has been so often repeated,
didn't spring merely from the fortuitous coming together of a personal
interest of Azorín's with the fact that in *Del vivir* Miró shows an obvious affection for the work of St. Teresa. Finally, the 'hálito de la
divina Grecia', of which there is rather little evidence in *Del vivir* itself,
is interesting as an illustration of the firm bond between Greece and
beauty that existed in the minds of writers of the time, including Miró.

After *Del vivir* Miró published little until 1908, the year in which
his father died and which he later called 'mi primer año de desamparo,
y de profesión de escritor retraído en una paz horaciana mentirosa'. [13]
The year 1908 also saw recognition of Miró as a writer take a considerable step forward, for it was the year in which he won with *Nómada*
a prize offered by *El cuento semanal*. This prize and the celebrations
following it were the occasion of a number of articles, a growth of
interest that was continued later in the year by the publication of
La novela de mi amigo. In 1907 the *Heraldo de Madrid* had printed
a favourable piece by Cristóbal de Castro (5 August 1907), describing
Miró as a pantheist writer with a Franciscan love of nature. The same
paper, announcing the prize won by *Nómada* (22 January 1908), pro-

---

[12] *Obras completas*, VI, 992-3.
[13] *Del huerto provinciano*, 1912; see preface to *Nómada*.

duced the earliest version of the kind of off-the-peg judgement required on such occasions. Miró was 'una de las figuras más interesantes de los intelectuales jóvenes'. The paper went on: 'Conocedor a fondo de los clásicos y enamorado de la forma, constituyen sus novelas hermosos estudios en que la Naturaleza parece descripta con ricas tonalidades de color.'

Almost a month later, on 15 February 1908, a banquet was held for Miró in Madrid. Valle-Inclán and Baroja, as members of the jury of the competition, were present, as was Benavente. But *modernista* writers were much more strongly represented: Martínez Sierra, Villaespesa, and Cansinos-Assens among them. As E. L. King has pointed out, the generation of '98 did not consider Miró one of themselves. [14] *El Mundo* (16 February 1908), reports that 'toda la juventud literaria asistió al banquete', but that several of the 'maestros' were also present; that is, Baroja, Valle-Inclán, Benavente, Trigo, and so on. The line between the already established writers and the new group that supported Miró could hardly be more clearly drawn. Bernardo de Candamo, writing about the banquet later, emphasised how different Miró was from the other guests, a difference that Eugeni d'Ors had also noted. [15] Candamo writes: 'Todo el aspecto del novelista joven ofrecía yo no sé qué apariencia de timidez mal disimulada, de cortedad y de provincianismo. Destacábase la figura de Miró entre la de los demás comensales como más saludable, más sencilla y más ingenua.' [16]

Candamo goes on to review *La novela de mi amigo*. He praises Miró's originality and humility, comparing him with St. Francis of Assisi, and criticises an 'exceso de descripción', calling Miró a 'descripcionista'. This objection has always been a stock one but it is often curiously hard to justify, not least in *La novela de mi amigo* itself where even the most mechanical approach would surely not reveal an overwhelming proportion of 'description'. With whom is Miró being compared? Pereda, Azorín, the French realists? 'Description' (though the term begs a number of questions) was surely accepted as part of the nineteenth-century novelist's trade, so that the objection here (and Candamo hints as much) is more to the fact that Miró deals with the interaction of observer and observed than to 'description' as such. Candamo refers to writers whose obsession with 'descripción' is 'enfermiza'.

The genre of Miró's works, too, caused difficulty from the beginning: Candamo speaks of 'un libro novelesco', and another reviewer, in *El Liberal* (Madrid, 14 October 1908), of a book which 'tiene ... corte de novela de nuevo género, de novela-poema'. This latter review

[14] 'Gabriel Miró y «el mundo según es»', p. 122.
[15] 'Del novecentista Gabriel Miró', *Diario de Alicante,* 8 April 1911.
[16] 'La novela de mi amigo', *El Faro,* 18 Oct. 1908, p. 450.

solves the critical problem by the assimilation of novel and poetry: the charm of *La novela de mi amigo* lies not in the plot but in 'el perfume de poesía que exhala la pluma del narrador'. Another example of the decorative approach to style: Miró adds the perfume of poetry to a basic structure that is as necessary and as uninteresting as the paper and the printing ink. The question of genre is thus but another facet of the critical problems set by Miró's work, the problems of the nature of his language, and the structure or lack of structure of his work.

However, Andres González-Blanco had by now lost his doubts on the score of genre. 'Dentro de unos años barrunto que ha de ser nuestro gran novelista' he declares, making it clear that he looks upon himself as the discoverer of Miró. [17] The genre problem is settled by using the term 'la novela fragmentaria', which is 'de escritura artística a lo Goncourt, pareciéndose a *Azorín* y Baroja' (pp. 859-60). The point about the Goncourts is interesting, for Miró does use stylistic devices employed by the brothers, such as abstract nouns to replace verbs and adjectives, though the route by which he acquired them is far from clear.

Not only in Madrid was Miró's work now becoming better known. Reviews begin to appear in Barcelona too and often they are a good deal more sympathetic. Xenius, Eugeni d'Ors, for instance, lays claim to discoverer's honours on behalf of Catalonia. In the article in which he recounts that in Madrid in 1908 Miró clearly did not belong to the capital's literary society (*Diario de Alicante*, 8 April 1911), he writes that Miró has visited Barcelona and that he felt himself a brother to the *novecentistas*. A letter writen by Maragall to Miró a few months later expresses the sympathy that was felt on both sides. [18] The reactions of Miró's Catalan friends in the second decade of the century are more reminiscent of the early Alicantino comments than of the more conservative Madrid criticisms. Maragall puzzles over the prose/poetry problem and concludes: 'Pero no, queda prosa teniendo dentro toda la luz de la poesía.' He adds that 'una embriaguez de expresión' distracts him from the 'asunto'. But this is not style for style's sake: 'La acción queda como absorbida en la figura poemática de Félix.' 'El sello de sus creaciones', he writes to Miró, is in 'esa ultrarrealidad que tienen, que hace usted ver tan fuertemente el mundo y los hombres, que se les ve el más allá.' Another friend, Suriñach Sentíes, offers a similarly empathetic view: 'Penetra les vides i els paisatges i posa les ànimes en descubert totes palpitants en les paraules

---

[17] *Historia de la novela en España*, p. 1012.
[18] *Obres completes*, p. 1720.

15

caldes, pures í lluminoses d'un castellà únic' (*La veu de Catalunya,* 22 November 1913).

But the response Miró found in Barcelona seems to have had little effect on the stereotype emerging in Madrid. Reviewing *Las cerezas del cementerio,* Juan Pujol wrote in the *Heraldo de Madrid* (17 June 1911) of 'labor de taracea', and a 'novela [que] sólo tiene de tal el hilo de una asordada intriga'. 'Como un orfebre trabaja Miró el idioma de Castilla.' Shortly after this Ramón Tenreiro, Miró's most regular critic, wrote his first review of Miró in *Lectura* (November 1911), on *Las cerezas del cementerio.* He sees the novel as an exploration of man's determination by the forces of heredity and environment, but regrets that Miró 'extravíase persiguiendo a las pintadas mariposas del estilo galano' (p. 326). 'Su prosa ... resplandece entre las más insignes que se producen hoy, [pero] no iguala a la forma el fondo' (p. 327). A note in *La Tribuna* sums up the public view: 'Ha estado en Madrid Gabriel Miró el exquisito literato, maestro del estilo.' [19]

By way of contrast it is worth looking at the note of Marcel Robin, probably the earliest foreign critic to write on Miró, in *Mercure de France* (16 September 1912). In the atmosphere of a France that was passing beyond the Symbolism whose Spanish variant was still having to battle with the realist tradition, Robin is as unconcerned with decorative style, structural inconsequence, excessive description and the rest of it, as the Barcelona *novecentistas.* Félix's tragedy is one of progressive disillusionment: 'Il doit bientôt douter même de sa jeunesse et de sa liberté: ces dernières illusions ne résistent pas à l'acuité de son analyse' (p. 431). Miró is an 'écrivain sobre et lucide, mais précieux néanmoins, psychologue infiniment pénétrant, réaliste d'une vigueur surprenante' (p. 432).

From 1911 to 1915 there was once again little public attention paid to Miró. He himself published mainly newspaper articles. When in 1915 a major work, *El abuelo del rey,* appeared Tenreiro was again the reviewer in *Lectura.* Miró's characters were all 'fracasados' to be related to Antonio Azorín and the hero of Baroja's *Camino de perfección.* Hence he sees Miró as 'el Benjamín de la generación literaria de 1898', a suggestion that is only comprehensible in the context of the contemporary confusion over the new-found label of 1898. Again Tenreiro refers to 'el escaso asunto'. 'Lo que importa es ... sobre todo el carácter personal y vivo de la prosa en que está narrado el libro.' [20] The words 'en que' reveal Tenreiro's premise: style is clothing. Tenreiro repeats his remarks on Miró's characters, à propos of Sigüenza, in a later review (*Lectura,* 3 (1918), 70-1): 'Sigüenza es

[19] In 'Día tras día', *La Tribuna,* 13 Feb. 1913.
[20] 'El abuelo del rey', *Lectura,* reprinted in *Diario de Alicante,* 1 Oct. 1915.

como un hermano menor del Antonio Azorín de la primera época y del protagonista barojiano de Camino de Perfección.' In fact, contrary to Tenreiro's assertion, the main characteristic of Sigüenza is the irony with which he constantly pricks his own vanities, while the heroes of Baroja and Martínez Ruiz take themselves seriously. This is precisely the difference between the generation of 1898 and Miró: the serious search for what is wrong with Spain and her people is replaced by a sceptical analysis of the idealist himself. To compare Tenreiro's critical ideas with those apparent even in the sketchy remarks of the Catalans or of a Frenchman such as Robin, is to be aware at once of a considerable critical lag. To read Miró in terms of a model derived from Zola or the 98 generation, as Tenreiro did, led inevitably to misunderstanding.

Again and again Miró met with incomprehension of his work, often accompanied by the sort of praise that he did not find welcome. Julio Bernácer, the son of a close friend, wrote: 'Sus amigos sabíamos cuanto le molestaba —más tarde, ya reía de ello indulgentemente— que lo catalogasen entre los estilistas. Como si su esfuerzo de superación idiomática y constructiva fuese un mero alarde de artífice y no una resultante lógica de su afán de precisión, que tantas veces llevóle a ser antigramático.'[21] But understanding was mostly only forthcoming from the fringes of the literary establishment. Even the leading *modernista* propagandist, Cansinos-Assens, in *La nueva literatura,* praises Miró as a regional writer, a variant of the 'description' theme: 'En Gabriel Miró la literatura regional por la merced de la nueva voluntad estética, se redime de la garrulería tradicional, de los antiguos cánones y de las antiguas visiones' (II, 203). This is praise, but praise that relegates Miró to a minor category.

All this criticism, naturally, was confined to a very small circle of readers following literary matters closely. During Miró's stay in Barcelona even the initial surge of interest after 1908 had died away. As Xenius remarked: 'Ninguna singularidad, ninguna nota pintoresca supo mantener a su favor despierta la curiosidad de la villa y corte. Miró no era un escritor fecundo. No escribía para el teatro. No era tan solamente un pederasta. En aquellas condiciones, su estrella debía amortiguarse en poco tiempo' (*Diario de Alicante,* 8 April 1911). By 1916 Vicente Díez de Tejada could write, after mentioning Miró as once winner of the *Cuento semanal* competition: 'Y los valores nuevos, con el empuje creador de su savia nueva, yacen postergados, ahogados.'[22]

When renewed interest came it was of a new kind, for in 1916 and 1917 Miró published the two volumes of *Figuras de la Pasión del*

[21] 'Estampa mironiana', p. 8.
[22] 'Crónica: Señales de los tiempos', *El Liberal* (Madrid), 16 April 1916, p. 1.

Señor. The clerical opposition that this work aroused at once changed the nature of discussion of Miró's work. Inevitably, once right-wing clerical groups had condemned the *Figuras,* Miró's work, entirely against his will, was thrust into the violence of the struggle over the Church, with its amosphere of irrational fears and hatreds. The campaign against Miró at this time has not been investigated with any thoroughness, and there is little evidence about it in the press of the time. Its effects, however, are quite obvious in the controversies surrounding *El obispo leproso* in 1927 and the few years following. Miró's work then became so deeply involved in clerical controversy that it became the occasion for abuse and counter-abuse between the left and right wings of the press.

But in the years immediately after publication of the *Figuras* the campaign was more subterranean, only surfacing publicly in the trial of Valdés Prida, editor of the Gijón newspaper *El Noroeste,* for publishing a chapter of the *Figuras,* an offence for which he was jailed. The right-wing *El debate* reported the case, and a few days later congratulated the Gijón judges on a series of further sentences for blasphemy and pornography (28 April 1917), a comment typical of the papers of the 'Buena Prensa' movement founded early in the century, and gently mocked by Miró in *Las cerezas del cementerio* (*OC,* pp. 349-50).

The offending passage appears in 'Mujeres de Jerusalén':

> La mujer judía pronunciaba confiadamente el nombre del denodado nazareno; y la mirada del esposo o del padre conturbó y apagó su fé. El nazareno se vanaglorió de una austeridad que arruinaba a los mercaderes humildes; y en su ímpetu había proferido una blasfemia abominable contra el Templo del Señor.

(*OC,* p. 1370)

A woman on the point of belief has her doubts reawakened by the suggestion that Christ has blasphemed. The judge in the case took the second sentence to be the comment of Miró, instead of the accusation of husband or father, and found 'la más grave injuria que puede verterse contra la Divina Persona de Jesucristo Nuestro Señor y Redentor, ultrajando y menospreciando con ello a la augusta Divinidad, ofendiendo en lo más íntimo y hondo los sentimientos de todos los cristianos'. The judge quite explicitly rejected the obvious interpretation: 'No son palabras puestas en boca de los judíos, sino expresadas por él mismo ... el escritor conocidamente erético (falta la h), Gabriel Miró.' (The details are taken from Miró's article on the episode, 'La potestad de un juez', *Diario de Alicante,* 10 May 1917.) A decision so absurd was obviously not arrived at without clerical efforts behind the scenes. That an exceedingly stupid judge could miss the point through the typically Mironian compression and use of *le style indirect libre* is conceivable, but that he should wilfully reject it can only be attributed to partiality. It is ironical that Miró's opponents should use a misinterpretation of literary technique to gain their ends, adding a new dimension to misunderstanding of what Miró was about. Miró naturally defends himself: 'Es toda mi obra un propósito de evocación, de reconstitución del primer horizonte cristiano. *Todo* participa de aquel tiempo.' He defends himself in detail, quoting 'el doctor Sepp, teólogo alemán — es alemán y todo', an appeal to the Germanophile right from one who was an 'aliadófilo'. [23] Miró himself places discussion of his work in a political context, a clear sign of the change produced by the *Figuras*.

In part thanks to this defence and a later one given in a lecture in Gijón, Miró's intentions in the *Figuras* are far better documented than in his earlier work. In a letter to relatives he writes: 'Describo toda la preparación de la Pascua y la última cena de Jesús, sin omitir ni los nombres de las yerbas amargas ni de los cereales que componían el pan ázimo, ni aun la manera de asar el cordero. Creo que todo eso, que estaba esparcido en libros fríos de eruditos, interesará al devoto, al seglar y al artista.' [24] Many other letters present the same intention of reconstruction, a new departure in Miró's writing but one that the reader could easily grasp. Differences of opinion could only be expressed over whether the whole enterprise was disrespectful, or over whether Miró's interest in language made him ignore the spiritual realities of the Passion he described. Attacks on these lines do not become public much before 1927, but Miró's defenders constantly imply such criticisms. Antonio Maura, for instance, thanks to whom Miró found a job in Madrid, writes, breaking with his usual impartiality as Director of the Academy: 'Paréceme a mí que no se lesiona con esto la piedad de los creyentes, puesto que la pluma profana no pierde el respeto ni un solo instante; y no acierto a reputar vedada a la pluma una artística reproducción en que los pinceles de los más afamados pintores se ejercitaron siglo tras siglo, por encargo y bajo el patrocinio de las mayores autoridades de la Iglesia.' [25]

This passage is taken from pages at the end of the first edition of Miró's *Niño y grande*. Tacked onto the end of Miró's text are comments on the *Figuras* by three eminent men, evidently designed to combat the clerical accusations. Alongside Maura, whose presence would allay the fears of large sections of the right, were Unamuno

[23] See for instance Sebastián de la Nuez, 'Cartas de Gabriel Miró', p. 80.
[24] Letter in the possession of the Miró family.
[25] G. Miró, *Niño y grande* (Madrid, 1922), p. 206.

and Azorín, both offering whole-hearted tributes. Unamuno writes: 'Las *Figuras de la Pasión del Señor* están realzadas por toda la histo- ria, estéticamente penetrada, del pueblo judío, por la intuición de su paisaje —comprendido al través de nuestros paisajes levantinos— y por una fuerza de visión que a las veces recuerda la de la Beata Cata- lina Emmerich ... Y hay además una honda exégesis poética, de pro- fundo valor espiritual.' [26]

Underlying the attacks, and this too was to become clear in 1927, was something more deep-seated than the question of respect for the figure of Christ: the fear of the senses. In this, of course, there was no misunderstanding, and in this attack the clerical and political opposition joined hands with a new (as far as Miró was concerned) conservative literary opposition. Hostility to the 'decadence' of modern literature had existed throughout the century, but had not been applied specifically to Miró until Julio Cejador attacked his work, most compre- hensively in his *Historia de la lengua y literatura castellana.* Before Ce- jador, reviewers had been few but generally favourable (even if mis- understanding), criticising particular aspects of particular works. Ce- jador is sweeping: 'Es de los escritores a quienes por su afeminada educación a la francesa desalentaron los acontecimientos de 1898.' (So much for Jesuit education.) 'Es Miró pesimista decadente ... en los asuntos y manera de tratarlos.' The *Figuras* demonstrate 'el pru- rito de ser original y de parecer infantil y primitivo'. [27]

In *Nuevo Mundo* (25 April 1919), Cejador had condemned Miró and Valle-Inclán as 'sensacionistas' who, 'sección de los simbolistas france- ses, se han empeñado, sin embargo, en expresar sensaciones por medio del lenguaje. Vano y estúpido empeño'. 'Para expresar ideas se hizo el lenguaje.' Incomprehension here reaches even dimmer depths, but the new direction criticism of Miró takes after the publication of the *Figuras* is clear. He ceases to be a coterie writer and by antagonising a section of the Church draws more attention to himself and arouses the kind of literary judgement that temperamentally belongs with the clerical objections: both are founded on mistrust, deepening into fear, of the senses.

This was the situation in 1920, when Miró moved to Madrid. The second decade had brought little change in the understanding of Miró's work, excepting only the injection of religio-political complications into critics' minds. But with the start of the twenties new movements were about to get under way that were to produce new attitudes towards

[26] *Niño y grande,* pp. 207-8.
[27] *Historia,* XII, 38-9.

Miró. At the same time, with the publication of major new works and Miró's presence in the capital, the more important critics began to take an interest. In 1920 *La ilustración española y americana* reprinted from *El Sol* an article by Enrique Díez-Canedo (8 May 1920, p. 272). The magazine introduced the article with the words: 'Gabriel Miró, un interesantísimo escritor español, casi desconocido, encuéntrase en Madrid.' Díez-Canedo, reviewing *El humo dormido,* takes up the theme: 'No goza, necesario es decirlo, Gabriel Miró de la popularidad — ciñendo esta palabra al restricto significado que puede tener en las letras españolas — que hubieron debido conquistarle sus libros, que ya pasan de la docena. Tiene, sí, la consideración de cuantos siguen atentamente nuestra producción literaria; su alejamiento de la corte, en que tanta cuenta se hace de lo individual, aun dando a esa estimación unanimidad perfecta, no ha hecho que llegue al punto de entusiasmo y cordialidad oportunos.' Equally usefully he sums up the critical situation in 1920: 'Los que juzguen a Miró de ligero, llamándole con cierto desdén «poeta en prosa» — lo cual también pudiera decirse en justicia y sin asomo de desdén —, no han percibido, sin duda, el vivo latido humano con que palpitan sus páginas.' Díez-Canedo at once looks back over the past and forward to a more fruitful understanding.

Díez-Canedo was one of the first Madrid critics to see Miró as something other than an 'estilista'. He was also one of the earliest Spaniards to devote serious attention in modern times to Góngora, so that his name raises an interesting and suggestive parallel to the history of Miró criticism — that of contemporary attitudes to Góngora. The year 1927 was to be the tercentenary of his death and the occasion of the famous celebrations in his honour prepared by the leading young poets: Gerardo Diego, Salinas, Alberti, Lorca, Dámaso Alonso, Jorge Guillén and their friends. It was also the year in which interest in Miró reached its peak, with the publication in late 1926 of *El obispo leproso,* the candidature of Miró for the Academy early in 1927, and his failure to win either election or the Academy's Fastenrath prize. And in 1927 the national competitions of the Ministry of Public Education were devoted to Góngora, at the instigation of Miró, secretary of the competitions. Dámaso Alonso writes that in 1927 'el poeta proscrito entraba por primera vez en las «esferas oficiales» de su patria, tan arisca. Que así fuera se debió por entero al desvelo y al entusiasmo de Gabriel Miró'. [28]

Young writers in the twenties, Miró himself, and his most sympathetic critics, all shared a common enthusiasm for Góngora. Miró him-

[28] *La lengua poética de Góngora,* p. 7.

self, speaking in Gijón in 1925, said that 'es más de nosotros que de antaño la lírica de Góngora'. [29] So that a comparison of attitudes to Miró and Góngora helps to fix the critical ambience more clearly. Elsa Dehennin's fascinating *La Résurgence de Góngora* makes the comparison possible, again and again suggesting detailed parallels.

To go back to the period of Miró's earliest work, Dehennin shows that the *modernistas* were often lukewarm in their appreciation of Góngora, with the sole exception of Darío, and to a large extent uncomprehending of the later poems. But there is no such ambivalence about the attitude of the 98 writers: with the exception of Azorín, they all disliked Góngora as much as their nineteenth-century predecessors did. Maeztu, Baroja, Machado, Unamuno, and Valle-Inclán all expressed ignorance, indifference, or hostility. [30] The parallel between these attitudes and the same writers' views of Miró is remarkable. Only Unamuno diverges sharply for as we have seen he was an enthusiastic admirer of Miró. Azorín 'comprend un certain Góngora' (Dehennin, p. 47): he also praises a certain Miró. But Baroja is hostile: 'A mí me parece que Miró no es un hombre cuya obra tenga una raíz fuerte en la realidad' he is reported as saying in 1946. [31] And Maeztu, though devoting more space to Miró, is equally critical: 'La insuficiencia del bello estilo se hace patente cuando Miró plantea un asunto de interés general.' [32] Machado never mentions Miró, while Valle-Inclán, as befits a writer who bridges the 98/*modernista* division, is half-hearted. In 1908, along with Baroja and Trigo, he awarded the *Cuento semanal* prize to Miró (we have already seen how much that weighed in Baroja's estimate of Miró) and at the same time presented two of his own books to Miró (*Romance de lobos* and *El resplandor de la hoguera*). Both contained inscriptions that are merely formal: one is 'como testimonio de consideración literaria', the other is presented 'muy cordialmente'. Thereafter contact ceased until in 1927 in reply to the *Heraldo de Madrid* (18 January 1927), the Galician writer praised, without much warmth, Miró's 'renovación del léxico' and 'la capacidad sensible que tienen algunos de sus personajes para el sentimiento de la naturaleza'.

Most of these comments are of a late date which weakens their value as evidence for Miró's early critical reception, but it remains fascinating to see not only the parallel with Góngora but also how views,

[29] Ramos, *Literatura,* p. 305.
[30] All quoted in Dehennin: Maeztu, p. 39; Baroja and Machado, p. 40; Unamuno, p. 31; Valle-Inclán, p. 47. All in reply to *La Gaceta Literaria,* 1 June 1927, except Unamuno, *Helios,* 7 (1903), 475-80.
[31] Romano, 'Pío Baroja nos habla del escritor Hermann Hesse', *Madrid,* 20 Nov. 1946, p. 3.
[32] *Las letras y la vida,* p. 175. First published in *La Prensa* (Buenos Aires), 9 Sept. 1930.

such as those of Baroja and Valle-Inclán just quoted, which originate in an earlier period, were carried forward intact into the years when Miró's reputation was at its highest (and this in spite of Valle-Inclán's own transformed aesthetic). It must have been by some similar process that from 1927 to 1930 Miró was still largely subject to the same criticisms that had pursued him earlier, the intervention of the aesthetic upheaval of the twenties notwithstanding.

The relationship between *modernismo* and Góngora was more confused. Attacks on *modernismo* commonly coupled it with Góngora. Unamuno calls *modernista* poems 'gongorinadas de hoy',[33] showing, incidentally, that for him Miró was quite distinct from the *modernistas*. As for the *modernista* poets themselves, Dehennin concludes that 'même à l'époque moderniste ceux qui goûtent l'essentiel des oeuvres gongoriques — les *Solitudes* — sont infiniment rares. Sans doute ne sait-on pas encore comment les décortiquer' (p. 32). Typical is E. López Chavarri who protests at the assimilation of 'modernista' to 'lo gongorino y decorativo, en vez de lo poético sincero' (p. 33). 'Lo decorativo' echoes very clearly the tenor of early Miró criticism. Both the outright opposition of an older school and of the writers of 1898, and the semi-comprehension of *modernistas* are represented in the cases of both Miró and Góngora. If not an explanation of why Miró, springing from a *modernista* atmosphere, was poorly understood by his contemporaries, at least Góngora's case shows that Miró's was not unique.

In the second decade of the century Góngora criticism, after the initial impetus given by Rubén Darío, lay nearly dormant as did writing on Miró, disturbed only by the *Figuras*. Again Dehennin's book is helpful: Alfonso Reyes, the Mexican critic, 'el primer gongorista de las nuevas generaciones', according to Foulché-Delbosc, in 1911 wrote of Góngora as 'arrebatado por su lirismo, [empeñado] en retratar con palabras sus musicales y coloridas emociones, sin afligirse del descuido en que iba dejando las ideas' (Dehennin, p. 24). Dehennin comments: 'A ce moment il était encore imbu des théories traditionelles.' Reyes's words are illuminating — here is a scholar working against the prejudices of the majority and in a field that requires a considerable adjustment of outlook ahead of his contemporaries: yet his praise for Góngora is in terms that again echo the critical vocabulary used to praise and blame Miró.

Leaving the Góngora parallel for the moment and returning to the main narrative, 1920 finds Miró settling in Madrid for the last, crucial, decade of his life. In 1921 he published *Nuestro padre San Daniel,* his

---

[33] Dehennin, pp. 31-2. Quoted from *Helios* (1903).

finest novel so far, and it was the occasion for one of the most careful reviews yet written about his work, that by Julio Casares published in *ABC* in 1922.[34] That this review was superior to any other study yet published says a great deal by itself. Nevertheless, Casares, from a middle-of-the-road standpoint, writes with fairness and intelligence, though without much penetration. He avoids the old clichés about decoration and incoherence, and deliberately sidesteps the religious and political issues. For Casares a writer either explores the mind of a character or describes his 'proyección exterior'. Miró is of the second type — his style follows from this : 'Si decimos ahora que el señor Miró pertenece a esta última categoría de escritores y que en su lenguaje constelado de imágenes predominan las visuales (sensaciones de luz, forma y color), quedará explicado el alcance del calificativo «pictórico» y habremos determinado de paso la característica principal de su estilo.'

The avoidance of the old clichés and the probity of the argument form a welcome advance, but they only thinly veil the fact that this is the old view in more up-to-date dress. Miró's style is for Casares the consequence of the choice of a particular method, rather than an integral part of his exploration of reality. And phrases such as 'un albúm de deliciosas acuarelas' imply the inconsequence of the novel's structure. In his more detailed remarks on style there also appear more sophisticated versions of traditional reservations : Miró uses 'las más atrevidas y desconcertantes metáforas'. Miró's vocabulary is extensive, 'pero también en esta virtud cabe exceso'. Miró's syntax goes beyond 'el límite ordinario de la sobriedad y de la concisión'. In fact Miró's faults 'nacen de la exageración de cualidades excelentes', a theme that was to be repeated over and over again, and which was applied during the same years to Góngora: 'Un excès de lumière spirituelle, comme on aimait le répéter en 1927' (Dehennin, p. 11).

Casares's position was a traditional one, but since 1918 a new aesthetic outlook had been developing. In that year Vicente Huidobro, the founder of *creacionismo,* arrived in Madrid and the many variants of *ultraísmo* were just beginning to appear. These new aesthetic theories offered the possibility of more fruitful approaches to Miró's work. It was in the same year that Miró's dictum, 'la palabra es la idea hecha carne' — thought and word are indissoluble — found its classic expression in *El humo dormido*:

> Hay emociones que no lo son del todo hasta que no reciben la fuerza lírica de la palabra, su palabra plena y exacta. Una llanura de la que sólo se levantaba un árbol, no la sentí mía has-

[34] *Crítica efímera*, pp. 78-86. First published in *ABC*, 3 May 1922, pp. 3-5, and 6 June 1922, pp. 4-5.

ta que no me dije : 'Tierra caliente y árbol fresco.' Cantaba un pájaro en una siesta lisa, inmóvil, y el cántico la penetró, la poseyó toda, cuando alguien dijo : 'Claridad.' Y fue como si el ave se transformase en un cristal luminoso que revibraba hasta en la lejanía. Es que la palabra, esa palabra, como la música, resucita las realidades, las valora, exalta y acendra, subiendo a una pureza 'precisamente inefable', lo que por no sentirse ni decirse en su matiz, en su exactitud, dormía dentro de las exactitudes polvorientas de las mismas miradas y del mismo vocablo y concepto de todos.

(*OC*, pp. 692-3)

Jorge Guillén, naturally enough, quotes this passage in his *Language and Poetry*, and comments : 'And form, the revelation of content, is something more than revelation. Form discovers — and remakes, creates' (p. 161). Is this not a direct echo from the years of Guillén's own poetic education? And a reminder of the more extreme statements of the new outlook, such as Huidobro's, that propose poetry as creation :

> Por qué cantáis la rosa, ¡oh Poetas!
> Hacedla florecer en el poema. [35]

For Huidobro a poem was a created object, a phenomenon, a new fact, independent of other phenomena. This new artefact was, of course, created largely by means of that magical instrument the metaphor, an instrument so insisted upon by some poets that little else was present in their work. All these ideas were much more akin to Miró's practice than were surviving nineteenth-century ideas and they paved the way for a new appreciation of Miró. Miró was no 'creacionista', though he used the word 'creacionismo' in the early twenties (*EC*, XII, 185). Rather, he used words to recreate, to discover, to take possession, and to define. But one of his favourite instruments was the metaphor, so that it is not difficult to understand why the poets of the twenties should show great respect for Miró. In any case, they could respect him in ways that suited themselves. The Góngora of the propagandists was a rather special version of Góngora, and in the same way the poets selected among Miró's qualities those that suited their aesthetic. Their preoccupations meant that the 'estilista' argument was superseded, but Miró the novelist, the organiser of large-scale works, remained, by and large, unrecognised. For these young admirers the question of overall structure was simply not interesting; their attention was centred on

[35] Huidobro, *Obras completas*, I, 255.

Miró the linguistic creator. We shall see how this new, equally partial, but more serviceable stereotype developed.

It emerged amidst the continuation of a more traditional approach, and indeed until 1926 there is little direct evidence for it in the press. Yet Giménez Caballero could remark in 1926: 'La neofortuna literaria de Gabriel Miró —tras la gran guerra— ha sido uno de los fenómenos más destacados y menos apercibidos que han emergido por nuestras letras.' [36]

Among the few serious articles on Miró appearing between 1920 and 1926, an interesting example of the way attitudes were developing is Juan Chabás's article of 1924. [37] Though of an age with the new poets of the twenties, he does not entirely belong with them — his remarks on Miró include both conventional criticism and the preoccupations of his contemporaries. Miró is to Chabás, after Juan Ramón Jiménez, the most perfect contemporary 'prosista' (the term 'prosista' is itself a valuable clue — the derogatory 'estilista' is replaced by a word that is neutral about questions of genre and decorative style). The most significant quality of modern prose is exactitude while one of the major conquests of Miró is his expansion of the use of metaphor. But Chabás is bothered about Miró's status: is he a novelist? 'Sí y no.' On almost every count Chabás clearly demonstrates an enormous shift of emphasis towards the new aesthetic. The values of precision and metaphor are paramount so that Chabás does not mean total condemnation when he says: 'Como siempre, los trozos menos novelescos son los mejores' (p. 13).

In 1927 C. Rivas Cherif remarked: 'Hay lectores de Gabriel Miró ... que le creen, sin duda, viejo ... . Los jóvenes, en cambio, los jóvenes literatos, le tienen por joven.'[38] But the evidence for the admiration of the younger poets for Miró is best found in Miró's library. A glance at Section Fourteen of the Appendix is enough to show the preponderance of young writers of the twenties. This is not surprising. Traditionally, young writers sent their work to established masters, though only to those whom they respected. But a glance at the inscriptions shows at once that these presentations are no mere formalities: 'toda la admiración', 'más devota admiración', 'profunda admiración', appear side by side with repeated testimony to the mutual affection between Miró and these writers. Once again the parallel with the revaluation of Góngora is relevant. Miró owned books presented by Salinas, Alberti, Marichalar, Bergamín, Dámaso Alonso, Guillén, and Gerardo Diego. Of those who met in April 1926 to plan the tercentenary celebrations,

[36] 'El obispo de Miró', *El Sol*, 21 Dec. 1926, p. 2.
[37] 'Crítica concéntrica: Gabriel Miró', *Alfar*, March 1924, p. 14.
[38] 'Autobiografía sin comentarios', *Heraldo de Madrid*, 18 Jan. 1927, p. 4.

only Lorca, of the leaders, is not represented, and of the secondary figures only Fernández Almagro (who later wrote several articles on
Miró), J. Moreno Villa, J. M. Hinojosa, and G. Durán are missing. (As
another Gongoristic coincidence Miró owned books presented by Díez-
Canedo and the Mexican writers Alfonso Reyes and M. L. Guzmán,
between them responsible for the important 'Contribuciones a la bibliografía de Góngora' of 1916-17. [39]

Dehennin picks out six men as most 'dévoués à la cause de Góngora': Salinas, Alberti, Lorca, Alonso, Guillén and Diego (p. 74). Their
grasp of form as meaning enabled them to unlock some of Góngora's
secrets, and that same grasp was essential to an understanding of Miró.
All except Lorca wrote about Miró after his death, and all retained
their enthusiasm for his work. It is a sign of why they respected Miró
that all of them start from the verbal precision and magic that were
their own ideals. The most important study has been that of Jorge
Guillén discussing Miró's 'Adequate language' in *Language and Poetry*.
We have already seen that Guillén's starting-point is Miró's principle
that (in Guillén's words): 'Form discovers — and remakes, creates' (p.
161). From here he develops a splendid discussion of the ways in
which Miró's language discovers and reveals, a discussion of the place
of the senses, of the exploration of time and space and memory, of
cruelty and pain and beauty. It is only after all this that Guillén goes
on to deal with Miró's narrative irony and his success as a novelist.
His essay covers thirty-nine pages: five are devoted to the ironical
aspect of Miró's work which, Guillén writes, is 'possibly as important,
or almost as important, as the lyrical' (p. 189). To Miró as a novelist
he devotes one page, even though he writes: 'And Miró, so well aware
of his lyrical gifts, poured all his ambition into narrative writing.
The effort was successful. His capacity for describing landscapes is
so exceptional that it seems to overshadow his vigor as a novelist. It
pained Miró that his tales should be read as if they were no more
than a collection of descriptive and lyric pieces. Let us not commit
this error' (p. 194).

This is not intended as criticism of Guillén — it would be a mean
response to so penetrating a study, and, after all, his subject is Miró's
use of language. The point is that Guillén exemplifies perfectly a stage
in the development of Miró criticism. Guillén and his contemporaries
of the 1927 generation understood Miró better than any previous group
of readers, yet they naturally viewed him through their own interests.
In this way, paradoxically, their better appreciation of him led, in the
longer term, only to a slight modification of the earlier accepted view.

[39]   *Revista de filología española*, 3 (1916), 171-82, and 4 (1917), 54-64.

For these poets, with their dispersal at the time of the Civil War, suffered a swing of taste against them that labelled them heartless and obscure manipulators of words. Not only was Miró also a victim of this change of taste, but the stress laid by his younger friends on language made it all the easier to dismiss him along with them. Miró had been rescued from the pigeon-hole of 'estilista' only to be thrust back into that of 'deshumanización', as that word was abused by opponents of the achievements of the twenties. As for Miró the master of irony and the builder of complex full-length novels, where there had previously been incomprehension, the case was now largely to go by default.

Salinas provides an excellent example of this lack of interest in novelistic structure; in a lecture given in 1931, he presents Miró as having rescued prose from its servitude to narrative. [40] Miró has broken away from the tradition of narrative structure and Salinas sees no need to replace it with any other kind of structure. Simply, 'Miró es en nuestra literatura el máximo ejemplo de la lucha por la palabra, del triunfo sobre el lenguaje'. Miró has destroyed genres by writing prose that is also poetry, by raising prose from 'su rango ancilario'. By a new route, 'la palabra', we are back at an old conclusion — Miró the 'poeta en prosa' (though Salinas speaks rather of Miró's 'posición lírica' and Guillén tells us that Miró disliked being called a poet; Guillén himself, in his inscription in Miró's copy of *Cántico,* got round the difficulty by calling him 'el único gran poeta que no quiere serlo'.). For Salinas, Miró is a poet by virtue of his linguistic triumphs, whereas for an older school he was a poet by virtue of his 'poetic feelings'. The latter implies distinguishable genres and that Miró has chosen the wrong one; the former implies nothing about large-scale form.

Nor, for Salinas, is Miró 'poetic' in the sense of being a descriptive or regionalist writer. Regionalist prose 'a lo Pereda' would be 'humanamente separatista', and for Salinas, as for Guillén, poetry was intensely human. The word 'humano', of course, is always used in awareness of Ortega's 'deshumanización', the term that, Guillén tells us, 'rang false from the very beginning' (p. 209). Elsewhere Salinas writes: 'La obra de Miró es profundamente humana sin estilización pintoresca o costumbrista' (EC, VII, xiii), while Gerardo Diego writes of 'palabras humanizadas, gabrielizadas, que recrean la tierra, el aire, la luz, las plantas, las bestias, los hombres, para infundir en el reflejo de su ontológica hermosura la vida, el alma, el cuerpo físico mismo de Gabriel Miró'. [41]

---

[40]   Reports in *El Sol* and *ABC,* 14 Nov. 1931.
[41]   'Gabriel Miró', *Cuadernos de literatura contemporánea,* Nos. 5-6 (1942), 201.

If 1927 was an important year for this new group of poets, it was also a crucial year for Miró. The attention he received in the press in the early months of the year bears comparison with all the attention he had so far received put together. The initial occasion for all this writing was the publication of *El obispo leproso,* the continuation of *Nuestro padre San Daniel,* and among the reviews one is of overriding importance: that of Ortega y Gasset. 'Deshumanización' has already been mentioned; the famous coining that Guillén thought 'rang false from the very beginning'. Guillén goes on: 'The poets of the twenties could have brought suit before the courts of law for the damages and prejudices caused by the use and abuse — in this case identical — of that novel phrase as a supposed key for the interpretation of their poetry' (*Language and poetry,* pp. 209-10). The damage and prejudice was caused because the new term offered a weapon to opponents of the new poetry — they took the word at its face value, a sense in which Guillén conclusively shows its absurdity. But though Ortega chose a word that could only lead to misunderstanding, the essay on 'Deshumanización' shows a good deal of understanding of what had occurred. Ortega grasped something of the new feeling for form as meaning. But the extreme way in which he states his case is only applicable to a very few poets and perhaps even then only to their theoretical statements: those of a Huidobro, say (Ortega's analysis is often more reminiscent of Cubist theory than any practice). He was still only feeling his way towards an explanation of the art of his time.

Ortega offers the example of a dying man surrounded by people taking various degrees of emotional interest in him. Furthest away is a painter, emotionally quite detached, trying only to get the colours and the design right on his canvas: 'Sólo atiende a lo exterior, a las luces y las sombras, a los valores cromáticos.'[42] Ortega lays himself open to the charge of oversimplifying the creative process, of presenting a painter who is literally inhuman in his detachment from another's death. (It was the choice of examples like this that made it possible for others to use the term dehumanisation in so crude a way later.) The concept of art underlying the example is instructive. For Ortega any work of art contains aesthetic elements and non-aesthetic elements. The artist's aesthetic attitude operates to see reality at a contemplated distance, without emotional involvement. But the objectification of his vision on, say, the canvas, will unavoidably retain a non-aesthetic residue that the spectator must disregard by means of a special mode of perception (looking at the glass, rather than at the scene beyond). In spite of Ortega's air of modernity, the principle underlying the theo-

[42] *Obras completas,* III, 362.

ry is not so very different from Mudarra's concept of literature as 'la bella expresión del pensamiento humano por medio de la palabra'. For both, form and content are sharply separated and the business of art is form. Content is nonaesthetic. If we return now to Ortega's example of the painter, it might be objected that the artist only disregards the dying man qua artist; as a man he is moved by the scene. But this interpretation still emphasises the sense of separation between art and reality that Ortega cultivates, a separation that does violence to our experience of the puzzling yet manifest interrelationship of life and art. The decision to paint a death-scene rather than a bowl of fruit is not meaningless; nor is the spectator indifferent to whether he sees depicted a nude or a side of beef. Ortega's artist turns out to be nothing but an 'estilista'.

Ortega's approach, then, is fundamentally old-fashioned, a more sophisticated version of earlier criticism of Miró. This deep-seated conservatism is clearly visible in his review of El obispo leproso. [43] Ostensibly the bulk of the review attacks the conventionality of Miró's characters. They are types, 'cabezas de cartón', through whom Miró speaks, always with the same diction. This 'convencionalismo permanente ... suena sin remedio a falsedad estética'. The types correspond to everyday conceptions and are the 'simplistas falsificaciones' of reality that the novelist should avoid. For, Ortega implies, superficially drawn characters indicate a superficial view of life on the part of the novelist. But this attack is part of a more comprehensive one, for Ortega speaks of 'un magnífico lirismo descriptivo — que es probablemente la auténtica inspiración de Miró y no la de novelista'. Miró is a 'gran escritor'; he has written a 'libro espléndido', but his novel 'no queda avecinada entre las buenas novelas'. This is because the book is written without a 'centro único', but, rather, in sentences that are somehow perfect but do not lead on one from the other. The effect is static and the book demands an effort from the reader to provide the continuity.

Amidst the praise of other critics for Miró's magnificent language, Ortega asks a logical question: if these are Miró's qualities, then why did he choose to write novels? Yet the question is based once again on a misunderstanding of Miró's own premises; once again the style-content division has asserted itself. This is made particularly clear in Ortega's review, written at about the same time, of Henri Massis' Réflexions sur l'art du roman. Ortega writes: 'Hoy todos los escritores son estilistas.' [44] And 'el estilista [as opposed to the novelist] es un incansable Narciso literario'. 'El señor Massis subraya certeramente

[43] Obras completas, III, 544-50. First published in El Sol, 9 Jan. 1927, p. 3.
[44] Obras completas, III, 568-9.

la incompatibilidad de la novela con el estilismo.' The old term of abuse 'estilista' accompanies the traditional view of the place of language in the novel. In an interview Miró remarked: '¿Dice usted estilista? No; yo nada tengo de estilista. Vamos, de lo que toman por estilista.'[45] And elsewhere he commented on Ortega's article: '¿No justificará la pereza de técnica en los autores y de atención en los lectores, afirmar que una prosa de las calidades otorgadas por Ortega, sea tan penosa de leer?'[46] Even Miró's admirers often made the same mistake as Ortega. In an interview with Miró Benjamín Jarnés remarked: 'Acaricia usted con más deleite una palabra que un espíritu.' Miró replied simply: '¡Hombre!'[47]

Beside the devotion of the young poets and the traditional criticism brought up to date in Ortega, there was also outright opposition, represented most forcibly by Luis Astrana Marín. After a series of five weekly articles in *El Imparcial* devoted to a violent onslaught on Góngora, he turned to 'El estilo leproso' (*El Imparcial*, 27 February 1927). A week later came 'Más sobre el estilo leproso' and, after another week, 'El homosexualismo en nuestras letras', described as 'esta otra lepra literaria'. The last two articles do not mention Miró, but the titles follow on from week to week. The three articles are an extraordinary display of the paranoid style in Spanish life. Miró's style, gathered up with all the other 'ismos', is clearly, for Astrana, part of a national disease. 'Bajezas inconcebibles' and 'ironías a todo lo noble y bello' characterise 'el arte de los neutros' (13 March 1927). All the 'ismos' are 'de importación'; there is nothing 'nacional'. Young poets disdain 'nuestro Parnaso gloriosísimo'. If they turn to any poet it is 'al más decadente, a Góngora' (6 March 1927).

As for Miró, his style is 'una enfermedad contagiosa y terrible, aunque cutánea — por cuanto su mal se nota en la superficie'. In the novel 'nada sucede'; instead it possesses 'hinchazón, afectación, falta de naturalidad y sencillez, ausencia de gallardía y de gracia, desconocimiento de la agilidad del diálogo, carencia del sentido de la proporción, inarmonía de pensamiento, colorismo enfermizo y por demás redundante y pesadez abrumadora' (27 February 1927). All this connects back directly to Cejador and the clerical opposition to the *Figuras*. The fact that Astrana links Miró and Góngora shows that the parallel between them is not fortuitous; and the fact that atheism was a traditional accusation against Góngora points to the nature of the

[45] González-Ruano, 'Un sillón vacío en la Academia', *Diario de Alicante*, 28 Dec. 1929.
[46] Jarnés, 'De Sigüenza a Belén', *La Gaceta literaria*, 15 Jan. 1927.
[47] Ibid.

link between clerical opposition to Miró and the attacks of conservative literary critics. Homosexuality, too, was associated in the public mind, and especially since Oscar Wilde, with decadence and aestheticism, in turn identified with a concern with language.

The remaining reviews of *El obispo leproso* revolve around the topics already discussed. Chabás and Tenreiro are enthusiastic, as are the majority of reviewers, some of whom discuss whether the novel implies any social criticism. But chiefly it is the cluster of arguments associated with the concept of 'estilismo' that preoccupies critics.[48] One example will suffice of the power of the stereotype of Miró and the hesitancy of critics in withstanding it. The critic of the Barcelona paper *La Vanguardia* notes: 'Es el estilo, es la forma, es el lenguaje que nos seduce, nos sugestiona y nos maravilla.' Then he ventures: 'Si fuésemos dados a los símbolos, cosa que tal vez no pasó por las mientes del novelista, diríamos que el obispo leproso simboliza el bien, la tolerancia, el amor, la máxima bondad, frente a la intransigencia, a la ruindad, a la tortuosidad de las conciencias cerradas a toda humana expresión.'[49]

But the controversies were not only literary, for the sudden attention paid to Miró set off wider circles of argument. Nine days after Ortega's article (18 January 1927), the *Heraldo de Madrid* published a whole page devoted to Miró, including the first part of a favourable review by González Olmedilla, an interview by C. Rivas Cherif, an article by Rafael Marquina, and a section entitled 'Miró juzgado por los escritores'. Rivas Cherif reports that Miró 'abomina de la supuesta exquisitez de estilo con que se suele motejar galantemente al escritor preciosista, horro de sentido humano'. He stresses that Miró admires St. Teresa, soon to appear in the text proposing Miró for the Academy. The section giving writers' opinions included contributions from thirteen writers, almost all enthusiastic for Miró's work, though in different ways. The only hostile comment is from Juan Ramón Jiménez; he finds Miró's prose 'lenta, prolija, monótona, de poca espontaneidad y menos dinamismo'.

This tribute from the *Heraldo de Madrid* aroused the opposition: in *El siglo futuro,* on the far right, R. Alcover attacked the rumoured suggestion that Miró should receive the Academy's Fastenrath prize. He recounts how Miró has been attacked in 'un soleado rotativo' and how

[48] Chabás, 'Un libro nuevo', *La Libertad,* 10 Dec. 1926, pp. 6-7; Tenreiro, 'Gabriel Miró: el obispo leproso', *Revista de Occidente,* Jan. 1927, pp. 114-23; González Olmedilla, '«El obispo leproso», novela de Gabriel Miró', *Heraldo de Madrid,* 18 and 25 Jan. 1927, pp. 4 and 5; Precioso, '«El obispo leproso», por Gabriel Miró', *El Liberal,* 18 Jan. 1927, p. 1; Fernández Almagro, 'Una novela de Gabriel Miró', *La Época,* 18 Dec. 1926, p. 3; Aguado, 'Boletín de literatura', *La ciencia tomista,* 19 (1927), 243-5.
[49] 'El obispo leproso', *La Vanguardia,* 26 Feb. 1927, p. 15.

the *Heraldo de Madrid* replied. He attacks *El obispo leproso* for its emptiness and style, and for being a satire on the Jesuits: 'Y eso es lo que le ha robado el corazón al Heraldo.' Of course the *Heraldo* does not admit to this, but, Alcover continues: 'Para eso estamos aquí nosotros ... para avisar a todos los católicos del carácter sectario, tendencioso, y gazmoñamente inmoral de la obra del señor Miró.' [50]

On 24 February further fuel was added to the controversies by the publication of the proposal of Miró for the Academy by Azorín, Palacio Valdés, and Ricardo León. Publishing the text *El Sol* added its support, as if to make up for Ortega's article: 'En todo momento y circunstancia la encontramos justa' (24 February 1927). It was three days after this that Astrana Marín published the first of his articles on 'el estilo leproso', in which he attacks the proposal, written, he presumes, by that 'bobo' Azorín.

A few days later *El Debate,* slightly less far to the right than *El siglo futuro,* published a violent attack by Nicolás González Ruiz. Miró was a pornographer, a Freudian and 'perfectamente repugnante'. [51] When the votes were counted at the Academy Miró won neither membership nor prize, a direct result, his friends believed, of the campaign against him. Miró's new-found fame collapsed around him, though he continued to receive more attention in the press than before these trying days. The ripples of the controversy spread through the provincial press and the Madrid press produced occasional interviews and general articles. But all the elements of Miró's later reputation were established: Ortega's endorsement of the traditional view of great writer/bad novelist, coupled with the enthusiasm for language of Miró's most understanding supporters, overcame the voices of those who asserted otherwise, such as Chabás, Tenreiro, and González Olmedilla, or, later, Pedro Sainz Rodríguez, who attacked 'el tópico del «estilismo»'. 'No es', he wrote, 'esta obra una serie de descripciones, ni un largo poema lírico en prosa. Es una «novela» con figuras vivas, de carne y hueso; con una psicología honda y compleja, personajes de una «acción»; pero todo esto llevado a cabo, no con un realismo de primer plano sino con una técnica deliberada y consciente.' [52]

Shortly after this, in April, there appeared the most sustained defence of Miró against the right-wing critics: three articles by Ricardo Baeza, a personal friend, in *El Sol.* He finds that the perfection of Miró's prose 'reside en una modalidad sensitiva, en una manera de ser personal, que, como en los verdaderos poetas, funde fondo y forma en una intimidad tan íntima — hipostática podríamos decir — que hace

[50] 'El gallinero literaria', *El siglo futuro,* 25 Jan. 1927, p. 1.
[51] 'Las ideas y el estilo de Gabriel Miró', *El Debate,* 4 March 1927, p. 8.
[52] 'El momento de Miró', *El Liberal,* 5 April 1927, p. 1.

casi imposible aislar la segunda'. [53] As a result, though one could parody Valle-Inclán or Azorín, Miró could never be parodied. Baeza sees this unity of form and content exemplified in vocabulary, which is never mere show, and in imagery: he describes Miró as the greatest 'innovador de la imagen' alive, excluding only those who reject grammar and logic. But he criticizes Miró's style for its occasional inadequacy, 'por razón de sus mismas cualidades, para la expresión de la dinámica espiritual y de la vida interior' and for 'la inferioridad manifiesta del diálogo'. [54] Baeza's enthusiasm is based on an uneasy compromise between critical attitudes of different generations.

The generally accepted view of Miró can be seen clearly in 1930, immediately after his death. Obituaries are the occasion for majority opinion to be codified as fact, and Miró's case was no exception. His death won him a far greater number of mentions in the press even than the events of 1927; looking only at the unsigned comments the expected words and phrases abound: 'un estilista ... un escritor preciosista' (*La Noche,* Barcelona, 28 May 1930); 'el prototipo del escritor puro' (*ABC,* 28 May 1930); 'el tipo de escritor puro en la más extensa y efectiva acepción de la palabra', 'únicamente un esteta puro, para quien los temas bíblicos eran el pretexto por el cual llevaba a cabo una grandiosa creación artística' (*El Sol,* 28 May 1930); 'prosa suntuosa y magnífica', 'nadie como él ha sabido comprender y descubrir el paisaje' (*La Libertad,* 28 May 1930). The various papers missed no opportunity of scoring political points off each other. *El Debate* (29 May 1930) condemned Miró's 'ideología' and 'técnica', but respected 'la actitud estética de Miró'. But *El Debate* was sharply ticked off by the quasi-Carlist *El siglo futuro: El Debate* had failed to point out that Miró's books 'merecen condenación terminante', and should not be read (31 May 1930). On the other side *La Libertad* (30 May 1930) accused *El Debate* of 'pequeñez de alma'. The provincial Catholic press echoed the quarrels in Madrid over whether Miró had taken the sacraments on his death-bed, thus renouncing his earlier 'attacks' on the Church.

In *La Libertad* (8 October 1930) José Montero Alonso reported an interview with a *Puerta del Sol* bookseller; of Miró he says: 'En vida era un autor que vendía muy poco. Con motivo de su muerte nosotros hemos vendido unos dos mil ejemplares de cosas suyas.' The bulk of the references to Miró in the press reflect this: at last there is an 'incident' in Miró's career that draws public attention to him, and the press from now on publishes little but the most ephemeral

[53] 'Prosa de Gabriel Miró', *El Sol,* 14 April 1927, p. 1.
[54] 'La prosa pura y Gabriel Miró', *El Sol,* 16 April 1927, p. 1.

articles, though in much larger quantities than before his death. At last Miró is news for the general public, news spiced with politico-religious controversy. The anniversaries, the square-, street-, and park-naming keep his name in the public eye: in Orihuela the fact that *mauristas* were devoted readers of Miró was thought helpful in a campaign to have a bust erected in the town that was the model for Oleza. And occasionally left-wing writers tried to appropriate his authority: Juan Gil-Albert refers to Miró's 'labor socializadora' [55] and Francisco Pina writes that 'de ningún trabajador oriolano salieron palabras duras para enfocar la obra o la persona de Gabriel Miró'. [56]

Of the personal reminiscences, few are of much value. José Guardiola Ortiz's biography, published in 1935, aroused a certain amount of interest, but the book itself, though it provides useful material, is riddled with errors. [57] Only the prologue to *El abuelo del rey* (*EC*, IV, vii-xv) by Augusto Pí Suñer, and an article by Julio Bernácer, the son of a close friend, tell us very much. Both insist on Miró's gentle irony. For Pí Suñer it was a defence: 'Escéptico, amablemente escéptico, por tu inteligencia y por las enseñanzas de la vida — para ti no siempre fácil — buscabas defenderte por la reacción que es la ironía, esta leve y buena ironía de tus obras mejores.' Miró himself has, through Sigüenza, spoken of his use of irony in a passage in 'Simulaciones' not included in the *Libro de Sigüenza*: 'Valga la ironía como episodio, como recurso, como consolación, como sutileza que evite o mitigue lo rudo, lo torvo, lo descarnado, lo cruel y lo ridículo. Pero ironía siempre, empacha sin dejar substancia. El sentido irónico exclusivo ya tiene menos encanto que la elementalidad de lo literal. Ironía siempre, equivale a lo redicho y chistoso' (*EC*, VII, 254). This is precisely Miró's practice. His irony is never all-pervading — the reader is never left without 'lo literal' to provide a context that gives direction to the irony.

Pí Suñer's essay is a far more helpful introduction to Miró than almost any of the criticism that argues endlessly and vacantly about 'prosa pura' and the rest. He writes: 'El mundo se le muestra a Miró en su multiplicidad contradictoria y en la mente de Miró se organiza y encuentra un sentido. Revive el pasado y se objetiva el presente, en una recreación expontánea de la realidad universal y eterna. La vida adquiere veracidad y entonces la realidad se hace novela.' Or again: 'Sensitivo, organizabas esas sensaciones y como nadie sugerías la complejidad, el placer, la melancolía de la vida humana. Lleno de intuición

---

[55] *Gabriel Miró* (Valencia, 1931).
[56] 'Orihuela y Gabriel Miró', 28 May 1932.
[57] *Biografía íntima de Gabriel Miró*.

psicológica, creabas personajes vivos; penetrado del mundo, creabas los paisajes.'

Pí Suñer was a close friend of Miró in Barcelona. Germán Bernácer was a close friend from much earlier days. His son writes (*Eco,* May 1934): 'Se le admiraba por muchos más por lo externo de su arte que por la emoción de su obra, y cuando le llegaban loanzas en tal sentido, ¡qué poema también el de su risa, entre asombrada, burlona y compasiva! Que le clasificasen entre los estilistas, como si fuese la forma lo mejor de su arte, arrancábale una franca risa, después de un leve gesto de enojo.' In 1927, he records, Miró wrote to the Bernácer family: 'Me parece la novela lo más costoso de nuestro arte. En ella se multiplica y acumula la humanidad del escritor, y no para volcarla, sino para destilarla.' And lastly, Miró's irony: his 'tierna y humana ironía — pareja, en el fondo, a la de Cervantes'.

The polarisation of Spanish life in the early and mid-thirties, followed by the catastrophe of 1936, totally altered the cultural situation. Many of Miró's admirers were scattered across the Atlantic and the new writers who began to emerge in the forties were uninterested. *ABC,* in 1945, reports Cela as saying of Miró, when asked about his influence: 'Su interés lo juzgo, realmente, muy escaso.'[58] And in spite of a number of critics who have been dissatisfied with the stereotype Miró, the textbooks and the standard works continue to record 'la incapacidad de Miró como novelista'[59] and that 'lo grave es que cada fragmento, casi cada frase entre sí, son «autónomos», no se completan ni ensamblan, no se «necesitan» entre sí ni respecto al conjunto'.[60] There would be little point in a tedious gallery of opinion since the Civil War: the arguments have for the most part been conducted along lines laid down long ago. What has been absent from the discussion on almost every side has been concentration on individual works and an awareness of Miró's irony and humour. Even those who are dissatisfied with the standard view usually answer it by studying some aspect of Miró across the whole of his work, thus implicitly lending support to the idea that his pages are a mere succession of independent passages, connected only by the writer's personality. Studies of how the language and imagery work within the structure of a particular novel, article, or *estampa* have been rare, and it is largely because of this that Miró's pervasive irony been missed, for context is essential to grasping irony. Essentially the failure has been one of not tackling Miró's works as wholes.

[58] Marquerie and Fernández Almagro, 'Valle-Inclán, Azorín, Baroja, Miró, Gómez de la Serna', *ABC,* 11 Nov. 1945, pp. 8-9.
[59] Torrente Ballester, *Panorama,* I, 265.
[60] Nora, *La novela española,* I, 465-6.

It is noticeable that those who insist on Miró's irony are often his close friends, who insist at the same time on the interdependence of personality and writing. The more one reads of Miró's less formal work — his newspaper articles that were not republished, and his letters — the more the rich and gently sceptical complexity of his personality is seen reflected in the *Obras completas*. The solemn aesthete of popular opinion disappears entirely. In a sense such considerations are irrelevant to the understanding of Miró's work. The author's personality and utterances, his reading and his aims and intentions may be considered inadmissible evidence. But a glance at the criticism shows that violent divergences exist as to the value of Miró's work and that outside evidence may be helpful. The following chapters try to discover a little of what sort of writer Miró was and to place him in his literary context. Ricardo Gullón has written: 'Gabriel Miró no está de moda. Quizá no lo estuvo nunca; pero yo me siento en deuda con él.' Gullón speaks for all those who feel themselves 'en deuda con él' when he says a little later: 'Si en los primeros treinta años de esta centuria existe en España un escritor de veras humano, con las cualidades y atributos espirituales inherentes a la condición de hombre, ese escritor es Gabriel Miró.'[61]

[61] Gullón, *La invención del 98*, pp. 113 and 117.

4

II

MIRÓ'S LIBRARY

In a peaceful and always deliciously perfumed room in her Madrid flat, Doña Olympia Miró, Gabriel Miró's elder daughter, kept her father's library almost as it was the day he died. Miró's table and chair stand in one corner by a small bookcase holding classical translations and important works of reference. A bureau with a glass-fronted bookcase holds editions of Miró's own works, and two large bookcases hold the bulk of his library, with the books arranged two deep on most shelves. Also in the room, in other bookcases, are the books gathered by members of the family, chiefly Doña Olympia's husband, Dr. Emilio Luengo: a collection of about the same size as Miró's. Some of Miró's books have become transferred into these bookcases over the years, but otherwise they are quite separate.

When Gabriel Miró died in 1930, he and his family were living in a flat in the Paseo del Prado. Since then, the family has moved, so that the library has left its original home. But, thanks to the care of Clemencia, Miró's younger daughter, who died in 1953, and the respect of the family, it is certain that the books are much as Miró left them. Clemencia at some time compiled a list of the books in her father's library; the books were found still arranged essentially as in this list, which gives them in shelf order. A simple list of titles and authors, it includes the following note at the end:

> Muchos libros pasaron a la biblioteca de Emilio. Algunos se regalaron a amigos de G. M. La Biblia que estaba en su mesa de trabajo se colocó en la vitrina, lo mismo que el ejemplar de 'El Obispo Leproso' encuadernado por H. Alsina Munné. Otros libros que estaban en su mesa pasaron a su lugar correspondiente en las librerías.

This gives a good impression of the care that the family took and the character of the library as it was preserved: Clemencia's objective was obviously to keep things as they were, as with the books put back in their correct places on the shelves. The fact that the list is arranged by shelves also speaks for Clemencia's assumption that preservation was the first priority. Again, the books themselves, with the appealing litter of forty years' reading, such as bookmarks, notes, tram-tickets, postcards, silver paper and so on, immediately suggest that to keep all just as it was left was the main aim of the family.

When one compares Clemencia's list in detail with the library a certain number of discrepancies appear — books listed by Clemencia have disappeared, others that obviously belonged to Miró are not listed. Yet overall these discrepancies, though puzzling, are not very important. [1] What we know of Gabriel Miró's books from Clemencia's list and from the present collection is, almost certainly, close to what he actually possessed at his death. But is what we know of Miró's library also representative of his reading over his whole life? Personal libraries can be very heterogeneous things, haphazardly collected and dismembered, but there are several reasons why one can take Miró's library with a seriousness that might otherwise be unjustifiable. There is no suggestion that there was ever in Miró's life the kind of upheaval that might have involved the loss of many books. There is among the books a very high proportion acquired when Miró was a young man: as he got older he acquired less and less books until the twenties, when his new position as a fairly well-known author living in Madrid led to a new rise in the rate at which his library grew. To suppose that many early-acquired books have disappeared or have been discarded would be to suppose an even greater imbalance in Miró's habits of collecting books at different stages of his life. Again, even with Miró's earliest writings there is a remarkable correspondence between his quotation of other authors and the library as he left it. Finally, the occasional duplication of titles suggests that Miró was not in the habit of discarding books. His library was in any case never of such a size that pressure of space would have forced him to cut it down. But when all this is said, the real basis for the conviction that Miró's library is important as offering a portrait of his interests and development is the subjective argument that as one works in this library, one comes to accept as self-evident that this is in the main a purposefully constructed, intensively used, and very personal collection of books.

The library includes something over a thousand volumes — a small library compared with the more than five thousand of Baroja and the four thousand titles of Galdós. [2] It is roughly grouped on the shelves

---

[1] The discrepancies are discussed in the Appendix (pp. 206-7).
[2] Alberich, *Los ingleses*, p. 39; Berkowitz, *La biblioteca de Benito Pérez Galdós.*

by subject-matter or by the nature of the edition. Some of the more obvious groups are the *Biblioteca de autores españoles,* the Spanish translations from the classics of the *Biblioteca clásica,* books of Biblical scholarship, books presented by their authors, books with the same binding and so forth.

In order to present the evidence on which later arguments are based, a list of the books has been included as an Appendix. It is usual in such lists to arrange them either by subject-matter, or in a single alphabetical list. However, in this case the books have been arranged according to a classification that attempts to place Miró's acquisitions in rough chronological order. Gabriel Miró lived from his birth in 1879 until 1914 almost entirely in Alicante. In 1914 he moved to Barcelona and in 1920 to Madrid where he remained, except for summer periods in Alicante province, until his death in 1930. In each of these three places he naturally used different binders for books he had acquired unbound, so that the various styles of binding allow these books to be allocated to the appropriate periods of his life. It is by using this fact as a starting-point that the books have been tentatively classified in order of acquisition.

First, all books that show written evidence of having been presented by their authors, editors, or translators, have been grouped separately. The books listed by Clemencia but now missing have also been grouped together, as have the volumes of the *BAE* and a set of books from Miró's adolescence. Next, five groups have been drawn up to include all books that have been privately bound for Miró, in the five binding styles that he used during his life. Of the remainder, all books published from 1928 to the end of Miró's life have been listed separately, because he acquired during those years of comparative fame a mass of books that is largely irrelevant to his work. Lastly, all other books have been classified according to whether they are in publisher's bindings, unbound, or privately bound, and according to their dates of publication. [3]

This classification allows the development of the library to be studied. Amongst the books bound privately for Miró, for instance, it is clear that the first three types of binding were used while Miró lived in Alicante. The fourth type always carries the label (except where it has clearly fallen off) of 'Subirana, Barcelona', so that these books must have been bound between 1914 and 1920, or perhaps a little earlier (Miró made several journeys to Barcelona before settling there). The fifth type carries the label of 'Raso, Madrid', and obviously belongs to the period after 1920. The question remains, do the dates of binding

[3] The list of categories is set out in the Appendix (p. 205).

offer firm evidence as to when Miró acquired these books? First, of course, they give a date before which he must have possessed them — 1914 or 1920. Together with the *terminus a quo* of the date of publication this often offers useful limits for possible dates of acquisition. In addition, the bindings probably also offer evidence of the date after which books were acquired. The problem here is that a period of time may have elapsed between acquisition and binding, but the character of each type of binding viewed as a whole is against this, for each type offers a kind of house-style within which are found the minor variations consistent with the books having been bound a few at a time, with slight differences in each new batch. More than a dozen variations of the third type exist, for instance. This hardly suggests that large accumulations of long-possessed books were taken to the binders. A quite different interpretation is also possible: that the books in the Subirana and Raso bindings, at least, were purchased ready-bound in the usual style of the bookseller, the initials 'G. M.' being added after purchase (Subirana was a bookshop as well as a binder's — Raso was a 'papelería'). But even in this case it seems very plausible that Miró would buy in Madrid when living in Madrid and in Barcelona when living in Barcelona.

Some books are bought purposefully, others more casually, as a result of browsing or as opportunity offers in second-hand dealers. It is reasonable to assume that books that Miró had bound were bought for the most part new and purposefully. But books in publisher's bindings are more problematic since the evidence is missing, and books that were acquired privately bound are almost certain to have been collected second-hand and therefore, on the whole, more casually. It seems sensible to try a further classification on these lines, and the results are illuminating: for instance, only four titles classified as privately bound other than for Miró were published in this century. Second-hand bookshops naturally tend to stock in the main books that are a good many years old, but even so the suggestion seems strong that only the young Miró made much of a practice of picking up odd second-hand books. Certainly the distribution of publication dates in this group is so radically different to that of the books that are in publisher's bindings that it becomes at once clear that this latter group must, on the whole, have been bought new rather than second-hand and purposefully rather than casually. In such ways the classification by bindings seems to show up several basic facts about the library.

These rather abstract assertions can only be filled out and the evidence for them presented in a detailed study of the library, category by category. The remainder of the present chapter is therefore essentially a commentary on the list of the books in the library drawn up in the Appendix; it uses the categories established in that list. In this way it proves possible to suggest a partial reconstruction of what Miró read and when and why he read it. At the same time a great deal of incidental information emerges, showing that the library is indeed an excellent guide to Miró's reading, and contributing to a portrait of Miró the writer.

1. Books from Miró's childhood

(a) First type of binding: leather spine marked 'G. MIRÓ'

Amongst all the books one small group of seven volumes calls out for separate classification. All are bound in the same way with 'G. MIRÓ' on the leather spine. They may well have been bound by the binder responsible for the second type of binding, but they are clearly separate. All seven are large volumes published in Barcelona by Montaner y Simón from 1885 to 1887. Palau comments on the volume of Larra's *Obras completas* that it is the most complete available: '¡Lástima que por su gran tamaño no es manejable!' The same comment can be applied to the other volumes.

The title page of *Las plantas que curan y las plantas que matan* is covered with childish doodles. Was this a book given early to Miró by his parents, or are the doodles by Miró's own children? Very likely the whole set was bought for Gabriel Miró by his parents who would have had it bound for him, hence the leather binding, more expensive than the cloth used on most of Miró's early books. The notion that these were childhood books is confirmed by the fact that with one exception none of the five authors is ever mentioned by Miró in his written work. The exception appears in his short 'Autobiografía' written in 1927:

> Mi padre era Ingeniero de Caminos. En su biblioteca, además de los libros de Ciencia, tenía otros de viajes, de Historia, de Mística, las obras de Larra, del Duque de Rivas, una 'Divina Comedia', un 'Quijote', una Biblia.
>
> (*EC*, I, x)

According to Clemencia Miró's list, the bottom two shelves of the small bookcase housed the most important reference works (*Diccionario Valenciano*, Roque Barcia's *Diccionario general etimológico*, Lafuente and Valera's *Historia general de España*, the *Crónica general de España*, and the Academy dictionary), together with four other volumes — large two-volume editions of *La Divina Comedia* and of *Don*

Quijote, the former of 1884, the later undated but according to Palau of 1879. Surely these would be volumes passed from father to son; but in that case why does Miró mention Larra and Rivas along with them? Without further evidence one cannot choose between a variety of possibilities. Did Miró confuse his own early Larra and Rivas with his father's books? Or were the Larra and Rivas the property of his father, later passed on and then having 'G. MIRÓ' added to the spine? Or did the father simply express his own taste by giving to his son editions of his own favourite authors? Whatever the answer is, the picture we get is of a middle-class liberal background and a father whose outlook was in the tradition of the liberal Romantics of the thirties and forties. For Gabriel Miró himself the contrast is strong between the continuing powerful influence of Cervantes and the enduring interest in Dante, and the quiet discarding of the Spanish Romantics. Even Larra, for all the interest of Miró's older contemporaries and in particular of Azorín, clearly meant little.

(b) Others

This group of books has been, perhaps, somewhat arbitrarily separated from other groups, but in the library it is physically separate in that it is kept on the back of a shelf among Dr. Luengo's books. None of the books in this group is listed by Clemencia Miró, yet it is reasonable to assume that all were Miró's, since more than a third contain his youthful signature and all are kept together. However the element of doubt about the unsigned ones is another reason for keeping them in a separate group. All are in publisher's bindings and of similar format to each other; all are published in Barcelona, the majority from 1882 to 1887. Apart from signatures and a note about Miró's friend Adelardo Parrilla in one volume, only the Victor Hugo is marked in any way — with a number of doodles. Cervantes and the *Celestina* appear in the library again in the *BAE,* the duplication serving to emphasise that this group represents some of Miró's earliest reading, well before he acquired the Rivadeneyra collection.

2. «BIBLIOTECA DE AUTORES ESPAÑOLES»

To Spain's classics Miró turned early and with continuous enthusiasm. The *Biblioteca de Autores Españoles* forms the basis of the whole library and clearly Miró built his collection around it. His friend Francisco Figueras Pacheco tells us that between the summer of 1899 and November 1901 (the month of Miró's marriage), whenever he and Miró went into the centre of Alicante their 'propósito común consistía por regla general en cumplir cualquiera de estos tres objetivos: comprar libros viejos, oír buenos sermones o ir al Teatro'. He goes on: 'La temprana entrada del Rivadeneyra en el despacho de mi amigo hizo innecesarias muchas búsquedas, tanto en las librerías de lance como en las restantes.' [4]

Rivadeneyra's *Biblioteca de Autores Españoles* started to appear in 1846, continuing to be published until 1880 when the seventy-first volume, of indexes for the set, appeared. As required, individual volumes were reprinted. Miró's complete set of the seventy-one volumes is uniformly bound, with a binding unlike any other bindings in his library, and carries no initials on the spines. Probably it was bought bound. E. L. King has stated that 'Miró adquirió la «Biblioteca de Autores Españoles» en 1900. De ella leía trozos a un amigo ciego, don Francisco Figueras Pacheco, quien aún lo recuerda'. [5] But the dates of publication of these volumes run from 1858 to 1902, so that either Figueras Pacheco's date is a little out, or else the set was acquired volume by volume over a few years. The last eleven volumes, published from 1869 to 1880, are first editions; the earlier volumes are, with three exceptions, reprints, including four dated 1902 and three dated 1901. A complete and reliable list of all the reprints of the *BAE* might cast some light on how Miró's set was made up and acquired, but this is not available. In general it looks as if the bulk of Miró's copies are the latest editions in 1900. One can therefore guess that he probably bought the set new; however all we know for certain is that if Miró bought the set complete, it must have been in 1902 or later — but by then he was twenty-three and for this reason and in view of Figueras Pacheco's evidence it seems an unlikely possibility. The volumes published in 1901 and 1902 (there are none from 1900) are the two volumes of *Dramáticos posteriores a Lope de Vega,* Lope's *Comedias escogidas,* I, II, and IV, Calderón's *Comedias,* I, and *Novelistas posteriores a Cervantes,* II. So it seems fairly certain that Miró acquired his set over a period, leaving the volumes that he found less important (or, possibly, out of print) till last. 'Yo no he sido un gran lector de teatro', he remarked in *ABC* in 1927. [6] This needs modifying since he clearly read widely in the Golden Age drama in his youth, but it could explain why Lope, an author he only mentions once in his writings, might have been among the last to enter Miró's set of the *BAE*. Miró, then, probably acquired the bulk of the set before he started publishing his work

[4] Ramos, *Mundo,* p. 23.
[5] 'Gabriel Miró y «el mundo según es»', p. 123.
[6] '¿Por qué no escribe usted para el teatro?', *ABC*, 16 June 1927, pp. 10-11.

in 1901. How long before this he started collecting the set is impossible to determine; ten of the volumes were published from 1897 to 1899, but the latest before that are of 1886.

The complete set of the *Biblioteca de Autores Españoles* offers an excellent illustration of Miró's reading habits as they appear from his library; a quick glance at the less important features will stand for the whole library. Miró rarely wrote comments in his books — usually the only marks are crosses or vertical lines in the margins and lines marking off passages in the text. In the seventy-one volumes of the *BAE* there appear to be only three comments. In volume LVII (*Poetas castellanos anteriores al siglo XV*), against stanza 147 of the *Libro de buen amor:*

> Al mancebo mantiene mucho en mancebés,
> E al viejo fas perder mucho la vejés,
> Fase blanco e fermoso del negro como pés,
> Lo que non vale una nues, amor le dá grand prés,

Miró has written: 'La cristalización de Stendhal', a reflection of his intense interest in Stendhal that reached its peak in his late twenties. In volume LXV, amongst the aphorisms culled from Seneca, Miró points out two that are mutually contradictory (p. 75), and in the first volume of St. Teresa Miró has written a remark explaining to whom St. Teresa was referring in a passage in the *Libro de las Fundaciones.*

The remnants of thirty years' reading are more in evidence : pieces of paper serving as bookmarks — half of them cut from Miró's father's notepaper — a couple of Miró's visiting cards and one of his friend, the architect Juan Vidal. Here is a letter from his doctor friend Pittaluga; here a postcard from Heliodoro Carpintero in Granada in 1930; elsewhere a couple of *estampas,* or a piece of silver paper still being flattened. In volume VII (Calderón's *Comedias,* I) is a piece of paper reading: 'Querido Juan. Ahí va el Sr. Calderón. El tomo de la *Celestina,* lo tendrá Ud. dentro de unos días. Hasta mañana. Le abraza y saluda a todos—Sigüenza.'

The *BAE* provided Miró with an invaluably large range of Spanish authors; it 'hizo innecesarias muchas búsquedas'. But it is not vastly illuminating to know that an author had probably read widely among the classics of his own literature before he began to write himself. Fortunately the books themselves offer a little more evidence as to their owner's interests : evidence in the shape of markings of passages, sheets of paper with quotations of various kinds, and uncut pages.

Uncut pages are a surprise in bound volumes: they only occur where the cut of the guillotine has not fallen inside all the folds in the paper. Usually this is due to some of the folds being out of place and the effect is that at regular intervals parts of folds are left to be cut. In volume LXVIII (*Crónicas de los Reyes de Castilla,* II), for example, sufficient folds are regularly uncut for it to look as if the book has scarcely been read. The second volume of *Poetas líricos del siglo XVIII* (LXIII) and *La gran conquista de Ultramar* (XLIV) are similar. A few pages in the volume of Quevedo's poetry (LXIX) are also uncut. In volume XXVII a few pages at the end of San Juan's *Cántico espiritual* and in *Llama de amor viva* are uncut, as are pages throughout almost the whole of Zárate's *Discursos de la paciencia cristiana.* On the whole the impression is that the least used volumes were those of history.

More important are the volumes that, to judge by the markings in them (much more common than the rare written comment), seem to have been of especial interest. The usual form of marking used by Miró is a cross (X) in the margin. Habitually this is a large cross extended to cover roughly the whole of the passage of interest, sometimes the whole margin. But there are also much smaller, quite different crosses; these are repeated below each other as long as the marked passage continues. These different markings are especially common in volume LIII, the first volume of St. Teresa's *Escritos,* and here they support a likely explanation. At first sight the copious markings of Miró's copy of the *BAE* St. Teresa seem to be evidence for his very special attachment to her work. But in the early twenties Miró started to prepare an anthology of St. Teresa and it is clear that much of the annotation in the St. Teresa volume has to do with preparation for this work. [7] The composer, Oscar Esplá, has also written: 'En la última temporada veraniega de Polop, planeamos una ópera sobre Santa Teresa.' [8] Since the markings may have to do with the anthology or the libretto they cannot be used by themselves as evidence for Miró's admiration for St. Teresa. Yet by distinguishing between large and small crosses something can be salvaged. Sheets of paper lying in the volume suggest that the small crosses are associated with the systematic selection of passages, while on the other hand Miró's books in general suggest that the large cross was the usual youthful practice. It is likely, then, that the small crosses are the practical markings of the older Miró, while the bolder crosses are those of the young reader, marking passages that strike him as 'fine thoughts'.

It seems a psychologically normal progression to start by enthusiasti-

---

[7] I owe to E. L. King this information, which modifies his earlier view that the markings are evidence for Miró's devotion to St. Teresa: see 'Gabriel Miró y «el mundo según es»', pp. 123-4.
[8] *Evocación,* p. 25.

cally marking striking lines, and then slowly to drop the practice of marking at all and to use it only when practically necessary. If this is right, and perusal of the library constantly suggests it, there is a fascinating parallel with the development we find in Miró's writing. Compare, say, *Del vivir* (particularly the first, 1904, edition), with *Nuestro padre San Daniel*. In *Del vivir* both Sigüenza, the hero, and Miró, the author, are obviously impressed with the quoting of other authors and in particular with direct ethical statements. In *Nuestro padre San Daniel* this practice has entirely disappeared: the central problem of despair at men's lack of love for each other is still there, but instead of confronting it with the aphorisms of notable authors, Miró presents his theme through character and plot and the marvellous control of his language. To some extent the young man is still hopeful of finding plainly-stated answers, the mature writer knows that the truth can only be sought in the whole of his novel.

The comparison is unfair to *Del vivir* for often its quotations are a part of the whole, but it is surely true that the impression it gives of being here and there constructed out of prefabricated parts closely parallels Miró's search in his reading for thoughts fine enough to approach the status of answers, a search that comes across in his markings as a young man. Again and again it is the plain prose content of passages that has obviously attracted his attention. And so remote is this kind of thing from the qualities that one most admires in Miró that it is yet another confirmation that this marking of books was confined to his earlier reading years. Figueras Pacheco writes: 'Los versos rotundos le subyugaban ... Años más tarde, le seducirían los saturados de ideas y sentimientos hondos, fuesen o no sonoros y brillantes, pero en aquella época ... el ritmo y el vigor, la justeza y la fuerza de expresión conquistaban fácilmente el corazón de mi amigo.'[9] When Figueras speaks of 'versos rotundos' this would be just before the beginning of the century; the search for lines 'saturados de ideas y sentimientos hondos' clearly corresponds to the period of reading as a search for truths. It is after this period is over that the fully mature writer emerges.

But to return to St. Teresa. Her works occupy volumes LIII and LV of the *BAE,* the second volume consisting entirely of letters. In volume LIII the only section showing no sign of interest is *Escritos breves.* All the major works are marked both with the large youthful crosses and the smaller repeated crosses. In addition a number of sheets of paper lying in the volume make the situation clearer still. These papers probably indicate a further stage in the preparation of the anthology. For instance, in the *Vida* is a sheet of paper headed: 'Para la no-

[9]   Ramos, *Mundo,* pp. 23-4.

ticia preliminar de Teresa de Jesús.' Then follow passages copied from the *Vida,* up to page 26. On page 32 the first small crosses begin. In the *Libro de las fundaciones* the small crosses end at page 200. At page 202 is a pile of about a dozen sheets mostly copying out marked passages from the *Libro de las fundaciones* up to page 200. The *Avisos, Camino de perfección, Moradas,* and others also reveal a close correspondence between the small crosses and the passages copied out. All this reinforces the conclusion that the small crosses belong to the twenties. If they are disregarded, leaving only the large crosses (that show no relation to copied passages), we can see the extent of Miró's youthful interest clearly: as a young man he marked St. Teresa as much as he marked almost any other book, particularly in the first quarter of the *Vida* and in *Camino de perfección* and the *Moradas.*

At the end of the *Modo de visitar* a sheet reads: 'Se ha creído que la Santa no leía lo que llevaba escrito de otros días. Se fundan en lo que ella declara en pág. 297, 1.ª columna. «Modo de visitar los conventos.»' The reference is to Vicente de la Fuente's 'Preliminares' in volume LIII, where in the section on 'Estilo y lenguaje de Santa Teresa' he writes: 'En la multitud de ocupaciones que la asediaban, ni aun tiempo tenía para leer lo que llevaba escrito, cuanto menos para corregirlo' (p. xii). It is clear from other volumes that Miró read the introductions to them carefully; and from his library as a whole that for many authors they were his chief source of information. It seems that he rarely sought out books even about the writers in whom he was most interested, but instead relied on material like these *BAE* prefaces. Did Miró write out this note in protest against the preface-writer's insistence on Teresa's 'gracioso desaliño'? Finally, in volume LV, eighteen letters of St. Teresa are marked.

As for the rest of the *BAE,* about a dozen volumes have markings such as crosses and sidelines, the rest being unmarked. In volume XIII, the first of the *Epistolario español,* half-a-dozen of the letters of the *Centón epistolario,* now accepted to be a forgery, are marked. This is a curious case; Miró wrote an article entitled 'Figuras de antaño — La del físico del muy poderoso e sublimado rey Don Juan el Segundo de este nombre', and published it in the *Diario de Barcelona* on 1 October 1911. The whole piece is based on the *Centón epistolario* and clearly Miró's one source was this volume of the *BAE,* whose introduction rejects the suggestion that the *Centón* is a forgery. It looks from Miró's piece as if he accepted this defence, but it probably did not concern him overly. In the article Miró quotes liberally from the *Centón,* but only once from a marked letter. He calls its author Fernán Núñez instead of Fernán Gómez and he calls him 'babchiller'. Is the intrusive 'b' a repeated misprint (it occurs a score of times), or is it a strange attempt by Miró to archaize further? The whole article is a mixture of near-*modernista* prose and deliberate delight in the archaic, an extreme example of tastes that occasionally led to comparisons with Ricardo León. The opening sentences give the flavour: 'Desde la fenestra contempla el babchiller los pinares de Castilla, que han recibido la gracia y la pureza de la nevada. El Pisuerga rasga y pasa mansamente la blanca llanura. El cielo es de humo de frío que baja al amor de las calladas aguas' (p. 13752).

Straight history did not interest Miró very much but something like the *Centón,* a personal historical document, could act as a trigger for that side of his art that attempted to evoke and reconstruct, as in the *Figuras de la Pasión del Señor.* The last sentence of 'Figuras de antaño' — the earliest attempt of this kind — reveals the nature of Miró's interest in history: 'Y nosotros sabemos de su vida [Fernán Núñez] por lo que él se afanó y contó doctamente de las ajenas.' In his lecture delivered in Gijón in 1925 Miró makes a complementary point: 'Se ha reconocido que las figuras distantes tienen para el artista un encanto y fuerza siempre poderosos, porque la distancia las despoja de todo lo que en ellas puede haber de episódico y de transitorio, deján-doles la verdad profunda sobre la que acciona el Arte' (Ramos, *Literatura,* p. 303). At the same time that Miró attempts to bring historical figures nearer to us as individuals, he makes use of the distance naturally offered by his subject-matter. Perhaps part of the explanation of Ortega's failure to grasp what Miró was doing is that he saw only the distancing, in accordance with his own theory of modern art as distance, and like so many other critics missed the paradoxically accompanying involvement. But it is ironical that this first attempt at historical recreation (and the first use of the title 'Figuras') should start from a forgery written nearly two centuries after its purported date, and doubly so that in the twentieth century Miró should archaize on a seventeenth-century imitation of the archaic.

The next volume in the *BAE* with a cross is volume XVI, the second volume of the *Romancero general.* Here there is a single cross against Alfonso de Alcabdete's 'Yo me levantara, madre' (p. 497). Again this is an interesting illustration of Miró's habits. He quotes the first six lines of the poem in the chapter of *El humo dormido* entitled 'San Juan, San Pedro y San Pablo' (*OC,* p. 729). The fifth and sixth lines read:

> Sola lava y sola tuerce,
> sola tiende en un rosal,

lines that are used again by Don Magín near the end of *El obispo leproso:* 'Yo, hija de mi alma, lavo, tuerzo y tiendo mi vida al sol' (*OC,*

p. 1060). Perhaps it is worth adding that there are paper markers both at the page containing Alfonso de Alcabdete's poem and at the pages in volume I of the *Romancero general* containing the two other ballads quoted in 'San Juan, San Pedro y San Pablo'.

Another marked volume is *Escritores del siglo XVI,* I (XXVII). This is the volume containing San Juan de la Cruz, Malón de Chaide, and Hernando de Zárate, and its markings are directly interesting. In Malón de Chaide's *La conversión de la Madalena* there are three crosses near the beginning (this is a common pattern, indicating either that books were often left unfinished, or that as the reader settles into the book the flow of reading takes over and marking is forgotten). The crosses mark these passages : 'Por el entendimiento conocemos, por la voluntad amamos' (p. 284), 'Hasta agora habemos tratado cómo se ha el amor con las criaturas intelectuales, que son los ángeles' (p. 285), and 'Y con irnos tanto en acertar a asentar el amor, es una potencia que no puede estar parada' (p. 286). In the introduction to San Juan the following words are marked : '«Distingo en mi alma, decía él mismo en una carta, las almas de los que más amo»' (p. xi). Another kind of mark, a vertical line in the margin, is made against four of San Juan's 'Avisos y sentencias espirituales' (nos. 129-131 and 135). All four deal with the contrast between spiritual and sensual love. The only other markings in San Juan are in the *Subida del Monte Carmelo,* including passages used in *La palma rota* and in *Las cerezas del cementerio,* both dealing once again with aspects of love. [10] In marking San Juan Miró could scarcely fail to mark passages dealing with 'amor', and the early pages of *La Madalena,* too, are extensively concerned with love. But one is struck, as elsewhere, by Miró's persistent interest in writings and passages that deal with 'amor' and 'amar'. Very often the word 'amor' is enough to arouse his interest, regardless of the sense in which it is used. Many critics, and especially A. W. Becker, [11] have pointed out 'falta de amor' as a leading theme in Miró's work, but here one can be more specific. The 1904 edition of *Del vivir* included a very lengthy footnote, full of quotations, on 'falta de amor', which was removed from later editions. *Del vivir* essentially turns around the problem of why men fail to love each other — in the character of Sigüenza and, more prosaically, in the footnote, Miró explores how this should be so. While this failure to love was to remain prominent in Miró's work, it was around the time of the writing of *Del vivir* that Miró's interest in philosophical statements about the many kinds and aspects of love was at its keenest. Miró's interest in 'amor', as seen in these markings and in *Del vivir,* fits well with the notion that most of his markings were made as a young man.

[10] *BAE,* XXVII, 7 and 17: cf. *OC,* pp. 220 and 346.
[11] *El hombre y su circunstancia,* Chap. III.

The same attraction to the very word 'amor' turns up again in the next marked volume, *Poetas líricos de los siglos XVI y XVII,* I (XXXII). In Herrera's own preface to his poems the following is lined right round: 'Y si he de decir verdad, no ha tenido pequeña parte en mi determinación el amor, que es tan natural en todos los que escriben, de querer ver sus obras en alguna estimación y cuenta' (p. 256). Of itself a comforting thought for a young writer: but the structure of the sentence, forcing into the forefront of our attention the word 'amor', must surely have caused it to strike Miró with double force.

Apart from Herrera, Hurtado de Mendoza is also marked (at Sonnet VI), along with nine poems of Góngora, four sonnets, one *canción,* three *letrillas* and an *epigrama.* Seven of these nine are used in a manuscript note on Góngora that has been left in this volume and which most probably is connected with the 1927 celebrations for the Góngora tercentenary, so that the marking of these poems (with the small crosses) is not of great importance.

In Volume XXXIV, Lope's *Comedias escogidas,* II, there are two crosses, and again the passages deal with 'amor'. The first is in *La Dorotea,* I, v: Julio says: 'La raíz de todas las pasiones es el amor: dél nace la tristeza, el gozo, la alegría, y la desesperación' (p. 10). The second is from the same work, II, ii: 'Dorotea: Amor no es margarita para bestias: quiere entendimientos sútiles, aborrece el interés, anda desnudo, no es para sugetos bajos; después de muerta, quiso y celebró el Petrarca su bella Laura' (p. 15). Once more, statements about the nature of love are what interest Miró, love in all its senses.

Volume XL, *Libros de caballerías,* is marked twice in passages from *Amadís de Gaula* dealing with the loves of Perion and Elisena, and El Doncel del Mar and Oriana. Of less interest are five markings in Volume LI, *Escritores en prosa anteriores al siglo XV;* all are in Juan Manuel's *Libro del caballero,* and four of them are aphoristic. There are three markings in Feijoo's *Obras escogidas* (LVI), all in an essay entitled 'Causas de el amor'. Two of the passages are long and deal with love. The third is typical of the kind of maxim that Miró noted: 'Hay asuntos que piden más penetración para encontrar lo verosímil, que se ha menester en otros para hallar lo cierto' (p. 411). The previous article in the volume has an uncut page: clearly Miró was attracted to read just this one essay by the title. Volume LXII, the second of the *Epistolario español,* is marked four times at the first and second letters by Juan Lorenzo Segura de Astorga (purporting to be from Alexander to his mother) and at the first letter of Pedro López de Ayala.

The only other two volumes to be marked are of more interest and extend the impression of the young Miró as a seeker of aphorisms. The first is the volume of *Poetas castellanos anteriores al siglo XV* (LVII). The *Poema del Cid* is unmarked, as are Berceo and the *Libro de Alexandre*. But in the *Libro de buen amor* no less than thirty stanzas are marked, all in the first half. Twenty-five of Sem Tob's *Proverbios* are marked, mostly in the first fifth, together with five passages from the *Rimado de Palacio*. By now it is becoming clear that the books marked fall in general into two categories: writing before the Golden Age and philosophical and religious writing. The former was, of course, an enthusiasm shared with most of Miró's contemporaries, the latter a more personal interest that is further confirmed in the other marked volume *Obras escogidas de filósofos* (LXV). Apart from Vives's remark that 'todo el resto de la vida cuelga de la crianza de la mocedad' (p. 240), all the markings are either in the Senecan *Libro de oro* or in Setanti's *Centellas*. Fifty-six of Seneca's and fifteen of Setanti's sayings are singled out. The principles lying behind the selection of these are hard to formulate: this is the case, too, with Sem Tob's proverbs, though in Juan Ruiz, not unexpectedly, stanzas about 'amor' dominate. What is obvious is the interest in maxims: the marked passages are mostly wise sayings. Perhaps Seneca comes closest to exemplifying the kind of thought that most appealed to Miró — the stand against being made bitter by a world of injustice, the sceptical view of conventional values, and the genuine goodness and humility that all come across in a collection of sayings from Seneca: these, together with that superior knowingness that is a part of the whole business of maxims and aphorisms, are what one finds in general in thoughts that Miró found noteworthy as a young man.

Finally in dealing with the *BAE* there are a certain number of sheets of paper to be found in the volumes which cast light on Miró's methods of working. Some of the cases in which quotations from the volume concerned are copied out have been mentioned. The others include Cervantes's *El licenciado Vidriera* (I), Mariana (XXXI), *Diálogos de apacible entretenimiento* by Gaspar Lucas Hidalgo (XXXVI), and Luis de León's *La perfecta casada* — warning wives to act as wives, not as nuns (XXXVII).

Another kind of manuscript is that with notes or sketches for future writing. In Volume I, at the end of the *Quixote,* are a couple of sheets, one with a score of lines of phrases describing the port of Alicante, the other a short description of Catalan character. There is virtually nothing else of this kind anywhere — Miró's manuscripts and notes in general do not exist. It is sometimes asserted that he wrote without any notes at all, in contrast to Azorín always jotting down what he saw. The assertion, as with so many made about Miró, is probably derived from what he says about a character, in this case Sigüenza:

'No recuerda ahora Sigüenza dónde ha leído — el no anotar, el no marginar el estudio, dejándolo que se le transfunda como elemento de la propia sangre, le incapacita para ser erudito o crítico — (...)' (*OC*, p. 655). Probably these notes in Volume I are in the nature of drafts with writing in view, rather than notes made as a response to particular scenes and events.

More interesting are four other sheets of paper, in Volumes II, III, XXXVI, and LVII, listing single words. The size of Miró's vocabulary has been a subject for much argument and criticism. His most serious detractors alleged that he was a comber of dictionaries, while defenders claimed that he gathered words directly from people who used them. The truth must be that Miró was far more eclectic: certainly local terms and expressions were gathered locally, but Miró's reading must inevitably have played a very large part in the formation of his vocabulary. Hence the interest of these lists of words. Were they noted down to be looked up afterwards? Or did Miró find them particularly attractive or useful and record them for later use? One of the lists is such as to suggest the latter. But Miró notes the words down without reference or context: either the word itself appealed to him or else he relied on his memory for the particular context in which he found it. In any case the probability is that at least at some stage of his career it was his habit to make aide-memoires of this kind. The few that are left are probably no more than representatives.

The longest lists are found at the end of the *Celestina* in Volume III (*Novelistas anteriores a Cervantes*), and in Volume LVII (*Poetas castellanos anteriores al siglo XV*). Almost all the words in the first list can be found in the volume concerned; it looks as if the list was not intended for checking later, but rather as a record of interesting words — one would hardly read over three hundred pages in the *BAE* before looking up words!

The list is as follows (I have added references to the pages of *BAE*, III on which the words appear):

> junta la puerta (37) — amanojar (40) — diacitrón (40) — ronces (61) — escotar (62) — avahadar? (?) — humero (81) — falsopeto (81) — golosmear (81) — recuesta (81) — espadañadas (94) — almohazar (94) — [After this the words are scattered in confusion on the paper, some written in ink, others in pencil] — cimojes (112) — cuja (320) — ochavado (289) — bajamanero (298) — baharí (298) — mohatra (301) — mozuelo (288) — moyuelo [should be 'hoyuelo'] (220) — antipodio (338) — tueros (320) — nesgas (296) — gorguerán (307) — recentar (311) — [At this point the words begin again to be placed in order] — mochiller (113) — barrachel (113) — en porreta (118) — madaga-

53

ñas (122) — alhorinas [should be 'alhorines'] (124) — cabezalero (125) — pelechar (127) — bancal (128) — en cerro (189) — sonrodado (190) — asterin [should be 'arestín'] (191) — molletes (195) — cisiones (220) — mariscar (221) — empachado (221) — haronear (224) — atabal (237) — azacaya (237) — alcarria (243) —ahilar (250) — cóndito (264) — ax (263) — entrevar (288) — acebruchales (338) — jerosilla (?) — perulero (?) — desguijavar (?) — flocaduras (?).

In the middle of the list is a quotation: 'Celestina: Es un fuego escondido, una agradable llaga, un sabroso veneno, una dulce amargura, una deleitable dolencia, un alegre tormento, una dulce y fiera herida, una blanda muerte.' Under this is written: 'Se acabó el aceite y ardían las torcidas.' The first quotation, which appears on page 46, looks as if it was written down before any of the words were added, the paper with the quotation later being used as a word-list.

What immediatedy appears from this list is that for the most part the words are in the same order as in the book. The first five are from the *Celestina*, then 'humero' to 'recuesta' are from *Lazarillo*. The next two are from the anonymous second part of *Lazarillo*. Then a number of words are packed in without much order around the quotation in the middle of the sheet, before resuming again with 'mochiller' in Luna's continuation of *Lazarillo*. The next seven words, up to 'bancal', are all from Luna, and the remainder, except for the four unidentified words at the end, are taken from *Guzmán de Alfarache*. Although the exact order of the words in the middle of the sheet is not clear, all but two of them belong between 'entrevar' and 'acebruchales' at the end of the list. We can picture Miró, then, reading through the volume, noting down words neatly above and then below the quotation, and finally, after page 288 going back to fill up the space in the middle.

Some of the words in the list occur more than once in the volume, but in that case the page has been given that preserves the sequence. The pattern is quite clear: Miró read systematically through the *Celestina*, *Lazarillo* and its continuations, and then, possibly omitting *El patrañuelo*, *Doce cuentos de Juan Aragonés*, and *El sobremesa y alivio de caminantes*, went on to *Guzmán de Alfarache*, Parts One and Two. Seemingly he stopped there, or at least stopped taking notes (there follow the spurious Part Two of *Guzmán*, *Historia de los amores de Clareo y Florisea*, *Selva de aventuras*, *Historia del Abencerraje*, and *Guerras civiles de Granada*).

Where does all this lead? First, we know that Miró read these works attentively, and it is most important to show this of the picaresque novels especially. Most obviously in *La novela de mi amigo*, but also in, say, *Nómada* and *Niño y grande* he learned from their structure. Secondly, we discover that the fact that a book is unmarked is no evidence as to Miró's lack of interest in it. Knowing that Miró used slips of paper like this we can surmise that this was quite a common habit and perhaps that he adopted it at a different period from that when he was making enthusiastic crosses. Or, at the very least, a different technique corresponds to a different purpose. Either way, the direct marking of books clearly has a restricted place in Miró's reading habits.

Thirdly, the list of words provides more evidence for Miró's psychology as a reader. More often than not the words he notes down come from the beginning or the end of a chapter. He is not a systematic student of vocabulary, but rather starts reading slowly, interrupting his reading to make notes; then, as he becomes involved in the text, the flow of reading takes over and particular words seem to catch his attention less. Until at the end of a chapter the break allows him to note down a word or two he has just read. In spite of appearances and with the exception of the *Figuras de la Pasión del Señor,* Miró is not an erudite or systematic reader. He tends to find material by coming across it more often than by searching for it. The abundance of quotations and the constant use of literary and other sources in his works are not there because he painstakingly sought them out to ornament his prose, but because he came across them and fell for them. These aspects of Miró's character constantly emerge from his library; they are of essential importance in view of the widespread assumption that Miró is a cold jeweller with words.

This assumption has a bearing on the fourth kind of conclusion to which this list of words leads us: the reasons why Miró picked out these particular words. The common view is that Miró culled words painstakingly as rare ornaments, and that he was interested in their sound, quite apart from their reference to any other reality. Mariano Baquero Goyanes writes:

> La agudizada sensorialidad mironiana, orientada literariamente bajo un signo modernista, puede percibirse en mil aspectos. Por ejemplo, en la eufonía de los nombres. Miró se deja atraer por seductoras cortezas verbales. Hay nombres —de personas, de pueblos, de cosas— cuyo sólo enunciado, cuya sola agrupación misteriosa de vocales y consonantes, provocan en el escritor sensual deleite. [12]

He uses as evidence the following passage:

> Agres, Ondara, Alcalalí ... ¿Es la delicia de la palabra por ella misma? Pero es que la palabra no sería deliciosa si no signifi-

---

[12] *Perspectivismo y contraste,* p. 150.

case una calidad. Y estos nombres rurales en boca de sus gentes dejan un sabor de fruta, que emite la de todo el árbol, con
sus raíces y su pellón de tierra, y el aire y el sol y el agua que
lo tocan y calan.

(*OC*, p. 1134)

Miró's passage makes, in fact, exactly the opposite point to that
made by Baquero Goyanes, who has allowed the stereotype to obscure
what Miró actually says. Form and content for Miró are indissoluble
at every level, and this applies just as much to individual words and
names as to larger structures. It is ironical that in quoting this passage from Miró Baquero Goyanes omits the word 'no' before 'sería deli-
ciosa', thus making the passage rather odd, but apparently in support
of the commonplace view. But Miró's love of unusual words was not
aimed at impressing, nor at mere aural enchantment. Richness and
precision were what he looked for, which is why his greatest admirers
were among the generation of poets of 1927, the men who admired
Góngora and constantly strove for precision and control in their vocabulary.

Several kinds of interest are visible in the list of words itself. Most
of the words are unusual, though sometimes their meanings are plain
enough; presumably Miró had not come across the particular form before: 'amanojar', 'ronces', 'escotar', 'humero', 'golosmear', 'mozuelo',
'cabezalero', 'bancal', 'ahilar', are obvious examples. There are three
phrases: 'junta la puerta', 'en porreta', and 'en cerro'. With these clearly belong words that were particularly interesting for their use in
phrases: 'almohazar (los oídos)', '(pudieran echarme) nesgas (al pelle-
jo)', '(traer los) atabales (acuestas)', 'entrevar (la flor)'. Another class
of words belongs to *germanía* or is associated with picaresque life, not
surprisingly, since all come from *Lazarillo* and *Guzmán:* 'falsopeto',
'bajamanero', 'barrachel', 'mariscar', 'entrevar'. Others clearly appealed to Miró's sense of the precise word: 'diacitrón', 'espadañadas', 'ocha-
vado', 'cuja', 'baharí', 'antipodio', 'gorguerán', 'mochiller', 'barrachel', 'alhorines', 'sonrodado', 'mollete', 'azacaya', 'alcarria', 'acebuchal'. All these
words have very precise meanings, and Miró was always delighted to
find single words for things usually described more circuitously. Unsurprisingly, some of these words have an archaic flavour, but chiefly
it is their exactness that attracts Miró. Finally, there are words that
are rarer terms for some commoner expression. Here the interest is
in the avoidance of cliché: 'mohatra', 'tueros', 'recentar', 'madagañas',
'pelechar', 'arestín', 'ciciones', 'empachado', 'haronear'. Very many of
these owe their attraction to the fact that they are metaphorically used,

so that they not only replace a cliché, but offer a wealth of connotation for the writer to use.

The other fairly lengthy list of words is to be found in Volume LVII. Though slightly longer, it is more straightforward. All the words in it are taken from the *Libro de buen amor* and are noted down in more or less correct order, covering most of the poem. This confirms what was evident from the markings, that Miró read Juan Ruiz with attention, and it reveals the same interest in finding words that offer unusual forms, interesting phrases, and precision with the avoidance of the commonplace. The remaining volumes of the *BAE* yield three more scraps of paper with a total of eight words, not enough to be easily traced, and which add nothing to the general conclusions about these word-lists.

There is one other set of papers to be found in the *BAE* that must be mentioned, since it casts light on many of the questions raised so far. In Volume XXXII (*Poetas líricos de los siglos XVI y XVII*, I) are two sheets of paper on which Miró has written some remarks about Góngora, quoting from eight of Góngora's poems. The first words are: 'Ahora, releyendo a Góngora, me paraba más en los versos de amor.' The rereading is probably in 1927 in connection with the Tercentenary celebrations. There follow the quoted poems and then this passage, which beautifully expresses one aspect of what has been discussed:

¿Cómo se influyen los escritores tan a distancia de los años y de sus escritos?

Góngora, además de ese idioma poético que se le atribuye, y que él no niega, es un descubridor de la sensibilidad, de la sensibilidad en contacto con mucho que entonces no tenía palabra o forma exacta. Góngora se precia del hallazgo de una palabra que equivale al hallazgo de las nuevas realidades de sensación —pues sin palabra no existirían— la misma creación sale de la nada en virtud del verbo divino —y Góngora es y quiere ser el que pronuncia y denomina felizmente las nuevas cosas sin duda porque otros, casi todos los poetas de su tiempo lo han intentado sin aquella fuerza y claridad de sentidos con que está él dotado.

Góngora es el que llega a nosotros como un inmediato antecesor de nuestra técnica. Pero su influencia, su enseñanza, no es ejercida, no debe serlo, al dictado de la erudición, de la lectura prolija y difícil de la obra. Ese estudio de Góngora, esa afición a Góngora ha venido después de nuestro parecido. Es casi lo biológico que así da.

How do writers influence each other? Miró delicately indicates the mysteries in this process that often make the apparently most precisely stated connections the most dangerously unreliable in the study of influences. Here Miró's belief in the power of the word is displayed: stated in the classic passage in *El humo dormido* (*OC*, pp. 692-3), these notions are implied in his whole use of words. The word is creative ('sin palabra no existirían'). The word is precise ('palabra o forma exacta'). The word always reaches out for more subtle distinctions of sensibility ('nuevas realidades de sensación'). Miró finds exactly in Góngora his own greatest talents, talents that his young contemporaries in the 1920's found admirably expressive of their own poetic aims. Hence, of course, Miró can talk of Góngora being 'antecesor de *nuestra* técnica'. The 'nuestra' surely refers not to the generation of '98 or to Ortega's generation, but to the poets of 1927. Finally, Miró indicates his own relationship with the Spanish classics, a relationship made tangible in his copy of the BAE. It does not rely on the 'dictado de la erudición', but 'es casi lo biológico que así da'.

Some general conclusions are possible. The *Biblioteca de Autores Españoles* has a particular interest, not only because it is clearly the most consulted part of Miró's library, but also because, being a complete collection, it is possible to judge both what interested Miró and what he left to one side. Above all Miró was a reader of prose fiction and of religious and philosophical works. Drama was of less interest. Poetry he read with most interest when it was from before the Golden Age, though Golden Age poetry itself he also read. Historical works, by contrast, clearly form the least-read section of the library. In more detail, the *BAE* volumes suggest that Cervantes, the *Celestina*, the picaresque novels, and Juan Manuel were important among the prose fiction. In fact, among the volumes of prose fiction only Volume I of *Novelistas posteriores a Cervantes* and the volume of Isla are entirely without evidence of reading. Amongst the religious writers, St. Teresa stands out, followed by Luis de León, San Juan de la Cruz, and Malón de Chaide. But Luis de Granada and Rivadeneira are quite without evidence of reading. Seneca and Setanti of other prose-writers aroused Miró's interest. Less clear-cut cases are Vives, Feijoo, and Floridablanca, with a few signs of being read, and Saavedra Fajardo, Fernández Navarrete, Jovellanos, and Quintana with none.

The dramatists are only represented, as far as evidence of reading goes, by the Moratín volume and one each of Calderón and Lope. The remainder of Calderón and Lope, Tirso, Ruiz de Alarcón, Moreto, Rojas Zorrilla, and the volumes of *Autos, Dramáticos posteriores a Lope de Vega*, and *Dramáticos contemporáneos a Lope de Vega* are without sign of having been read. Among the poets the volume of *Poetas castellanos anteriores al siglo XV* is well marked, while one volume each of the *Romancero general* and the *Poetas líricos de los siglos XVI y XVII* are paid some attention. Quintana, Quevedo, and Castellanos are without evidence of reading, as are the *Poemas épicos,* the *Romancero y cancionero sagrados,* and the three volumes of eighteenth-century poets.

Summing up, the set suggests that Miró acquired the *BAE* from about 1900 to 1902, read it intensively during the next few years, and steadily thereafter. As a young man he is fascinated by the power of words and absorbed by the problem of men's lack of love for each other; he is interested in any idea casting light on it and he marks up ideas that strike him. Naturally enough he looks for such ideas especially in prose writers, both of fiction and of philosophical and religious works. This must of course only be one of many special interests and a part of the general enthusiasm for literature; the important point is that he looks for formulas with which to answer the world, a youthful tendency that he soon leaves behind.

3. SECOND TYPE OF BINDING: CLOTH SPINE MARKED 'G. MIRÓ' OR 'G. M.'

The acquisition of the *BAE* can be assigned to a fairly closely defined period. The present category of books cannot be restricted in the same way: it must include some books, perhaps a majority, acquired in the last years of the nineteenth century, as well as some that entered the library after the *BAE.* From 1896 to 1900 Miró was studying for a law degree at Valencia and Granada universities. In 1896 and 1897 he passed examinations in 'Historia Crítica de España', 'Metafísica', 'Literatura General Española', and 'Economía y Estadística'. After this all the passes are in law subjects. It is not known what reading Miró undertook for these courses and it is not easy to connect many of the books in his library directly with these subjects; but it must be born in mind that his knowledge of history, philosophy, and literature underwent this formal training, as well as the more important independent reading evidenced in his library. Probably the university work played a very minor part: a pass in economics would hardly be guessed by the most careful reader even of his essays on contemporary topics. Yet his pass, 'aprobado', was the same as that in Spanish Literature.

Essentially the present group of books is made up of those that were privately bound for Miró with bindings entirely cloth-covered (all his later bindings have leather spines). There are several different varieties of binding, with variations in cloth, colour, end-papers, and decoration of the spine, but all stand out at once as by the same binder.

Exceptionally, three books have also been included that, though they have leather spines, are otherwise similar to the rest of the books · Euripides, Valera's *Juanita la larga,* and a copy of the Bible.

The value of classifying by bindings becomes visible with a glance at the list: quite a few of the books were published in 1901, but not a single one is dated later than this. Of the undated volumes a very few do not appear in Palau until later, but then omissions of editions in Palau are not uncommon. So this group of books must belong to the period up to 1902, when Miró had not yet found his personal style. They must include some of the books that most interested him at the time, though Miró's apparent practice at this time of having all his unbound books bound means that not necessarily all of this group are especially important.

The hundred-or-so titles are easily classified by subject-matter, the most obvious and important class being classical literature, consisting of classical texts, with the exception of González Garbín's *Literatura clásica latina.* González Garbín was professor at Granada University when Miró was a student there and his book was published in 1896. This is as near as we come to finding Miró's higher education reflected in his books. But it is confirmation that this group of books relates to Miró's reading during his student years. For the rest, classical literature is represented by more than thirty titles, most of them from the *Biblioteca clásica* first published during the late nineteenth century, and all of them in Spanish translations without the original text. The range of authors covered is considerable: from Aeschylus to Xenophon, including the work of almost fifty writers.

Manuel Fernández-Galiano has traced the course of Miró's relationship with the classics; he points out that Miró had almost all of the *Biblioteca clásica* volumes and how Miró quotes from them. As he notes, the bulk of the classical references in Miró's work are very early. At a later stage these student recollections turn into deliberate erudition in the *Figuras.* And Fernández-Galiano frankly dislikes Miró's 'mundo helénico' after the move to Barcelona in 1914: '¡Qué diferencia entre esta Jerusalén de cartón y aquella Oleza de piedra y carne y hueso y sangre!'[13] It is interesting to see confirmed in the library what Fernández-Galiano notes, and what is evident in the works: that, more overwhelmingly than with any other group of authors, Miró's interest in the classics was an early enthusiasm, the results of which always remained with him, but which did not prolong itself beyond the earliest years of the century. After this, Miró acquired almost no further classical works. From the lavish name-dropping of 'Vulgarida-

[13] 'El mundo helénico de Gabriel Miró', *Ínsula,* 15 May 1950, p. 1.

des', an early essay pleading for a return to the classical literary virtues, and the extensive quotations of *Del vivir,* there is a headlong decline. Only in the *Figuras* do the classics reappear to any great extent and here the motive is quite different: conscious recreation of an age rather than the exhibition of enthusiasms.

But this early collection of classical texts was clearly very important to Miró. It is placed in a separate bookcase where almost all the volumes are kept together. The proportion of books marked is, as in the *BAE,* higher than the average for the library. Seneca's *Tratados filosóficos* in two volumes are perhaps more extensively marked than any title in the library other than St. Teresa. In *De Providentia,* IV, where Seneca speaks of how bearing ills patiently strengthens a man, Miró has added the comment: 'Pero el cuerpo combatido por frecuentes enfermedades no es el más vigoroso y fuerte', a remark referring doubtless to Miró's own supposed ill-health. There is another comment a few pages further on, and there are marks in *De Ira, De Clementia, De Beneficiis, De Consolatione ad Marciam,* and *De Consolatione ad Helviam,* and sheets of paper copying passages from *Naturales Quaestiones* as well as from the two last-mentioned essays.

Plutarch, Cicero, and Florus are somewhat less extensively marked; Plutarch in the lives of Alexander, Mark Anthony, and Artaxerxes, including a sheet of notes on the first two; Florus mostly against descriptions of brutalities, doubtless of interest as background to the *Figuras*; and Cicero in Volumes II to V, including *Brutus, Orator, De Natura Deorum, De Finibus bonorum et malorum, De Officiis,* and *De Amicitia.* Marcus Aurelius and Publilius Syrus are occasionally marked, usually at epigrammatic lines, while Lucian and Herodotus both are marked once or twice near the beginning of the first volume and then no more. Lucan is unmarked, but contains a paper copying out a passage.

In the *Iliad* are two more of Miró's rare comments in the margin. In Book VI at the speech of Hector to Andromache and the meeting with his baby son, he has written: 'Estas dos páginas son encantadoras.' Later, in Book XVI, he writes: 'Homero arrebata a Hector la gloria de dar muerte a Patroclo y cubre de vilipendio a Apolo haciendo de él un rufián, un asesino asqueroso.' A last interesting mark is in the volume of *Poetas bucólicos griegos.* Fernández-Galiano suggested that Ignacio Montes de Oca y Obregón, the bishop-translator of Theocritus, Bion, and Moschus, was the model for the first bishop in *Nuestro padre San Daniel.* [14] The similarities are plausible and the argument is almost clinched by the fact that Miró refers to his bishop as 'el buen Ipandro

[14] 'El mundo helénico de Gabriel Miró', *Ínsula,* 15 May 1950, p. 1.

de Oleza' (*OC*, p. 793) — Montes de Oca's pseudonym was Ipandro Acaico. In the volume possessed by Miró the first page of a note entitled 'Un obispo poeta', dealing with Montes de Oca, is sidelined in red. The only doubtful point is that Miró rarely used red pencil for marking his books; perhaps a later reader, spotting the link, marked the passage. But it is an unlikely possibility and the line seems to confirm the interest of Miró in the Mexican bishop. If the argument is correct the reference remains an odd one. Few readers, surely, would understand anything by the reference to Ipandro, even though Miró tells us that his bishop, too, translated the Bucolics. This is by no means the only occasion on which Miró introduces a near-private allusion with an air of innocence, as if he were writing only for himself.

Leaving the classical texts, the remainder of the books in this group can be classed, with a very few exceptions, as either Spanish or foreign literature. In Spanish literature Miró was acquiring the *BAE* at the same time, so that, unsurprisingly, only five items are from before the nineteenth century. Three are by Quevedo and are from the *Biblioteca clásica* (which was not confined to the ancient classics). These volumes from a trusted series, together with *Persiles y Sigismunda* and Gracián's *El héroe* and *El discreto,* also probably belong to the days before the *BAE*.

Among nineteenth-century Spanish writers only Clarín and Valera claim more than one item. E. L. King has reported that Valera was recommended to his daughters by Miró and has shown that he was beyond doubt Miró's most admired nineteenth-century predecessor. [15] His evidence is based in part on the library: the present group of books includes five titles by Valera, whilst a sixth, *Pepita Jiménez,* in which Miró's inscription '¡Bendito seas!' appears under the frontispiece portrait of Valera, was bought second-hand during this period. Of the other five titles, *Doña Luz* and *Genio y figura* were purchased in Granada; though Miró studied at home he naturally had to visit Granada several times. Finally, the copy of *Juanita la larga* is a delightful witness to the esteem in which Valera was held in the Miró household. Extremely battered and with loosened pages, it is full of children's doodles. Titles are pencilled in under the illustrations and Don Paco and his two children by Juanita have been drawn in. The date 1920 is added, with the words: 'Juanita la larga. Su esposo y sus dos hijos.' For one or both of Miró's daughters it was an evident first favourite.

Of the rest of the Spanish volumes, Campoamor's *Poética* bears a note showing that it was given to Juan Miró (either the father or the brother of Gabriel): even among these bound volumes we can never

---

[15] 'Gabriel Miró y «el mundo según es»', p. 124; see also King, *Humo,* pp. 31-3.

be sure that Miró obtained them deliberately. A volume of Bécquer, another known favourite of Miró's, [16] is marked once, in Rima III. But by far the most interesting item is the nine-volume set of Menéndez Pelayo's *Historia de las ideas estéticas*. Dated from 1884 to 1891, every volume is marked. At the beginning of the fifth volume Miró has written : 'Signos : X frases que más me interesan. —Lo subrayado indica lo que deseo consultar, leer. X ( ) — paréntesis = curiosidad.' This is hardly any use as the key it sets out to be, since Miró failed to stick to it. It looks like a good resolution early on, just as Miró starts an individual book eager to mark. But it does reveal what Miró looked for and clears away the doubt that these markings might be directed towards University studies. To mark 'Frases que más me interesan' is not the practice of an indifferent student with exams in mind. The word 'interesan', too, is helpful; not 'lines that I agree with', but 'lines that interest me most'. As for underlining, he very rarely uses it — perhaps the simpler practice of sidelining took over from it.

The markings themselves are full of interest; clearly this was Miró's chief source of the history of aesthetic theory, as well as a fertile source of quotations from authors on a variety of subjects, as we shall see in the next chapter. In the first volume there are copious markings in the chapter on Plato, especially the central pages dealing with the relationships between love, beauty, and the good, confirming the suggestion that Miró's early aesthetic outlook was essentially Platonic. In the next volume it is Lull and Sabunde and March who draw his attention, together with Santillana; it is noticeable that Miró usually marks quotations, not Menéndez Pelayo's own words — he uses *Ideas estéticas* as a source-book. In the third volume (II in Miró's set), León Hebreo is marked almost continuously. In succeeding volumes there are still a good number of marks, but they are more scattered, though in III, i Lessing, Arteaga, and Piquer are marked more thoroughly than others. Undoubtedly Miró owed much of his knowledge of eighteenth- and nineteenth-century literary history and theory to Menéndez Pelayo, and it must be remembered that he was reading this extraordinarily comprehensive work at a time when he was, or had just been, discussing with his uncle Casanova painting and literature together, so that the whole of Menéndez Pelayo's field would be meaningful to him. But above all Miró seems to have acquired from Menéndez Pelayo some knowledge of the philosophy of such men as Lull, March, and León Hebreo.

There remains the modern foreign literature and one of the most striking characteristics here is that only two of the thirty-odd items

[16]   Ibid.

are in French, all the others in Spanish. Miró was, of course, as E. L. King puts it, 'at home in the little society in Alicante in which French was spoken and French books were read and discussed, even though his efforts — apparently he was by nature a poor linguist — to speak French, like his efforts to speak Valencian, were the occasion of some mirth among his family and friends' (*Humo,* p. 22). Whatever his reading ability, Miró clearly at first preferred translations whenever available. Later on he acquired more and more works in French, often reading English and German works in that language. Many of these were rather more specialised than the books he was reading before 1901 and therefore not obtainable in Spanish. Again, his bibliographical awareness grew slowly: later, there is evidence that he ordered from specialist bookshops, and chased up particular studies, especially for the *Figuras,* but at this time he was buying what he found available — the preponderance of the Barcelona and Valencia publishers who would dominate the Alicante market confirms this. Of his books of French literature in this group, two are published in Paris, two in Madrid, three in Valencia, and seven in Barcelona. In other sections of this group Madrid is more prominent, but the sample is roughly indicative. Sempere of Valencia and Maucci of Barcelona were publishers active in French translations who are often represented in Miró's library.

Among the French authors, nineteenth-century writers are the great majority. Only Le Sage and Bossuet (a volume in the *Biblioteca clásica*), are outside the century in which Miró was born. Sénancour and Mme. de Staël, Chateaubriand and Lamartine, Flaubert, Zola, and Maupassant, are each represented by one item, only the first two being marked in any way. Letters VI to XX of *Obermann* are extensively marked; it is hardly surprising to find Miró interested in the stoicism and romantic nature-description of Sénancour. The important author here is Daudet, with four titles, a large number for one author in this library. But it is not easy to clarify Miró's interest in Daudet. *Tartarin de Tarascon,* the only work from which he quotes in his writings, is missing; instead, the naturalist works *Jack* and *El Nabab* are present.

English literature is scantily represented, with the exception of three titles by Scott, another youthfully enjoyed writer. German literature offers a further six titles, but a much more predictable selection of authors. Two titles by Nietzsche (one slightly marked), accompany Schopenhauer, while Goethe's *Faust* and *Werther* go with Heine's poems. In literature the great works of romanticism, in thought the newest ideas: these were Miró's guiding interests in foreign literature. Heine, not unexpectedly in one fond of Bécquer, is liberally marked.

Large numbers of whole poems or single verses are marked, and against number six of *El regreso* Miró has noted: '¿A quién no le ha pasado lo mismo?'

Amongst the remaining works of foreign literature, three books by Sienkiewicz stand out as another special interest. In *Hania* Miró has marked the list of the author's other works with the letter L against *Quo vadis?, Sin dogma, Hania, A sangre y fuego,* and *El diluvio.* If 'Leído' is meant, only two of the five are in the library and the remainder must have been borrowed or lost. The same situation must apply to many other authors where the evidence is missing. But it is interesting to see Miró already with a taste for the recreation of Christian history. Not only has he Sienkiewicz, but also Merezhkovsky's *La muerte de los dioses,* a successful (at the time) portrayal of Julian the Apostate.

Leaving aside literature, two of Miró's other special interests are foreshadowed among these books. Apart from the Bible and St. Augustine's *La ciudad de Dios,* there appears the first title by Renan, to remain an author for whom Miró felt great sympathy, and who perhaps comes closest to expressing Miró's own attitude to religion. Later Miró was to acquire a large collection of Renan in French; for the present he owns one title, in Spanish, published by Maucci of Barcelona. The other enduring interest seen here, psychology, is one that grows over the first ten years of the century and then disappears as far as the library is concerned. Often the interest is in popular or semi-popular works; Miró is never very concerned about the scholarly status of his sources. And often the interest goes hand in hand with absorption in the theme of 'amor'. *El amor libre* by Charles Albert, a French writer, is a work that deals with sexual relationships in a social context, and from a socialist point of view. For Albert capitalist society vilifies the relationship between the sexes. It is a work that has everything to do with 'amor' and rather little with psychology even taken in a wide sense. But it belongs to an interest of Miró that was shortly to develop along psychological lines. At this time he is bothered about the barriers that convention erects against the aims that sexual love would pursue. In his second novel, *Hilván de escenas,* like his first more of a search for a personal means of expression than a valuable novel, this interest in social barriers is obvious. The novel can be seen in some respects as a thesis, an attack on the unfair difficulties placed in the way of the illegitimate, and the stigma of illegitimacy. It was for Miró at this time a matter of a simple conflict between petty social restrictions and the man (often an artist), who rose superior to them and so freed himself of the need to pay them attention. The topical theme of the artist to whom the 'ordinary' rules did not apply was very much present in Miró's early outlook, and doubtless there is also a good share of the perennial young man's fancies in these beliefs. These linked themes of the superman-artist and the injustice of social convention never left Miró, but they became merged into a more complex understanding of human nature. One aspect of this development was the interest in psychology of the next few years and this is why it seems right to place Albert's *El amor libre* and Mantegazza's *Fisiología del amor* as the earliest evidence of this particular interest. Albert's book is heavily marked; it was obviously a book that aroused great interest in Miró, and it would otherwise be unjust to pay it much attention. The third book in this group is more strictly psychological: Condillac's *Traité des sensations*. It is tempting to speculate on possible links between Condillac and Miró's vision of the world around him as his own sense-perceptions, but the book is quite unmarked and gives no encouragement to such speculation.

4. THIRD TYPE OF BINDING: LEATHER SPINE MARKED 'G. M.'

Some time after 1901 Miró changed the style in which he had his books bound. The main feature of the new style is a light brown leather spine with the initials 'G. M.' (the only exception is Chekhov's *Vanka*, with Miró's initials, but a unique binding — though details allow it to be placed in this group). There are variations within the style, chiefly of details of decoration on the spine, and it is possible to group the books into over a dozen sub-styles. Unfortunately when this is done the publication dates of these sub-groups show no kind of pattern, so that we are left only with the firm knowledge that these books were bound after 1901, before 1914, when Miró moved to Barce-lona, and, obviously, after their date of publication. In the group as a whole there are notable changes in emphasis from the earlier years. Marking comes near to disappearing. Half-a-dozen titles have an oc-casional cross, while the lines marked are now even more obviously and consistently epigrammatic, dealing most commonly with the artist, the great man, love, or more general moral themes. Only Stendhal's *De l'amour* is extensively marked in the earlier style, and here the crosses stop suddenly at Chapter Thirty. None of the volumes have bookmarks or other papers in them, except for a volume of Flavius Josephus where Miró heads a sheet 'Herodes — fuentes que me faltan ...' and lists a number of sources including Josephus.

Miró is reading far more in French now — almost half these volumes are in French and very few of the books by French authors are in translation. The subject-matter, too, has changed in emphasis.

Only just over half the titles are literary, and of these the bulk belong to French literature. Two titles by Clarín, and Cervantes's *Teatro* (missing from the *BAE*) are the sum total of Spanish literature, over-shadowed by a completely new enthusiasm, Stendhal, and a lesser one, Anatole France. The dates of the Stendhal volumes give little clue as to when Miró bought them. The last of them is from 1909, the year in which he published 'El presagio', which mentions Stendhal's psychology, the earliest reference that can be dated. The markings in these volumes suggest that Miró discovered Stendhal when his main ideas were fairly well established and that his enthusiasm came from the way in which Stendhal's ideas corresponded with and strengthened his own. The notions of the artist as a superior soul in search of beauty and sincerity, and of passion overriding convention are examples of ideas that occur earlier in Miró being marked by him in Stendhal.

The rest of the literary works do not offer anything very striking. The Goethe volumes probably belong to an interest in Goethe that continued from the previous group of books into the early years of the century. The fact that there are only three volumes of contemporary Catalan literature is slightly surprising since Miró began during this period to visit Barcelona and make the acquaintance of Catalan writers.

Outside the works of literature another later interest of Miró that is still only slightly represented (Josephus and Tertullian), is the history of Christianity. Much more impressive is the growth of interest in psychology. As before, the borderline between 'el amor' and psychology proper is blurred. At one extreme are Stendhal's and Michelet's books on 'l'amour'. At the other are works by writers as important as Ribot, Binet, and Taine. The title of the first of Binet's *Etudes de psychologie expérimentale,* 'Le fétichisme dans l'amour', offers a concrete example of the fusion of 'amor' and scholarly psychology in Miró's preoccupations.

Another concern that emerges is with the will. Not for nothing was this the period of Azorín's *La voluntad,* and the many other novels of 'abulia'. Miró himself often used the theme; in *Del vivir* it is a main-spring of Sigüenza's actions (or lack of them). In *El abuelo del rey,* the hero is a classic *abúlico.* The subject was immensely topical: Payot's book *L'Education de la volonté* (Miró's copy is of 1906), offers practical advice to the layman on how to strengthen his will-power.

Miró's choice of writers on psychology follows a logical pattern. Taine's achievement had been to overthrow the highly theoretical, metaphysical French psychological tradition that had held the field after Condillac. Taine denounced everything between himself and Condillac, and so paved the way for a new school of empirical psychologists including Ribot, Paulhan, and Binet. Miró already possessed Condillac, so that his new acquisitions in this group continued logically his view of psychology. How this came about is hard to determine — probably by reading in journals and newspapers. Miró's editions of Ribot's books are of 1905 and 1906. Two of the titles had been reprinted several times, so that Miró probably acquired these books fairly soon after these dates. It must have been at around this time that he went through a period of especial interest in contemporary psychology.

Linked with this interest are two others: philosophy and biology. Schopenhauer, to the reading of whom the 'abulia' of the generation of '98 eventually goes back, Kant, and Nietzsche, are all represented, along with the lesser, but fashionable figure of Guyau, the title of whose *Esquisse d'une morale sans obligation ni sanction* fits in exactly with Miró's interests. As for biology, the three outstanding evolutionists, Darwin, Haeckel, and Lamarck, are all represented. Taken together these books suggest a coherent picture of Miró interested in man as a part of the world of phenomena. In evolutionary theory, man is a part of the whole network of nature. In empirical psychology, man's mind becomes an observable phenomenon, the subject of scientific investigation in a manner in no way different from that applied to other phenomena. And shortly Miró was to take up modern Biblical scholarship, in which the events of the Bible are no longer seen as unique and independent of the rules that govern the rest of the world, but in the context of their historical setting, and in which Biblical texts are dissected in the manner applied to ordinary human documents.

In all these three areas, evolution, psychology, and Biblical modernism, that so upset the Church and her view of man and the Bible as unique, Miró was consistently open to the modern view. Miró's perception, in his writing, of men as objects, and of the things of nature as human, is closely connected with this general habit of mind.

5. BOOKS PUBLISHED BOUND BEFORE 1914

The books in this group are less useful as evidence of Miró's development. Some are obviously important but about many we can conclude little, for mostly their acquisition cannot be dated with any accuracy. Using the bound groups as a yardstick, many of these volumes, especially those on the Bible and Christian history, belong after 1914, and this is confirmed by the fact that four such titles, those by Cabrol, Hello, Joly, and Kellner, were bought in Subirana's bookshop in Barcelona. A few other volumes can be roughly dated by linking them to particular interests of Miró, and Dante and Cervantes, as we have seen, are early acquisitions, perhaps family possessions before they became

Miró's. Another early book is Diego de Yepes's *Vida de Santa Teresa,* signed in Miró's youthful hand, and in all respects similar to the books in Section 1 (a).

Over half of the group are concerned with religious and ancient history and scholarship; none of them is marked, and most of them are in Spanish. Amongst the volumes of literature most tie up with interests already noted: Sienkiewicz's *Quo Vadis?,* Renan's *Souvenirs d'enfance et de jeunesse,* and two volumes each of Flaubert and Balzac.

6. BOOKS LEFT UNBOUND, PUBLISHED BEFORE 1914

About half the books in this group also are on religion. The remainder are very miscellaneous and the possibility of second-hand purchase makes dating hazardous. Three items by Azorín are important: a battered first edition of *Antonio Azorín,* a copy of *La evolución de la crítica* inscribed 'Para D. Lorenzo Casanova', and Azorín's preface to Luis Pérez Bueno's *Artistas levantinos.* E. L. King has surmised that these last two were influential in the formation of Miró's style in *Del vivir;* [17] it is interesting to note that his copy of *La evolución de la crítica* was that of his uncle, the painter Lorenzo Casanova, who, according to Pérez Bueno, devoted far more time to reading than to painting. No doubt Miró discussed Azorín's book with his uncle just as he certainly discussed with him artistic and literary theory in general.

7. BOOKS PRIVATELY BOUND, BUT APPARENTLY NOT FOR MIRÓ

Presumably these are almost all second-hand books, so that their dates of publication mean rather little. Only four were published in the twentieth century, suggesting that Miró probably bought fewer and fewer second-hand books as time went by, a probability that is indirectly confirmed by Figueras Pacheco telling us that Miró visited the Alicante second-hand bookshops frequently in his youth.

The subject-matter of the books is about equally divided between Spanish literature, French literature, and religious topics, with a very few others to complete the list. A few of the books on religious history are marked (De Saulcy's *Histoire d'Hérode* and Lenormant's *Manuel d'histoire ancienne de l'orient*); otherwise there is little sign of Miró's presence. But there is one volume of especial interest;

[17] 'Gabriel Miró y «el mundo según es»', pp. 129-33. See also King, *Humo,* p. 34.

bound, with the initials 'J. L.', it includes, along with four other titles, *Santa Teresa de Jesús y la crítica racionalista*, by Juan Maura y Gelabert. This Maura was the cousin of Antonio Maura, the statesman, Director of the Academy, admirer of Miró, and the man who got Miró a job in the civil service in Madrid. Juan Maura published this work in 1883, when, as the title-page tells us, he was 'Lectoral de la Santa Iglesia de Mallorca'. In 1886 he became bishop of Orihuela where he remained until 1910. Miró was at the Jesuit boarding school in Orihuela from 1887 to 1892, and would certainly be familiar with the figure of Bishop Maura. Inside the volume is a dedication to Julio López (the 'J. L.' of the spine), from 'El obispo' in memory of a 'Velada literaria' in 1888. How or when Miró acquired the volume is unknown, but what is certain is that Juan Maura, a man interested in social affairs and liberal ideas, and author of a monograph on Miró's favourite, St. Teresa, was the model for 'el obispo leproso'. An extraordinary cluster of coincidences — did the book play a part in keeping alive Miró's sympathy for Maura, or did he get hold of the book after starting on *El obispo leproso?*

Among other types of book, several volumes of Balmes and Rousseau indicate two further authors possibly of interest to Miró. In Rousseau, Miró has not only marked passages, but twice has added comments. In *Les Rêveries,* in the third 'Promenade', Rousseau writes : 'J'en ai beaucoup vu qui philosophaient bien plus doctement que moi, mais leur philosophie leur était pour ainsi dire étrangère.' Miró has added : 'Yo lo pensé también.' Later, in the eighth 'Promenade', speaking of his 'amour-propre', Rousseau comments that 'il s'est contenté que je fusse bon pour moi'. Miró adds: 'Mucho antes de conocer yo esta frase de Rousseau díjemela frecuentemente y a ella sujeté mis pensamientos y acciones.'

Two other volumes contain sheets of paper written in Miró's hand. The first is Millot's *Histoire littéraire des troubadours;* this is dealt with later. The other volume is Pascal's *Cartas provinciales,* where we read on a piece of paper an extract from the ninth letter: '¿Qué importa la puerta por donde entramos en el paraíso, si el caso es entrar?', a thought that could well be Miró's own.

8. FOURTH TYPE OF BINDING: BY SUBIRANA OF BARCELONA

Returning to a group of books that can be dated more accurately, we leave Miró's youth behind. In 1914 Miró was 35 and in the same year he moved with his family to Barcelona. From now on almost all the books listed must have been acquired after this move. Six years later he moved on again, this time to Madrid, so that these books, bound in Barcelona, can safely be assigned to 1915-1920. These titles should represent an important part of Miró's significant acquisitions during those years, the years during which he wrote and published the *Figuras de la Pasión del Señor*. The books reflect Miró's intense work on this recreation of the context of the Passion. Only two titles do not belong to religious and ancient history and many of the books are scattered with markings indicating material on the civilisation and events of New Testament times. Sometimes a note indicates the particular part of the *Figuras* for which a fact is singled out; at other times, appropriate subjects in the index are marked with a cross.

These are not books of devotion, nor works of conservative apologetics, but contemporary scholarship. Many of the books are fairly specialised works, and over half are in French, indicating that Miró by now knew exactly what he wanted and where to find it. This was the period during which he worked as editor of the abortive Catholic Encyclopaedia planned by the Barcelona house of Vecchi y Ramos. He came into contact with Christian scholars who could guide him through the latest literature: indeed a good part of his work as editor would involve him in getting to know it. Miró never became a scholar, nor even a very scholarly reader; nevertheless the character of his library has changed radically from the famous literary texts with their enthusiastic markings to these works of learning with their factual and practical annotations.

9. BOOKS PUBLISHED BOUND FROM 1914 TO 1918

This is another mixed group, all of which must have been acquired after Miró moved to Barcelona, and a good number of which probably entered the library before 1920. About half are on religious history and religion.

10. FIFTH TYPE OF BINDING: BY RASO OF MADRID

With very few exceptions all the books listed from now on were acquired after the move to Madrid. This particular group is of interest in that they were the only books Miró chose to have bound during the last ten years of his life. Unlike his earlier practice, the majority of new books are now left unbound, so that presumably these books, beautifully bound by Raso, are of some importance. It is conceivable that the books were bought already bound, but the first volume of

Flaubert's correspondence is stamped 'Fé Librero', and Renan's *Les Apôtres* was bought in Buenos Aires, so they at the very least were bound after purchase. And since Raso seems to have been primarily a *papelería*, it is safe to assume that these books were singled out for binding after purchase by Miró. Once more works of ancient history and religious scholarship predominate, while Renan, always a favourite author, is now repurchased in a splendid binding. A number of these books were to provide quotations and material for Miró during the twenties, both in his published work and, presumably, in the further series of *Figuras* on which he was working. A comparison of his work with the library shows clearly that the books bound by Subirana and Raso form the nucleus of that part of the library used for such reference purposes.

11. BOOKS PUBLISHED BOUND FROM 1919 TO 1927

None of the books in this heterogeneous group is marked. A preponderance of them are published by Atenea, Miró's own publisher for a time in the early twenties, run in part by his friend Ricardo Baeza, so that they are likely to be presented copies and of little importance in studying Miró's interests.

12. BOOKS LEFT UNBOUND, PUBLISHED 1914 TO 1927

A similar situation, though a more complicated one, arises with this group of books. Living in Madrid, Miró now had more literary friends and contacts, and it becomes increasingly difficult to tell which books he chose to acquire and which came through these connections. For example, twenty-two items here are published by Calpe and seven by Biblioteca Nueva or Atenea (both publishers of Miró). Well over half the remainder have some obvious connection with a friend, and careful investigation would doubtless reveal further links.

13. BOOKS PUBLISHED 1928 TO 1930

After the publication of *El obispo leproso* late in 1926 Miró's work and the author himself were suddenly paid much more attention than before. The rate of growth of Miró's library increased dramatically, and much of this is evidently due to Miró's changed situation. Many of these books would be given by acquaintances and publishers and tell us nothing sure about Miró himself. A few are uncut. At the same time, Miró's published work was more or less complete. Only *Años y leguas* and a few articles were to come, and the former had already appeared for the most part in newspapers. In spite, therefore, of the interesting presence of Husserl, amongst others, these books can be set aside as of no possible influence on the major published work, though some of them may give an indication of the way Miró's ideas were developing.

14. BOOKS INSCRIBED BY THEIR AUTHORS, TRANSLATORS, OR EDITORS

The largest group of all is that of books presented to Miró by their authors, translators, or editors. In this group books have only been included in which an inscription shows this to be so; many of the books in the previous three groups almost certainly would be in this category if the evidence were conclusive. The picture given of Miró by this collection of books is of quite a different kind from the earlier groups. Here what interests us is not the books but the list of those who admired Miró, and in this sense the list is instructive. Almost all the writers are literary men, with Alvarez del Vayo and Araquistain as exceptions from the left of politics and Angel Ossorio y Gallardo from right of centre. Others were close personal friends not otherwise well known: Germán Bernácer, Augusto Pí Suñer, Gustavo Pittaluga.

But most are writers by profession, and they correspond to various clearly defined periods in Miró's life. First come a group of Catalan writers (the dates are those of the inscriptions): Maragall (1911), Carner, Massó-Ventós, López-Picó (1915), Frederic Clascar, Joaquín Ruyra, Ramón Turró, Suriñach Sentíes (1912), and Xenius (1911). Miró was in touch with all of these in Barcelona both before and during his residence there, and he has written about all except Clascar.

But there were others who admired Miró sufficiently to send him their books fairly early, though in most cases there is a special link. Azorín, one of the first to praise Miró, sent three books published in 1909 and 1912. In two of the three dedications Azorín uses the word 'amigo', though it is not known when he and Miró first met. Later Azorín supported an attempt to get Miró elected to the Academy in 1927. This is the occasion for a renewed friendship confirmed by three more books.

Valle-Inclán sent two volumes of 1908 and 1909; he had been on the jury that awarded Miró a prize for *Nómada* in 1908. After that, there are no more. Ricardo León sent three volumes at the same period (two dated 1908 and 1910, one published in 1912). Andrés González-

Blanco, who boasted that he had discovered Miró, sent a volume of his *Los contemporáneos* in 1907. Rather later, Ramón Gómez de la Serna sent him the second volume of *La sagrada cripta de Pombo*.

Two other friendships appear to rise and fall a little later still. Jacinto Grau sends four titles from 1917 to 1921, and then no more. Juan Ramón Jiménez, to whom Miró was introduced around this time, presented three volumes in 1919. But the friendship very soon cooled, more due to Juan Ramón than to Miró, and again, there are no further presentations. Finally two volumes by Larbaud complete the more interesting books before 1920. Larbaud and Miró never met, but Larbaud did much for Miró in France, having lived for a time in Alicante after Miró had left.

After 1920 a few more Catalan names occur and those of some French admirers, along with odd volumes by a dozen or so Latin-American men of letters. But the most striking characteristic is the support of the new young poets. Almost the only writers to contribute more than one volume are Salinas with four, Jarnés (four), Gerardo Diego (two), Juan Chabás (two), Bergamín (two), and Dámaso Alonso (two). Alongside them Alberti, Mauricio Bacarisse, Jorge Guillén, and Marichalar appear with one volume each: altogether a remarkable group of those associated with the Góngora revival of 1927. Díez-Canedo, one of the few early admirers of Góngora, appears also. Miró contributed in a valuable way to the 1927 celebrations, as we have seen, and quite obviously felt at home with these young men. But the mutual sympathy was not a mere reflection of the events of that year, for Alberti, Diego, Salinas, Jarnés, Chabás, and Bergamín all made presentations before 1927.

Young writers naturally send their work to established authors, but they do choose the recipients with care, and this particularly iconoclastic group would hardly send their work to Miró with such unanimity unless they recognised him as a writer they could admire. They were seemingly united in viewing Miró as someone with whom they were artistically in touch. For a short time Góngora was the touchstone by which those of whom they approved were marked off from those who were to be rejected, and it is appropriate that they should meet Miró in this admiration and in just this situation. So that having followed Miró's interests as he builds up his library, we end with a tribute from the new generation to the work that had made so much use of that library.

III

MIRÓ AND OTHER WRITERS

In his classic *Problems and methods of literary history,* André Morize sets out five 'principal fields for the investigation of sources'. [1] The first of these, 'reconstruction and study of the private library of an author' is the concern of the last chapter and the check-list of Miró's library included as an appendix. The second field, 'information about the periodicals ... to which the author may have subscribed', is fairly inaccessible in Miró's case. Very probably he read the journals to which he contributed regularly. Indeed, his newspaper articles sometimes refer to, or comment on, events reported in the same paper a day or two earlier. But apart from occasional references by Miró to particular articles by other writers this is the only sort of evidence available about the pattern of Miró's reading of periodicals.

Morize's third field is 'compilation of the reading done by the author from clues given by himself in his correspondence and other writings'. Miró's work, more than most authors', abounds with quotations and references to his reading, and the present chapter deals with this field insofar as it relates to published work in books and periodicals. Lastly, Morize suggests two more areas for investigation: the 'study of any biographical elements that throw light on the desired sources' — these elements are mentioned in the present chapter as and when they seem helpful — and the 'enumeration of the books or documents that a writer working on a given subject at a given time might have consulted'. The comparison of the library and quotations with the books that one might have expected Miró to read provides a useful check, and at once, for instance, brings out the astonishing and almost total lack of contemporary writing in Miró's library. And in turn the question is again raised as to how representative the library is of Miró's reading.

Some arguments from the nature of the library itself have already

---

[1] Pages 128-9.

been offered, suggesting that it is unusually representative; now a comparison with quotations in Miró's work provides another check. Miró's library is a smallish one and it would be reasonable to suspect that he might have done a good deal of reading in borrowed books or in libraries, at least once he reached Barcelona, for in Alicante a good public library was not available. Miró's library might conceivably only be the visible tip of his reading. Taking Miró's published work together more than one hundred authors are quoted in their own words (or what purport to be their own words). Of these about nine out of every ten are represented in the library. The correspondence is particularly complete with authors of works of Biblical and religious historical scholarship — it looks as if an exhaustive comparison of the *Figuras de la Pasión del Señor* with its sources would show almost all of them to be available to Miró in his own library. On the other hand, among the two hundred or so further authors who are either mentioned or briefly paraphrased, the proportion represented in the library is somewhat lower. Two opposed conclusions are possible: either that the close overall correspondence between library and reference proves that the library covers the bulk of Miró's reading, or that the less close correspondence among writers not directly quoted suggests that Miró tended to quote when the source was at hand, but to paraphrase or merely mention if it was not. This might imply that much of his reading simply does not appear in his writing because he could not refer to it at the time. The business of quotation would depend on the availability of sources rather than on the wish to quote a particular author. Logically, we are left helpless to judge between the two possibilities, yet further facts suggest that the library does give a good picture of Miró's reading.

Miró was not particularly interested in accurate quotation: the notes, for instance, to E. L. King's edition of *El humo dormido* show this clearly, as do Miró's quotations from the Bible, sometimes assembled out of the three main Spanish translations, sometimes adapted to improve their language, without, of course, reference to the originals. On occasion, even if a text was in his library, it seems Miró would rely on his memory to produce a paraphrase, in which another's words were made more his own. So it is quite probable that Miró would find no barrier to 'quoting' from another in not having his text at hand. Again, many of the authors mentioned but not in the library are the contemporary Spanish writers so curiously missing from Miró's books. If we disregard this special case, the degree of correspondence between authors referred to and the library becomes much more like the correspondence between authors quoted and the library. As the distinction between quotation and mention becomes less crucial and more blurred, so quotation and library each reinforce the argument for the other's representative character. Taking all the arguments together it looks as if from the library and quotations we know at least a very significant portion of Miró's reading; but a more accurate assessment can only be reached by a more detailed look at his quotations, taken by authors rather than as a whole. This study by authors is the main object of this chapter.

1. CASTILIAN LITERATURE

The mass of names is perhaps handled more easily if the authors are classified in some way and one turns first to Castilian literature, including in this broad category all the peninsular writers in Castilian used by Miró. The overwhelming majority of these are writers that can properly be placed under the heading of Castilian literature; the remaining few do not form a coherent or significant group so that it is practical to include them here. The order of the writers is roughly chronological, but not strictly so where deviations from strict order allow the facts to be more clearly presented.

Miró was, naturally enough for a man of his period, interested in Spanish writing of the Middle Ages: this is clear from his quotations. The *Poema de mío Cid,* Berceo, Lull, Juan Manuel, Juan Ruiz, Sem Tob, *La danza de la muerte,* are all quoted or referred to. In *Hilván de escenas,* for instance, lines 1, 2, 8, and 9 of the *Poema de mío Cid* are used to head a chapter (p. 179), while at the other end of Miró's career, the Cid reappears in a passage from *Años y leguas (EC,* XII, 283) that was removed from the final version, to provide evidence of the costume of his day.

Berceo is quoted at more length, but under rather exceptional circumstances: a longish extract from the *Vida de Santo Domingo de Silos* is used in the 'Estudio histórico del templo de San Vicente, de Ávila', a monograph written by Miró in connection with his work as a civil servant in Madrid, and not published until 1952. [2]

> San Viçent avie nombre un martir ançiano,
> Sabina, e Cristeta de ambas fo ermano;
> Todos por Dios murieron de violenta mano,
> Todos yaçien en Avila, non vos miento un grano,

is the first of fifteen stanzas quoted. [3] Miró tells us that he has copied 'puntualmente', and apart from odd spelling and accentual changes this

[2] *Clavileño,* No. 16 (July-August 1952), pp. 65-72.
[3] *BAE,* LVII, 48, Stanzas 262-76.

is true. In the same essay on San Vicente, Miró also makes use of the 'Preliminares' of the *BAE* volume from which the quotation is taken. Tomás Antonio Sánchez there reports that Fray Prudencio de Sandoval tells that Berceo knew people concerned with the burial of San Vicente in Ávila (*BAE*, LVII, xxiii). This information is quoted verbatim by Miró, except that he changes 'se hallaron a esta traslación' into 'se hallaron en esta traslación'. We shall see again and again that not only does Miró quote Spanish writers almost exclusively from the *BAE*, but that most of his information about them derives from the introductions and footnotes of these volumes.

The most important exception is the use Miró made of Menéndez Pelayo's *Historia de las ideas estéticas,* a work copiously marked by Miró. The earliest Spaniard quoted from Menéndez Pelayo is Lull; since a small selection of his work appears in the *BAE*, we shall, with apologies to Catalonia, deal with him here. In the first, 1904, edition of *Del vivir,* Miró writes of 'la exclamación ardiente de Ramón Lull: «¡Cuán grande daño es que los hombres mueran sin amor!»' (p. 187). In the *Ideas estéticas* Menéndez Pelayo quotes: '«¡Cuán grande daño es (exclama con frase ardentísima) que los hombres mueran sin amor!»'[4] (The passage is marked with a large cross). Miró, in quoting, takes in Menéndez Pelayo's words as a part of his material. There are two further references to Lull, in *Dentro del cercado* (*OC*, p. 288), and *Las cerezas del cementerio* (*OC*, p. 373). The first of these is a vague one, but the second alludes to the famous episode of 'aquello de descubrirse los cancerosos pechos la dama perseguida de Raimundo'. The episode appears in the Introduction to the *BAE* volume that includes Lull (LXV, xv); the introduction itself is marked in several places. Again we find Miró using a *BAE* introduction as a source of material.

The *BAE* texts of the works mentioned so far are all unmarked, but Juan Manuel, the next writer, is marked in the *Libro del caballero*. Miró quotes from another of his works, *De las maneras de amor,* in *Del vivir:*

> 'Amor es amar solamente por amor; et este amor nunca se pierde nin mengua ..., más dígovos: que este amor yo nunca lo vi fasta hoy.'
>
> (*OC*, p. 56)

It is worth comparing the original in the *BAE:*

> Et de las maneras vos digo: que amor es amar home una persona sola solamente por amor, et este amor do es nunca

---

[4] Second edition, I, ii (Madrid, 1891), 188-9. In Miró's set of the *Ideas estéticas* the first two volumes are of the second edition, the rest of the first. References are to Miró's set.

se pierde nin mengua. Mas dígovos que este amor yo nunca
lo ví fasta hoy.

(LI, 276)

The periods after 'mengua' in Miró's version might be taken to indicate
a cut; exactly the opposite — it is merely a change of punctuation,
while the cuts actually made are not shown. The periods after 'mengua' are a favourite Mironian device: Juan Manuel's text is tailored to
suit Miró's taste. Literal accuracy in quoting was simply not a thing
of overriding importance for Miró. Likely enough we must see him not
as taking carefully weighed decisions about the justification for touching a sacred text, but as assimilating material to his own work and
passing it all through his own processes of literary judgement and creation, without the need to consider any barrier of scholarly respect.
We have already seen how, even in the quite factual study of San Vicente, he does not reproduce spelling exactly.

The same lines from Juan Manuel appear in Menéndez Pelayo's
Ideas estéticas. [5] Menéndez quotes exactly the same sentence, making
'amor', as Miró does, into the first word of the sentence. The suspicion
immediately is that Miró took the quotation from the *Ideas estéticas,*
but *BAE* and Miró both write 'dígovos', while Menéndez Pelayo writes
'dígoos'. Miró, having read some of Juan Manuel, would certainly
have turned to a work headed *De las maneras de amor,* but it remains
very probable that Miró was directed to this particular remark by Menéndez Pelayo — the chapter in which he quotes it is extensively
marked. The precise source would be unimportant but for the fact that
on several further occasions Miró clearly used the *Ideas estéticas* as a
source-book; together these quotations confirm that Menéndez Pelayo's work was one that Miró used intensively. Miró made one later
reference to Juan Manuel: this time in a short story called 'Crónica de
festejos', first published in *El Imparcial* in 1909 and then included in
Del huerto provinciano in 1912.

Another author for whom Miró evidently felt enthusiasm was Juan
Ruiz, who appears in a variety of situations, and first in *Nómada* in
1908. At the start of his writing career Miró used large numbers of
quotations as decoration or as prefabricated units of thought, but by
1908 the flood had abated. Nevertheless, this use of Juan Ruiz is in
the earlier manner. The hero of *Nómada,* Don Diego, has lost his wife
and daughter and turns to a 'vida de escándalo'. This is how Miró
tells us that sex entered into it:

> Don Diego, siempre robusto, ahito de casino, pensó con
> Juan Ruiz:

[5] Second edition, I, ii (1891), 223.

...que una ave sola nin bien canta nin bien llora,
el mástil sin la vela non puede estar toda hora,
nin las verzas non se crían tan bien sin la noria... [6]

Y aunque no había leído ni el nombre del famoso arcipreste, conoció mucho a Doña Venus, y hubo hembras placenteras.

(*OC*, p. 167)

In part this suggests evasion of the difficulties of finding exactly the right tone, but this was probably not a conscious evasion, for on the other hand it has virtues of expression in terms of certain nineteenth-century standards. But essentially bringing in Juan Ruiz adds nothing to our understanding of the hero; it merely turns a narrative corner with a Valera-like elegance, concealing a possible rough joint with an ornamental surface.

A mention of Juan Ruiz in *Nuestro padre San Daniel* (1921) provides a perfect contrast. In general, this longish novel is almost free from references to other authors, except for erudite references by the characters. The new bishop has arrived in Oleza and, seeing Don Magín, enquires: '¿Pertenece a la parroquia aquel sacerdote que está oliendo unas flores?' Magín's opponents, who are with the bishop, 'se apresuraron a decirle que sí'.

Y todos aguardaron que hablase. ¿Habría llegado para el Joan Ruiz de Oleza el riguroso don Gil de Albornoz?
Enjugóse el prelado las sienes; y, al retirarse y pasar junto a don Magín, acogió su reverencia gratamente. Hasta parece que le sonrió. Algunos lo vieron, y se miraban, confesándose su asombro.
Ya el buen arcipreste dijo que 'A veses cosa chica fase muy grand despecho.' [7]

(*OC*, p. 809)

In the first place this is a quotation in a book where they are rare, but in any case the reference to Juan Ruiz is here carefully made a part of the whole text. The question '¿Habría llegado (...)?' is, of course, the thought of those standing around the bishop, eager to see Don Magín put in his place, but not daring to express any criticism. They think of him as the licentious archpriest. Miró makes deliberate use of the ambivalence of the *Libro de buen amor*: to Magín's critics, Juan Ruiz is dangerously licentious, just as they believe Magín to be. Since their interpretations of Magín and Juan Ruiz run parallel, Magín

[6] *BAE*, LVII, 230, Stanza 101.
[7] *BAE*, LVII, 249, Stanza 707.

is assimilated to the ambivalent archpriest. The conflict between the liberal Magín and the Carlist-inclined clergy is illuminated by the reference to the conflict between different views of Juan Ruiz. The reference is valuable in itself and closely controlled: the ever-present danger of quoting, that the reader's possible reactions are very numerous and that the author may let control of the reader slip from his grasp, is here skilfully avoided. In the light of all this, the elegant circumlocution 'Ya el buen arcipreste (...)' is entirely acceptable as a pleasant piece of decorative comment, akin to the use of Doña Venus in *Nómada,* but transmuted by what goes before. Even then Miró takes advantage of the line to slip in the adjective 'buen' to qualify the archpriest and to indicate his own warmth towards Magín.

There are two more quotations of less interest: the first a piece of oratorical decoration of the 'as ... said' type in a speech made in honour of the composer Oscar Esplá in 1911, the second a paragraph paraphrasing passages from Juan Ruiz, in an article on Lent published in 1930.[8] Miró clearly used the *BAE* edition of the *Libro de buen amor,* though of the quotations only the one in *Nuestro padre San Daniel* is marked.

Another mediaeval poet who appears in the same volume of the *BAE,* whose poems are also marked, and who is quoted by Miró, is Sem Tob, one of whose four-line epigrams is used to close the short story 'Día campesino', first published in 1908. Further lines appeared at the head of the piece in the original version (*EC,* IX, 305). It was published in the same year as *Nómada,* and there is the same rather unsatisfactory fit between the quotation and its surroundings, resulting this time from the difficulty of integrating so large a unit.

The story deals with a typically Mironian character, a 'romántico' who feels compassionate towards all creation because he is at peace in the countryside. He takes pride in his own goodness and is immediately presented with a situation in which a trivial incident shows up the hypocrisy of his self-praise, although it is an incident so trivial that his companions are not even aware of moral issues in it. He therefore despises them for their insensitivity, while at the same time he despises his own weakness. The story ends:

> Acabó el día campesino, comenzado alegremente por un hombre que se creyó bueno y amable, porque compadecía, según el salmista...

> Sol claro, plasentero
> Nuue lo fas escuro,

---

[8] Esplá, *Evocación,* p. 13: cf. *BAE,* LVII, 227, Stanza 4; *Glosas,* p. 104: cf. *BAE,* LVII, p. 277, Stanzas 1581-5, p. 268, Stanza 1313, p. 261, Stanzas 1079-92.

De un día entero
Non es onbre seguro,

escribió el judío Sem Tob.

(OC, p. 97)

Miró's words suggest the hero's humbug, but the lines from Sem Tob seem to suggest that the hero is in the hands of powers outside him, that he has no control over his circumstances. It is possible to marry this to the point of the rest of the story but only at the cost of an effort by the reader to select a meaning that will suit what has gone before. Requiring effort from the reader is no bad thing, but here his only reward is to fit in a piece that adds very little to the whole, and even tends to narrow the range of the story. Miró, still somewhat attached to the decorative quotation, tries to make it functional, but fails to control his material fully. In the end, the quotation is almost as gratuitous as the adjective 'judío' before Sem Tob. Much later, in *Años y leguas,* Miró used another of Sem Tob's epigrams, whose appropriateness makes the point by contrast *(OC,* p. 1157).

Also in *BAE,* LVII, is *La danza de la muerte.* Miró must have read this, since in 'Los dejos de los días: Almas medianas' he mentions it, tells us that the text is from 'el códice del Escorial' (information gleaned from the *BAE* introduction or footnotes), and continues with six short extracts, showing how all the characters react in the same way to death. [9]

The original seventy-volume set of the *BAE* did not include fifteenth-century poetry and it is another sign of Miró's dependence on the set that he refers to no fifteenth-century poetry except for Jorge Manrique's *Coplas* (which are slipped into the *BAE* by way of volume XXXV, the *Romancero y cancionero sagrados*) and three ballads — the *romances* had two volumes to themselves in the *BAE.* In the piece 'El río y él', published in *El ángel, el molino, el caracol del faro* in 1921, a river is described as it flows to the sea; and though Jorge Manrique is not mentioned by name, he is referred to by the river as 'el poeta, que comparó mi vida a la de los hombres' *(OC,* p. 756). The *Coplas* are so well known that there is no need to mention their creator, and Miró acknowledges this also on the other occasions on which he quotes them: neither in *El obispo leproso (OC,* p. 1061) nor in *Años y leguas (OC,* p. 1120) does Manrique's name appear. Indeed, in *Años y leguas* Miró relies on the reader knowing the poem for after a brief quotation he starts the next paragraph: 'Vengamos a lo de ayer.' The

[9] *La Publicidad,* 2 Nov. 1919, p. 1.

volumes of the *Romancero general* provided three quotations for *El humo dormido* where they appear together in a chapter on 'San Juan, San Pedro y San Pablo'. [10]

Miró's quotations from mediaeval literature show, as did his library, that his major interest was poetry. As we move forward in time the emphasis shifts considerably: from León Hebreo to Moreto the largest group are the religious and moral writers, with poets, dramatists, and writers of fiction some way behind. León Hebreo himself, the oldest of them, does not appear in the *BAE*. Nor does Miró appear to have possessed any other copy of his works, but instead he must have relied on the extensive description and quotation provided in Menéndez Pelayo's *Ideas estéticas*. Although Miró refers to León Hebreo in *Niño y grande* (*OC*, p. 467), his only direct quotation is in the first edition of *Del vivir* (1904), in the footnote excluded from later versions: '«El fin singular del amor es la delectación del amante en la cosa amada» — afirma León Hebreo' (p. 187). This same quotation appears in the *Ideas estéticas* underlined by Miró [11] — confirmation of his dependence on this work.

Straightforward works of history seem not to have interested Miró very much. Their neglect in the library is confirmed by the few references in the writings. Rodrigo Jiménez de Rada is mentioned briefly (*OC*, p. 730) and Hernando del Pulgar, the chronicler of the Catholic Kings, is quoted, but from his letters, not his chronicle, as we shall see shortly. On another occasion Miró refers to Francesillo de Zúñiga, court buffoon to Charles V, whose satirical *Crónica* appears in *BAE*, XXXVI. The first chapter describes the arrival of King Charles in Spain; hence Miró, mentioning the visit of Alfonso XIII to Alicante, compares himself with Don Francesillo in 'El favor de su majestad', though, as he tells us, he writes 'con distinto estilo' (*Amigos*, pp. 67-8). Doubtless Miró the illpaid and sacked *cronista* always felt sympathetic towards the profession. Nevertheless it is not until we reach Mariana that there is any evidence of Miró reading history: for Zúñiga's account is scarcely a chronicle in the ordinary sense.

For Miró personal documents, and especially letters, revealed much more about the past. His use of the *Centón epistolario* as the basis for an article has already been discussed. [12] It appears in the *Epistolario español* in the *BAE*, two volumes that Miró used on a number of other occasions. In 'Plática que tuvo Sigüenza con un capellán', first

---

[10]   *OC*, pp. 728-9: cf. *BAE*, X, 57 and 121, and *BAE*, XVI, 497. The third ballad was also used in *El obispo leproso* (*OC*, p. 1060): see pp. 49-50.

[11]   First edition, II (1884), 61.

[12]   See pp. 48-9.

published in 1911 and later included in *Libro de Sigüenza,* Miró quotes from Hernando del Pulgar's letters. The *capellán* refers to Pulgar's phrase 'la mala condición española', words that Sigüenza rejects, saying that 'la mala condición' is universal, not a unique Spanish disease. [13] On another occasion Antonio de Guevara's *Epístolas familiares,* also in the *Epistolario español,* are quoted twice in 'Cartas vulgares'. [14] Both quotations are remarks about jealousy, used to illustrate the article which is a letter of warning and advice to a friend suffering from envy. In *El obispo leproso,* too, there is a reference to the *Epistolario,* for Don Magín appears 'leyendo en un volumen del licenciado Cascales la epístola al licenciado Bartolomé Ferrer Muñoz *Sobre la cría y trato de la seda*' (*OC,* p. 947). The letter appears in the second volume of the *Epistolario* (pp. 509-11) — Miró often brings books from his own library into his fiction in this way.

A last quotation shows directly how appealing Miró found the personal view of history that these letters provide. In the chapter 'Ochocentistas: Lectura y corro', in *Años y leguas,* Miró starts by presenting Sigüenza spending Sunday afternoon browsing in the *Epistolario,* and he quotes at some length from letters of 1637 from the section of correspondence from Jesuits in Volume Two. Sigüenza reflects idly on the passages he reads and then the chapter moves on to describe how the peasants in Sigüenza's village spend Sunday. After recounting their names and conversation, Miró concludes the chapter: 'Principió Sigüenza la tarde de domingo con una lectura desganada, y el rolde de lugareños tejía sus asuntos en el paño viejo del Epistolario' (*OC,* pp. 1108-12). Again there is a remarkable contrast between, say, the long, long footnote of quotations in *Del vivir* in 1904 and these lengthy extracts in a piece first published in 1924. The former are explanatory, distracting, and destructive of the author's control over the reader's thought; the latter are woven into the narrative and contribute directly both to revealing Sigüenza's thought and to making Miró's point about history. The quotations are not used for what they say in themselves, but as a part of the whole texture of meaning.

Letters do not appear only in the *Epistolario* volumes of the *BAE.* Another volume (XXII), for instance, includes Cortés's *Cartas de relación,* and these Miró uses in the essay 'De España y de América' first published in 1911. But here the use is merely documentary: a quotation from the *Cartas* serves to illustrate the commercial nature of Spain's interest in America (*Glosas,* p. 28).

The writers of poetry and fiction of the period are poorly represented. Two lines by Garcilaso and three from Boscán, both quoted in

[13] *OC,* p. 634: cf. *BAE,* XIII, 46.
[14] *El Ibero,* 16 Jan. 1902, pp. 43-5: cf. *BAE,* XIII, 146 and 100.

chapters for *Años y leguas* — though the Garcilaso quotation never reached the book version — are all the verse there is. [15] The *BAE* contains very little of Boscán, but Miró possessed a 1917 edition of Garcilaso and Boscán. As for fiction, there are simply two quotations from *Amadís de Gaula*. In 'La señora que hace dulces' (*Libro de Sigüenza*) Miró writes : '«¡En fuerte punto sus ojos le han mirado!', puede clamar, como Amadís' (*OC*, p. 620). The actual passage (*BAE*, XL, 11) reads : 'En fuerte punto mis ojos la miraron', while in *Dentro del cercado* Miró offers another version : '¿Cómo es aquello de Amadís de Gaula, lo del doncel? ... «En fuerte punto mis ojos miraron ...» Ya no recuerdo' (*OC*, p. 313). The interest of this reference is that it might help to date *Dentro del cercado*, first published in 1916, but written a good deal earlier. [16] 'La señora que hace dulces' was first published in 1913. Perhaps both were written at roughly the same time when Miró had recently read or re-read *Amadís*. Unfortunately, Miró dates 'La señora que hace dulces' as of 1909, so that, even if the supposition is correct, we are still left with the years 1909 to 1913 as possible dates for *Dentro del cercado* (even though the dates Miró added to the ends of his pieces are often unreliable).

A more interesting quotation is one from Vives in the short story 'La niña del cuévano' of 1908. In *BAE*, LXV, Vives's work is entitled *Introducción a la sabiduría*. But Miró states that he is using 'una de las primeras máximas de la *Introducción y camino para la sabiduría*' (*OC*, p. 83), and the words he quotes do not appear in the *BAE*. Miró writes : 'Procure siempre lo bueno y huya de lo malo, porque la costumbre de hacer a la continua bien se le volverá en naturaleza.' The nearest to this in Vives is : 'Sus apetitos y deseos confórmeles con la razón; huya con gran diligencia de los que della se desvían y tuercen; porque esta costumbre en bienhacer, refrenando las pasiones, se apegue tanto, que casi sea tan natural, que ya no haya cosa que le traiga a hacer mal, si no fuese forzado y traído como de los cabellos arrastrando' (*BAE*, LXV, 239). Did Miró quote from memory, or paraphrase because the original was too cumbersome? From what we have seen, when he used the easily-accessible *BAE*, he normally only altered details, so that this complete rewriting, more in the manner of his work in the twenties, would be unusual. Perhaps he used a different translation of Vives's Latin work, that does not now figure in his library.

The use to which the quotation is put is also enlightening, for it

---

[15] *EC*, XII, 270; *OC*, p. 1082.
[16] After the title-page of the first edition Miró has added a note that includes the following : 'Yo de mí sólo digo que, ahora, no escribiría ya estas páginas; pero, también, os confieso que no me pesa haberlas escrito' (*Dentro del cercado* [1916], p. 5).

is an example, quite early, of successful use of quotation as part of the fiction. A group of friends out in the country are asked by a girl to buy a basket. They ask her about her miserable family background and then the narrator remembers Vives's maxim and determines to attempt to spread 'amor' to this girl's life. He instructs the girl to love her family. She listens attentively, quashing an incipient sense of his own pomposity in the speaker's mind. Finally she gets up: 'Nosotros estábamos conmovidos, al·borozados. ¡Habíamos redimido un alma del pecado de no amar!' The girl replies: 'Pero, ¿me merca usted el cué-vano u qué?' (*OC*, p. 83). The puncturing of the narrator's hypocrisy is made all the more dramatic because not only was his advice theore-tical, but it was not even his own theory; instead it was a piece of bookishness acquired from a stout volume in the peace of his study. Throughout the story the friends are paralleled by insects; now the girl ends the piece by stamping on an 'hervidero de hormigas' who are busy burying a large insect that she had killed with a stone earlier on.

Discussing influences on Miró, Vicente Ramos writes: 'Creemos que, al nivel influyente de Cervantes y Santa Teresa, hay que situar a Fray Luis de Granada, cuya ascendiente se muestra, tal vez, más rele-vante en orden a las concepciones mironianas de la Naturaleza y del amor' (*Mundo,* p. 25). This judgement may on the surface be an at-tractive one, but there is little evidence to support it either in Miró's library or in his quotations. In general terms his quotations and mark-ings show little interest in nature — they are chiefly on moral or philo-sophical subjects. Obviously nature was important to Miró, but it looks as if this aspect of his art arose from direct experience; where it was influenced by reading, the relevant authors are the Romantics and their successors. This is not to say that Miró did not read and enjoy Luis de Granada; merely that Luis's attitude to nature coincided (at points) with Miró's, rather than influenced it. Certainly the three volumes of the *BAE* devoted to Luis's works are almost entirely un-marked, and the Dominican is mentioned only three times, quite insig-nificant alongside the pervasive references to Cervantes and Santa Te-resa.

The hero of *La mujer de Ojeda,* Miró's first, repudiated novel, reads Luis de Granada (p. 14); probably in imitation of his creator. The long footnote on 'amor' in *Del vivir* also includes a paragraph of quotation and paraphrases from Luis's *Guía de pecadores* (II, xvi), dealing with the problem of how men are to be persuaded to love each other. We must work at loving our neighbour, and we must reflect that we are all one and all made in God's image: this is the only way in which men can be induced to love each other (pp. 185-6). In the style of this footnote, Luis's ideas are introduced as a straightforward commentary on the problem, a commentary that is novelistically of little relevance.

The third mention of Fray Luis de Granada compares Creation to a book whose reader is man. In 'Plática que tuvo Sigüenza con un capellán', the *capellán* offers the following platitude as a comment on a group of peaceful birds: 'La Creación —escribe Fray Luis de Granada, y lo han repetido otras plumas — es un libro inmenso y glorioso, cuyo lector es el hombre' (*OC*, p. 634). The idea is a commonplace one, but Miró may have been drawn to it once again through Menéndez Pelayo, who quotes related but differently worded passages from the *Símbolo de la Fe*. He also mentions, rather like the *capellán,* that Luis derived his essential ideas on this subject from earlier authors. [17]

No sooner has the *capellán* spoken, than war breaks out amongst the birds over a dead worm, and, with references to contemporary politics (the title in the first edition of *Libro de Sigüenza* was 'Plática que tuvo Sigüenza con señor capellán después de algunas revueltas en el país'), Sigüenza points out how the gulf between the priest's words and reality is connected with his hypocrisy towards other men, revealed a page later. This article was first published in 1911; the *capellán* is, of course, doing what Miró himself did as a young writer — trying to explain the world with texts. The two uses of Luis de Granada, this one and the one in *Del vivir,* make the point about Miró's aesthetic development neatly.

Along with Luis de Granada, a considerable number of Renaissance religious writers are represented in Miró's works; foremost among them is St. Teresa. When Azorín, Palacio Valdés, and Ricardo León proposed Miró for the Academy in 1927 they included the following words in their proposal: 'De Santa Teresa procede la prosa límpida y exacta de Miró. La gran mujer de Ávila es quien, predominantemente, ha marcado su sello en el estilo del escritor levantino. De Santa Teresa ha extraído, en gran parte, su vocabulario psicológico Gabriel Miró. Y en cuanto a lo material, a la realidad cuotidiana, tiene el novelista, por todo lo que le rodea, la misma viva simpatía, el mismo amor que alentaba en la autora de *Las Moradas'.* [18] This idiosyncratic description of Miró's writing is the work of Azorín, and it must be seen in its historical context, a campaign of vilification of Miró as a decadent anti-catholic. But its effect has been considerable, and repeatedly the St. Teresa-Miró link appears in critical comment. Clearly there are many possible approaches to the problem, for it was not pure fancy on Azorín's part to stress St. Teresa as the one supreme

---

[17] *Ideas estéticas,* first edition, II (1884), 133-4; the passages are from *Símbolo,* I, 2.

[18] 'Gabriel Miró, propuesto para candidato', *El Sol,* 24 Feb. 1927, p. 1.

influence. False as this stress is, it relies on Miró's obvious affection for the Saint, already seen in his annotations in the relevant volume of the *BAE*. The most obvious route to follow would be an analysis of style, and it is interesting to note in this connection that in *Pepita Jiménez,* the immediate source for Miró's *La mujer de Ojeda,* R. E. Lott finds that Valera parodies the mystical, ascetic, and theological language of St. Teresa. [19]   However, for the present the object is to see whether Miró's use of St. Teresa in quotation is at all enlightening.

There are some eighteen quotations from or references to St. Teresa in Miró's published work : a high number for a single author, but about half the direct references to Cervantes, the author most often mentioned. The references to St. Teresa almost all appear between 1901 and 1913, but this is not especially significant since it was during this period that Miró's use of quotation in general was most frequent. The quotations are evidently drawn from the two *BAE* volumes (LIII and LV), the first of which is the most heavily marked volume in the library. A comparison of these markings with the passages used in Miró's work shows little relationship between the two. Seven times Miró quotes St. Teresa verbatim, and on three occasions the passage quoted is unmarked. Two further quotations, short ones, are drawn from passages that are marked at length with small crosses : clearly they were not marked with the quoted extracts in mind. Another quotation, used on two separate occasions, is the only one to be specifically marked. But taking the evidence of quotation and marking together it is clear that St. Teresa was read thoroughly and repeatedly. There are quotations from, and references to, the *Libro de las constituciones,* to *Camino de perfección,* the *Vida,* and the letters. References to, or quotations from, St. Teresa appear in work published in 1901, 1903, 1904, 1907, 1909, 1910, 1911, 1912 and 1913, as well as 1921 and 1926. [20]

Perhaps the most striking thing about Miró's use of St. Teresa's words is the respect he shows them. On most occasions his only departures from the *BAE* text are in punctuation, in written accents, and capital letters. Otherwise, 'via' becomes 'veía', 'alazena' becomes 'alacenas', 'diere' becomes 'diera', and 'que ya parece ha empleado su fuerza' becomes 'que parece que cumplió su fuerza'. [21]   The replacement of one verb by another in the last example is all the more surprising in the context of respect elsewhere. Whatever other qualities Miró found in St. Teresa, he obviously valued her style very highly; certainly

---

[19]   *Language and psychology in 'Pepita Jiménez'.*
[20]   References to St. Teresa not dealt with in the following pages: *OC,* pp. 27, 57, 253, and 583; *EC,* IX, 283; *Mujer,* p. 14; *Hilván,* p. 123; 'Historia que no se cuenta', p. 20; *Hijo santo,* p. 6.
[21]   'Santo Tomás', pp. 67-8: cf. *BAE,* LIII, 102; *Amigos,* p. 72: cf. *BAE,* LIII, 274; *Amigos,* p. 73: cf. *BAE,* LIII, 276; *OC,* p. 350: cf. *BAE,* LIII, 47.

it is a style that cannot be tampered with. The contrast with Miró's eclectic use of Bible translations makes the point very well. Yet there is an important exception; by the twenties Miró had become far less respectful towards his texts, and this included even St. Teresa. In *El obispo leproso* Miró quotes the same passage he had used fifteen years before. St. Teresa's version reads: 'El Señor dará gracias a algunas para que den recreación a otras', and this, in 1911, was faithfully copied. But in 1926 it becomes: 'El Señor dotará de gracias a una hermana para que sea nuestra recreación.'[22] The change from 'algunas' to 'una hermana' is made in order to suit the context.

The references to St. Teresa naturally offer examples of all Miró's various ways of using such references. The most interesting are those in *Las cerezas del cementerio* and 'El favor de su majestad'. The former was published in 1910, but Miró had been working on it for a number of years. It is the most *modernista* of all Miró's major works and St. Teresa is brought in as a part of the fashionable fusion of sex and religion. 'Fashionable' is perhaps a harsh word, for Miró's sincerity is self-evident, but *Las cerezas del cementerio* is very much a book of its time. Félix, the hero, is introduced to his cousin Isabel whom he has not seen since both were children. She tells him that his reputation is of an 'atolondrado' and he replies:

> —¡Yo obtuve de mí mismo abrir las puertas de la alegría de sentirme vuestro, y se me ha quedado el alma 'con un desgustillo como quien va a saltar y le asen por detrás, que parece que cumplió su fuerza y hállase sin efectuar lo que ella quería hacer'!
> —¿Qué le vas murmurando? —preguntó risueñamente don Eduardo.
> Y Félix siguió:
> —¿Yo atolondrado? ¡Y le hablo a Isabel con palabras de una santa doctora!
>
> (*OC*, pp. 350-1)

The passage quoted is from Chapter XII of St. Teresa's *Vida* (*BAE*, LIII, 47). For all his admiration for the saint, Miró reverses the terms of mystical literature and uses religious experience to illustrate sexual feelings. This, of course, begs the important question: is the narrator not merely illustrating the character and outlook of Félix? The answer is not a simple one; one of the unsatisfactory features of *Las cerezas del cementerio* is Miró's failure to establish a consistent position for his narrator, and his use of St. Teresa

---

[22] *Amigos*, p. 73, and *OC*, p. 964: cf. *BAE*, LIII, 276.

illustrates this well. Later on, for instance, Félix entertains his aunt Lutgarda with stories of saints and miracles. She is innocently and deeply pious, but his attitude is much more aesthetic: he shocks his aunt by telling her:

> Tus palabras tienen adorno, dulzura y hasta coquetería de función religiosa de iglesia rica ...
> —¡Pero, Félix! — y ahora fué tía Lutgarda la que pareció ruborizarse —. Déjame que te hable de nuestro Santo Cristo, y te pido que creas que es de milagrosa eficacia su patrocinio y advocación ...
> —Lo creeré; lo creo todo ... ¿Sabes lo del Cristo de Navarra, que sudaba y todo cuando San Francisco Xavier padecía trabajos en la India? Pues, ¿y aquella otra imagen de Jesús que le crecían los cabellos y las uñas? ... Más te agradarán los milagros primorosos, como el de las rosas de Santa Casilda y los que sucedieron después de la muerte de Santa Teresa de Jesús ... ¡Milagros póstumos, tía Lutgarda!

(OC, p. 373)

The contrast between the two attitudes makes that of Félix perfectly plain. He then relates some of the miracles concerning St. Teresa and 'contaba los místicos coloquios y la limpia, seráfica amistad de Teresa de Jesús y Juan de la Cruz'. The word 'místicos' is spoken by the narrator, but in this context its straightforward descriptive meaning is swamped by *modernista* connotations, as if Félix himself were using it. Throughout Félix and the narrator seem to merge into each other. The narrator tells us that Tía Lutgarda is 'arrobada por el devoto cuento de Félix'. The narrator himself appears to be 'arrobado' by Félix's sentimentalising of mysticism.

So far it has always been Félix who introduces St. Teresa. But earlier, the narrator introduced her: 'Cuando mentaba a Isabel no le daba título de señorita, sino que le decía *Belita* nada más, diminutivo usado por tía Lutgarda y que ya hizo la santa madre Teresa de Jesús para nombrar a una predilecta novicia, todavía rapazuela muy graciosa, hermanita del padre Jerónimo Gracián. Bueno; pero esto no se dice que lo supiera doña Lutgarda' (*OC,* p. 363).

The last sentence points directly to the question of narrative technique. This last comment is the narrator's — it is he who is knowledgeable about St. Teresa and introduces this anecdote by the way. Miró and narrator are indistinguishable. But more importantly, there is a related link between Miró and Félix. The latter is a Miró-figure, an exaggerated, partial Miró, just as Sigüenza and so many other early Miró heroes are. We have seen how Miró used quotation early on: he was interested in ideas and inserted them bodily for their own value into his texts. He lacked sufficient detachment from his quotations to use them novelistically. The case of Félix and the narration of *Las cerezas del cementerio* is a parallel one. When Félix addresses his cousin Isabel with words from St. Teresa, we as readers cannot sufficiently distinguish between Miró, narrator, and Félix. When the narrator comments on Belita, the comment might as well be the thought of Félix, who knows his St. Teresa, as it might be Miró's own. When Félix recounts miracles, the narrator handles his story so that we are constantly presented with Félix's viewpoint; it is as if another Félix were telling the story. The opening of the novel is an excellent example of this. All the scenery is presented through Félix's eyes, while the everyday men who scoff at his fancies are presented as vulgar and despicable. The weakness throughout is Miró's own lack of detachment. The contrast between this *modernista* fusion of sex and religion and the magnificent exploration of the psychological links between sexual and religious emotions in *Nuestro padre San Daniel* is bound up with the detachment achieved in the latter, expressed in the sure narrative control.

In 1907 Miró published in the *Heraldo de Madrid* (5 August) an extract from *Las cerezas del cementerio*. It is clearly recognisable as the last part of Chapter Eighteen, but it is written in the first person, as a letter from Félix. If much of the rest of the novel was also originally in the first person it would explain the peculiarities of the narrative method in the novel as it stands. It would explain why the events are consistently seen as if through Félix's eyes; and the presumption of an original first-person version would much clarify how the three passages we have looked at came into existence in their final form. Miró's first novel, *La mujer de Ojeda,* technically an imitation of Valera's *Pepita Jiménez,* was in part in epistolary form. It seems likely that Miró started *Las cerezas* very early trying a similar technique, so that we have in a novel of 1910 the signs of his earliest struggles to master narrative. The difficult task of converting a first-person narrative into a third-person one without a total rewriting would in part account for the long delays in completing the novel, as well as for the fact that the viewpoint of Félix melts into that of the narrator, a danger that Miró successfully avoided in, for instance, *Del vivir* with its constant gentle mockery of the hero. If Miró was attempting a treatment of his heroes as ironical as Valera's treatment of Luis de Vargas in *Pepita Jiménez,* then he was better served by the invention of Sigüenza than by the attempt in *Las cerezas del cementerio* to imitate Valera's technique directly followed by an unsatisfactory process of adaptation.

Finally, compare with the passage above, where the *narrator* introduces the details about Belita, the following passage from *Nuestro padre San Daniel:* '¡Si se perdía [Don Magín], que se culpase a su olfato! En la nariz, al menos en la suya, se ocultaba el más fiero y delicioso enemigo del hombre. En la nariz aposentaron los antiguos el pecado de la ira. Allá ellos; en la suya hizo residencia un diablejo infatigable que le puso hechizos, como aquel religioso redimido por la santa de Ávila los traía en el ídolo de cobre que le colgó del cuello una mujer de perdición ...' (*OC,* p. 800).

Again St. Teresa, again an anecdote, but this time the homogeneity of the passage is left intact. The narrative hovers in a delicate balance between assertion by an omniscient author and the following of Magín's own thoughts on the matter. The 'que se culpase' and the curious learning (the assigning of anger to the nose is from a footnote in Miró's Theocritus) both suggest that we are dealing with Magín's view of himself. Miró has detached himself from the materials of his creation and masters them in the interests of that creation as a whole.

'El favor de su majestad', first published in 1911, is a short narrative using material from St. Teresa in a different but equally instructive way (*Amigos,* pp. 65-78). Miró recounts how he visited a local convent posing as an architect's assistant. He is told by the prioress that 'Su Majestad' holds him in high favour. Miró thinks she means Alfonso XIII and only later discovers his error. The convent is not of St. Teresa's order: Miró speaks of 'monjas, me parece que clarisas'. But clearly a good deal of the atmosphere of the description of the visit is derived from St. Teresa's *Libro de las constituciones,* in which she describes how unavoidable visitors are to be handled. Miró quotes St. Teresa to the prioress: spotting 'arcaces viejos', he remembers her 'Ni tengan arca ni arquilla, ni cajón ni alacenas' (*BAE,* LIII, 274). Then he recalls that St. Teresa permits a period of conversation after the midday meal. But 'juego en ninguna manera se permita, que el Señor dará gracias a algunas para que den recreación a otras' (*BAE,* LIII, 276 — the passage is marked). Miró wonders who is the nun here 'dotada de celestiales agudezas'.

The whole piece, on a small scale, is a good example of Miró's way of assembling the material of everyday life into a story that, once assembled, becomes a piece of fiction. Here he uses a visit to a convent, a recent visit by Alfonso XIII in which he was interested as *cronista,* and his reading of St. Teresa as raw materials. Imagination plays little part in the supply of these primary materials: its place is in their selection and ordering. At the end Miró brings in his recent sacking as *cronista,* and this too enters the fiction. It is this undisguised use of autobiographical detail that has misled Miró's biographers into using his work as an authoritative source for facts about his life. They have failed to note that the work itself remains fiction, not autobiography.

In *Del vivir,* Sigüenza is told that a group of olive trees is over three hundred years old. He reflects that they 'empezaron en edad que cautiva amorosamente su alma' (*OC,* p. 8). In spite of the perils, just mentioned, of attributing Sigüenza's deeds and thoughts to Miró, it is fair to assume that this refers to Miró's love of the sixteenth-century religious writers. His personal affection for the character of St. Teresa emerges in the references and quotations. Most of them are not theological; they consist of details of convent life, personal anecdotes, miracles and superstitions, and psychological observations. The contrast with St. John of the Cross, from whom Miró takes remarks on theology and mystical practice, is marked. The distinction between Miró's feelings towards the two saints is seen clearly in Félix, who expresses Miró's admiration for St. Teresa as a person, but, like other characters, experiences the insights of St. John as a condemnation of himself.

During this period non-religious writers are poorly represented. Montemayor is mentioned in *La mujer de Ojeda* (p. 82). The name of Bernardino Miedes appears in *Años y leguas* (*OC,* p. 1153) and that of Juan Carrillo, one of whose books forms part of a library, in *El obispo leproso* (*OC,* p. 1028). Miró possessed works by neither: it is unlikely that he read their work. Huarte de San Juan is referred to in an article of 1909. [23] Returning to the religious writers, Rivadeneira is one of those read by the hero of *La mujer de Ojeda* (p. 14) — probably reflecting an early interest of Miró. Even among these little-mentioned writers the correspondence with the library remains close: Rivadeneira and Huarte de San Juan appear in the *BAE,* while Miró possessed a separate copy of Montemayor's *Diana.*

A more constant companion was Luis de León. Like other Christian writers he is mentioned as a favourite author by the hero of *La mujer de Ojeda* (p. 14) and the young Miró's fondness for his works is confirmed by two references in *Hilván de escenas,* a quotation from *De los nombres de Cristo* and a reference to 'Vida retirada'. [24] In 1909 a piece called 'Galeote de su fama' included an extract from the *Exposición del libro de Job,* faithfully repeated in essentials. [25] Later again, in *El humo dormido,* Miró quotes from *La perfecta casada* and

[23] 'Del salón de retratos', *Gérmenes,* 15 March 1909.
[24] *Hilván,* pp. 53-4: cf. *Nombres,* I, vi (*BAE,* XXXVII, 89-90); *Hilván,* p. 66. The second reference mentions the dependence of Luis de León on Horace. Miró found information on their relationship as well as Luis's Horace translations in *BAE,* XXXVII, and used the latter elsewhere: *OC,* p. 164.
[25] *Los Lunes de el Imparcial,* 15 Feb. 1909: cf. *BAE* XXXVII, 296.

from Luis's poem on the Ascension.[26]   In no case is there an associated marking in the *BAE* volumes.

Mariana, too, appears in *El humo dormido,* amidst a host of other authorities for details of the legend of Santiago.   Though the reference is to a passage in Mariana's *Historia* it cannot be taken as evidence that Miró read Mariana's work, as he could have found the passage through the index of chapter-headings if he was searching for material on St. James.[27]   A quotation from Mariana had earlier appeared in *Del vivir* (*OC,* p. 61), used to express a leper's longing for death.   The passage is from Mariana's essay *De Morte et Immortalitate,* a work not available to Miró in translation.   However, the quoted passage appears, translated, in Pi y Margall's introduction to *BAE* XXX (p. xiv), though Miró shortens it somewhat.   Once more we find Miró studying a *BAE* introduction, but the only evidence that he read Mariana himself is a number of bookmarks left in the second *BAE* volume.

San Juan de la Cruz is another who is a favourite of Carlos, the hero of *La mujer de Ojeda* (p. 14).   Further mentions of San Juan all appear in work published in 1909 and 1910, in *La palma rota,* in *El hijo santo,* in an article on Francisco Figueras Pacheco,[28] and in *Las cerezas del cementerio.*   In *El hijo santo* Miró portrays a young man forced to become a priest by his mother, thus frustrating both his ambition to be a singer and his sexual nature.   In a scene with a wealthy and attractive young widow passages from the Song of Songs keep coming into the priest's mind, not applied in the traditional spiritual sense, but with their overt meaning directed towards the widow.   In this context Miró makes use of San Juan: the priest reflects on his past attempts to live the spiritual life forced upon him:

> ¿Y era su alma, la que buscando la no gastada quietud y ansiando la áspera subida al Monte Carmelo *'en una noche obscura, estando ya su casa sosegada',* se hería el corazón con los martillazos de aquellos opresores y durísimos avisos del místico: 'Para gustarlo todo, no quieras tener gusto en nada; ... para venir del todo al todo, has de negarte del todo en todo.' ¡Si ahora la lumbre de los cielos y el aire campesino y la alegría de las criaturas, le dejan en los ojos y en la boca encantos de Paraíso y gusto de mieles, y lejos de negarse y de negarlo todo, todo es para él jugosa afirmación de bienaventuranzas![29]

---

[26]   *OC,* pp. 685-6: cf. *BAE,* XXXVII, 238; *OC,* p. 725.
[27]   *OC,* pp. 729-30: cf. *BAE,* XXX, 203.
[28]   'Del salón de retratos', *Gérmenes,* 15 March 1909.
[29]   *Hijo santo,* IV: cf. *BAE,* XXVII, 18 (commentary on first line of 'Subida del Monte Carmelo').

The priest, Ignacio, finds an agonising conflict between the idea of a necessary dark night of the senses and the 'encantos de Paraíso' that the senses offer him. The conflict has already been indicated in Ignacio's use of the Song of Songs: where San Juan used nature as a metaphor to explain spiritual life Ignacio has reversed the procedure and applies traditionally spiritual words, the Song of Songs, to nature and to the erotic. This awareness of the tension between the rejection of the senses as obstacles and acceptance of the pleasures they bring as an 'afirmación de bienaventuranzas' must correspond to a tension in Miró's own mind between his admiration for the mystics and his own perception of Nature as a route by which hints of Paradise might be discovered. For San Juan Ignacio would simply be a man not strong enough to undertake the rejection of the senses; for Valera, so much admired by Miró, Ignacio might be, in the fashion of Luis de Vargas, a young man in need of finding the right course for himself; but Miró goes further: Ignacio has intimations of an alternative route to salvation.

The Golden-Age religious writers who so obviously enchanted Miró solved the problem of the clash between nature as God's creation and nature as an obstacle to reaching God in hierarchical fashion — the delights of the soul were superior to the pleasures of the body, but the bodily senses were necessary as a starting-point. Bodily pleasures would be discarded in the face of higher ones and must be deliberately avoided if the love of them clashed with the achievement of the aims of the soul. This is clearly reflected in distorted form in this passage from *Las cerezas del cementerio*:

> Doña Beatriz partía con sus dientes un pedacito de pan como un diminuto terrón de nieve, y Félix, enloquecido, se lo quitó y volviéndose lo besó, y aún pudo gastar la humedad dejada por la fresca y encendida boca de la mujer. Beatriz le había sonreído con tristeza ...
>
> Esta era la adorable y gustosa reliquia que ahora tocaba con ardimiento y voluptuoso fetichismo. Y al contemplarla y besarla mucho, notó que sabía a pan viejo, y que la menuda y perfumada huella de los blanquísimos dientes estaba ya seca y rugosa. Y entonces se cumplieron en Félix los avisos del abrasado carmelita Juan de la Cruz, y probó los malos dejos del apetito satisfecho. [30]

In the memory, past satisfaction of physical appetite has turned as stale as day-old bread. But San Juan would hardly recognise the treatment his ideas receive. The deliberate fusing of sex and religion in

---

[30] *OC*, pp. 345-6; cf. *BAE*, XXVII, 17 (*Subida del Monte Carmelo*) — the passage is marked in Miró's copy.

'pan', 'adorable', 'reliquia', 'fetichismo' offers the *modernista* view, so that in this context San Juan's assertions have to be distorted to suit the case. Indeed, the passage continues by describing Félix as 'este mozo sensual y místico'. Only *modernista* usage could couple those two adjectives that explicitly reject San Juan's hierarchical solution. Perhaps this poor fit between St. John and his new surroundings is again to be explained in terms of the earlier first-person version. For the narrator's tone is, in the circumstances, oddly moralising, oddly sure of itself: 'Probó los malos dejos.' Once more Miró's narrative technique in this novel seems to offer problems. The opening sentence of the second paragraph quoted presents these most acutely. Who says the bread is a 'reliquia'? Who says Félix is guilty of 'voluptuoso fetichismo'? Evidently the latter is the narrator's judgement. But if 'reliquia' is also the narrator's choice of word, then the narrator is party to the confusion of sex and religion and cannot be commenting on Félix. On the other hand, if 'reliquia' presents Félix's thought, then the narrator is pointing out that the confusion is the fault of Félix; but this alternative involves a shift of point of view within the sentence. It is evident from the novel as a whole, as we shall see when we deal with Cervantes, that Miró criticises Félix, that there is considerable distance between them. The difficulty is that often, as we saw with St. Teresa, Miró fails, technically, to place his narrator at a distance, partly because so much of Miró has gone into Félix, and partly because of the first-person origins of the novel.

The quotation from San Juan in *La palma rota* is a useful contrast: 'Vacilaba la voluntad de Aurelio; la sentía reducida por otra ancha, fuerte y dominadora. «El que ama criatura, tan bajo se queda como aquella criatura, y en alguna manera más bajo, porque el amor no sólo iguala, más aún, sujeta al amante a lo que ama.» Y estas recordadas palabras de San Juan de la Cruz le hirieron, viéndose rendido. Protestó en su corazón embravecido y altivo. El, sí; él amaba, pero sin pérdida ni menoscabo de sí mismo' (*OC,* p. 220). The technique is quite different — the quotation, from the *Subida del Monte Carmelo* (*BAE,* XXVII, 7), is introduced by the character, not the narrator, and the views throughout are stated by the character. The comment to the reader is implicit rather than explicit. It looks as if this passage is a maturer piece of work than the quoted part of *Las cerezas del cementerio* (novelistically it certainly works better than the smudgy effect that results there). But the approach to San Juan remains the same: Miró is not interested in San Juan's contrast of earth and heaven, but in his understanding of earthly psychology.

How did Miró view all these religious writers that he read so avidly? Miró was not only devoted to nature but, more importantly, to the effort to capture precisely through his own fleeting sense-perceptions the world around him. He was interested in his own experience of the world, in the phenomenon as his senses perceived it, so that he took seriously not merely what was transitory, but a unique and subjective experience of it. How is this interest to be reconciled with the reader of St. Teresa and St. John? The conventional answer is that Miró had a 'Franciscan' attitude — he loved nature and delighted in descriptions of it. On this view, Luis de Granada is an important writer to Miró. But there is no evidence to suggest that he was. Indeed we have seen how ironically Miró uses Luis's notion that Creation is a book in which we read of God. What seems to emerge more clearly from the evidence is that Miró was interested in human nature and in ideas and interpretations of it. He found the religious writers profound observers of their own minds and this was surely what attracted him. For this reason it is interesting to see that when he uses St. Teresa and St. John in his fiction they are used to further psychological understanding. But the purpose that they had in mind, turning man to God, was either ignored by Miró, or accepted conventionally, or confused by the insertion of sexual notions. It is only in work after this period up to 1910 that Miró achieves his own solution to the problem of the senses and the spirit, a solution that is summarised in the figure of Don Magín in *Nuestro padre San Daniel,* a priest significantly, who accepts the pleasures that his senses offer him, but within a context of love for others. Just as in this novel Miró achieves a balanced exploration of the links between sexual and religious emotions, so he inserts his love of the world into a larger spiritual framework of rejection and acceptance. Though his conclusions differ from those of the religious writers, he moves on from merely using their descriptions of the mind, to a whole view of life that has its parallel in theirs.

Cervantes and Alemán were both born in 1547. We have seen that Miró read Alemán with attention, but a single reference to Guzmán de Alfarache (*OC,* p. 838) is the only evidence of it in his works. The contrast with Cervantes is total. He is the last Spanish writer whom Miró mentions extensively, but also the one who appears most frequently, for Miró was devoted to him. When he entered the competition that he won with *Nómada,* his motto was 'el bachiller Sansón Carrasco', and a pseudonym he used later was Tomé Cecial; and Oscar Esplá tells us of Miró reciting passages from the *Quixote* aloud from memory in his youth. [31] There are about forty references to Cer-

---

[31] *Evocación,* p. 15.

vantes or Don Quixote to be found, ample confirmation of Cervantes's supreme place (with the exception of the Bible) among Miró's reading. But the use to which Cervantes is put is rather different from the cases of the earlier writers. Cervantes is hardly ever quoted; when he is it is to remind the reader of some episode from the *Quixote* or to introduce some piece of advice given by Quixote to Sancho. The carrying of the reader's mind back to some well-known episode of the *Quixote* is, in fact, the usual purpose of all Miró's references to Cervantes. This follows naturally from the special position of *Don Quixote* — Miró relied on his readers being well-acquainted with the book. Since there are so many references to Cervantes, only a selection from them will be presented.

Sometimes we are offered a straightforward adaptation: '...Y la del alba sería de un día de marzo, cuando salí, bien apercibido de los dineros que me quedaban, de aquel lugar de la Mancha, de cuyo nombre tampoco quisiera acordarme y nunca se me olvida' (*OC*, p. 460). The use of Cervantes in this way allows Miró to stress particular words by making them differ obviously from the original; for instance, 'quisiera' for 'quiero', together with 'nunca se me olvida', draws the reader's attention to the speaker's longing to forget, by contrasting it with Cervantes's original wilful assertion of his power over what he writes.

More often Miró simply remembers an episode: '¿No están al pie de los palacios de Aldonza Lorenzo? Y aunque lejos del Toboso, ha de surgir para su mirada la figura larga, cansada, estrecha del valiente y enamorado caballero, transido de emociones, guiado por el embuste y bellaquería' (*OC*, p. 608), or: 'Pasaba un amigo, hombre aficionado a curiosidades como el famoso estudiante que Don Quijote tomó por guía para visitar la cueva de Montesinos' (*OC*, p. 615).

These are typical examples of uses that are usually decorative or at most illustrative on a small scale in their immediate context. Occasionally, however, references are made to work harder, and these are more useful in assessing Miró's view of Cervantes. A good example is found in *La novela de mi amigo*. The 'amigo', beginning the story of his life, is making the point that for him 'las cosas no son grandes ni menudas, sino indiferentes'. He continues:

> Humanizaré el ejemplo. ¿Conocerá usted la *Ilíada*, verdad? ¡La conozco yo! Elija usted la hazaña que más le plazca y entusiasme de Aquiles, Héctor o Agamenón, y póngala junto al lanceamiento que hizo Don Quijote en el rebaño que tomara por huestes de Pentapolín, o al lado de otra aventura de nuestro caballero. ¿Son las primeras empresas superiores a las segundas?... ¿Distintas, dice usted? ¡Nunca, nunca!... ¡Si

para el delirante hidalgo eran hombres enemigos y desaforados los mansos corderos! Los hechos se trenzan indiferentemente...

(*OC*, p. 120)

First of all there is an oddity here. Don Quixote believed he was defending Pentapolín and therefore charged the other flock, that which he presumed to be the army of the pagan Alifanfarón. Either the 'amigo' or Miró has suffered a lapse of memory, confusing the two adversaries. Given Miró's apparent habit of quoting from memory on occasion, and his fairly frequent alterations, intended or otherwise, to the texts he quotes, it is impossible to decide whether the lapse is intended to show the confusion of the 'amigo', or is Miró's error. Nevertheless the reference makes its point. In the first place it offers an apology for the subject-matter of the story, an apology from the 'amigo' to the narrator, and implicitly from Miró to the reader. But as such apologies usually do, it points out that the subject-matter is not the area where the reader should be concentrating his attention. The *Quixote* is the equal of the *Iliad* in spite of the descent from the noble to the grotesque.

More importantly, the passage introduces a major theme of the story: the validity of the subjective, a notion that immediately ties up with an essentially Romantic view of the *Quixote*. In the third chapter the 'amigo' shows the narrator a portrait and the narrator exclaims:

—Pero ¿eso que usted ha pintado no es un fraile?
—Fraile, fraile es.
—¡Si usted dice que su modelo fué una moza!
—Y es cierto. Moza era; pero la fuí viendo fraile, y me gustó hacer un lego en faena huertana. Esto me sucede con frecuencia. No es informalidad artística; tampoco inquietud. Todo modelo delante de mí se modifica en un proteísmo irresistible..., y, además, he pintado ya muchas campesinas.

(*OC*, p. 136)

Federico, the 'amigo', is a poor artist. He allows his imagination to transform what he sees of reality and then paints the result of this transformation. This is just one of the most striking examples of the way in which he makes the subjective absolute for himself. The individual's experience of the world is more true than any supposedly objective construction. Hence, of course, the point of introducing Don Quixote. The knight transforms reality and acts on his version of it, just as the painter paints it. For 'el delirante hidalgo', the sheep *were*

99

men, hence Don Quixote's battle is the equivalent of those of Achilles, Hector, and Agamemnon.

Now this is, of course, not the sense in which Cervantes intended us to look at Don Quixote. For Cervantes there was an absolute objective reality outside ourselves, so that Don Quixote erred in deluding himself about it. But Miró cannot escape his Romantic inheritance with its notions of the mad genius and the validity of the uniquely personal. Yet Miró's understanding of Cervantes was not a simply Neo-Romantic one, and the last words of the passage quoted, '..., y, además, he pintado ya muchas campesinas', are subversive in the genuine Cervantine manner: 'El quedó satisfecho de su fortaleza y, sin querer hacer nueva experiencia de ella, la diputó y tuvo por celada finísima de encaje' (a passage recalled a few pages later — *OC,* p. 147).

Usually, Miró's use of Cervantes is not as directly significant within its context, but instead the repeated references to Don Quixote point to Cervantes presiding over the work as a whole. This is particularly evident in *Las cerezas del cementerio,* which includes six direct references to *Don Quixote,* most of them in themselves of the kind previously described as decorative — pleasant embellishments of the narrative. *Las cerezas del cementerio* is on the surface the least Cervantine of all Miró's work, but it was written at a period when Miró's references to Cervantes appeared most frequently. As with St. Teresa, references peter out after 1915, in parallel with references to other authors. *Las cerezas del cementerio* will serve as an example of the overall presence of Cervantes in Miró's work.

As with St. Teresa again one obvious route into the subject would be a study of style, and Joaquín de Entrambasaguas, the critic who makes most of the Cervantine influence (it is not commonly put very high), suggests such a study and comments: 'Cervantes le dio, con el Quijote, fundamentalmente, un vocabulario y una sencillez sintáctica, verdaderamente áureas.' [32] In addition, Entrambasaguas speaks of 'el espíritu quijotesco que captó Miró quizá mejor que nadie en aquellos tiempos del centenario cervantino y de la obra cumbre de la novela'.

Early in *Las cerezas del cementerio,* Félix, bored with his father's advice, exclaims: '¡Si es que tu predicación (...) me trajo el recuerdo de los consejos del señor don Quijote a su criado!' (*OC,* p. 336). A little later his uncle mentions Félix's rigid aunt Doña Constanza: 'Al punto enmudeció Félix, lo mismo que el Roto de la mala figura cuando por la reina Madasina le interrumpió en su historia el antojadizo hidalgo' (*OC,* p. 347). Further on, Miró, to avoid difficulties over the confusion between the narrator and Félix, writes: 'Y llegando aquí

---

[32] *Mejores novelas contemporáneas,* IV, 662.

el *Cide Hamete* de esta sencilla historia, jura solemnemente que el labriego cometió bellaquería' (OC, p. 376). Far from Cervantes's destruction of reliability, Miró's use of Cide Hamete is to offer the reader total assurance about what really happened.

Shortly afterwards Félix is wandering in the open: '¡Es que estaba solo; se había perdido en el inmenso y oscuro valle, bajo los fantasmas de los olivos! Pensó en Ulises, en Dante, y luego se le apareció el hidalgo de la Mancha. Tuvo que reírse, porque, ¡Señor, si no era verdad que se hubiese perdido!' (*OC*, p. 380). Here Cervantes makes more of a point; indeed the chapter is called 'De lo que aconteció a Félix en su primera salida por los campos de Posuna'. Like Don Quixote, Félix suffers illusions that are frequently of a literary origin. He imagines, on the slightest pretext, that he is lost, and immediately Ulysses and Dante seem to him to be suitable parallels for his plight. Then reality destroys the delusion, but through the next literary image that crosses his mind, that of the deluded Quixote.

One of Félix's illusions is that he is like his romantic uncle Guillermo 'que pasó por la vida hendiéndola como un águila, como un arcángel trágico!' But the illusion keeps breaking down in the face of reality for he finds that he himself 'se regalaba trazándose un sosiego aldeano semejante al del «caballero del verde gabán»' (*OC*, p. 387). The reference to Cervantes is little more than embellishment, but it does point to the link between Félix's illusions and those portrayed by Cervantes.

Lastly, there is a more extended series of allusions, a passage that, more than any other in Miró's work, refers continuously to Cervantes. Félix, coming down the hillside, meets a group of shepherds and eats with them. They offer him a stone on which to sit, but 'Félix prefirió un dornajo [Don Quixote sat on a 'dornajo'], y parecióle que se alzaba una ideal figura mostrando un puño de bellotas a los hermanos cabreros ['bellotas' are the starting-point of Don Quixote's 'Edad de oro' speech]. ¡Oh, poderoso ingenio, aquel que supo trazar la vida con tanta sencillez y verdad, que, cuando nos hallamos en momentos que tienen semejanza a los del peregrino libro, acudimos al sabroso recuerdo de sus páginas para sentir mejor la hermosura que vemos!' (*OC*, p. 413).

For the next page or so the parallel continues until in an incident in which two dogs fight and then are separated brutally by a shepherd, the dogs are likened to men, and a man to the dogs. Baquero Goyanes has dealt with this passage and points out that it is an amalgam of *Don Quixote* and *El coloquio de los perros*. He also sees in the destruction of Félix's fond illusions about the shepherds' Arcadia by the confusion of man and beast, an example of a naturalistic attack on 'el

8

viejo tópico... del menosprecio de corte y alabanza de aldea'. [33] But there is no need to bring in Zola, for the clash portrayed is a clash between Félix's illusion and reality — a Cervantine clash, as Miró hints. Miró is not saying that, contrary to general belief, country folk are brutal, but that Félix is such a dreamer, so taken up in his reading, that he tailors the world to his visions until reality becomes too obviously at variance to be ignored. The point is an important one, for Miró is a purely descriptive writer far less often than most critics suggest. Cervantes is a far more helpful comparison than Zola.

Miró, then, offers us a scene in which Félix, as so often, dreams and is rudely awakened. First, the shepherds' talk becomes vulgar, and then, as the dogs fight, the shepherds cheer them on. But Félix's disillusion goes further: 'Félix se maldecía sorprendiéndose gustoso y conmovido de esa lucha.' He asks the shepherds to stop it, and immediately a shepherd separates the dogs by a savage bite at the muzzle of one of the dogs. Félix's action to calm his guilty conscience leads directly to a man becoming a beast: step by step his dreaming has led him down to this.

These six passages illustrate clearly the ways in which Miró used Cervantes's work directly. Taken with Cervantine chapter-headings and phrases such as 'La amorosa pestilencia' (which occurs in Don Quixote's 'Edad de Oro' speech), they offer convincing evidence of the continuous presence of Cervantes as Miró wrote. This is not a matter of mere interest, but one essential to understanding *Las cerezas del cementerio*. Again and again, we are presented with Félix as a modern Quixote, but without Miró pointing this out directly. In the second chapter Félix sets out to be a labourer and naturally enough is soon exhausted. He cannot be a real labourer because he can stop when he wants to. Or, more obviously Quixotic: 'Junto a un ribazo halló dos rapaces hermanitos que se estaban escupiendo, peleándose por una vara de regalicia. Los sosegó; les repartió la mata. Los chicos se quedaron mirándole, burlones y medrosos. Después volvieron a escupirse' (*OC*, p. 420). There are endless small-scale examples of this kind, but through the whole book runs the theme of Félix's recurrent self-identification with his mysterious and romantic uncle Guillermo. There is no space for detail, but the climax of this theme is obvious. Guillermo died in a fight with a Dutchman, Koeveld, who bit Guillermo in the throat (like the shepherd and the dog). Félix meets a neighbour he dislikes; the neighbour trips, Félix tries to help him up, but falls and suffers a heart attack:

[33] *Perspectivismo y contraste*, pp. 97-9. Also '*Las cerezas del cementerio*, de Gabriel Miró', in Alarcos, *El comentario de textos.*

> Félix dio un grito inmenso y angustioso:
> —¡Koeveld!
> Una zarpa de fuego torcía su corazón; un puñal de dolor
> le desgarraba desde el hombro hasta el codo izquierdo, y la
> boca de un oso le mordió apretadamente en la garganta... Se
> ahogaba.
>
> (*OC,* p. 421)

Félix is so obsessed with his own grandeur that even a heart attack seems to be the brutal death his uncle suffered.

For a short while Félix recovers and, convalescing, his illusions disappear. Chapter XX is headed '«En el nido de antaño, no hay pájaros hogaño»', and the whole chapter describes the process of Félix coming to his senses, clearly parallel to Quixote's recovery of his sanity. The climax of this recovery is stated like this:

> Solo y señero de su ánima hallábase Félix; los nidos de qui-
> meras quedaban vacíos de los engañosos pájaros de antaño;
> y ya no tenía calor para llenarlos de águilas ideálicas y *suyas*...
>
> (*OC,* p. 424)

Shortly after this, Félix dies. The parallel with Alonso Quijano could hardly be more obvious. In his last speech, after he has said: 'Pues ya en los nidos de antaño no hay pájaros hogaño', Quijano says: 'Yo fui loco, y ya soy cuerdo.' In this way Miró places Félix's life firmly into a framework of moral responsability. Félix's illusions have evidently been less harmful and less absurd than Don Quixote's (this reflects the Romantic view of Don Quixote as a mad genius), but they have led him into moral folly nonetheless. They are illusions derived from others; from reading Byron or from believing himself pursued by a fate that makes him like his uncle. Hence Miró italicises '*suyas*' — up to now Félix has never had his own moral ideas.

This moral framework, in part the result of the influence of Cervantes, differentiates Miró from many *modernista* contemporaries. Miró was well-acquainted with fashionable views of the artist as a superior being and therefore unbound by the conventional morals of lesser men. They provided an essential theme for his earliest work. The point of *Las cerezas del cementerio* is the assertion that, after all, such a belief is an illusion, and the matter of the novel is largely an exploration of Félix's mind in order to see how the sensitive, artistic mind works and how, if it fails in its responsibilities, it can let its virtues be warped and degraded.

If the return to sanity of Félix is the key to the novel, it remains to be explained why even critics who have pointed out the connections with Cervantes have failed to go the whole way and see Félix as a character upon whom Miró comments, not merely a figure with whom we are presented (though G. G. Brown, in his recent volume of *A Literary History of Spain,* is a notable exception). The answer must in part be that Miró's failure to master the problems of narration has been responsible. The effect is to leave a minimum of distance at many points between the narrator and Félix, and this is why Félix is invariably treated as a version of the author, and both praised or criticised together. This kind of appreciation was made all the more likely in a literary climate accustomed to the presentation, as such, of extreme aesthetic characters.

But the differences between Miró and Cervantes, the differences between the ways in which they use the clash between reality and illusions, should not be omitted. If Cervantes works beneath the dome of heaven, Miró relies on no stable system of values into which his writing fits. Regardless of his view of Christian doctrine, he does not invoke it as a standard by which to judge either the whole or parts of his narrative. When Félix is restored to sanity, we have no system of values to which we as readers can relate this event, other than the values that emerge from the book itself. Hence of course the figure of Félix is constantly ambivalent in a sense that Don Quixote is not. The latter is mad; Félix is only intermittently deluded. Even when Don Quixote talks sense, it is in a context that modifies it; but often Félix expresses feelings that impress us quite directly without the intervention of the narrator. There are, too, the many obvious surface differences, including the immaturity of *Las cerezas del cementerio.* But this comparison is not concerned with evaluation, but with showing that Cervantes offers a key to the understanding of this novel, and that it was from his continued reading of Cervantes that Miró learned a good deal of his moral and psychological subtlety.

After the religious writers and Cervantes, few Spanish authors of any kind appear with any frequency in Miró's work. The Golden-Age dramatists are notably absent. In a piece first published in 1923, '¡Mañana es Corpus!', Miró mentions, as authors of *autos,* Joan Timoneda, Josef de Valdivielso, fray Gabriel Téllez, Lope de Vega, don Agustín de Moreto, don Pedro Calderón de la Barca (*Glosas,* p. 91). Moreto is quoted in the long footnote on 'amor' that appeared in the first edition of *Del vivir* (pp. 186-87), and there is a solitary reference to *La vida es sueño* (*OC,* p. 946). These are the only occasions on which Miró mentions Golden-Age drama. The passage from Moreto is simply a quotation to illustrate a point about 'amor'. It is copied from the *BAE* edition of *El desdén con el desdén* (XXXIX, 9) with an accuracy that includes taking over a faulty reading. Much more interesting is '¡Mañana es Corpus!', for the mention of the dramatists' names offers a clue from which Miró's mature methods of composition can be closely followed.

The piece was originally published as a part of the series that was later made into *Años y leguas*; it appeared first under this title in *La Nación* of Buenos Aires, but was dropped in the book version. In it Miró attempts to express Sigüenza's feelings aroused by the sentence '¡Mañana es Corpus!'. The six dramatists he mentions all appear in Volume LVIII of the *BAE* (*Autos sacramentales*), making up the bulk of the volume. Miró's copy is unmarked but this article shows that he read, at the very least, the introduction and a good number of Calderón's *autos*. The authors he has mentioned 'producen su apologética del Santísimo y solazan a la multitud con las gracias y conceptos de los recitantes que han de encarnar y vestir peregrinas figuras: el Sosiego, el Cuidado, el Desabrimiento, la Noche, el Hebraísmo, la Culpa, el Afecto 1°, 2°, 3°, 4°, 5°, 6°, 7°, Máscaras, la Lascivia, Isaías, las Potencias del alma, la Serpiente de metal, el Ateísmo, los Reyes Magos con hachas encendidas, Hugo el Hereje, que se engulle una forma porque quiere averiguar «si en este día este pan tiene sabor de carne»...' (p. 91). Every one of these characters appears in the *autos* in this volume, with the exception of 'la Noche', who is mentioned in the Introduction. All but the first four and Hugo el Hereje appear in Calderón, but they do not seem to be in any order that corresponds to their order in the book. 'Los Afectos', 'Máscaras', 'las Potencias del Alma', do not appear in the lists of characters, but only in the headings to scenes. The 'hachas encendidas' and Hugo el Hereje's words— from Moreto's *La gran casa de Austria* (p. 559) — also show that Miró did not merely leaf through the volume before writing the piece. He goes on: 'La jarcia escénica es de una simplicidad laberíntica. En la memoria de las tramoyas de «La Divina Filotea» se advierte que en una mitad del cuarto carro ha de aparecer «un jardín (...)».' He continues to quote the rest of the highly involved instruction, with minor changes in the wording.

But Miró did not just use the texts of the *autos*. The introduction to the volume is by Eduardo González Pedroso and this too provided details for '¡Mañana es Corpus!'. It offers a history and description of the *autos,* but also information about the celebration of Corpus Christi, especially in Madrid. The tone is strongly anti-protestant and stresses above all the rôle of the *autos* in combatting the protestant denial of transubstantiation. Luther appears 'llevando a su manceba de una mano y empuñando con la otra la *santa botella*' (p. xviii). In response Miró includes the following passage: 'Ya se aborrecían herejes y creyentes con cada latido de su sangre. El dogma se hizo patria. Las hogueras expiatorias y las luminarias eucarísticas alumbran las ciudades. La Caridad no puede regocijarse mucho, aunque lo diga Urbano IV' (p. 90). (Miró has earlier quoted Urban IV's words on instituting Corpus Christi: 'La Caridad se regocije.') Miró's irony gently rebukes the violence of González Pedroso's account, without ever mentioning it. His reading has directly stimulated his development of the piece.

He goes on:

> ¿Será todo eso el Corpus, Sigüenza?
> Y por si acaso no lo fuera, se pone a imaginar: pompa de trono, atuendo de galanía, carros de la farándula, morteretes, tonadas y danzas en que

> Era cada cascabel
> de un danzante, silogismo
> contra el apóstata infiel... (p. 90)

The lines are quoted from González Pedroso's introduction and the scene conjured up is evidently seventeenth-century Madrid as described by González Pedroso, who on page xxx of his Introduction recounts details of the procession laid on for the visit of the Prince of Wales to Philip III. Miró uses details from this description, but completely reorders and reworks them:

> La tarasca, enanos y gigantillas, cruces de parroquias, banderas, guiones, mangas y ciriales; oro de casullas, coleto de plebe, paño de los gremios, jerga de sayales, capa de mendigo, blancura de túnica, de sobrepelliz y de manto de cruzado caballero, brocado y felpa de ropillas, libreas de lacayos, muceta de cardenal, estofas de Indias, terciopelos, paramentos, relumbrón de la Guardia española, alabardas, bandas, plumas, vellones y nieblas de los incensarios, centelleo del viril, la llama de la cima de la Custodia. Catorce arrobas de plata pesa la de la corte; trescientos noventa y dos kilos la de Cádiz; quinientos seis la de Sevilla...
> Pero ¿es que recordará Sigüenza puntualmente las cifras?

> (p. 90)

González Pedroso's passage is too long to quote, but some of Miró's changes can be presented. 'Colchas y paños de la India' become 'estofas de Indias'. 'Pendones, cruces, estandartes, guiones, mangas y ciriales... anunciaban de lejos el lugar que a todos correspondía' becomes 'cruces de parroquia, banderas, guiones, mangas y ciriales'. 'La inmaculada blancura de los mantos en que iban pomposamente envueltos los caballeros de los órdenes militares' is turned into 'blancura de túnica, de sobrepelliz y de manto de cruzado caballero'. 'Los variados colores de las guardias española, alemana y de archeros' becomes 'relumbrón de la Guardia española'. Miró's description of the host's surroundings is derived from these words: '...el cual entre nubes de incienso, al son de las músicas de la capilla real, puesto en su relicario de oro y diamantes, a dos haces, dentro de una custodia de plata que pesaba catorce arrobas...' Earlier Miró has transformed the moral attitude of González Pedroso; here he transmutes his descriptive attitude into something entirely his own. Miró's passage is concerned with the sense of sight, and he rigorously excludes all else. González Pedroso contrasted the different costumes to demonstrate the order ruling the procession. Miró converts the costumes into the materials from which they are made — he wishes to convey visual sensations. Almost every change confirms this: 'paños', the articles, become 'estofas', materials. 'De la India' indicates a geographical origin; 'de Indias' indicates a quality. The crosses that for González Pedroso pointed out the origin of each group, are for Miró 'cruces de parroquia', a type of cross. 'Blancura', typically, loses its article — note the almost total absence of articles in Miró's passage, a favourite device for concentrating attention on visual qualities. With similar intent, 'los variados colores' become 'relumbrón', and 'nubes de incienso', clouds *of* incense, become 'nieblas de los incensarios', clouds *seen* emerging from the censer. Again, 'centelleo' and 'llama' replace concrete nouns. And the music that González Pedroso mentions is simply excluded.

The sudden mention of the weight of silver throws the whole scene into perspective with the gentlest of digs at the vulgarity of mind that rates the status of a city by the weight of its 'custodia'. The weights slip into kilos — Miró must have been reading something contemporary, perhaps a seasonal newspaper article that he has not to hand — hence the '¿es que recordará (...)?'. Next, another anecdote from the following page in González Pedroso continues the theme of the vulgarity of mind that lies behind the visual splendour (none the less splendid for that):

> Ni el rey reposa la siesta de Corpus. Ha pedido de comer en la casa de un vasallo. Así lo hizo el señor don Felipe III en la del duque de Uceda, quien le sirvió un refrigerio de doscientos manjares.

In the original it is 'un almuerzo compuesto de doscientos diferentes manjares' — 'refrigerio' is a favourite Mironian word.

So far the material is all from the *BAE* volume of *autos,* but in the case of '¡Mañana es Corpus!' it is possible to go further, constructing something like a complete inventory of Miró's written sources. The piece opens with three paragraphs dealing with Sigüenza's attempts to analyse his emotions before Corpus. Then follows a longer paragraph on the origins of Corpus, derived from works of reference in Miró's library: Kellner's *El año eclesiástico* provides most of the facts, with others coming from González Pedroso. It is at this point that Miró implicitly rebukes the unmentioned editor of the *autos*. For the next page all the material is drawn from his work — we have seen how Miró adapts it. Next comes a paragraph on the *autos* themselves, mentioning authors, characters, and settings. Again the source is the *BAE* volume, but Miró adds four lines on the origins of the *autos* which have a different source, but which, by chance, can be traced. Boissier's *El fin del paganismo* states that 'en la Edad Media [la *Psychomachia* de Prudencio] ha dado nacimiento a toda una literatura', and mentions in the same context 'los vicios y las virtudes librando una batalla: la Fe contra la Idolatría, el Pudor contra la Lujuria', but without mentioning the *autos*.[34] Left in Miró's copy is a slip of paper on which Miró, drawing his own conclusions, has written: 'Los autos sacramentales que traen un origen de los primitivos poemas cristianos como la *Psychomachia* de Prudencio, donde contienden los vicios y virtudes personificados; la Fe con la Idolatría, el Pudor con la Lujuria — T. 2.° — Fin del Paganismo — 134.' He has assumed that 'toda una literatura' includes the *autos,* either remembering something he has read elsewhere, or without further evidence. It is this slip that he then uses to write '¡Mañana es Corpus!' where he speaks of 'los Autos Sacramentales, que parecen originarse de los primitivos poemas cristianos, como la «Psychomachia», de Prudencio, donde contienden los vicios y las virtudes: la Fe con la Idolatría, el Pudor con la Lujuria' (p. 91). The essential modifications of Boissier are made in the transitional version on the slip of paper which is then incorporated almost intact in '¡Mañana es Corpus!'.

Exactly what purpose this kind of note served is hard to establish; perhaps it was Miró's way of collecting material before writing, although it seems odd that he should bother to copy out when he was using only a very few sources for a particular article. It may well be that the thought that Boissier's 'toda una literatura' included the *autos* struck him before he had started on '¡Mañana es Corpus!', and that he wrote it down in order not to lose it. Since he never wrote in his books except when young, this may sometimes have been his way of making marginal comments. Whatever the explanation, we are offered a rare glimpse of the transition from source to finished work, including a typically Mironian 'improvement' on the way.

[34] G. Boissier, *El fin del paganismo* (Madrid, 1908), II, 134.

After the passage on the *autos* Sigüenza goes on to deal with Corpus in his own day and region: this part, except for a short quotation from Stendhal, relies on observation. '¡Mañana es Corpus!' is a short and unimportant piece, but it reveals more than most how it was composed. In Miró's later work quotation becomes less common than 'before and we are offered less clues as to the material he used, so that on this count also this piece is worth examining. As a young man Miró tended to take over material from other authors more or less directly, but here everything is fused into Miró's own style. This is a corollary of the observation that as he matures as a creative writer he becomes less and less respectful of the texts he quotes. It is also once again clear how much Miró depended on his materials, be they from reading or from observation.

One other author in the *BAE* volume of *autos* is mentioned elsewhere. In 'Los dejos de los días: Almas medianas' [35] Miró refers to 'Juan de Pedraza, tundidor, natural de Segovia', and mentions some of the characters in his *Danza de la Muerte,* adding: 'Todos acaban de la misma mediana manera.' All the details he mentions are found in the volume of *Autos* (p. 41).

Few Golden-Age writers remain to be dealt with. Góngora, in spite of the interest revealed in the relevant *BAE* volume, is only mentioned once: in the talk given by Miró in Gijón in 1925, 'Lo viejo y lo santo en manos de ahora'. He says: ' Por fortuna y por justicia, la modernidad no se somete a los cómputos y límites de la cronología. Por eso es más de nosotros que de antaño la lírica de Góngora, y son futuras las concepciones de Goethe.' [36] The comment itself, its date, and the lack of earlier references all confirm the idea that Miró came to understand Góngora's achievements fairly late.

Quevedo is mentioned on three occasions, none of them particularly interesting. [37] Miró possessed *Biblioteca clásica* editions of Quevedo as well as the three volumes of the *BAE.* The state of the volumes, the presence of bookmarks, and three mentions together all make clear that Quevedo was carefully read. Another writer whom it seems Miró read is Saavedra Fajardo, whose work appears in *BAE,* XXV, and who is referred to in an article of 1909 and in a piece for *ABC* (quoted by José Guardiola Ortiz, but not otherwise seen) where Miró presents a passage from the *Empresas.* [38] Castillo Solórzano is mentioned once when a town is called 'La Garduña' after *La Garduña de Sevilla.* The

[35] *La Publicidad,* 2 Nov. 1919, p. 1.
[36] Ramos, *Literatura,* p. 305.
[37] *Hilván,* p. 49; *Amigos,* p. 65; *EC,* IX, 266.
[38] 'Del salón de retratos', *Gérmenes,* 15 March 1909; Guardiola Ortiz, *Biografía íntima,* p. 191.

reference makes it clear that Miró had read the story.[39] Another reference suggests that Miró had read, in the same *BAE* volume, Luis Vélez de Guevara's *El diablo cojuelo* and Francisco Santos' *Día y noche de Madrid*.[40]

Baltasar Gracián is of more importance. Miró possessed in Volume LXV of the *BAE,* where Gracián receives a minor place, *El héroe, El discreto,* and the *Oráculo manual.* All these are unmarked. He also possessed a copy of *El héroe* and *El discreto* published in 1900 and bound for him, and a two-volume *Obras* of 1700. These volumes, too, are unmarked, yet the fact that Miró possessed them is interesting, as duplications of works in the *BAE* are not common. E. L. King states that Gracián was 'one of Miró's favourite writers when he was a young man' (*Humo,* p. 172), but other commentators rarely mention Gracián as a favourite author, while Quevedo appears in their lists several times. Yet Miró mentions Gracián more frequently than Quevedo. Clearly much of Gracián would have appealed strongly to the young Miró intent on moral epigrams. When he quotes Gracián he does so in a way that makes Gracián appear as unambiguous a moraliser as any other favourite of Miró's. 'Formidable fué un río — escribe Gracián — hasta que se le halló vado', he writes in 1911.[41] The two earliest quotations appear in 1901 in *La mujer de Ojeda.* One is from *El discreto,* while the other, praising books, is from the *Criticón,* suggesting that Miró had already acquired his 1700 edition of Gracián's *Obras* at this time.[42] Nine years later Miró opened 'Glosas de Sigüenza' with a sentence from *El discreto:* 'Una gran capacidad no se rinde a la vulgar alternación de los humores ni aun de los afectos; siempre se mantiene superior a tan material destemplanza.' He goes on: 'Recordadas estas rígidas palabras, Sigüenza amohinóse con el sabio jesuíta. ¡Sigüenza no era gran capacidad!' Sigüenza was a marvellous instrument for dissecting the ambivalences Miró found within himself when he looked back to his own youthful enthusiasms and aspirations.[43] But interest in Gracián continued for he is quoted again in *El humo dormido* (this time from the *Criticón*), though the reference is to Miró reading Gracián as a student.[44]

Feijoo is another writer whose work Miró possessed in early editions, as well as in the *BAE* (LVI) which offers selections from the

---

[39] 'Galeote de su fama', *Los Lunes de el Imparcial,* 15 Feb. 1909: cf. *BAE,* XXXIII, 169.

[40] 'Nuevas jornadas de Sigüenza: I — Lector: La nariz', *La Publicidad,* 1 Sept. 1920, p. 1.

[41] 'Oradores en el «huerto provinciano»', *Diario de Alicante,* 16 Jan. 1911.

[42] *Mujer,* pp. 38 and 8: cf. *BAE,* LXV, 541, and *Criticón,* Pt. II, Crisi IV.

[43] *Glosas,* p. 20: cf. *BAE,* LXV, 556.

[44] *OC,* p. 676: cf. *Criticón,* Pt. I, Crisi VI.

Teatro crítico. Miró refers on three occasions to Feijoo, never with any great enthusiasm. Two references are early, in 'Del natural' and in the first edition of *Del vivir*. [45] The third is in *El humo dormido* and illustrates well Miró's attitude both to Feijoo and to religion:

> El Padre Feijoo no creyó en las lámparas perennes del se-
> pulcro de Palante, de Máximo Olybio, de Tulia, de los tem-
> plos gentiles … Otros varones eruditos o rudos tampoco
> creerían en la realidad de estas luces perpetuas (…); pero
> las lámparas siguieron encendidas para muchos, aunque no
> creyesen. Porque un hombre puede sonreír delante de la con-
> seja que ya no cree y 'todavía' podrá gozarla. Menos el Padre
> Feijoo, que hizo un discurso contra las lámparas perennes y
> las apagó definitivamente para sus ojos. [46]

The remainder of the eighteenth century is quickly dealt with. Carlos, in *La mujer de Ojeda* (p. 14), reads Isla (*BAE*, XV). Alfonso Verdugo y Castilla is mentioned in *Nuestro padre San Daniel* where a poem of his is ludicrously adapted by *Alba-Longa* to celebrate Paulina's marriage. [47] A title by Campomanes appears in a library in *El obispo leproso* (*OC*, p. 1028). Vicente de los Ríos is joked against in *El humo dormido*. [48] Cadalso is alluded to in the 'Noticia preliminar' of *La mujer de Ojeda* (p. xii). And 'el muy grave y dulce don Juan Meléndez Valdés' is mentioned in *El humo dormido*. [49]

The only eighteenth-century writer of more interest is Juan Sempere y Guarinos, whose *Historia del luxo* Miró possessed, and which he twice used as a source-book of quotations. In a chapter of *Libro de Sigüenza* first published in 1914, 'Sigüenza, los peluqueros y la muerte', the first five paragraphs are entirely taken from Sempere's book, and a page later almost two more paragraphs come from it. Eight years later, in an article called 'Lujo y nobleza', Miró drew again on Sempere, this time being, as usual, noticeably less faithful to his original. [50] This was the kind of history Miró appreciated, in which details that contributed little to the wide panorama of history yet revealed the enduring sameness of human nature.

[45] *El Ibero,* 16 March 1902; *DVi*, p. 192: cf. *BAE*, LVI, 402.

[46] *OC*, p. 724: cf. *Teatro crítico*, IV, 'Lámparas inestinguibles' — not available to Miró in *BAE*.

[47] *OC*, p. 855: cf. *BAE*, LXI, 132.

[48] *OC*, p. 726. Cf. King, *Humo*, pp. 199-200, who suggests Miró's father possessed an Academy edition of *Don Quijote* that included Vicente de los Ríos's commentary. It is at least as likely that the source was Miró's own copy of de los Ríos's *Análisis del Quijote* (Barcelona, 1834).

[49] *OC*, p. 729: cf. *BAE*, LXIII, 136.

[50] *OC*, pp. 636-7: cf. Sempere, *Historia* (Madrid, 1788), II, 121-5; *Glosas,* pp. 84-6: cf. Sempere, II, 2, 13, and 17. Miró's copy of Vol. II contains slips of paper and markings that relate to 'Lujo y nobleza'.

The first nineteenth-century figure to appear is José Somoza, whose poems are in *BAE,* LXVII together with his 'Recuerdos e impresiones'. From one of these, 'Una mirada en redondo', Miró drew a remark that must have been very close to him. In *El humo dormido* he writes: 'Había plenitud en el sentimiento del paisaje del escondido Somoza, que confesaba no comprender más que el campo de su país, porque de este campo suyo de Piedrahita se alzaba para sus ojos y sus oídos la evocación y la comprensión cifrada de todo paisaje' (*OC,* p. 666). He repeats these words almost exactly in his Gijón *conferencia* in 1925, starting from 'confesaba (...)',[51] and refers again to Somoza in *Años y leguas* (*OC,* p. 1157). In fact Somoza said rather less than Miró attributes to him: 'El campo que no es de mi país, no es comprensible para mí, ni me da casi placer' (*BAE,* LXVII, 454). Miró's attachment to the retiring Somoza is shown by the fact that he used his name as his motto in the competition for the Mariano de Cavia prize that he won with 'Huerto de cruces' in 1925.

The Romantics are entirely absent except for Miró's remark in his 'Autobiografía' that his father's library included the works of Larra and Rivas (*EC,* I, x). Instead the anti-romantic Valera, hero of Miró's youth, makes one appearance in an article of 1913, 'Comentado', where the opening lines of 'Primavera' ('un hermoso trabajo del admirable D. Juan Valera, olvidado de muchos'), are quoted in a comment on an accusation of plagiarism made against Benavente by Gómez Carrillo.[52]

Perhaps it is a little surprising to see Valera's name only once, but with him we have reached writers still alive in Miró's day — Valera was fifty-five years older than Miró — and the ways in which Miró brings in living writers are quite different from those we have seen up to now. Plenty of names from the literary world appear — well over thirty — but with the sole exception of Núñez de Arce, who figures in *El humo dormido,* they are all in work not included in the *Obras completas.* The vast majority are in the more ephemeral of the newspaper articles. As a result, a perusal of Miró's major work would show a complete contrast between the constant references to the Spanish classics and the total absence of his contemporaries. A study of the uncollected material changes the picture somewhat, but a new contrast emerges. Most often these references are not used to illustrate points, or as the raw material of fiction, but as part of comment on contemporary literary affairs. Accordingly the names are many, but only two of them appear more than twice.

[51] Ramos, *Literatura,* p. 315.
[52] *Diario de Barcelona,* 21 Feb. 1913, p. 2558.

Miró's involvement in contemporary literature is a subject full of obscurities. Contemporary writers, with a few clear exceptions, are strikingly absent from the library until the period in the twenties when so many of the young poets sent Miró their work. Miró's biography is scarcely more helpful. Unlike most of his contemporaries, typically moving from the periphery to Madrid, Miró stayed in Alicante until he was thirty-four, and then he moved not to Madrid but to Barcelona with its specialised atmosphere of continuing Catalan renaissance. At the age of forty, finally, he moved to Madrid, only to repeat over and over again that he was unfitted for the conventional literary life. In a recently published letter to Rafael Romero, written at the end of 1922, Miró says: 'Todo me afirma cada día en el convencimiento de que no soy un escritor o no he sabido serlo profesional, sino de devoción.' [53] This is merely an extreme version of the words that close the 'Auto-biografía': Miró says he does not look ' con malhumor a los que bullen y se afanan por alcanzar sus deseos. Ellos ejercen verdaderamente su oficio de escritor. Si yo no lo hago no es por humilde ni por orgulloso, sino probablemente por carecer de aptitudes' (EC, I, x).

The portrait of Miró as a man withdrawn from the literary squabbles, from the *tertulias* and the self-advertisement of so many of his contemporaries is correct enough, but there remain to be accounted for the fashionable features of his style and the obviously contemporary links of his thought. Miró may not have taken part in the literary scene, but he knew it well enough: this his references to contemporary writers make clear.

The most surprising thing of all about Miró's references to his elders and contemporaries is that very few are represented in the library. This is in complete contrast to the close parallel between library and quotation with the classics. The following writers are not represented in the library by any title at all: Teodoro Llorente, Núñez de Arce, Pardo Bazán, Palacio Valdés, Rueda, Dicenta, Benavente, Vicente Medina, Blasco Ibáñez, Baroja, Maeztu, the Machado brothers, Villaespesa, R. Marquina, Martínez Sierra, Muñoz Llorente, Eugenio Noel, and Martínez Cuenca. Yet all these are mentioned by Miró, mostly in a context that suggests some reading of their work. Galdós and Ortega only appear in the library in 1930 and 1929 respectively; Unamuno in 1925 in Italian. Books by Valle-Inclán, Ricardo León, Andrés González-Blanco, Tomás Morales, and Rafael Romero, other mentioned writers, are all presented by their authors. Of all the literary figures that Miró mentions, only Valera, Pereda, Alas, Ganivet, and Azorín have titles in Miró's library other than late or presented copies. The

[53] Sebastián de la Nuez, 'Cartas de Gabriel Miró', p. 95.

conclusion is inescapable that the absence of contemporaries in the library is almost meaningless insofar as it might tell us about whether Miró read them or not. The absence of any author of the period, whether mentioned by Miró or not, cannot be taken as any kind of evidence.

Why this should be so is another question. Miró must have read a good deal in newspapers and magazines. Newspapers, of course, carried daily contributions from the most important writers in Spain, and much important literary work in the field of poetry and the short story appeared in magazines rather than in books. We have little evidence as to what periodicals Miró read, but presumably those to which he contributed regularly were read at least.

As for books, it is hard to choose between various possibilities. Did Miró simply not keep contemporary writing in his library unless it was particularly important to him, either in itself or because it had been presented? In this context Valera, Clarín, and Azorín are the only authors mentioned by Miró who are represented in the library by more than two titles (if we except three books presented by Ricardo León). It is plausible that if Miró only kept what was most important, these would be the three who stood out. The same would apply if Miró had read contemporary work in borrowed volumes, which would be another way of accounting for its absence. Yet both explanations are a little odd. Either Miró got rid of books he owned, which does not look very plausible from the general character of the library, or else he borrowed contemporary work, but not earlier work or foreign literature or non-literary work, all of which are represented in a way that corresponds closely to the pattern of quotation in Miró's work.

In themselves these references to contemporaries are mainly interesting for the light they throw on Miró's tastes. He devoted an article to Teodoro Llorente, the Valencian translator of Goethe, Byron, and Hugo, who wrote both in Catalan and Castilian. [54] But mostly the references are no more than epithets: we have seen that Valera is 'el admirable'. Pereda, from whom Miró quotes briefly, is 'el insigne autor de «El sabor de la tierruca»' (a work Miró did not possess). [55] The only other reference to Pereda is to 'quesos con el título de algunas novelas de don José María de Pereda'! [56]

Núñez de Arce is the only contemporary literary figure to appear in a major work and his position is correspondingly less straightforward. In *El humo dormido* Miró remembers his return from Valencia University on vacation: 'Repetíase el gozoso regreso de las vacaciones. Leía-

---

[54] 'La coronación del maestro', *Diario de Alicante*, 13 Nov. 1909.
[55] 'Domingo Carratalá', in *De mi barrio*, ed. Mendaro del Alcázar.
[56] 'Los dejos de los días: Pan y queso', *La Publicidad*, 3 July 1919, p. 3.

mos el *Idilio,* de Núñez de Arce' (*OC*, p. 675). The literary favourite of 1896-97 needs no comment of Miró's for the reader to pick up the distance in taste from then to 1918, the date of this chapter.

To Galdós Miró devoted an article in 1907. E. L. King has pointed out that Miró felt none of the aggression of his close contemporaries towards the great nineteenth-century figures (*Humo*, pp. 29-33). He was content to admire them while moving on from their position. Miró, of course, realised how this attitude differed from those who talked of the 'estilo garbancero', and he himself, in this article, ties this in with his remoteness from the conventional literary scene: 'Los que por humildad, resignación o fuerza están en apartamiento, lejos de la vida amada, que sin gozarla nunca, la contemplan remota, perdida como una costa vaheante y azul, los que se han formado solitaria-mente, sin avisos ni ejemplos, aman un maestro.' [57] Galdós appears again in 1911, in an article devoted to literary relations with Spanish America, in slightly unexpected company. Spanish America, Miró tells us, still admires 'los libros de Palacio Valdés, Galdós, Valle-Inclán y otros de limpia ejecutoria literaria' (*Glosas*, p. 30). Palacio Valdés and Valle-Inclán are mentioned nowhere else.

Another interesting, and entertaining, piece is a 'Plática' published in the *Diario de Barcelona* with the title 'El alto asiento. — Cajas de fósforos vacías' (9 May 1912). With a quietly malicious attack on Mariano Catalina, secretary of the Academy, Miró writes about the vacancy to be filled amongst the immortals: 'Estos días se han pro-nunciado los nombres de los merecedores o aspirantes del «alto asien-to». Los cuales son: el de Jacinto Benavente, el de Mariano de Cavia, el de *Azorín,* el de la condesa de Pardo Bazán, el de Ricardo León, el de D. Juan Navarro Reverter y D. Augusto González Besada.' Later he continues: 'Confieso que de todos los candidatos al «sillón» no es la condesa mi predilecto; es verdad que no llegan a cinco los libros que de esa esclarecida dama he leído; pero, ¿quién se atreverá a negar sus grandes partes, su macizo entendimiento, su copiosa obra, los triunfos, en fin, que adornan una rancia ejecutoria literaria?' The choice of adjectives is hardly flattering; the 'no llegan a cinco los libros (...)' is suspiciously cryptic. La Pardo Bazán was obviously no favourite. Earlier, in the 'Cuartillas' read by Miró at the banquet held in his honour after he had won a prize with *Nómada,* he referred to 'un artículo de doña Pardo Bazán'. [58] It is not uncommon to find

[57] 'A don Benito Pérez Galdós: El maestro', *La República de las Le-tras*, 22 July 1907.
[58] 'Cuartillas de Miró', *Heraldo de Madrid*, 16 Feb. 1908. Text in Ra-mos, *Vida*, p. 122.

references like this to newspaper articles: they seem to have formed a good portion of Miró's reading.

More respected by Miró was Leopoldo Alas. In 1911 he wrote of 'Clarín, a quien cada día admiro más' (Glosas, p. 120). Alas was evidently a constantly admired figure; another, Salvador Rueda, was for a shorter time the object of intense enthusiasm. In April 1908, the poet, the Spanish forerunner of some of the changes that swept in with Rubén Darío, arrived in Alicante in order to stay on the offshore island of Tabarca. Twenty-two years older than Miró, he was welcomed with the traditional celebrations by a group of young enthusiasts including Miró. At the Ateneo, amidst speeches, music, and readings, Miró presented his 'cuartillas', entitled 'Ofrenda', extolling Rueda's art, but more especially art in general, in his most modernista manner: 'Salvador Rueda es grande, simbólico. Pero no nos satisfagamos con esto y hasta tropezar en los muros del sacro recinto donde sólo su alma, antes ablucionada como un Sumo Sacerdote, pasa, se angustia y goza en la eucaristía del Arte, penetremos descalzándonos de toda grosería a escuchar amorosos.'[59]

At the opposite end of the scale of intensity is a reference to Maura, Blasco Ibáñez, and Dicenta. They appeared, in the first edition of La palma rota, as part of a barber's small-talk, only to be removed in later editions (EC, III, 300).

Of all the writers alive during Miró's lifetime, only Unamuno and Azorín are referred to more than twice. Miró's stimulation by, and admiration for Azorín is well-known; several articles in Glosas de Sigüenza show this eloquently. But Miró's view of Unamuno is less clear. In the first place, there is no title in Spanish by Unamuno in the library. Yet one of Miró's last articles is 'Una fotografía de don Miguel' (Glosas, pp. 146-8), a complex and touching tribute. In 1908 and 1909 there appear three fairly casual references to Unamuno as an established public figure.[60] In 1914, in 'De una conferencia del Doctor Ingenieros', Miró writes: 'Un discurso de Unamuno, afirmando o negando — da lo mismo — que nuestros primeros padres Adán y Eva hablaron en eúskaro bajo el hermoso manzano del Paraíso, sería tan sugestivo, tan íntimo, tan inquietador, de tan gustoso jadear de toda el alma, como otra oración del glorioso rector de Salamanca tratando de los caminos vecinales' (Glosas, p. 137). In his lecture in Gijón in 1925, Miró refers to Unamuno as 'el maestro', and a further reference

[59] Diario de Alicante, 21 May 1908. Text in Ramos, Vida, p. 130. Rueda is also mentioned in 'Altamira en su huerto provinciano', Prometeo, 3, No. 15 (1910), 15.
[60] Glosas, p. 13; 'El presagio', Heraldo de Madrid, 4 April 1909 (text in Huerto, pp. 125-32); 'Crónica de festejos', El Imparcial, 27 July 1909 (text in Huerto, pp. 95-101).

appears in a piece written in 1926. [61] Clearly the admiration for Unamuno was one that grew steadily, unlike, say, that for Azorín, which was an early and sustained respect. Equally clearly, what Miró appreciated was the personality of Unamuno rather than his ideas, insofar as they can be separated.

By contrast, Miró's mention of Ganivet tells us little of what he thought of him [62]; the same is the case with Miró's reference to Benavente when he comments on Gómez Carrillo's charge of plagiarism. [63] But with another, obscurer figure, Vicente Medina, the Murcian regionalist poet, there is once more enthusiasm. Miró speaks in the 'Cuartillas' read at the *Nómada* banquet of the recent emigration of Medina to South America — 'un hombre bueno y artista admirable'. [64] Without his poetry, says Miró, he would have been unable to face separation from his own region.

The major figure, on the other hand, of Baroja raises no apparent enthusiasm (*Glosas,* p. 18). It is only with Azorín that profound admiration reappears. The main expression of this admiration is found in two articles of 1911 and 1912 included in *Glosas de Sigüenza* (pp. 117-124). Here the emphasis of Miró's remarks is in a quite different direction from those on Unamuno. The qualities that are brought out are Azorín's use of language and his 'serenidad'.

The first article ('El párrafo; la palabra. «Azorín»'), contrasts the nineteenth-century use of the paragraph as the basic unit of prose with the twentieth-century return to the word. In this change Azorín occupies a key position: 'El renacimiento de la *palabra literaria* en España se debe principalmente a *Azorín*' (pp. 118-19). If Miró seems to exaggerate, it is probably because of the pivotal position of Azorín's writing in Miró's personal development. E. L. King has argued plausibly that the sudden fixing of Miró's style that appears in *Del vivir* was precipitated by Azorín. [65] Summarising the argument, he writes: 'When Miró learned this lesson [«el paso del párrafo a la palabra»] from Azorín, when he realized that his admiration for Galdós and Valera did not oblige him to look at life through their eyes or to use the literary language they had worn out, he was suddenly ready to speak for the person that he truly was in the volume *Del vivir*' (*Humo,* p. 34).

This is perforce to simplify, but perhaps the importance of Azorín

---

[61] Ramos, *Literatura*, p. 314; *Glosas,* p. 143.

[62] 'Pláticas: De las corridas de toros', *Diario de Barcelona*, 28 Nov. 1912, p. 17543.

[63] 'Comentado', *Diario de Barcelona*, 21 Feb. 1913, p. 2558. Benavente is also mentioned in 'Pláticas: El alto asiento', *Diario de Barcelona*, 9 May 1912, p. 7390.

[64] 'Cuartillas de Miró', *Heraldo de Madrid*, 16 Feb. 1908. Text in Ramos, *Vida*, p. 123.

[65] 'Gabriel Miró y «el mundo según es»', pp. 129-33, and King, *Humo,* p. 34.

early on is confirmed not only by Miró's handsome compliment in this article of 1911, but by the careful qualifications that, at a distance of about ten years, are added. Miró repays his debt, but reserves his own position:

> Que *Azorín* haya resucitado el íntimo valor de la palabra, entregándonosla, en la pureza y hermosura de su desnudez, de su transparencia, y que en *Azorín* se halle el origen de nuevas y escondidas bellezas, no significa que a él le deban las plumas todo su ímpetu y enjundia.
>
> Esas plumas han ensanchado el descubrimiento léxico de *Azorín.* Y con abundancia y sencillez idiomática han iluminado zonas de vida que para aquél permanecen apagadas, quizá voluntariamente y por reconcentración, por la intensidad de su temperamento, nunca por enjutez de sus 'entrañas artísticas', como algunos han dicho.
>
> (*Glosas,* p. 119)

Miró's second article on Azorín is a eulogistic review of *Castilla* (*Glosas,* pp. 121-4). Not surprisingly he sees among Azorín's chief merits some of the techniques and aims he himself has used: 'Cuenta enlazando dulcemente la imaginativa y la reconstitución ... En el «viejo tronco» de la crónica reverdece la nueva vida' (p. 122). He concludes: 'Lector: no hay prosista que más sabiamente aplique las riquezas de una hacienda idiomática tan inmensa como la que este hombre posee y suministra' (p. 124). [66]

Most writers younger than Azorín receive mentions so brief that they are merely useful as evidence of acquaintance in the face of the library's silence. Maeztu and Ortega are mentioned as examples of men who have read a great deal (*Glosas,* p. 55). Elsewhere Miró refers to 'la generación literaria, brava y luminosa, de los Villaespesa, los Machado, Muñoz Llorente y otros elegidos poetas y prosistas'. [67] (Villaespesa was editor of *Revista Latina,* in which Miró published work in 1907 and 1908. Miró met him in 1905 when in Madrid for *oposiciones.*) Ricardo León is given as an example of how sometimes a young man can triumph in a world dominated by the old. [68] Marquina is praised for his translation of Xenius's *La bien plantada.* [69]

[66] Passing references to Azorín: *Glosas,* pp. 30 and 50; 'Pláticas: El alto asiento', *Diario de Barcelona,* 9 May 1912, p. 7390; '¿Por qué no escribe usted para el teatro?', *ABC,* 16 June 1927, pp. 10-11.

[67] 'Las últimas vestales', *Diario de Alicante,* 7 January 1911.

[68] 'Comentado', *Diario de Barcelona,* 21 Feb. 1913, p. 2559. León is also mentioned in 'Pláticas: El alto asiento', *Diario de Barcelona,* 9 May 1912, p. 7390.

[69] 'Jornadas y comentarios de Sigüenza: De la lectura de «La Bien Plantada»', *La Vanguardia,* 19 April 1914, p. 13.

Eugenio Noel is referred to for his campaign against bull-fighting, which Miró supported in general terms though he was sceptical as to its success. [70] Salvador Martínez Cuenca is mentioned without comment in Miró's speech at the *Nómada* banquet. [71]

Two writers closer to Miró in spirit are written about in more detail: Martínez Sierra and the Canaries poet Rafael Romero. The occasion for the first piece was the presence in Alicante in 1911 of Martínez Sierra as 'Mantenedor' of the local 'Juegos Florales'. Miró contributed 'cuartillas' to the *Diario de Alicante,* praising the 'Mantenedor' and explaining that his hearers should not expect 'las frases redondas, que retumban como esferas vacías, las palabras de pólvora oratoria, de cuerno de caza tribunicia' (2 August 1911).

The second piece, 'Rafael Romero: *Alonso Quesada',* was written in 1926, a year after Romero's death, but not published until 1944. [72] Both it and the recently published collection of letters from Miró to Romero make clear his affection for the Canaries poet. Miró mentions also Tomás Morales, another island poet, both in the piece on Romero and in the correspondence. Romero, Morales, and another young Canaries writer, Saulo Torón, are represented in Miró's library by presented books.

This gallery of modern writers is completed by a number who are not strictly figures from literature, but personal friends, journalists, critics, and scholars of various disciplines. For instance, Luis Pérez Bueno, *alcalde* of Alicante and writer of a preface to Miró's *La mujer de Ojeda,* is 'cifra y archivo de las más finas partes y virtudes', while Miró's first biographer, José Guardiola Ortiz, is a *'precioso vaso de elocuencia,* según le llama el poeta Salvador Rueda'. [73]

The journalist Mariano de Cavia appears once as an 'aspirante del «alto asiento»', [74] while Ricardo Blasco and Luis Bonafoux, Paris correspondents respectively of *El Imparcial* and *Heraldo de Madrid,* are brought into 'Glosas de Sigüenza' (*Glosas,* p. 24). Evidently Miró read the papers to which he contributed, for 'Glosas de Sigüenza' was first published in 1910 in *Heraldo de Madrid,* while both newspapers took the bulk of his output in 1908 and 1909.

Few critics are mentioned by Miró. Menéndez Pelayo, whose *Ideas estéticas* we have seen Miró read thoroughly, is mentioned by name

---

[70] 'Pláticas: De las corridas de toros', *Diario de Barcelona,* 28 Nov. 1912, p. 17542.

[71] 'Cuartillas de Miró', *Heraldo de Madrid,* 16 Feb. 1908. Text in Ramos, *Vida,* p. 121.

[72] *Glosas,* pp. 142-5; written as a preface to Romero's *Obras completas,* but included instead in his posthumous *Los caminos dispersos* (Las Palmas, 1944).

[73] 'Altamira en su huerto provinciano', *Prometeo,* 3, No. 15 (1910), 15.

[74] 'Pláticas: El alto asiento', *Diario de Barcelona,* 9 May 1912, p. 7390.

and quoted in Miró's 'Estudio histórico del templo de San Vicente'. [75] Other critics briefly mentioned are Gómez Carrillo, Candamo, and Andrés González-Blanco, 'que no tiene quien le iguale en agudeza y fecundidad literaria'. [76] As for other scholars, Miró rarely quotes Spanish scholars of any kind, usually relying, as we shall see, on French or other foreign authorities. However, he owned Lafuente's popular *Historia general de España,* completed by Valera. He evidently used it for historical material in compiling his novels. This is clear from slips of paper left in it, and a quotation confirms it : a character in *El abuelo del rey,* referring to the French forces of occupation in Madrid during the Peninsular War, says : '¡Bando draconiano, dice Lafuente, y no le falta razón!' (*OC,* p. 526). From the library it is evident that Lafuente was Miró's chief source for Spanish history. The only other historian mentioned is Altamira, to whom Miró devoted an article in 1910. [77] Although the article is a eulogy there is no evidence in it that Miró had read any of Altamira's work; nor does the library include any of his books. [78]

From this mass of detail, a clear-cut pattern emerges. Miró's reading of Spanish authors up to the eighteenth century is almost entirely in the *Biblioteca de autores españoles.* After this he was well-acquainted with the nineteenth century and his contemporaries but their works are absent. Even so it is clear that while he read Spanish contemporary literature, he rarely made use of Spanish writers on other subjects. Spanish scholars, with the notable exception of Menéndez Pelayo, were only used where specifically Spanish subjects were involved — Spanish history or architecture. Later we shall see how foreign writers filled the gaps that Spanish authors could not cover.

[75] Cf. *Historia de los heterodoxos,* II (Madrid, 1917), 17-21: copy in Miró's library.

[76] 'Comentado', *Diario de Barcelona,* 21 Feb. 1913, p. 2558; 'Cuartillas de Miró', *Heraldo de Madrid,* 16 Feb. 1908: text in Ramos, *Vida,* p. 121; *Glosas,* p. 120.

[77] 'Altamira en su huerto provinciano', *Prometeo,* 3, No. 15 (1910), 14-18.

[78] Miró also mentions or quotes from the following scholars, listed for the sake of completeness: Mudarra, the literary theoretician, dealt with earlier (see above, pp. 10-11); Estanislao Sánchez Calvo, author of *Los nombres de los dioses,* a work in Miró's library, quoted in *El humo dormido* (*OC,* p. 728); and the authorites used in the 'Estudios históricos' of two Ávila churches: Padre Flórez, *España sagrada;* Manuel Gómez-Moreno y Martínez, author of the Ávila volume of the *Catálogo monumental de España,* published by the Ministerio de Instrucción Pública y Bellas Artes where Miró worked; José María Quadrado, author of a volume on *Salamanca, Ávila y Segovia,* and another of whose books, possessed by Miró, is mentioned in *El humo dormido* (*OC,* p. 715); and Enrique Repullés y Vargas, architect, author of *La basílica de los santos mártires Vicente, Sabina y Cristeta en Ávila,* and, in 1890, restorer of the facade of San Vicente.

2. CATALAN AND AMERICAN LITERATURE

In 1914 Miró moved from Alicante to Barcelona. He had made a number of friends in Catalan literary circles and since 1911 had been writing for Barcelona newspapers. Although the move was made for personal reasons, he must have felt that in Barcelona he would at least be among friends who understood and appreciated his work. Above all he had admired Maragall who had died in 1911, an admiration that was handsomely returned. The steps by which Miró's Barcelona friendships developed can be clearly traced in his writings. Only two of the authors he mentions (three if we include the Valencian Teodoro Llorente) are much older than himself — most are contemporaries or slightly younger. The two older men were Maragall, and a writer who used to spend the winter in Alicante, and whom Maragall asked Miró to visit, Joaquim Ruyra.

In Maragall's *Obres completes* (Barcelona, 1947) are three letters to Miró. The first, dated 14 January 1909, thanks Miró for signed copies of *Del vivir* and *La novela de mi amigo* and praises them highly and sincerely (p. 1719). Evidently Miró had sent these copies to Maragall, as he sometimes did send his work to well-known figures, and from this a friendship started. Early in 1911 Miró made a trip to Barcelona and evidently made useful contacts, for on 8 September his first article appeared in the *Diario de Barcelona,* of which Maragall was 'secretario de redacción'. The piece, entitled 'Pláticas: La paz lugareña', begins: 'Estas sencillas pláticas que, desde hoy, me dejan mantener con los lectores del *Diario de Barcelona,* quería yo titularlas con una gustosa quimera que ya puse de epígrafe a mis crónicas publicadas en periódicos madrileños: «Del huerto provinciano».' Instead he calls the series 'Pláticas', a series that was to be continued until August 1913.

The very next day the second article appeared: 'Joaquín Ruyra'. Miró writes: 'Hace algunos años, don Juan Maragall, ese dulce maestro que va dejando en todas las almas levadura de amor y las prende a la suya con gustoso acatamiento, me escribía una carta buena y sencilla que encendió la fe en mí mismo y derramó gracia y alegría en mi apartada vida (...). En lo postrero de esa carta decía el maestro: «¿Estará ahí nuestro Ruyra también este año? ¿Se conocen? Es un hombre angelical»' (*Glosas,* p. 114). The letter referred to is the one of 14 January 1909, and includes the sentences quoted by Miró.

Miró's gratitude to and admiration for Maragall are evident. Ruyra himself, two years older than Maragall, and a lesser figure having not written in Catalan until over thirty, is also praised by Miró at length in this article and in terms that make it clear that Miró's own artistic attitudes are now confidently held. This article is a mark of respect for an older man viewed in one's own terms; Miró speaks of 'la íntima y siempre encendida ascua de amor por lo grande y por lo humilde, la adivinación de la palabra precisa, armónica, prócer o llana que se hace carne con la idea y con ella se funde hasta quedar insepa-rables en fondo y expresión como en la música' (*Glosas*, p. 116). In all Miró's relationships with Catalan writers, it is less appropriate to speak of influences than of affinities. Miró reveals himself as he comments on the work of his friends.

He speaks of Ruyra as 'el autor de «Marines y boscatges»', and this is the volume that he possessed in his library (Barcelona, 1907), com-plete with Ruyra's dedication 'al excellent narrador de la real y doloro-sa historia «La novela de mi amigo»'.

Two further letters from Maragall follow these articles. On 19 Sep-tember 1911 the Catalan writer says he has enjoyed them, that he has not yet obtained *Las cerezas del cementerio* and reproves Miró for hav-ing suggested he no longer liked him (p. 1719). On the first of October Maragall has received a signed copy of *Las cerezas* and has read it. He praises it as poetry in the guise of prose and, mentioning Miró's charac-ters, speaks of 'esa ultrarrealidad que tienen, que hace usted ver tan fuertemente el mundo y los hombres, que se les ve el más allá. ¿Y no es eso la esencia de la poesía?'. He talks of discussing particular pas-sages: 'En presencia viva yo no haría sino mostrárselos y sin una pala-bra nos entenderíamos' (p. 1720). This last remark is a splendid ex-pression of the sympathy for each other's ideals felt by Maragall and Miró at this stage.

In March 1911 Maragall had presented to Miró (perhaps in connec-tion with Miró's first visit to Barcelona) a copy of his *Artículos* (Bar-celona, 1904) inscribed 'A Gabriel Miró, quien tanto le admira y le quiere Juan Maragall'. The volume is the only one by Maragall in the library, but Miró had it leatherbound in his current style. He was well-acquainted with Maragall's work through the press — the absence of books in the library is just another example of the almost systematic exclusion of contemporaries.

This swiftly-forged bond of sympathy between Miró and Maragall makes it interesting to compare their notions of verbal art. A good example of Maragall's outlook that Miró may have known is his 'Elo-gio de la poesía', [79] and in it the coincidences between Maragall's theory of art (expressed in a much more organised way than Miró's), and that

---

[79] *Obres completes*, pp. 819-27.

of Miró, are fascinating and the divergences instructive. Maragall writes:

> Poesía es el arte de la palabra; arte es la humana expresión de la belleza; belleza es la revelación de la esencia por la forma; forma es la huella del ritmo de la vida en la materia...
> La vida es esfuerzo, esto es, alternación de acción y reposo, esto es, ritmo, que se manifiesta más o menos en la materia de las cosas y constituye sus formas...
> Son las formas, son el ritmo, el sello del esfuerzo de la vida por la revelación de su alma, que es Dios.
> El supremo logro de este esfuerzo en la tierra es el hombre. El hombre es la tierra en su mayor sentido de la revelación de Dios a través de ella. Y ésta es la gran dignidad y la gran tragedia humana: sentirse tierra y Dios al mismo tiempo, ser la cúspide anhelante.

Whether Miró was influenced by such ideas, or whether he came to them with evident delight when his own were already formed, they illuminate many aspects of works such as *Del vivir* and *La novela de mi amigo,* especially Miró's conception of man's relationship to his 'circunstancia'.

Maragall goes on to offer an example; he watches the sea: 'Soy la Naturaleza sintiéndose a sí misma.' He marvels: 'Es mi momento religioso.' He reflects: 'Es mi momento filosófico.' Then he thinks about the scientific aspects of nature; he sees a boat and reflects on the applied science involved. Then he ponders on the fishermen: 'Es mi momento moral.' Next he considers the social, legal, and economic aspects. Finally he contemplates the scene as pure form; this is the aesthetic moment: 'El arte es, pues, la belleza trashumanada devuelta a Dios de más cerca por la humana expresión del ritmo revelador que está en la forma natural.' Sincerity, spontaneity, and purity are needed to allow the divine will to reveal itself through form. Therefore, Maragall says: 'Si yo veo salir al mar la barca con sus pescadores y en mi sentimiento de su belleza se mezcla en aquel momento mi compasión —o mi envidia u otro interés cualquiera— por la suerte de aquellos hombres, mi emoción no será entonces puramente estética.' This is not to be inhuman 'porque el arte y la poesía traen en sí mismos su propia nobleza, justicia y piedad, su propia eficacia, que valen por sí solas todo lo que estos nombres pueden valer aplicados a otra esfera de actividades'. Once again, here is the notion that the aesthetic and the ethical are one and the same, the fundamental concept on which Miró's art is based. They are as indissoluble as form and content: 'Es falsa aquí la distinción entre

123

fondo y forma: poesía, propiamente hablando, no es más que la forma, el verso. La poesía no está en lo que se dice, sino en el modo de decirlo; o mejor, en la poesía, forma y fondo son una misma cosa.

There is much common ground here between the two writers, but the differences are significant for in Miró's work there is always a profound concern 'por la suerte de aquellos hombres'. For him the unity of the work of art as a whole is not destroyed by the inclusion of the other 'momentos', but instead they are seen as essential aspects of a more widely conceived aesthetic whole. This divergence from Maragall is expressed in Miró's attribution to Ruyra not only of 'la palabra (...) que se hace carne con la idea', but also of 'amor por lo grande y por lo humilde', the 'amor' in Miró's own personality that is the overwhelming concern of his work. Correspondingly, Miró's concept of form is wider than that of Maragall who can say poetry is essentially 'el verso'. Maragall is naturally puzzled that Miró writes prose — but to Miró of course the principles of poetry were the same universal principles that he applied to his prose. As with Ruyra, Miró's attitude is one of respect for a master to whom he owes some of his own starting-points. That, as befits a younger man, he has moved on, in no way lessens the expression of that admiration.

In late 1911 Maragall died. In one of his 'Pláticas' Miró paid his respects: 'El amor de las ciudades' recounts how Alicante has expressed its sympathy for Barcelona on the occasion of Maragall's death. The eulogy is not a literary one but is expressed in terms of admiration for Maragall as a man: 'Un poeta que era ascua de amor.' [80]

On three other occasions Miró mentioned Maragall. Once, before his death, in the original version of 'Plática que tuvo Sigüenza con un capellán' (EC, VII, 249), and on two later occasions in connection with Barcelona, with which Maragall was so firmly linked in Miró's memory. In February 1914 Miró moved to Barcelona and his first article written and published after the move was 'En la ciudad grande' in which he describes his reactions to Barcelona as a place in which to live. He concludes the article with Maragall's three beatitudes, each beginning, '¡Oh, feliz la ciudad que tiene una montaña al lado'. [81] The same thought, but reworded 'Dichosa la ciudad (...)', appears in 1919, in 'Barcelona necesita un río' (Glosas, p. 71).

Shortly after the article occasioned by Maragall's death, Miró wrote about two other Catalan writers, Francisco Sitjá and J. M. López-Picó (Glosas, pp. 125-8). Amongst the several Catalan authors to whom Miró devotes more than a few sentences, Sitjá is the only one whose books he did not possess. In itself this is not significant: the article

[80]   Diario de Barcelona, 18 Jan. 1912, pp. 871-2.
[81]   La Vanguardia, 27 Feb. 1914, p. 9.

does not comment on any specific work of Sitjá but deals with him more as a character. What is interesting is that in every other case Miró does possess at least one volume inscribed by the author. Quite evidently Miró's literary dealings with his Catalan contemporaries were very much on a personal basis. He possessed, for instance, a book by López-Picó presented in 1915; and of Sitjá he writes that he met him 'en los escasos días que estuve en Barcelona', that is, in 1911. This was a unique phase in Miró's reading, for it is only at this time that there is the give-and-take of reading, personal presentation, and criticism: affinities not influences.

Furthermore, it looks as if Miró took little interest in Catalan literature until stimulated to do so by personal relationships. Verdaguer's *L'Atlàntida* he owned in a copy published in 1902; after all, this was the obvious work if one had any curiosity at all about the Catalan renaissance. The next earliest date of publication is 1904 (Maragall's *Artículos*), followed by 1906 (Carner, *Els fruits saborosos*), and 1907 (Costa i Llobera, *Poesies,* and Ruyra, *Marines y boscatges*). Probably none of these was acquired until at least 1909, and from then on almost every work Miró receives is by personal presentation.

Josep Carner, for instance, presented copies of at least four of his works to Miró, probably all between 1911 and 1914. He had been responsible for the publication of *Las cerezas del cementerio* in 1910 and had, along with Maragall, also introduced Miró to Ruyra in Alicante (*Glosas,* p. 114). In 1912, in an article on Xenius, Miró recounts how Carner introduced him, at the offices of the *Veu de Catalunya,* to Eugeni d'Ors and Prat de la Riba (*Glosas,* p. 129).

Xenius, too, presented books to Miró, including a copy of *Glosari, 1906,* presented, like Maragall's *Artículos,* in March 1911. Miró refers to Xenius on half-a-dozen occasions: the article mentioned above deals with *La ben plantada* and d'Ors's work in general, while there are three passing references in 1913 and one in 1914. [82] Finally, in April 1914 an article is devoted to an account of a reading by Rafael Marquina of his Castilian version of *La ben plantada,* a reading to which Miró was invited by d'Ors. [83]

While Miró speaks with continuing appreciation of Eugeni d'Ors, he writes with enormous personal enthusiasm of the last Catalan writer to whom he devotes space: Suriñach Sentíes. [84] In 'Un libro' he

[82] 'Un libro', *Diario de Barcelona,* 11 Jan. 1913, p. 473; 'Cosas viejas y sabidas', *Diario de Barcelona,* 2 Aug. 1913, p. 10463; 'Jornadas de Sigüenza: La hermosa señora', *La Vanguardia,* 20 Dec. 1913, p. 9; 'Jornadas de Sigüenza: Nosotros', *La Vanguardia,* 13 March 1914, p. 9.
[83] 'Jornadas y comentarios de Sigüenza: De la lectura de «La bien plantada»', *La Vanguardia,* 19 April 1914, pp. 12-13.
[84] *Diario de Barcelona,* 11 Jan. 1913, pp. 472-3.

writes: 'De muchos libros he hablado con exaltadas alabanzas (...); pero de éste del señor Suriñach Sentíes quisiera hacerlo con tanta devoción y ternura que moviese a leerlo a todas las gentes.' The book is *Petites proses,* of which Miró possessed a copy presented in December 1912: clearly this review was a direct result of receiving the copy. In the same article he lists the names of those young Catalan writers that stand out at the end of 1912: Carner, Xenius, Bofill i Matas, Rucabado, López-Picó, Josep Massó-Ventós, and C. Jordá are picked out. Miró possessed presented copies of books by Massó-Ventós and López-Picó as well as Carner and Xenius.

If Miró's reading of Catalan was fostered by his personal meetings in Barcelona, his writing about his Catalan literary friends was confined to an even shorter period. Nothing before September 1911, and after April 1914 only one reference to Maragall. Curiously, the latter date is only two months after his arrival to live in Barcelona, though in part the explanation is that in June 1914 Miró gave up writing columns for the press, work which he did not resume until 1918.

There is one exception to the silence about Catalan writers after 1914. In 1919 was published Miró's translation into Castilian of Ramón Turró's *Filosofia crítica,* and in the library there appears a presented copy of the 1918 Catalan edition. In the first version of the chapter of *El humo dormido* entitled 'Mauro y nosotros', published in 1918, Miró quoted from Turró (*EC,* VIII, 274), and later, in 1922, he wrote an article about him though this has not been seen. Undoubtedly Miró felt a deep affection for Turró — in a letter he refers to him as 'mi amigo paternal'.[85] Turró was a medical scientist and it is clear that as Miró's interest in Catalan literature decreased so he turned in his personal friendships to men who were not professional writers: Turró, Granados, and Pí Suñer, a medical man and collaborator with Turró. There is a good deal of biographical evidence about this growing feeling on Miró's part that he was not truly at home among Catalan men of letters. However, for Miró's literary background it is the earlier Barcelona years that are of interest and the main features here are clearly enough established. Largely before settling in Barcelona, Miró developed considerable enthusiasm for Catalan literature, an enthusiasm that was in part diverted by the new interest in Biblical history, and in part simply waned. After all, after the literary give-and-take of 1911 to 1914, it is clear that in spite of superficial appearances and except for Maragall Miró was not profoundly influenced by his Catalan contemporaries.

* * *

[85] Letter dated 9 July 1926, to Eduardo Irles, in possession of Miró family.

Miró published work in South America as well as in Catalonia, but he shows no real interest in the writing of the New World. In an article published in October 1911 he writes: 'Es amarlo [nuestro idioma] también escribir páginas de oro como las que salen de las plumas de un Rodó, de un Larreta, y notables libros como «Juana de Asbaje», de Amado Nervo' (*Glosas*, p. 30). Miró owned copies of Rodó's *Motivos de Proteo* and Nervo's *Juana de Asbaje,* both presented by their authors. The only other Spanish-American writer mentioned by Miró is José Ingenieros, about a speech of whom he wrote an article in 1914 (*Glosas*, pp. 135-8).

3. CLASSICAL LITERATURE

'Cuando ya conocía muchos autores griegos y latinos (traducidos, pues olvidé estas lenguas) y había leído a nuestros clásicos, hice un volumen de artículos; en uno de los cuales me detuve tanto, que me salió un libro: la Mujer de Ojeda.' [86] So Miró wrote in reply to Andrés González-Blanco at the age of twenty-six. He went on: 'Grecia y Atenas han sido los pueblos en que con más veneración y amor he pensado. No los he visto nunca; no los visitaré. La idea de visitarlos como turista me ha repugnado, por irrespetuosa.' Miró's respect for the classics is so intense that tourism would be blasphemous: the religious term is exactly appropriate at the height of *Modernista* nostalgia for the sublimity of Greece. Only a few years earlier, at the very outset of his writing career, Miró had published 'Vulgaridades', a plea for a return to classical values. He wrote: 'La realidad de ahora es insípida, vulgar, oscura, anti-artística. Hasta el vicio parece hoy más asqueroso; no tiene aquel espléndido atavío con que antes se le acicalaba: esta repugnante desnudez podrá ser deseable y provechosa en el terreno de la moral, pero no en el campo del Arte.' [87]

The words are placed in the mouth of Polymnia, who speaks in the dream of a friend of the narrator. In 'Vulgaridades', a group of searchers after Art set out to find the Muses to enquire of them why the Republic of Letters is in so ruinous a state. On the way they encounter Pan who tells them that the muses have fled: 'Necia, enflautada y pegajosa muchedumbre, las obligó a pedir protección al Padre Zeus, por que las perseguían y atormentaban con sus ruegos y pretensiones. Cual, siendo vulgar, quería vestir sus sandeces con la delicadeza de Teócrito; cual, desnudo de ingenio, pretendía lucir el de Luciano; quien, careciendo de

---

[86] Andrés González-Blanco, *Los contemporáneos*, I, ii, 291-2, quoted in Cejador, *Historia*, XII, 37-8.
[87] *El Ibero*, 1 Aug. 1902.

ideas, imploraba el poder expresarlas con la elocuencia de Pericles' (1 July 1902). Miro's target is the attempt to decorate writing with a classical surface when underneath the surface there is a vacuum: what contemporary art lacked were subjects that were not 'vulgar' Aurelio Giménez, the hero of 'Del natural', written at about the same time, is another expression of the same idea: he suffers from an inability to find a satisfactory 'asunto'.

Miró's reverence for Athens, then, does not include admiration for purely formal classicism or for merely decorative skills. It is the spirit of classical literature that he reveres, the 'espíritu de Grecia' which Azorín found in his work that he seeks to transfer into his own time. 'Art for art's sake' is a widely used and abused label, and while Miró's aesthetic has obvious affinities with it, much clearer definition of his outlook is essential. 'Art for art's sake' is, of course, not a classical ideal, but is intimately involved with the admiration for Greece of writers from the Parnassians onwards. The exaltation of Beauty and Art, the rejection of bourgeois and commercial values, the disgust at the times: all these are present in the young Miró. Even the anti-Christian side of the admiration for pagan ideals is represented by the relative absence in the early Miró of Christianity. Renan, whose youthful 'Prayer on the Acropolis' contrasts the classical ideal with the oriental Paul in Athens, but who later devotes all his energies to Christian history, is an interesting parallel. Renan was, of course, a favourite author of Miró.

But though Miró shared in the fervour for Greece, the modification in favour of 'amor' and of concern, of the inner spirit rather than the outer form, must be made, just as Miró modified the pure aestheticism of Maragall. Perhaps another parallel is helpful. Nietzsche, an outstanding influence in general in Spain at this time, claimed that his judgements were always 'aesthetic'. It is because of this that he was often seen as a leader of 'art for art's sake', especially by his detractors in Spain. Yet he himself violently denounced 'pure' art: 'Die Kunst ist das grosse Stimulans zum Leben: wie könnte man sie als zwecklos, als ziellos, als l'art pour l'art verstehn?'[88] Nietzsche stood 'jenseits', on the far side of good and evil, he saw his judgements as aesthetic, yet it requires little knowledge of his work to see him as a moralist through and through. Miró was no Nietzschean, yet many of the German's ideas were common property. In 'Vulgaridades', Miró, we have seen, writes: 'La realidad de hoy es insípida, vulgar, oscura, anti-artística. Hasta el vicio parece hoy más asqueroso', and so on, notions very much in harmony with Nietzsche's. The German

[88] Quoted in Sobejano, *Nietzsche en España*, p. 56.

recommends objectivity and aesthetic distance, yet condemns art that is aimless. Ortega y Gasset has trained us to think of these points of view as contradictory: we tend to associate extreme emotional distancing at this period with poetry that is highly stylised and autonomous, self-consciously aspiring to the condition of music. But Nietzsche helps us to see into the quasi-moral character of what were declaredly aesthetic judgements, and to understand that a writer such as Miró could be rooted in the attitudes of 'art for art's sake', with its apparent escapism, and yet retain a burning concern. In our day, for instance, a preference for even the most hideous Victoriana over the most efficient functionalism, is not just a matter of decorative, of 'stylistic' preference, but of implicit protest of a moral kind. The exaltation of Athens, often couched in terms of Beauty and Art, and often condemned as escapist, was frequently in fact a statement of belief in a set of values that was diametrically opposed both to the 'slave ethic' (in the case of Nietzsche), and pharisaical versions of the Christian ethic (in the case of such as Miró).

Miró's reading and quotation of the classics have been studied by Manuel Fernández-Galiano. [89] He points out that at school in Orihuela Miró would have used the *Selecta ex classicis auctoribus graecia ad usum scholarum Societatis Jesu.* This volume opened with Aesop and ended with Homer, though Fernández-Galiano does not picture Miró getting very far into it. Indeed, after his school-days, he read the classics invariably in translation. Fernández-Galiano refers to Miró's use of this reading up to 1914 as student recollections. After 1914 these are replaced by erudition, erudition that he finds far less attractive and made worse by errors. But from 1920 onwards he suggests that Miró becomes less affected again in his use of the classics. These changes are of course bound up with the nature of the work Miró was writing. The years from 1914 to 1920 include the *Figuras* and *El humo dormido* with their historical recreations. Nevertheless, for Fernández-Galiano, Miró is far better versed in the classics than most of his contemporaries. One minor sign of this familiarity, one may add, is the frequent use of adjectives such as 'homérico', 'horaciano', 'geórgico', and 'epicúreo'.

Among particular writers, Homer is to the classics what Cervantes is in Spanish literature. More often mentioned than any other author (almost thirty times), Homer and his heroes rarely appear in quotations, but rather in more casual remarks that suggest an everyday acquaintance. In the early 'Vulgaridades' Miró uses 'la grandiosidad Homérica' as a standard ('grandioso' is a much-favoured term of praise). Elsewhere he

[89] 'El mundo helénico de Gabriel Miró', p. 1.

speaks of 'la tragedia bárbara, homérica' (*OC,* p. 132), or of 'las rudas y hermosas comparanzas que hace el padre Homero' (*OC,* p. 570). Homer is primitive, heroic, grandiose, and a touchstone of poetic sensibility: in 1912 an almond-exporter is despatched with: 'Ese hombre no ha leído a Homero' (*Glosas,* p. 39). Miró's reverence for Homer is a good example of the *modernista* classicism of his youth: in the 1904 edition of *Del vivir* he speaks of 'el divino Homero', but in later editions the epithet is dropped (*EC,* I, 261). Nevertheless, throughout the years from 1907 to 1914 when Miró was writing regularly for newspapers, Homer appears unfailingly and familiarly, sometimes even in the guise of the everyday adjective 'homérico'. Only occasionally is a reference to Homer more of a structural element, as in *Nómada,* where he is used to suggest that Diego's wanderings are an Odyssey (*OC,* pp. 174, 187).

In Miró's school text-book Homer was at the end that Miró presumably never reached. In *El humo dormido* he speaks of those who had: 'Los que ya traducían a Homero se acordaron de Polifemo' (*OC,* p. 677). (If Homer was at the end, Aesop was at the beginning, and a few pages earlier in *El humo dormido* [*OC,* p. 674], there is a reminiscence of the fables.) After leaving school Miró read Homer in the translations of the *Biblioteca clásica,* the copy of the *Iliad* being marked here and there.

Another essential element of the Greece Miró admired were the lyric poets. The volume of the *Biblioteca clásica* entitled *Poetas líricos griegos* includes, among many others, the *Anacreontea* and Simonides, while Pindar has a separate volume. All three are mentioned by Miró and the *Anacreontea* and Pindar at least were read by him, though they are unmarked. In 'Vulgaridades', Miró speaks of 'el arte de las ternuras y sensualidades Anacreónticas', and exalts 'líricos como Píndaro y Simónides'.[90] Once again, Miró's quotations from them are mostly youthful and enthusiastic. One chapter in *Las cerezas del cementerio* is entitled 'Anacreóntica': at the end of it Miró uses the story of Ode 40 to indicate the situation in his novel — Félix plays Cupid to Giner's wife's Venus (*OC,* p. 372). The chapter contains several other classical allusions, suggesting that it was written fairly early. A later mention of Anacreon exemplifies the historical uses to which Miró put his classical reading after the move to Barcelona: Pilate leaves his wife's company 'por escuchar a su lector el abejeo de los parrales de Anacreonte' (*OC,* p. 1321).

A quotation from Pindar provides an excellent illustration of Miró's familiarity with classical literature in translation. In 'En automóvil'

[90]   *El Ibero,* 16 June and 1 Aug. 1902.

Miró includes a quotation from the third Pythian ode, addressed to 'Gerón, vencedor con el caballo de silla':

> ¡Alma mía!
> No aspires más allá de lo posible,
> cual si fueras deidad ...

The driver of the car in Miró's anecdote becomes 'nuestro Gerón' (*OC,* pp. 77-8). But the quotation remained in Miró's mind, for years later without mentioning Pindar he has Don Magín say: 'No aspires, alma mía y alma de mi prójimo, a demasiada perfección' (*OC,* p. 1059). Untypically, Miró's other allusions to Pindar are in late work. [91]

'Vulgaridades', Miró's youthful lament over contemporary literature, is something of a register of the great names that made up the 'espíritu de Grecia'. Alongside the 'ternuras y sensualidades Anacreónticas', is 'la grandiosidad Homérica y Eschilea'. Alongside Pindar and Simonides are Sophocles, Euripides, and Aeschylus. [92] Euripides reappears in 'Los tres caminantes' (*OC,* p. 1213), while Aeschylus is mentioned or quoted in *Hilván de escenas* and *Del vivir.* In *Hilván de escenas* (pp. 197-8) the reference is included in a quotation from Aelian that is drawn from the introduction to Miró's volume of Aeschylus: the same use of introductions that was evident in the *BAE* reappears here. In *Del vivir* (*OC,* p. 46) the narrator quotes three lines from *Prometheus bound,* in which Prometheus declares he has made blind hope reside amongst men in order to allay their terror of death. In *Del vivir* only blind hope consoles the leper.

The roll-call of great names in 'Vulgaridades' also includes the historians: Herodotus and Thucydides appear alongside the lyric poets and the tragedians. Elsewhere they only occur in Miró's historical work, both of them in the *Figuras* (*OC,* pp. 1297, 1333), and Herodotus in 'Cuaresma' (*Glosas,* p. 95), and 'El turismo y la perdiz': 'No hay ojos que se hayan complacido tan generosamente en mirar como los de Herodoto' (*Glosas,* p. 108).

So far all the authors quoted or referred to by Miró are represented in his library. Indeed, the correspondence between quotation and library is remarkable. Occasionally one comes across a name not apparently in the library, but a source soon emerges in some favourite work. We have just seen how Aelian, for instance, appears in the introduction to Aeschylus. Another example is Isocrates, the orator, who is mentioned in an article in 1919 (*Glosas,* p. 71) but whose work does not appear in the library: it turns out instead that the remark

[91] *OC,* pp. 1146 and 1356; *EC,* XII, 291.
[92] *El Ibero,* 16 June and 1 Aug. 1902.

Miró uses is quoted by Montaigne (III, v). But there are limits to this sort of systematic correlation of library and quotation. After about 1912 Miró began serious reading about classical and Christian history and, naturally, there begin to appear in his work references to classical writers that derive from this reading rather than from direct reading of the classics. And because Miró was usually concerned in the *Figuras* with Roman and Hellenistic culture, almost all the references made after about 1912 to writers absent from the library, are to Roman or late Greek writers. What remains remarkable is that before 1912 only two writers are mentioned in all Miró's output who do not appear in an obvious source in the library: Longus and Petronius. Roughly speaking, it is clear that in his youth Miró went to the texts for the Greek classics, whilst later he went to modern historical works for background to the Passion.

In the roll-call of 'Vulgaridades' philosophers are represented by Plato, Socrates, and Theophrastus. [93] Miró mentions Plato on some fourteen occasions, but mostly rather late. He never quotes Plato, but mostly makes minor references that suggest little in themselves, but that taken together show Plato's considerable importance for Miró. The most interesting early reference is in *La mujer de Ojeda* (p. 243), where Plato's views on beauty are ridiculed by the pedantic and anti-artistic Joaquinito Manzano: Miró wants us to see that all true artists admire Plato. But a reference in the 1904 *Del vivir* to the Platonic doctrine of marriage (*EC*, I, 273), and a passing reference in *Las cerezas* (*OC*, p. 396), are the only other early cases. Also, the copies of Plato that Miró owned early are unmarked, but by contrast he acquired in the later twenties French translations of the *Symposium*, of *Phaedo*, and of *Phaedrus*, and had them handsomely bound. Only a few much-respected works received this treatment. But it must be remembered that Miró had early become well-acquainted with Plato's central ideas through Menéndez Pelayo's account of them in his *Ideas estéticas*.

In 1911, in a speech in honour of his friend the composer Oscar Esplá, Miró announced that 'la suprema Idea-música, (...) la Belleza apetecida de Diótima, se había hecho carne ... y estaba a nuestro lado'. After this Plato appears once in *El abuelo del Rey*, four times in the *Figuras*, once each in *El humo dormido* and *Años y leguas*, and twice in an article on Dante in 1922. [94] Miró's references to Plato are thus spread over his whole career, unlike the early concentration of Homer references. Plato's aesthetic doctrine must have been a vital and continuing element in Miró's outlook. Aristotle, by comparison, is

[93] *El Ibero*, 1 Aug. 1902.
[94] Esplá, *Evocación*, p. 12; *OC*, pp. 524, 1296, 1297, 1321, 1322, 671, and 1135; *Glosas*, pp. 74, and 75.

poorly represented; he is briefly quoted in *La mujer de Ojeda* (p. 56), and mentioned in *Nómada* (*OC*, p. 188), and 'Dante' (*Glosas*, p. 79).

Another volume of the *Biblioteca clásica* offers an interesting opportunity to see Miró at work. This is the *Poetas bucólicos griegos,* containing Theocritus, Bion, and Moschus. Fernández-Galiano has pointed out how Miró used the volume's preface in *Nuestro padre* (above, pp. 61-2). But 'Vulgaridades' shows Miró using the same volume in a different way. The seekers after beauty meet Pan who mentions 'el dulce canto de la cigarra'. [95] Miró adds a footnote quoting from a note by Ipandro Acaico, translator of his copy of the Bucolics, that 'el canto de las cigarras' was pleasant to the Greeks. (Ipandro Acaico's note is to the first Idyll of Theocritus.) A little later Pan refers to his own anger, and Miró supplies a further footnote, quoted from Ipandro Acaico's notes to the same Idyll, to the effect that Pan was famous for his anger, and that 'los antiguos colocaron en la nariz las pasiones violentas'. As with the *BAE* Miró is making use of both introduction and footnotes to his texts to construct his work. For Ipandro Acaico did not only serve in 1902; in *Nuestro padre San Daniel* (*OC*, p. 800) we read: 'En la nariz aposentaron los antiguos el pecado de la ira.' This occurs in a passage built on an anecdote from St. Teresa; here again is Miró's habitual technique of constantly rearranging reminiscences of all kinds into new patterns. The only other reference to Theocritus is in *Las cerezas del cementerio* (*OC*, p. 397).

A similar technique of quarrying materials from sources remote to the subject in hand can be seen in Miró's use of Diogenes Laertius. In 'Del natural' the hero, Giménez, 'halló en diversa obra una frase de Cleóbulo'. [96] The 'frase' in question appears in Diogenes Laertius (I, 92). A little later another character attacks Giménez with a quotation from Theophrastus, 'aquel sabio discípulo de Aristóteles'. The quotation and the name of Theophrastus's teacher appear in Diogenes Laertius (V, 35 and 40). When Miró refers in 'Vulgaridades' to 'retóricos como Empédocles' and 'dialécticos como Zenon Eleato', [97] it almost certainly again reflects his reading of Diogenes. Later Zeno appears again, in an anecdote in *Libro de Sigüenza* (*OC*, p. 586), taken once more, but twelve years later, from Diogenes (IX, 26-7). An anecdote about Diodorus Cronus (*OC*, p. 656) similarly appears via Diogenes Laertius (II, 111-12). Thales (*OC*, pp. 249 and 1356), Pythagoras (*OC*, p. 173), and Chrysippus (*OC*, p. 1322), who are

[95] *El Ibero,* 1 July 1902. The same section of 'Vulgaridades' contains a brief reference to Theocritus.
[96] *El Ibero,* 16 March 1902.
[97] *El Ibero,* 1 Aug. 1902.

mentioned too, also figure in Diogenes, but here the references could have been derived from many other sources. Epicurus's texts, too, appear in Diogenes but in this case, though a sentence is marked in Miró's copy, Diogenes does not appear to be Miró's source here. One of the references to Epicurus is a passing mention in 'Los tres caminantes' (*OC,* p. 1214). The other is a quotation almost certainly drawn from Seneca's *Epistulae morales,* XXV (*Glosas,* p. 36).

The only other Greek writers of the pre-Christian era are Euclid, brought into *El obispo leproso* for a discussion of editions of his work, a joke against erudition (*OC,* pp. 1003-4), Panaetius and Posidonius (*OC,* p. 1322), and Strabo (*OC,* pp. 1156 and 1309); there is no suggestion in any of these references that Miró had read these writers.

Plutarch, however, he evidently did read. The lives of Alexander, Mark Anthony, and Artaxerxes are marked in his copy, while those of Lycurgus, Demosthenes, and Pyrrhus are referred to in various places. [98] The reference to Lycurgus plays an important rôle in Miró's long footnote to *Del vivir.* He uses the Spartan régime to demonstrate how in the end even the Spartans failed to love each other, although they were equals in so many ways. Beyond this, the Spartan nation, even when internally at peace, violently attacked others: 'Siempre la preferencia en el cariño; nunca la universalidad', he concludes.

It is this interest of Miró's in moral thought that leads to his interest in the last group of Greek writers, the Stoic philosophers, and especially Epictetus. The sources from which Miró drew his knowledge of Epictetus are somewhat confused. In the first place he possessed a copy of the *Biblioteca clásica* volume *Moralistas griegos,* which included the work of Theophrastus, 'Cebes', Epictetus, and Marcus Aurelius. It also included Quevedo's short life of Epictetus on which Miró may have drawn. A second source was Quevedo's *Nombre, origen, intento, recomendación y descendencia de la doctrina estoica,* which was included in the second volume of Miró's Diogenes Laertius. Here, for instance, Quevedo presents as a quotation from Epictetus the words: 'Llueve, ¡oh Dios!, sobre mí calamidades', [99] words that Miró used in *Del vivir* (*OC,* p. 45). The quotation (which Quevedo repeats in his life of Epictetus, replacing 'Dios' by 'Júpiter'), does not appear in Epictetus's own work, though Miró does not point this out. It is useful to discover that Miró had read Quevedo's *Doctrina estoica* in connection with *Del vivir,* for Quevedo claims that Stoicism is derived from the Book of Job which in turn provides the quotation placed at the head of *Del vivir.* Epictetus, Aeschylus (*Prometheus bound*), and the book

---

[98] *DVi,* pp. 189-91 (*EC,* I, 273-4); 'Oradores en el «huerto provinciano»', *Diario de Alicante,* 16 Jan. 1911; *OC,* p. 1191.
[99] Diógenes Laercio, *Vidas* (Madrid, 1887), II, 309.

of Job, all of which figure prominently in *Del vivir*, were seen by Miró as interlinked studies of the problem of suffering.

The number of occasions on which Miró quotes directly from a classical author, as opposed to simple allusions, is rather few, yet with Epictetus we find that on every occasion Miró quotes, even if, as in the case above, the words are spurious. From the library alone it is clear that Miró felt strongly attracted to the Stoics; they are, also, almost the only philosophers whose words he quotes. It has often been pointed out that in the 'Autobiografía' of 1927 he chose to express himself in the words of Epictetus: 'Recordemos las palabras de Epicteto: «Compórtate en la vida como en un banquete. Si dejan un manjar delante de ti, toma honestamente tu porción; pero si sólo lo pasan cerca de tus ojos, guárdate de querer cogerlo; espera apacible que vuelva a ti»' (*EC*, I, xi). How was it that this man who was everywhere acknowledged to be extraordinarily sensitive to what was outside himself and who delighted to set it down was attracted to a philosophy of life that taught indifference to everything external? In the 'Autobiografía' it can easily be understood as referring solely to the circumstances of his life, especially his failure to enter the Academy. But it is a much deeper matter, and the common element in Stoicism and Miró's attitude to the world is the anguished consciousness of suffering. The Stoic response is a response to suffering; Miró's work is an exploration of suffering, the suffering caused by the 'falta de amor'.

Nor was Miró's interest in Epictetus something acquired as late in life as the 'Autobiografía' might suggest. In 'Cartas vulgares', of which only one appeared, Miró quoted from the *Encheiridion*: 'No te ofendas de que sienten a la mesa otro en mejor lugar que tú, ni de que le saluden primero o se tome su consejo y no el tuyo; porque si estas cosas son buenas, te has de holgar de que le hayan sucedido, y si malas no te debe pesar porque no te sucedan.' [100] And in *Del vivir*, as well as Quevedo's quotation mentioned above, Miró uses a genuine maxim from the *Encheiridion* (*OC*, p. 29). Marcus Aurelius, too, is quoted in 'Cartas vulgares', as well as in *Niño y grande* (*OC*, p. 460). The fact that on both occasions his words are quoted is further evidence of Miró's attachment to the Stoics. There are also references to him in 'Dos lágrimas' (*Huerto*, pp. 61-5).

Last among writers in Greek to be mentioned are Lucian, Dioscorides, and Longus. The last two are represented by references of little significance: Longus in *Niño y grande* (*OC*, pp. 443 and 481); Dioscorides in *El obispo leproso* (*OC*, p. 1015). Miró does not seem to have

[100]   *El Ibero*, 16 Jan. 1902.

135

possessed their works, though he did own those of Lucian, which he evidently read to some extent. [101]

The Latin writers are less numerous and less interesting. Publilius Syrus and Petronius are, respectively, quoted and mentioned in *Hilván de escenas* (pp. 128 and 195), and Lucan is mentioned in 'Vulgaridades'. [102] None of these appears again, though only Petronius is absent from the library. A further group are used for historical background only: 'Se comentan (...) los versos de Catulo, la prosa de Varron, el libro de Cayo Macio' we read in the *Figuras* (*OC*, p. 1214). No source can be assigned to such details where only the name of Matius, the writer on gastronomy, is unfamiliar.

Also in the *Figuras* are Pliny (*OC*, p. 1260), Suetonius (*OC*, p. 1322), and Florus (*OC*, p. 1289). Miró owned works of both Suetonius and Florus and both were marked. He speaks of 'el incendio de la ciudad que cuenta Floro', and 'los placeres de Capri, que relata Suetonio' — these works were clearly among the multitude of historical sources for the *Figuras*. Pliny Miró did not have, so that 'Los dátiles alabados por Plinio' are presumably drawn from a modern text. Similar kinds of reference to Pliny appear in 'El turismo y la perdiz' (*Glosas*, p. 112), and *El obispo leproso* (*OC*, p. 1015). Finally, in *El abuelo del rey* a pompous local scholar appears: not surprisingly he refers to texts such as Columella (*OC*, p. 552), and, once more, to Florus (*OC*, p. 496); the scholar is at work on a *Compendio de las hazañas de Serosca*, in imitation of Florus. As the narrator observes: 'Don César no tenía la culpa de que Roma fuese Roma, y Serosca, Serosca.'

Only in the case of five Roman writers does Miró show a deeper interest in their work: Cicero, Lucretius, Virgil, Horace, and Seneca. Miró had in his library at least sixteen of the seventeen volumes of Cicero in the *Biblioteca clásica* edition, and of these, the earlier volumes are quite extensively marked. Oratory was a particular interest of the young Miró before he started writing and many passages in Cicero dealing with the arts of oratory and rhetoric are marked. A reflection of this interest appears later when, in commenting on a political meeting in 1910, Miró quotes from Cicero advice on technical points of delivery. [103] But the main attraction of Cicero is made clear when in an article in the *Diario de Barcelona*, Miró refers to 'aquella templanza y dulzura que por Marco Tulio y Séneca era recompensa y condición de los cansados años'. [104] Cicero is linked with Seneca the Stoic — clear-

---

[101] Passing references in: *EC*, IX, 266; *OC*, p. 605; 'Vulgaridades', *El Ibero*, 1 and 16 July 1902.

[102] *El Ibero*, 1 Aug. 1902.

[103] 'Oradores en el huerto provinciano', *Diario de Alicante*, 24 Nov. 1910.

[104] 'Pláticas: Los estudiantes', *Diario de Barcelona*, 13 Dec. 1911, p. 18052.

ly Miró's early interest in Cicero was as another philosopher of personal dignity. Later, in the *Figuras,* Miró twice quotes from Cicero (*OC,* pp. 1322 and 1333), but one suspects these quotations are not taken directly from Cicero but from a modern text quoting them, for in one case the quotation is in Latin (though from *De natura deorum* [III, 39] which Miró had at least started to read in Spanish), and in the other the words, apparently from *De provinciis consularibus,* V, do not correspond very closely with Miró's translation. In *El humo dormido* Miró again quotes from *De natura deorum,* in the first place using an anecdote to indicate the religious doubts that will come to the children he is portraying, and in the second using a quotation to close the book with an ironical reflection on man's abuse of his gods. [105] An erudite allusion in *Años y leguas* (*OC,* p. 1156) completes the references to Cicero.

Miró's copy of Lucretius was unmarked and only two references to his work appear. Chapter Fifteen of *Las cerezas del cementerio* is entitled 'Vino dulcísimo en amarga copa', and it ends, like the chapter 'Anacreóntica', with a classical allusion that helps to indicate the situation. As Félix leaves Beatriz he is 'dichoso (...) pero en el vaso de su alma resbalaba una gota de hiel'. The narrator continues: '¡Acatado sea divinamente el poeta que supo cantar el amargor que nace del seno del placer, amargor escondido hasta en las mismas flores! Del sabio Lucrecio digo' (*OC,* p. 396). The reference is to *De rerum natura,* IV, 1133-4. Miró's edition translates the Latin very loosely indeed: 'Nada es bastante para endulzar la amargura que se experimenta, y de cuyo fondo surgen flores que se convierten en espinas', whereas the original reads:

> Nequiquam, quoniam medio de fonte leporum
> surgit amari aliquid quod in ipsis floribus angat.

Miró's summary in *Las cerezas* is nearer to the original, suggesting that he had seen another translation or, perhaps, the Latin. The pleasures Lucretius refers to are the pleasures of sex, against which he warns so dramatically. In this way Miró indicates both the nature of Félix's 'gota de hiel' and summons up the force of Lucretius's famous passage. In *Nuestro padre San Daniel* a further reference appears (*OC,* p. 813).

Of Virgil, Miró possessed early on a copy of the *Aeneid,* but only acquired his *Georgics* and *Eclogues* after 1924. Nevertheless it is the *Georgics* that are almost always in his mind when he mentions Virgil — the adjetive 'geórgico' appears dozens of times, though of course for this sort of allusion Miró did not need a copy of the text. He refers to his school studies of the *Aeneid* (*OC,* p. 572), and doubtless he early

---

[105] *OC,* pp. 688-9: cf. *De Natura,* III, 37; *OC,* p. 731: cf. *De Natura,* III, 36.

became aware of Virgil's other work as well. Virgil appears first in 'Vulgaridades' as one of the great writers of epic. [106] Later he is mentioned as Dante's guide in the articles of 1922 on Dante (*Glosas*, pp. 73-82). The remaining quotations and allusions are all concerned with the *Georgics*. In *Las cerezas del cementerio* (*OC*, p. 371), an examination of some beehives reminds Félix of Virgil. On other occasions agricultural scenes elicit a reference: in *Años y leguas* a quotation in Latin (*Georgics*, I, 178-9), is used to describe a labourer at work, while Miró points out that Virgil owed his ability to compose the *Georgics* to such illiterate workers (*OC*, p. 1085), and in the article 'Asuntos crematísticos' Sigüenza and a friend day-dream of living in the country reading the *Georgics*. [107] Virgil is then for Miró the creator of an archetype of rural peace and satisfaction, of communion with the earth through tilling it.

Inevitably, the place where Sigüenza and his friend would stay is an 'aposento horaciano'. The epithet is almost as common as 'geórgico' and direct reference to Horace is even commoner than to Virgil. Like Virgil, Horace is for Miró a reference-point, a standard, but there is an unusually wide variety of reasons why Miró should be especially attached to his work and personality. In Miró's youth, for instance, Horace is an 'adorador de la belleza' (*Mujer*, p. 230), and the model for the much-admired Luis de León, both associated with the planting of gardens (*Hilván*, p. 66). Miró had come to Horace in two different ways. He had evidently wrestled with his verse at school, for in *Niño y grande* he presents his hero at school studying and attempting to translate the first line-and-a-half of the *Epistola ad Pisones*. [108] He possessed in his library a copy of Horace in both Latin and Spanish with which to refresh his memory. But Miró also came to Horace through reading Luis de León in the *BAE*, thus associating Horace with the much-admired Luis de León and the ideal of rural peace, and Horace's poetry with Luis's splendid translations (perhaps the *Georgics*, too, were read here). The evidence is clear: in *Nómada* Miró writes of 'una castellana, tierna y hacendosa como la sabina o calabresa de Horacio' (*OC*, p. 164). The reference is to 'Beatus ille' (*Epode* II, ll. 39 ff.) where Horace speaks of Sabine and Apulian women, Apulian being replaced in Luis de León's version by 'calabresa'. When on another occasion Miró refers again to Horace's ideal wife it probably reflects his remembering Luis's version once more. [109]

[106] *El Ibero*, 1 Aug. 1902.
[107] *Diario de Barcelona*, 3 June 1913, p. 8202.
[108] *OC*, p. 438. Another quotation from *Ars Poetica* (372-3) appears in 'Los dejos de los días: Almas medianas', *La Publicidad*, 2 Nov. 1919, p. 1.
[109] 'Pláticas: Literatura feminista', *Diario de Barcelona*, 8 Oct. 1911, p. 14141.

It is the theme of rural peace that is most commonly associated with Horace. The examples seen so far, together with another in *Libro de Sigüenza* (*OC*, p. 585), derive from Miró's reading of the poetry. But two later references to the Sabine farm, in *Años y leguas,* typically enough derive from a work of scholarship, Gaston Boissier's *Nouvelles promenades archéologiques* (*OC*, pp. 1138, 1157).

Another way in which Horace was for Miró a point of reference as a writer was that he, unlike Miró, had a wealthy patron. The theme of the lack of money among artists, and, in particular, his own lack of money as an artist, is an obsessive one with Miró, though by all accounts he enjoyed dramatising his own problem. In 'La paz lugareña' he writes: 'No; no hay horacianas porque no hay Mecenas; y quizás no los hay porque tampoco nacen Horacios.' [110] The contrast between Horace's Sabine farm presented by Maecenas, and Miró's ironically titled 'Huerto provinciano' is unavoidable. The themes of the good wife and rural peace, Luis de León and 'Beatus ille', Maecenas, Art, and the *Ars poetica,* all were fused into what must have been a singularly appealing image. Not surprisingly, the picture is completed by quotations (in Latin) used as historical material in the *Figuras* and in 'Los tres caminantes'.[111]

We have already seen how Miró as a young man was obviously attracted to the writings of Seneca. The extensive markings in the appropriate volumes of both the *Biblioteca de Autores Españoles* and the *Biblioteca Clásica* show this clearly enough. Further evidence is supplied by Miró's allusions to Seneca, confirming the youthful interest, but also suggesting that, by comparison with the references to, say, Horace, the interest remained essentially youthful. We have seen that Miró coupled Seneca's name with Cicero's for their Stoic view of old age. [112] In *Hilván de escenas* an anecdote in *De ira,* III, 8, is referred to (p. 40), evidently copied from the version in Miró's *Biblioteca Clásica* set; the same anecdote is repeated in *El obispo leproso* (*OC*, p. 913). And in the 'Cuartillas' read in Madrid in 1908, Miró refers to a passage in *De beneficiis,* I, 2, that he had marked with a cross and oblique lines in his own copy. [113] There are only two further references after this (*OC*, pp. 658, 1327), neither of them adding anything to the relationship between Seneca and Miró already derived from the books in the library.

Miró's knowledge of the Greek and Latin classics was, then, exten-

[110] *Diario de Barcelona*, 8 Sept. 1911.
[111] *OC*, pp. 1351 and 1214: cf. Horace, *Satires*, I, iii, 119, and *Odes*, I, xii, 46-8.
[112] 'Pláticas: Los estudiantes', *Diario de Barcelona*, 13 Dec. 1911, p. 18052.
[113] 'Cuartillas de Miró', *Heraldo de Madrid*, 16 Feb. 1908. Text in Ramos, *Vida*, p. 113.

sive but not profound. It was a part of his youthful enthusiasm for
Art and also reflects his special interest in ideas, particularly moral
ideas. A few authors stand out for this reason — Plato, Epictetus, Cicero, Horace, and Seneca — but most of the writers scarcely emerge as
individuals from a generalised admiration of all things classical. This
is especially true of the Greek writers. And in keeping with the general pattern of Miró's development these largely youthful references
play little serious part in the works in which they appear. They are
largely decorative. This is related to the fact that Miró relatively rarely
uses classical mythology — as opposed to literature — though it had
been for so long an effective means for writers to extend the range of
meaning of their work. Rather than putting detailed knowledge to
work in an integrated way the young Miró attempts to capture the 'espíritu de Grecia' as a halo for his work.

4. FRENCH LITERATURE

Among modern foreign literatures French is naturally the one that
appears most frequently both in the library and among the quotations.
Miró acquired an understanding of the French language quite painlessly
in the household of the girl who was to become his wife, and though
his efforts at speaking the language were poor, he read French with
ease. [114] Yet translations into Spanish abound in his library, perhaps
because they were more easily obtained in Alicante. The authors quoted by Miró are overwhelmingly of the Romantic period and later:
this is natural since France was the source of what was modern and
up-to-date.

The earliest author mentioned is Rabelais, a copy of whose work
appears physically in 'Pastorcitos rotos' (OC, p. 606), a copy that Miró
probably possessed in 1911, the year of first publication of this piece.
Far more important is Montaigne. Miró owned a two-volume set of
the Essays, published in Paris in Spanish in 1899, and it is clear that
he read it extensively. There is a cross at Book II, Chapter 37, well
into the second volume, and the seven references to Montaigne in Miró's
work include quotations from, or allusions to, all three books. One
would expect Miró to read Montaigne for several reasons: for the
wealth of maxim-like sayings, for the constant reference to classical
literature, for the copious anecdotes, for the early Stoicism, and for
Montaigne's later acceptance of life and of nature. However the ear-

[114] King, Humo, pp. 21-2.

liest reference is not until 1909, in 'El final de mi cuento' (*Huerto*, pp. 103-110). Since Miró's copy of Montaigne is of 1899 and apparently second-hand, he may well not have acquired it until around this time. There follows a paragraph on friendship in the article 'Altamira en su huerto provinciano', though Miró disagrees with Montaigne's view that 'nos hallamos más ausentes del amigo cuando le tenemos delante'.[115] *Las cerezas del cementerio* mentions Montaigne (*OC*, p. 323), and in the article 'Del dolor' of 1912 (a reflection of Montaigne's 'De la tristesse'), Miró quotes the mayor of Bordeaux quoting his friend La Boëtie (*Glosas*, p. 35). A page later Miró tells us of 'los días de salud, «de ausencia de todo mal» —la felicidad según Funio—'. In Montaigne, immediately after the quotation from La Boëtie, comes one from Ennius: 'Nimium boni est, cui nihil est mali' (II, 12); Miró's 'Funio' must be a misprint for 'Ennio'. Miró is again quarrying quotations from other men's work and building an article out of a previous piece of writing.

Miró must have been constantly attracted by the wealth of classical anecdotes and sayings in Montaigne, and it is evident that several of his classical references are drawn from the *Essays* rather than from the originals. For instance, in an article of 1919, Miró quotes the orator Isocrates (*Glosas*, p. 71). The quotation (Miró possessed no work by Isocrates) appears in Montaigne, III, 5. Similarly, in Montaigne's 'De la tristesse' appears the anecdote concerning the Diodorus who died of shame when he failed to think up an answer (I, 2), an anecdote used by Miró in 'Simulaciones' (*OC*, p. 656), and which, as already mentioned, appears in Diogenes Laertius as well.[116]

The seventeenth century offers two French writers used by Miró, both very much to be expected, Pascal and La Bruyère. Pascal is only represented by a reference in *Las cerezas del cementerio* to the commonplace of faith arriving as the result of 'práctica religiosa' (*OC*, p. 370). Miró owned, not the *Pensées*, but a Spanish version of the *Lettres provinciales;* but clearly so common a thought could have been found in many places.

From La Bruyère, another writer full of maxims, Miró quotes three times. He possessed a copy of *Les Caractères* in French with a certain number of markings. It is undated but he acquired it early since he quotes in French from it in *Del vivir* (*OC*, p. 51), the quotation coming from 'De l'homme', 82. And in 'Del natural' Miró uses a remark of Theophrastus apparently drawn from Diogenes Laertius ('Si eres igno-

---

[115] *Prometeo*, 3, No. 15 (1910), 14-15: cf. Montaigne, III, 9.
[116] Further references to Montaigne: *Amigos*, pp. 153-60; 'Jornadas de Sigüenza: Nosotros', *La Vanguardia*, 13 March 1914, p. 9; 'Nuevas jornadas de Sigüenza: I — Lector: La nariz', *La Publicidad*, 1 Sept. 1920, p. 1.

rante obras prudentemente guardando silencio, pero si docto, imprudentemente.' [117]) but which could have been found in La Bruyère's 'Discours sur Théophraste', a preface to his translation of Theophrastus, included in the volume of *Les Caractères*.

On two occasions Miró translates La Bruyère into Spanish. In 'Cordialismo' (*Glosas*, p. 18) he translates straightforwardly from a passage he had marked in 'Du coeur', 68: 'Aborrecemos fieramente a los que hemos ofendido mucho'. 'Cordialismo' dates from 1908, but the thought stuck with Miró for in *El humo dormido,* without any mention of La Bruyère, he speaks in very similar terms of 'ese judío que las gentes aborrecen tanto porque le han ofendido mucho' (*OC,* p. 701): another excellent example of the eclectic ways of Miró's creativity. Later, in one of the articles on Dante of 1922, Miró takes a greater liberty. In 'Des ouvrages de l'esprit', 15, La Bruyère wrote: 'On se nourrit des anciens et des habiles modernes, on les presse, on en tire le plus que l'on peut, on en renfle ses ouvrages.' Miró writes simply: 'Dice La Bruyère: «Nos mantenemos de otros; les exprimimos»' (*Glosas,* p. 74). Miró adapts the remark of the French writer to his own purposes, ignoring the context of the battle between the *Anciens* and the *Modernes* that gives point to the comment. Once more as Miró grows older he becomes steadily less respectful with his sources.

Four eighteenth-century French writers appear in Miró's work. The first of these, 'el admirable Rousseau (J. J.)', as Miró calls him in *Del vivir,* is twice mentioned for his remark that 'l'homme est bon: les hommes sont mauvais'. In *Del vivir* the remark appears with the comment that Rousseau is 'un corazón exquisito, dolorido, férvido, de vibración pronta y tierna' (*EC,* I, 274), and his words are used approvingly. In 1909, in 'La vieja y el artista', Miró speaks of them as 'las agrias palabras de J. J. Rousseau' (*EC,* IX, 255-6), while the artist-hero of the piece, who is treated ironically, inverts Rousseau's thought, preferring humanity to individuals. But it is clear that Miró found Rousseau important early on. The quotation and comment in *Del vivir* seem to confirm what appears from the marginal comments in the *Rêveries* (above, p. 70), that Rousseau was very much a youthful enthusiasm.

The Abbé Barthélemy, the Abbé Millot, and E.-F. de Lantier are quite different figures. Barthélemy's enormously popular *Voyage du jeune Anacharsis en Grèce* appears in *El abuelo del rey* (*OC,* p. 560). The pompous antiquarian Don César is immersed in volume III. Miró possessed a copy of 1830. E.-F. de Lantier's imitation of Barthélemy, *Voyage d'Anténor en Grèce,* of which Miró owned a Spanish version, appears in *El obispo leproso* (*OC*, p. 1030). The Abbé Millot was responsible for publishing an *Histoire littéraire des troubadours* which Miró also possessed, this time in the first edition of 1774.[118] This is yet another book used as a source of material, but this one offers a unique example of how Miró extracted and arranged such material. Miró appears to have been in the habit of destroying his manuscripts so that the opportunity of studying how he polished his work is largely lost to us. But in Millot's history of the Troubadours Miró has left two sheets of paper on which he has summarised material from Millot's chapter on Guillaume IX. This material, in turn, has been used to write almost two pages of the second part of the article 'Cuaresma', published in 1930 and included in *Glosas de Sigüenza*. Thus Miró has left an opportunity to study not only how material from a source was used in published work, but also the stages of the actual process of converting the material into a piece of Mironian language. It also illustrates Miró's working methods — doubtless he habitually worked by filling pieces of paper with notes and references, later bringing them together. What is fascinating in this case is to see how the material has already been through a preliminary adaptation in the act of making notes.

In 1927, three years before 'Cuaresma' was published, Miró wrote: 'Creo que en «El obispo leproso» se afirma más mi concepto de la novela: decir las cosas por insinuación. No es menester —estéticamente— agotar los episodios' (*EC*, I, xi). To say things 'por insinuación' and not to exhaust the episodes are aims that Miró follows in several ways, but in this development from source to final article we can see at least one of those ways. The sheets copying material from Millot include several anecdotes, but 'no es menester agotar los episodios' — two examples will suffice to show how Miró handles his material. Millot's version of the first is as follows:

> On en peut juger, entre autres exemples, par une maison de débauche, construite à Niort en forme de monastère, divisée en plusieurs cellules, qui devoit être gouvernée par une abbesse, une prieure; c'est-à-dire, où l'on devoit jouer la vie monastique, & assaisonner, par cette espèce d'impiété, les désordres de la prostitution.
>
> (*Histoire littéraire des troubadours*
> (Paris, 1774), I, 3-4)

Miró notes this down as:

En Niort construye una gran casa, dividida, como un mo-

[118] Edited by Millot from the work of La Curne de Sainte-Palaye. For convenience I follow Miró in referring to Millot as the author.

nasterio, en celdas. La comunidad de mujeres galantes gobernadas por una priora, experta en delicias, es una morada de vicios.

The changes are obvious: 'débauche', 'impiété', and 'les désordres de la prostitution' are replaced by 'mujeres galantes', 'experta en delicias', and 'morada de vicios'. The moral values of the passage are entirely changed — even when the word 'vicio' appears it is softened in the romantically ambiguous phrase 'morada de vicios'. On the other hand, Miró's narrative skill is evident even in so simple a passage: his picture, though even more extravagant, is much more precise and self-contained. In Millot's account the monastery is a mere disguise for a brothel, in Miró the fusion of these two institutions is the essential point of interest and the writing reflects these contrasting aims. The final version runs as follows:

En Niort funda una enorme casa de celdas para una comunidad de mujeres, bajo el gobierno de una priora experta en delicias.

(*Glosas*, p. 103)

This is far better: the words all work much harder, so that the more explicit ones can be removed. 'Monasterio' is unnecessary with the introduction of 'funda' and the presence of 'celdas'. The word 'galantes' is unnecessarily directive, and the phrase 'morada de vicios', excessively sentimental. The picture is perfectly conveyed, yet direction to the reader is at a minimum — only the choice of words suggests a monastery, only 'experta en delicias' suggests a brothel, and the refusal to name either specifically makes it possible for the reader to imagine this new institution as a single whole, not a mixture of two institutions. Miró works, then, by making another's work his own, and then proceeds by a process of reduction, so that we are left with the 'thing itself' directly perceived and not described through the commonplace categories that so often we use as defensive barriers. The example in itself is a slight one, but it illustrates an essential Mironian technique. A little later Miró offers another anecdote from Millot about an 'encuentro con dos viajeras casadas'. All that we are told is:

El trovador se finge mudo. 'He aquí un hombre bizarro de quien puede fiarse una mujer.' Se le somete a la prueba del gato enfurecido. Y el lacerado grita, pero no habla.

(*Glosas*, p. 103)

Millot's summary of Guillaume's account takes about 260 words. Miró's version on the sheets of paper takes about 240. Yet the final version of the story takes only forty words: 'Decir las cosas por insinuación' could hardly be taken further. The first version is a rough and slightly shortened translation, but throughout the process of making the source one's own is clearly visible. Two examples will serve: Millot writes: 'On le mène ensuite a sa chambre; on le fait mettre au lit' (I, 9). Miró makes this: 'Y, en seguida, a la cámara bien iluminada; le obligan desnudarse, y a que se acueste.' Once the wretched troubadour is in bed they test his muteness by putting a cat in with him. Millot says they have the idea 'de prendre leur chat, de le glisser dans le lit de ce pauvre homme, de l'y tourmenter, de le rendre furieux. Le chat joue des griffes avec rage. Le muet, déchiré de la tête aux pieds, soutient cette épreuve en héros.' Miró improves the account thus: 'Lo enfurecen [el gato], y lo embisten al pobre mudo bajo las sábanas. El animal se revuelve, brinca, se le coge a las carnes del caballero, le araña y le muerde. El lacerado resiste heroicamente la prueba.' Miró again and again brings the sensual elements of the narrative into the foreground. Millot's 'déchiré de la tête aux pieds' is a plain statement of fact, while Miró's imagination has been caught and involved; he feels the scene, takes possession of it, takes possession of the reality behind the words. The essential elements are no longer the scandalous behaviour of the troubadour, but the powerful emotions of both the women and man, expressed through the horrible torture that they are willing to inflict, and he receive, as a result.

All this apparently disappears in the final version, but enough is taken over to show how the successive processes of possession and distillation work. The word 'lacerado' remains to stand for Miró's emotional involvement, while the sentence in inverted commas shows how Miró heightens the air of sexual tension. It is taken directly from the intermediate version, of which the original read: 'Voici un homme à qui l'on pourroit se fier' (I, 8-9). Miró adds 'bizarro' to the man, and turns 'se fier' into 'fiarse una mujer' — two simple alterations that convey the point of the story as he had made it his own.

Not only Guillaume IX is mentioned from Millot's book. Miró devotes a further paragraph in 'Cuaresma' to the monk of Montaudon: 'Peu de troubadours ont été plus libertins, ou ont écrit avec moins de décence que celui-ci', writes Millot by way of introduction (III, 156). Again Miró summarises, this time Millot's own summaries of the monk's verse. Lastly, a reference by Miró to Terence in this same article is also from Millot's account of Guillaume.

Montaigne, Pascal, La Bruyère interested Miró for their thought, and the two *abbés* for material they provided. But with the approach of Romanticism the situation changes somewhat. Miró remains interested in ideas and material but the writers are now more obviously linked to him in a continuing tradition. From Rousseau onwards almost all the important figures in French literature, at least in prose, are represented; for Miró was naturally conscious of the line that led to his own position from the Romantic movement. If Rousseau is significantly the only eighteenth-century writer quoted for himself, then, equally significantly, the next to appear are the two chief Romantic precursors, Mme. de Staël and Chateaubriand, along with a third, Sénancour.

De l'Allemagne Miró acquired early, and he marked it in a number of places. He refers to its authoress in the 1904 *Del vivir* (*EC*, I, 274), and again in articles of 1909 and 1911. [119] Mme de Staël appears, respectively, in connection with Rousseau, as a student of national psychology, and as the exponent of the 'dogma de la perfectibilidad'. Finally, in *El humo dormido* Miró appears to quote her work: 'Verlo y comprenderlo todo es una gran razón de incertidumbre' (*OC*, p. 683). E. L. King (*Humo*, p. 176) states that this remark does not appear in *De l'Allemagne* and suggests that it is adapted from *Corinne*. Very likely Miró found the quotation somewhere other than in Mme de Staël's own work, and quoted it from memory.

As for Chateaubriand, the evidence is scanty. Miró possessed early on an unmarked edition of 1895 of *Atala, René, El último Abencerraje, Viaje al Mont-Blanch*. At some time he acquired an apparently second-hand copy of the *Itinéraire de Paris a Jérusalem* (he probably used it for the *Figuras*) and refers to information from it in *El humo dormido* (*OC*, p. 687), and in 'El turismo y la perdiz' (*Glosas*, p. 108), though in the former case he misrepresents Chateaubriand (King, *Humo*, p. 179).

Sénancour's *Obermann* appears in Miró's library alongside *De l' Allemagne* and is also marked (from letter VI to letter XX). One marked passage is in letter VII, describing an excursion in the Alps, and it is a passage from this letter that is used in *Las cerezas del cementerio*. Félix prepares for his excursion to the 'Cumbrera'; his aunt carefully supplies him with the equipment she considers necessary: 'La manta dobladita; el cestillo de la comida, muy lleno, limpio y oloroso; los anteojos, sujetos a la cayada de cuento afilado; la linterna y unas viejas polainas.' When Félix discovers the care she has taken, he is moved, but immediately illusions capture him. His uncle Gui-

[119] 'El presagio', *Del huerto provinciano*, 1930, pp. 125-32; 'Las últimas vestales', *Diario de Alicante*, 7 Jan. 1911.

llermo would not have taken such things. And 'Obermann los despreciaría. Obermann abandona en su hospedería los dineros, el reloj, todo lo que pueda recordarle la pobre vida reglada de la ciudad, y trepa solo por los Alpes; hambriento, cegado por la nieve, se pierde y se abandona a un alud que cae con trueno de castigo bíblico sobre un torrente ... Féliz decidió no llevarse los gemelos' (*OC,* p. 407). The introduction of Obermann is beautifully judged. Félix's illusions are largely derived from literature; Obermann is a fictional character and in the Alps it would be insane to follow his example. But on the other hand, to visualise Alicante's mountains as the Alps is to day-dream. And when it comes to reality, Félix leaves only the binoculars behind. Other references to Sénancour are made in passing, in 'Las águilas' (*OC,* p. 114) and in Miró's article on Francisco Figueras. [120] All three allusions are made between 1908 and 1910.

Stendhal is another author whose work Miró marked. Yet there is considerable mystery about the position of Stendhal in his reading. E. L. King comments: 'Miró was an avid reader of Stendhal ... whom he admired and yet distrusted' (*Humo,* p. 181). And in an article in 1927, C. Rivas Cherif, reporting an interview with Miró, claimed that Stendhal was an 'autor admirado y de su mayor frecuencia'. [121] Miró's library includes no less than six volumes of Stendhal, and of these four have been marked, one of them, *De l'amour,* extensively. This suggests that Miró read Stendhal with great enthusiasm, and indeed he quotes him twice in *Las cerezas del cementerio.* Yet there is no conclusive evidence at all that Miró read Stendhal at any early date; the first reference is in 1909, in 'El presagio', but it does not necessarily imply that Miró had read any Stendhal. The first quotations, those in *Las cerezas,* provide the only limit: 1910. And since *Las cerezas del cementerio* was written over a period of perhaps eight years, these quotations are of little help in establishing when Miró started to read Stendhal.

Of the six volumes, five are in the third type of binding, that is, they are not among Miró's earliest books. The sixth, *La vida de Enrique Brulard,* is unbound, unmarked, and without date. It was certainly published later than the first five since it carries announcements of post-revolutionary Russian novels. Of the five titles bound in the same style, only one is a Spanish translation. It is *El rojo y el negro* and is unmarked and undated, though it appears to have been published in 1909. Whatever else may be concluded, Miró may well not have read any *novel* by Stendhal until that date. It is also perfectly plausible that the other four volumes were not acquired until shortly before that date.

---

[120] 'Del salón de retratos', *Gérmenes,* 15 March 1909.
[121] 'Autobiografía sin comentarios', *Heraldo de Madrid,* 18 Jan. 1927, p. 4.

Two of them, the *Vies de Haydn, de Mozart et de Métastase* and the *Vie de Rossini* (from which Miró quotes) are identical in every detail of binding to *El rojo y el negro,* though of course this is not conclusive proof that they were bound at the same time. Taken together the evidence suggests that Miró probably did not read Stendhal until, say, 1907 or 1908 at the earliest; but it is a conjectural conclusion that any single stronger piece of evidence could overthrow.

The conjecture is, of course, only of importance because of the importance Miró seems to have attached to Stendhal. The markings in four of the volumes show this clearly. None of them corresponds to Miró's quotations from Stendhal, but again the epigrammatic nature of the passages Miró chose to mark is clear. Connected with this is the fact that Miró had only one novel among the six volumes. Unfortunately Miró's quotations do little to make the situation clearer. In *Las cerezas del cementerio* Miró quotes twice from Stendhal in the same chapter, once in Spanish (*OC,* p. 392), and once in French (*OC,* p. 393). Curiously, in the first edition of the novel both the quotations were in French. The first of them is from the *Vie de Rossini* (Paris, 1892, p. 101), but the second has not been traced. In both cases the quotations are used to describe the state of mind of Félix (and therefore as instruments in a psychological study of a character who is treated with considerable irony), rather than as reflections with which Miró whole-heartedly agrees.

In the short piece 'El presagio' (*Huerto,* pp. 125-32), Stendhal is referred to as a student of national psychology. A little later Miró refers to Stendhal's 'étourderie' (*OC,* p. 649), just as in *El humo dormido* he mentions Stendhal in connection with the term 'cristalización' (*OC,* p. 692). A few pages later, without the author being mentioned, Miró agains draws on *De l'amour* when he refers to 'los árboles, como cristalizados en una salina' (*OC,* p. 714), an allusion to the salt mines of Salzburg from which Stendhal derived the notion of crystallization (King, *Humo,* p. 191).

Another passage which almost certainly owes a great deal to Stendhal, though his name is not mentioned, is the description in *El abuelo del Rey* of the death of Mozart after completing his Requiem. A comparison of this account (*OC,* p. 507) with that of Stendhal shows that it is entirely possible that Miró drew the whole anecdote from him. There is no detail in Miró's account that does not derive from Stendhal, other than the kind of embellishments that Miró himself would naturally add: details of the physical appearance of Mozart and his strange visitor and of Mozart's own feelings at the time. A good number of the details in Miró's version are indeed strikingly similar to Stendhal's. If the derivation is accepted it offers another glimpse of Miró at work, for he alters the story in a perfectly coherent manner, making it more dramatic and more romantic for the benefit of the character who narrates it in the novel.

In the twenties Miró twice more quoted Stendhal. In the first edition of *Niño y grande* (Madrid, 1922), he placed at the start of the work a quotation from *De l'amour:* 'L'amour est la seule passion qui se paye d'une monnaie qu'elle fabrique elle-même' (from 'Fragments divers', CXLV), a quotation removed in later editions, even though they were published after Miró's death. In '¡Mañana es Corpus!' there is a further quotation from Stendhal (*Glosas,* p. 92), though this has not been traced to its source.

The relationship between Stendhal and Miró remains tantalisingly unclear. Nevertheless the intense interest around, say, 1908, followed by the continuing series of references and quotations, makes it possible to conjecture that Miró probably learned a good deal about the analysis of erotic relationships from Stendhal, and in particular one would guess that he added to his own vocabulary and linguistic resources for dealing with them. Naturally, only a careful stylistic study could reveal whether such a hypothesis were true or false, but an unattributed quotation in *Años y leguas* is suggestive. Miró writes of 'una mujer moza *dans cette pose presque coupable, tant elle trahit ce que la femme a de plus enivrant dans les mouvements et dans les contours*' (*OC,* p. 1181). The quotation is remarkably Stendhal-like, yet it is by no means foreign to Miró's way of describing a woman. It is not known whether the lines are Stendhal's, but they do suggest an area of coincidence between the two writers that may well be the result of Stendhal's influence on Miró.

A much simpler case is Lamartine, whose *Voyage en Orient,* a work Miró possessed, is used as a source of material in 'El turismo y la perdiz'. Miró adapts Lamartine gently, omitting and adding, drawing from the early pages of the work, reducing the prolix narrative to a charming list and concluding (Lamartine is setting out for the Orient): 'Al levar anclas del puerto de Marsella, Lamartine ha de componer su *Adiós* de 17 estrofas' (*Glosas,* p. 109). This is the only specific reference ever made by Miró to French verse of any century; if he was a 'poeta en prosa', he seems to have taken little interest in the poetry of France. Even the Romantic concern with Nature appears only through the prose of such writers as Sénancour and Amiel.

Lamartine is mentioned on one other occasion, in company with Hugo, when Miró comes nearest to speaking of French Romantic poetry. In an article of 1909 on Teodoro Llorente he suggests that in the Valencian poet 'se copian (...) el vuelo fastuoso de quimeras, ansiedades, ternuras, audacias, y bizarrías dolorosas que formaron el corazón de Goethe,

Heine, Byron, Carducci, Hugo, Lamartine'. [122]   The remark is chiefly interesting for the light it sheds on how Miró thought of Romanticism — the language is remarkably like that used of Félix in *Las cerezas del cementerio,* which Miró, in 1909, was about to complete.   Hugo, in turn, is mentioned on one other occasion, but in a passage in 'La paz de la catedral' (*Glosas,* p. 62) derived from Menéndez Pelayo.   Musset, the only other poet mentioned, appears in a 'Plática' of 1911. [123]

Amiel was a writer who might have been expected to appeal to Miró, but it seems that he only came upon Amiel's *Journal intime* fairly late. There is no copy in the library and the two quotations, though both lengthy and used approvingly, are in work dating from 1924/5. [124] Probably Miró read Amiel for the first time about then.

The next great novelist is Flaubert, but it remains difficult to discover Miró's view of the 'master'.   He owned early a copy of *Salammbó,* followed by *L'Education sentimentale* bound in similar fashion to the third type of binding.   In the second decade of the century came *Trois contes* (probably 1911), and *La Tentation de Saint-Antoine* (1913).   A continuing but not necessarily very enthusiastic interest, and, of course, the absence of *Madame Bovary.*   Yet it is to this book that the only early mention of Flaubert refers : Miró makes the hero of *La novela de mi amigo,* racked by the memory of having caused the death of his sister as a child and suffering physical pain at the memory, say : 'Yo he leído en un libro francés que cuando Flaubert, ¿Flaubert?, sí, Flaubert, escribía el envenenamiento de Emma Bovary, se envenenó él mismo imaginativamente con tanta verdad, que sintió el gusto del arsénico y tuvo dos indigestiones reales, con vómitos y dolores atroces ... No soy piadoso. Me horrorizo de la ficción de mi tormento ...' (*OC,* p. 121).   The famous episode is recounted in the *Correspondance* in a letter of 1868 to Taine.   But Miró's copy of the *Correspondance,* though of 1887-1893, and including this letter, is bound by Raso of Madrid.   Probably he did not possess it when writing this passage, but doubtless the anecdote could have been drawn from many sources.   Naturally it would have a special interest for Miró, later to imagine so intensely the pains suffered by Christ during the Passion. But it remains unclear whether or not Miró was acquainted with *Madame Bovary.* Nor, indeed, do the two other references he makes to Flaubert tell us very much.   From *Años y leguas* it seems that Miró knew *La Tentation de Saint-Antoine,* for he adapts St. Anthony's last speech,

[122]   *Diario de Alicante,* 13 Nov. 1909.
[123]   'Pláticas: Literatura feminista', *Diario de Barcelona,* 8 Oct. 1911, p. 14140.
[124]   *OC,* p. 1144; Ramos, *Literatura,* pp. 312-3.

sticking fairly closely to the French original that was in his library, in order to contrast St. Anthony tempted by the longing to become matter, with Sigüenza's acceptance of the 'goce dolorido del propio contorno en la inmensidad' (*OC*, p. 1105).

Miró's final reference to Flaubert (*Glosas*, p. 108) is also drawn from the library, from the *Correspondance* which by now he possessed. The only markings in this set of four volumes are against letters of the same year as the one used, the year of Flaubert's journey to the Middle East. As we saw with Chateaubriand and Lamartine Miró had a special interest in accounts of Middle-Eastern travels. The letters referred to are of 12 March and 4 September 1850, and one of the sentences that Miró uses is itself marked.

After Flaubert no writer, with the exception of the Belgian Maeterlinck, is mentioned more than twice, though most of the chief writers of prose make a brief appearance. The poets are never mentioned: Baudelaire and Verlaine, for instance, are quite absent, as they are from the library. Gautier appears there only in a *Viaje por España* of 1920. Even among the prose-writers Miró never mentions any writer younger than himself and of his near elders only Rolland, Suarès, and Gide, together with Claudel, are mentioned. Yet one remembers the startling absence of Spanish contemporaries also. Neither library nor quotation can quite clear up the problem.

Glancing quickly at these remaining writers we find that the scorned Licenciado Trujillo of *La mujer de Ojeda* reads the two famous *feuilletonistes* Xavier de Montépin and Ponson du Terrail (p. 238). Neither appears in the library: evidently they serve as shorthand indications of disgust at Trujillo. Jules Verne also is mentioned once (*OC*, p. 1118), though no work of his is in the library.

His contemporary Taine is mentioned once without any great significance, [125] while Daudet, mentioned in *La mujer de Ojeda* (p. 71), is also quoted in 'Martín, concejal', of 1910 (*OC*, p. 90). Curiously *Tartarin de Tarascon*, from which Miró quotes and to which he referred in *La mujer de Ojeda*, does not figure in the library — perhaps it has been lost, since Miró evidently read it, and since he had four other works of Daudet. The quotation suggests a likeness between Martín who, after much talk, has to act on his socialist convictions, and the preposterous Tartarin. For both of them, 'il faut partir', they have to accept the challenge resulting from their talk.

Of Zola, Miró owned only *Germinal*. But when he mentions Zola in *Del vivir* (*EC*, I, 274), he refers to Zola's utopia in his late novel *Travail*,

---

[125] 'El presagio', *Del huerto provinciano*, 1930, pp. 125-32.

in which a new city is founded putting into practice the ideas of Fourier. *Travail* was first published in 1900-1901 as a serial: perhaps Miró read some review or article dealing with it.

At first glance Anatole France seems to have more in common with Miró and in the library are three of his works that were bought before Miró's move to Barcelona. Miró quotes from only one of these, *Opiniones de Jerónimo Coignard,* in two articles published in May and October of 1912. [126]

A writer one might suspect even more of being of some importance to Miró was Huysmans, yet the evidence is slimmer still. *A vau-l'eau,* from Huysmans' naturalist period, is the only work in the library, while the only reference to the creator of Durtal is in 'La paz de la catedral' (*Glosas,* p. 62), an article on the cathedral of Reims (severely damaged in the Great War), published in a special issue of *La Publicidad* to celebrate the treaty of Versailles. Miró opens the article by adapting a paragraph from Huysmans' *La Cathédrale,* but it remains unclear whether he had read this work or found it quoted elsewhere.

In the case of Maeterlinck, too, there is room for some doubts, though it is certain that Miró much admired the Belgian writer in the early years of his career. Antonio de Hoyos, writing in *Revista Latina,* the magazine directed by Villaespesa to which Miró contributed on three occasions, speaks of 'El Tesoro de los humildes que debiera ser el libro de horas y como el breviario de todas las almas sedientas de idealidad y misterio'. [127] This conveys exactly the remarkable importance to the *modernistas* of Maeterlinck, whom Miró quotes or refers to on six occasions. But Miró had in his library only one work by Maeterlinck, precisely *El tesoro de los humildes,* from which five of the six allusions are derived, all of them in the first decade. From the first reference, in *Del vivir* (*OC,* p. 59), it is clear that Miró had read Maeterlinck by 1903 at the latest, for the reference is to the first chapter of *El tesoro de los humildes.* It is also significant that Maeterlinck is used when Miró is at his most *modernista* as in *Las cerezas del cementerio* (*OC,* p. 343), and *El hijo santo* where he speaks of a 'frente sellada por el Misterio y la Muerte como los niños predestinados del libro de Maeterlinck' (p. 16). On two further occasions Miró uses the same quotation for both: 'No basta poseer una verdad; es necesario que la verdad nos posea.' [128] The sixth and later allusion appears in a footnote to

[126] 'Pláticas: El alto asiento', *Diario de Barcelona,* 9 May 1912, p. 7391; 'Pláticas: De los comerciantes', *Diario de Barcelona,* 23 Oct. 1912, p. 15643: cf. p. 161 and pp. 185-8 of Miró's copy of *Jerónimo Coignard.*
[127] 'Un gran creador de filosofía y estética', *Revista Latina,* 30 Oct. 1907, p. 35.
[128] *Glosas,* p. 17; 'Altamira en su huerto provinciano', *Prometeo,* 3, No. 15 (1910), 17.

Libro de Sigüenza that was added for the 1927 edition (*OC,* p. 642).
This quotation is in French and is taken from *La Vie des termites,* a
work that Miró did not own, so that once again it is not clear exactly
what Miró read of Maeterlinck, though it is obvious that he absorbed
the essential views of the Belgian dramatist through the essays of *Le
Trésor des humbles,* and probably through periodicals.

Born in the same year as Maeterlinck, Maurice Barrès is quoted
once in an early version of *Años y leguas.* The quotation, presented as
a thought that appeals to Sigüenza, is interesting: 'Avez-vous fait cette
remarque que la clarté n'est pas nécessaire pour qu'une oeuvre nous
émeuve? Le prestige de l'obscur auprès des enfants et des simples est
certain. Aujourd'hui encore, je délaisse un livre quand il a perdu son
mystère et je tiens dans mes bras la pauvre petite pensée nue' (*EC,* XII,
297). Miró possessed no book by Barrès.

Finally, Miró refers to a group of writers about ten years older than
himself. Claudel does not appear in the library, but is quoted at the
close of an article first published in 1918 (*Glosas,* p. 61). Romain Rolland, too, is not represented among Miró's books except by a copy of
his *Beethoven* of 1929. Yet E. L. King has suggested as a 'lema' for
Miró's work a saying of Rolland that he quoted in a letter of 3 March
1922 to Germán Bernácer and that he was fond of repeating: 'No hay
más que un heroísmo: ver el mundo según es, y amarle.'[129] The same
quotation, though differently worded, appears in an article of 1920. The
variation in the wording of the quotation (E. L. King offers two different
versions on the two occasions that he has referred to the remark,
so that we have three variations all told[130]), is evidence of Miró's habit
of quoting from memory. The whole passage, never reprinted, is a
fascinating comment on Miró's view of Sigüenza in 1920:

> Porque, a los treinta años, no me importaba que la óptica y
> los pensamientos de Sigüenza fuesen mellizos de los míos. ¿Qué
> digo importarme? Me importaba casi halagadoramente avenir-
> me hasta con la sonrisa de Sigüenza, viéndole como iluminado
> de las mismas claridades de Romain Rolland cuando éste es-
> cribe: 'No hay sino un heroísmo en el mundo: verlo según es
> y... amarlo.'
>
> Quizá Sigüenza no llegara a la perfección de amar el mundo
> como era, sino de interpretarlo a su antojo y aceptarlo sonriendo.
>
> A los treinta años, esa sonrisa, siendo honrada, se atribuye
> fortaleza, simplicidad y aun elegancia hasta delante de la pro-
> pia inaptitud.

---

[129] 'Gabriel Miró y «el mundo según es»', pp. 141-2.
[130] Cf. King, *Humo,* pp. 40-1.

A los cuarenta años es el principio de una arruga en el corazón, y de una mueca en la boca. ('Nuevas jornadas de Sigüenza: I — Lector: La nariz', *La Publicidad,* 1 September 1920).

The passage places Rolland's motto at the heart of what Sigüenza is about. What changes from 1910 to 1920 is the way in which it is used: the passage accurately sums up the difference between, say, Félix, of 1910, and Magín, soon to appear in *Nuestro padre San Daniel.* The early heroes saw the world 'a su antojo' and faced it with 'inaptitud', yet their position was honourable and they wore an elegant smile. Miró implies that he himself, too, saw the world as he wanted to see it, believing in Sigüenza; yet at the same time he understood what was going on in himself — hence the paradoxical treatment of a Félix who embodies many of the Mironian ideals, and yet is exposed as a self-deceiver, and a Sigüenza whose actions constantly belie his words. As Miró matured he became less indulgent towards smiling self-deception. In this article of 1920 he continues: 'La mansa rebeldía, el «escondido» aislamiento de Sigüenza como visionario y emotivo, era lo peligroso para mí, desarticulando mi vida de las realidades.' The distance travelled by Miró in his use of Rolland's maxim is from Sigüenza and Félix to the creation of the scene in which Magín ruthlessly exposes Cararajada's sentimental, self-excusing indulgence of his own faults (*OC,* pp. 832-9).

Of another contemporary of Claudel, André Suarès, Miró possessed four titles, two of them presented by their author. He quotes from Suarès twice in his article on Dante in 1922 (*Glosas,* pp. 73 and 75). Lastly, Miró quotes twice from Gide. In a part of *Años y leguas* first published in 1925, he uses the second and third sentences of *Les Nourritures terrestres* (*OC,* pp. 1164-5), a work he owned in an edition of 1924. And in his lecture at Gijón in 1925, he uses a saying of Gide again. [131]

André Gide was born in 1869: Miró mentions no French writer younger than him, so that he does not seem to have been at pains to keep acquainted with the French literary scene. Indeed, a pattern emerges in which, in the case of these writers only a little older than himself, Miró can be seen to be reading their work in the twenties or just before, and quoting from them soon afterwards. One has to go back to Maeterlinck to find the French writer nearest to Miró in age, who is also quoted in Miró's youth. And even Maeterlinck is a solitary figure, unaccompanied by the other writers of the symbolist period. It seems that for Miró the important area of French literature was that

[131]   Ramos, *Literatura,* p. 317.

from the Romantics to Daudet, Zola, and France: this period he had dipped into frequently by the time he was thirty. Then, as he became acquainted with Madrid circles around 1920, he seems to have read here and there amongst the fashionable writers of the day. This is not, of course, to minimise his reading in French, for it must be remembered that he read many of the scholarly works he used for the *Figuras* in French, and also many of the works of other foreign literatures that were only available to him in French.

5. OTHER EUROPEAN LITERATURES

Of other literatures Miró does not seem to have read a great deal, and what he did read is largely unsurprising. Only Shakespeare, Dante, Goethe and Heine appear in his work more than three or four times. The references to Shakespeare are, in their Spanish versions, too vague to be securely identified. Miró had, around the beginning of the century, *The Merchant of Venice, Romeo and Juliet,* and a volume of poems. The two specific quotations that he makes seem unlikely to appear in these volumes, but it is impossible to draw firm conclusions (*OC*, pp. 155 and 681). Two other references indicate some acquaintance with *Othello* and *Hamlet*. [132]

The remaining references to English literature are to nineteeth-century figures: Byron, Carlyle, Macaulay, Poe, and Pater. Byron was read in Spanish translation early on; Pater in French much later. The others do not appear in the library; except in the case of Macaulay we do not know where Miró came across them. The pattern is a little like that of the French writers: a concentration on the romantic period, with a later writer connected with the *fin de siècle,* Pater, being read in the twenties.

Byron figured in Miró's list of quintessentially Romantic poets in his article on Teodoro Llorente, [133] and, appropriately, he is chosen in *Las cerezas del cementerio* to assist in the depiction of Félix's self-delusions. Early on Félix learns that his romantic uncle, with whom he identifies, looked like Byron (*OC*, p. 331). Later he fancies himself to be Manfred, 'reflejo clarísimo del trabajado espíritu de Byron' (*OC*, p. 411), and he quotes from *Manfred* (I, i, 188-90). But then he reflects: '«Pero ¡válgame el Buen Angel!; ¿soy yo acaso Manfredo?» No; no era.' Miró's library included a translation of *Manfred* from

---

[132] *De mi barrio*, ed. Mendaro del Alcázar, p. 49; *OC*, p. 106. Passing references: *Glosas*, p. 75; 'Pláticas: Nosotros', *Diario de Barcelona*, 10 Dec. 1911, p. 17901.
[133] *Diario de Alicante*, 13 Nov. 1909.

which he adapted the words Félix quotes. Much later, in the later part of *Niño y grande,* there is a final reference to Byron in connection with Venice (*OC,* p. 483).

The references to Carlyle, Macaulay, and Poe are not very significant but for the fact that the quotation from Macaulay once again reveals Miró depending on Menéndez Pelayo's *Ideas estéticas.* In 1912 Miró writes: 'Macaulay escribió que «conforme avanza la civilización va declinando el Arte»' (*Glosas,* p. 48). The wording is rearranged, but still clearly from *Ideas estéticas* (IV, ii (1889), 94), where the remark has a cross against it in Miró's copy. The source, however, for Carlyle (*OC,* p. 176) has not been traced. Evidently Miró was acquainted with the theory of the hero, for he refers to it in his 'Cuartillas' delivered at the Madrid banquet in 1908: 'He de pensar mucho en un *heroísmo* que olvidó el gran inglés: ¡Virtud santa de llaneza, de generosidad, por un hermano que vive en apartamiento (...)!' [134] But it is not clear whether he had read Carlyle. Nor can anything be ascertained about Poe, since the reference (*OC,* p. 125) is quite enigmatic.

But in the case of Walter Pater it is quite clear that Miró did not read his work until the twenties although he then obviously was very much interested. He possessed *The Renaissance* in a French translation of 1917. In his essay on Dante of 1922 he quotes from Pater's first and third chapters: 'Todas las virtudes del arte íntimo y complejo están constitucionalmente en el de Alighieri, y las veo enumeradas por Walter Pater cuando escribe: «Desde el viejo casón de las orillas del Sena donde vive Abelardo, se expande ese espíritu de independencia (...); todo, en fin, lo que penetra en la vieja literatura de Italia, y que halla su resonancia en Dante»' (*Glosas,* p. 80). This is a somewhat loose translation from the French of the first chapter, 'Two early French stories'. [135] Miró immediately continues with a quotation that appears to come from the third chapter, 'Sandro Botticelli', although the reader of the article is given no clue that in the original the quotations are sixty pages apart, and that the second quotation is treated with a remarkable lack of respect. Pater wrote (in the French translation that Miró used): 'Giotto et ses successeurs ... n'avaient pas appris à mettre dans les choses matérielles, dans la lumière, la couleur ou la geste, cette signification profonde contenue partout dans la *Divine Comédie.* Aussi, avant le XVe siècle, Dante ne pouvait-il guère trouver d'illustrateur digne de lui' (p. 104). Miró's presentation of these sentences is: 'No encontrará —dice—, no encontrará el Alighieri, antes del siglo XV, un ilustrador que le merezca, porque nadie poseía ese gesto, ese «pneu-

---

[134] 'Cuartillas de Miró', *Heraldo de Madrid,* 16 Feb. 1908. Text in Ramos, *Vida,* p. 123.
[135] Pages 42-3 in Miró's copy (Paris, 1917).

ma» íntimo, esa significación profunda, que hace temblar cada palabra del enorme poema.' This is a typical example of the way in which Miró treated his sources in the later part of his career. Not only is the vocabulary altered, but a causal link established where Pater had none.

Yet Miró evidently admired Pater, since in 1924 and 1925 he quotes three times from *The Renaissance*. In a part of *Años y leguas* published in June 1924, Miró quotes, in this case fairly accurately, a long passage from the very end of Pater's last chapter, closing with the famous presentation of the theory of art for art's sake: 'Porque el Arte viene a nosotros sin otro propósito ni codicia que los de embellecer nuestras horas a medida que ellas pasan, y por el solo y único amor de esas mismas horas tan fugaces, tan veloces...' (*EC,* XII, p. 290). But Sigüenza is distrustful: 'Teme Sigüenza incluirse voluntariamente en una fórmula ideológica.'

A few months later, in March 1925, and again writing for *Años y leguas,* Miró quoted once more from the final chapter of *The Renaissance,* this time from the penultimate paragraph (marked in his copy) that begins with the equally renowned words: 'To burn always with this hard, gemlike flame, to maintain this ecstasy, is success in life.' The passage Miró takes from this paragraph, 'Ya que todo huye bajo nuestros pasos, qué mejor afán que el de asirnos a toda pasión exquisita (...)' (*EC,* XII, 315), is accurately translated and approvingly used. Pater seems to have spoken to Miró's preoccupations with time in *Años y leguas,* though both quotations were removed for the book version of this series of articles.

Only a month after the publication of this chapter Miró gave his address on the *Figuras* in Gijón, and here again he quoted Pater, using the same quotation that he had used a month before, but this time altering it considerably. It is possible that when preparing his lecture he referred to his *Años y leguas* chapter and reworked the quotation from his Spanish, but almost all the changes from the French seem to be independent of the earlier Spanish version, so that, more likely, Miró retranslated, but this time substantially altering Pater's words. Indeed, as elsewhere, Miró adapts the quotation to fit the context, though it is curious that in a lecture he should adapt, while in the more fictionalised *Años y leguas* he should copy faithfully. In the lecture several of his alterations go directly against Pater's original thought: 'Independientemente del amor al tema evangélico que se abre y florece en nuestra infancia, ¿no hay, recordándolo y proyectándolo ahora, un deseo de acogernos a una conciencia emocional de nosotros mismos de aquellos años, un deseo de revivirla que coincide con el de Walter Pater: «Ya que todo huye y desaparece bajo nuestros pasos, siquiera retengamos y prolonguemos toda pasión exquisita, todo conocimiento que ensanche nuestros confines, todo lo que liberte nuestro espíritu y conmueva nuestra vida»?'[136]   Pater had written: 'Pouvons-nous faire mieux que nous rattacher à toute passion exquise, à toute connaissance qui semble, pour un instant, élargir l'horizon et libérer l'esprit, a tout ce qui émeut nos sens' (p. 362).   Miró has added the idea of *prolonging,* removed 'pour un instant', and substituted 'vida' for 'sens', thus destroying the very insistence on grasping the instant that was Pater's chief point.

* * *

If one childhood affection was the New Testament, another, though on a lesser scale, was Dante. C. Rivas Cherif reports that Miró, in an interview, admitted the influence of 'una «Divina Comedia» leída ingenuamente como comentario a las estampas de Gustavo Doré, que llamaban su atención'.[137]   The work is still in his library, a two-volume edition in Italian with a Spanish prose translation, and Doré illustrations.   Published bound in 1884 by Montaner y Simón, it probably belongs, in the chronology of acquisition, with the books of the first type of binding, with Larra and Rivas; though we must remember also that Miró gave the *Divine Comedy* as one of the books in his father's library (*EC,* I, x). The Doré engravings must certainly have had a powerful effect on the young Miró's imagination.   Doré's portrayal of the suicides who appear to be trees (Canto XIII), for instance, at once brings to mind the tortured, personified trees that appear a number of times in Miró's work, notably *Del vivir*.   In fact in 'En un pueblo' Miró uses the episode directly, fusing man and plant in a long series of images: 'En el huertecito, los árboles deshojados, esqueléticos, tienden dedos largos, y parecen ansiosos de hundirse en mi ropa y retenerme. Una rama fina araña mi frente; yo rompo esa mano rígida de la planta, y frío de enfermedad se difunde en la raíz de mi cabello, como si hubiera oído la voz del precito que gritó a Dante: ¿*Perché mi schiante? ¿Perché mi scerpi?*'[138]   And in 'Paisaje' there is a reference to 'encinas viejas, monstruosas, apretadas' that are like condemned souls in Dante (*Amigos,* p. 146).

Miró also had a French translation of the *Divine Comedy* and the *Vita nuova,* a volume that included an essay on Dante by Charles Labitte. This book is marked both in the *Vita nuova* and in Labitte's essay. The first mention of Dante appears in *La mujer de Ojeda* (p. 233), a general reference to the *Inferno*. Then there are no more until

[136]   Ramos, *Literatura,* p. 316.
[137]   'Autobiografía sin comentarios', *Heraldo de Madrid,* 18 Jan. 1927, p. 4.
[138]   'En un pueblo', *Revista Latina,* 29 Feb. 1908, p. 29.

his work is mentioned in six separate titles published from 1908 to 1910. Two of these we have just seen, while a third is a simple reference to Dante (*OC,* p. 380). The other quotations are from the *Vita nuova,* suggesting that though Miró was thoroughly familiar with the *Divine Comedy* from very early on, he perhaps did not read or even acquire his second work by Dante until around 1908. In a speech in that year in honour of Salvador Rueda Miró refers to the episode in Chapter III, marked in his copy, where Dante has a vision of his Lord commanding Beatrice to eat of Dante's burning heart. For Miró the vision shows that 'si al comer la amada el corazón de llama del Poeta subía a dignidad gloriosa de amor, comía también fuego y angustias. Por eso el gran Padre llora.'[139] In the part of *Niño y grande* that is derived from *Amores de Antón Hernando,* Miró again quotes from *Vita nuova,* this time from Chapter II. The words are used to convey the quality of love felt by the fourteen-year-old Antón Hernando for Elena Bellver (*OC,* p. 439). And in 'El recuerdo' Miró paraphrases a sonnet from Chapter XL expressing Dante's sorrow at the loss of Beatrice.[140]

After this, there is once more no mention of Dante until 1922. At the beginning of that year, Miró published in *La Publicidad* three consecutive articles on 'Dante: El tránsito de la conmemoración'. The previous year had been the sixth centenary of Dante's death and Miró here adds his reflections: 'Llegamos los últimos. Ha salido ya la gente y cruje, casi apagándose, la lámpara del voto' (*Glosas,* p. 72). This is the only article Miró ever devoted to any writer other than one alive in his own time, and although the piece is largely constructed from other books, there is a good deal of interest in seeing Miró at the job of commenting on a great writer. 'El artista no crea de la nada. No crea de la nada, porque la nada es todo que aguarda, que necesita la forma que recibe del creador' (*Glosas,* p. 74), writes Miró, expressing his own theory of form and content. He then summarises some of the sources of Dante's work. His information here is a summary of Labitte, whose essay 'La Divine Comédie avant Dante' he possessed in his French edition of the *Divine Comedy.* A number of passages in this essay are marked, clearly in preparation for this article. Having completed this summary of Dante's sources, Miró makes quite clear his admiration for Dante and the manner of this admiration:

> La muerte, lo que ella nos oculta, el dolorido amor a nuestra personalidad, hambre de nosotros, de ser siempre nosotros, seguirá torturándonos en todos los tiempos. Pero ese mundo

[139] 'Ofrenda', *Diario de Alicante,* 21 May 1908. Text in Ramos, *Vida,* p. 131.
[140] 'El recuerdo', *Correspondencia de Alicante,* 24 Aug. 1909.

alucinatorio, con sus descendimientos a los abismos infernales, ya no eriza nuestra conciencia; ya parece una vejez o una infantilidad literaria que ha ido quedándose en las rinconadas de los siglos. Y el poema de Alighieri sigue estremecido, vivo, con la modernidad de lo cierto; eterno por su técnica, por su verdad de belleza, verdad del arte, 'verdad de la poesía más duradera y firme que la verdad de la historia', según el concepto de Aristóteles.

(Glosas, p. 79)

Quite contrary to what might be assumed from much comment on Miró he is not attracted to a writer such as Dante through a love of the archaic, but for the truth he finds even when the archaic is ignored. Miró expresses himself similarly but even more strongly about the Vita nuova: 'Este menudo breviario es el precioso documento de todo análisis y ciencia de amor, de toda exactitud de verbo y de idea de amor, de toda fuente lírica, de confesiones, de memorias, de ensayos, de glosas de sí mismo' (Glosas, pp. 79-80). And this 'amor', the great theme of Miró's work, is defined for us: 'Amor es la conciencia de nosotros mismos en lo amado; toda la creación nos rodea y se refiere, entonces, a nuestra vida' (Glosas, p. 81). A final reference to Dante, a few years after this tribute, is in El obispo leproso (OC, p. 944), where Magín mentions the leaden garments of the hypocrites of Canto XXIII of the Inferno.

As for Italian literature other than Dante, there is little evidence for Miró being acquainted with it. He mentions Castiglione on three occasions, [141] but these references do not necessarily suggest that Miró had read The Courtier, which he did not have in his library, though Menéndez Pelayo's Ideas estéticas once more offered the opportunity of acquaintance. The only other Italian writers mentioned are Carducci, listed with the great Romantic poets, [142] and Jolanda, the pseudonym of Maria Majocchi Plattis, who died in 1917. Miró devoted an article to her Le ultime vestali, published in 1908. The article, 'Las últimas vestales', refers to the Spanish translation and appeared in 1911. 'Yolanda, la patricia escritora italiana,' is an 'hermana buena y sabia a la generación literaria, brava y luminosa, de los Villaespesa, los Machado, Muñoz Llorente y otros elegidos poetas y prosistas'. [143] A few months later Miró wrote about her again: 'Es redentorista. Quiere redimir a la mujer de su cautiverio del hombre.' Miró repeats that she is close to his contemporaries (she was born in 1864), and speaks, somewhat unusually, of himself as taking part in literary activities: 'Toda mi generación literaria encontró en la solitaria marquesa de Platti una dulce

[141] OC, pp. 197 and 616; Glosas, p. 129.
[142] 'La coronación del maestro', Diario de Alicante, 13 Nov. 1909.
[143] Diario de Alicante, 7 Jan. 1911.

sonrisa de hermana, y sus cartas eran como palomas suaves y tibias que acariciaban nuestra frente. Unidos principiantes madrileños y provincianos fundábamos publicaciones que, recién nacidas, se encanijaban y morían por falta de pecho generoso que las mantuviese. Y en estas primeras empresas y jornadas de arte recibimos la compañía de *Yolanda*.' [144] Unfortunately the work of Jolanda has sunk almost without trace. Only the recording of such titles as *Amor silenzioso, Eva Regina, Il crisantemo rosa* remains. Miró himself left no works of hers in his library.

* * *

Goethe clearly occupied for Miró in modern literature something like the position of Homer among the classics. Not only is there a relatively large number of references, but they are like those to Homer in that Goethe's words are rarely quoted. He is above all a standard, a reference-point, a measure of excellence. Miró possessed *Faust* and *Werther* early on in Spanish versions, and a little later acquired *Hermann und Dorothea* and *Die Wahlverwandtschaften* in French. Among the references to Goethe only three are to specific books: two to *Werther* and a four-word quotation from *Faust* — Miró's only quotation from Goethe (*OC*, p. 442). *Werther* and *Faust* were certainly important works for the young Miró, though his copies of them are unmarked.

The earliest reference is in *Del vivir*: 'Werther tal vez no se habría pegado un tiro —a pesar de la distancia que mediaba entre él y los hombres— sin el ansia de una dulce y amplia reciprocidad amorosa, si su amor hubiera estado limpio de egoísmo' (*EC,* I, 272). The significant words here are 'la distancia que mediaba entre él y los hombres': for Miró Werther is par excellence the artist-superman, far above the vulgar herd, though, typically, this does not exempt him from the charge of self-interest. In *Las cerezas del cementerio,* Beatriz recalls how she and Guillermo, whom Félix later idolises, promise each other 'excursiones atrevidas, solitarias, a los lugares cantados por Goethe' (*OC,* p. 335). In the first edition the sentence went on: '[Goethe] el grande, el divino, el elegido entre todos los hombres según le llamaba Guillermo' (*EC,* II, 254). Similar, but fleeting, expressions of admiration appear elsewhere also at the same period. [145]

But by this time Miró's irony has developed: it is used, not to

---

[144] 'Pláticas: Literatura feminista', *Diario de Barcelona,* 8 Oct. 1911, pp. 14140-1.
[145] 'La coronación del maestro', *Diario de Alicante,* 13 Nov. 1909; 'Pláticas: La paz lugareña', *Diario de Barcelona,* 8 Sept. 1911.

undermine Goethe's name, but to laugh at Sigüenza: '¡Qué haría el mismo Goethe atado con mis sogas!», se dijo para disculparse de su mohina y cansancio. Nada se contestó de Goethe por no inferir el mal de la respuesta' (*OC*, p. 592). Goethe is not just an idol to be passionately praised, but an unquestioned master against whom Miró and Sigüenza can measure themselves. Later still, such commentary is developed further. In *Niño y grande,* in the part first published in 1922, Miró has the hero write: 'Me dejaba llevar de un nuevo engaño de melancolía y arrullo novelesco. Yo sería un Werther, que nunca se mata, sino que se resigna a ser un hermano pequeño, desgraciado (...)' (*OC*, p. 485). To model oneself on Werther is now not only an 'engaño' but the kind of illusion that romantic novel-readers suffer from. Miró's last reference to Goethe is in his 1925 Gijón lecture, where he picks up and develops his remarks made earlier in connection with Dante: 'La modernidad no se somete a los cómputos y límites de la cronología. Por eso (...) son futuras las concepciones de Goethe.' [146]

The other German writer for whom Miró felt enthusiasm was Heine, mentioned with Goethe in Miró's list of Romantic poets. [147] As a young man Miró owned a volume of Heine's poems which he marked extensively, and in the twenties he acquired the *Cuadros de viaje.* But all the references and quotations come from a relatively short period, 1907-1912, the earliest references (1907-1909) all being to poems in Miró's volume. In 'Historia que no se cuenta', 'D. Luis recordó la flor azul que viera Heine en la negra encrucijada de los suicidas', [148] a reference to a poem from *Lyrisches Intermezzo,* 'Am Kreuzweg wird begraben', that is marked with crosses in Miró's volume. Similarly in 1908 in his speech at the banquet in his honour in Madrid, Miró referred to another poem from *Lyrisches Intermezzo,* 'Ein Fichtenbaum steht einsam', also marked in his copy. [149] In *La palma rota,* published in 1909, the hero recalls reading 'aquel libro azul' (Miró's copy is bound in blue), and the heroine recalls two of the poems (*OC*, p. 203). This serves as an introduction for the mention of Heine's uncle Salomon Heine, and the nephew's rejection of his uncle's financial support. Miró's information clearly comes from the introduction to the volume he owned (the story is mentioned on p. xviii), and in the transmission Heine is transformed into yet another artist-hero, spurning money 'por no resignar su alma'. The story evidently impressed Miró for he repeats it two years later in a piece that eventually appeared in *Libro de*

---

[146] Ramos, *Literatura,* p. 305.
[147] 'La coronación del maestro', *Diario de Alicante,* 13 Nov. 1909.
[148] *Revista Latina,* 30 Oct. 1907, p. 22.
[149] 'Cuartillas de Miró', *Heraldo de Madrid,* 16 Feb. 1908. Text in Ramos, *Vida,* p. 120.

Sigüenza: 'El excelso poeta Enrique Heine (...), por desheredarlo su tío el banquero Salomón, logró la inmortalidad' (*OC*, p. 625). Heine and Salomon, and Horace and Maecenas are Miró's favourite literary figures when he turns to the subject he so frequently dwelled on, the financial difficulties of the artist.

On two other occasions Miró refers to Heine, the last of them in 1912. In *Las cerezas del cementerio* another artist-hero is found reading Heine; this time Félix has read to Beatriz of 'esa magna región del viejo Brocken' (*OC*, p. 335). And in 'Del dolor' Miró quotes at some length from the *Cuadros de viaje* (*Glosas*, p. 35). This is one of the few occasions where it is almost certain that Miró used a book not now in his library, for his copy of the *Cuadros* is of 1920-21.

* * *

Outside of Spanish and Catalan, and French, English, German, and Italian, references to modern European literature are rare. In the first edition of *Del vivir* Miró writes: 'Amar es preferir, no comprender, no abarcar. Así lo ha definido Tolstoi: El amor es una preferencia que siente un alma por otra' (*EC*, I, 273). Miró owned copies of *El matrimonio, La sonata a Kreutzer, Amo y criado,* and *Resurrección,* all in his personal binding, all from the turn of the century, and all unmarked except for the underlining of sentences in the first.

The Polish poet Slowacki is quoted at some length in Miró's first published piece. [150] The source of the quotation is not clear. Finally, Ibsen is mentioned in *Libro de Sigüenza* (*OC*, p. 597), and quoted in the 'Cuartillas' of 1908. [151]

6. WRITERS ON PHILOSOPHY, SOCIETY, SCIENCE, AND THE ARTS

Thus far we have dealt successively with Spanish writers and with classical and modern European literature. There remain two further groups of writers mentioned or quoted by Miró: roughly speaking, they can be described as philosophers, and writers on Christianity and its history. The categories are not just ways of imposing order on Miró's reading, but arise from the material itself. In fact it is surprising how straightforwardly most of the authors which Miró read can be put into groups that reflect his areas of interest. For example, one can group together writers in Spanish with no significant loss to the

[150] *De mi barrio,* ed. Mendaro del Alcázar, p. 49.
[151] 'Cuartillas de Miró', *Heraldo de Madrid,* 16 Feb. 1908. Text in Ramos, *Vida,* p. 122.

philosophers, or to the religious scholars, for Miró scarcely ever refers to Spanish writers on such subjects. The Spanish literature that mattered to him was classical, the European literature almost all nineteenth-century, and the scholarship on which he drew was largely non-Spanish.

Miró received a legal training and included philosophy amongst his university studies, so that it is not surprising that there are odd references to writers not appearing in his library, most of them very early on and never repeated. Grotius, for instance, appears in *Del vivir,* remembered perhaps from legal reading (of which scarcely another hint remains). However he appears in company that suggests perhaps some other reading: 'El reinado de paz de Grocio; esa casa de amor, el Falansterio, de Fourier; la ciudad infinita, amorosa, engendrada por gracia y poderío de la Ciencia, que nos presente Zola (...)' (*EC,* I, 274). By this time Fourier and his bizarre co-operativist schemes had long since passed into history; perhaps Zola's recent novel *Travail* had stimulated some article that remembered Fourier.

Other solitary references are to 'el malhumorado señor Hobbes' (*Glosas,* p. 25), to Descartes (*OC,* p. 728), to Voltaire and D'Alembert, with Voltaire writing to the latter: 'Con respecto a los españoles, no conozco más que *Don Quijote* y Antonio de Solís' (*Glosas,* p. 56), and to Lavater (*Mujer,* p. 56). Miró possessed no books by any of these authors except for one work each by Voltaire and D'Alembert, both published about eight years after the reference, and an old copy of a Spanish verse translation of *La Henriade.*

There remain five modern thinkers of more importance to Miró. Kant appears twice in his work, in *Del vivir* and in *Libro de Sigüenza.* The latter is merely a reference to Kant's famous punctuality (*OC,* p. 644), but in *Del vivir* a quotation from the *Groundwork of the metaphysic of morals* plays a crucial role in the analysis of Sigüenza and the problem of the 'falta de amor' (*OC,* pp. 55-6). This is described in more detail in the next chapter. It is not clear where and to what extent Miró read Kant: the only title in the library, the *Critique of judgement,* was published in 1914 and is unmarked, yet in *Del vivir* Miró quotes at length from a book he apparently did not own.

In Miró's day Kant was better known through Schopenhauer than through direct reading of his own work, and certainly there is more evidence for Miró having read Schopenhauer. He had a copy of *Sobre la voluntad en la naturaleza* published in 1900 and bound for him soon afterwards, and a copy of *La libertad* acquired a little later. In *La mujer de Ojeda* there is a reference to Schopenhauer's theory of the will (p. 34), and in *Del vivir* his opinions are mentioned twice (*EC,* I, 272 and 273). But after this the name does not reappear. These references in *La mujer de Ojeda* and in the long footnote in *Del vivir* do not suggest great enthusiasm, but rather are a part of that display of his reading that Miró fell into in his earliest work: no mention of Schopenhauer survives into the *Obras completas,* very much suggesting that this was something fashionable rather than a lasting influence.

The question of fashion in philosophical reading leads directly to Nietzsche (though if we adhere to strict chronology, mention must be made of the forgotten French philosopher Jean-Lucien Arréat, whose *Journal d'un philosophe* Miró owned and from whom he quotes on a favourite topic: 'Los sueños del artista harían la ruina de un comerciante' [152]). Nietzsche was, of course, one of the most important contemporary influences on writers of Miró's youth. Yet Germán Bernácer, one of Miró's closest friends, has written that Miró was never contaminated with 'snobismo nietzscheano' as a young man. [153] Doubtless this has a good deal to do with Miró's rejection of a privileged moral status for the artist, but it remains unclear when Miró read Nietzsche, for though he owned four of Nietzsche's works, all privately bound, he does not mention him until 1912 (*OC*, p. 253). After that follow quotations in 1913, [154] and 1922. The latter is introduced with the following words: 'Hay unas palabras de Nietzsche en las que creíamos y pensábamos antes de haberlas leído. Estaban en nosotros y nos faltaba su pronunciación. Nietzsche las pronuncia' (*Glosas*, pp. 82-3). Miró was no 'nietzscheano', but he clearly read and re-read the German philosopher with sympathy.

Finally, Guyau appears to have made a deep impression on Miró, at least in one particular passage. In *Esquisse d'une morale sans obligation ni sanction,* Guyau describes a dream in which he is carried up towards heaven and hears a torrent of prayers rising up from the misery on earth. In his copy Miró has added: '¡Dios mío, qué hermoso es esto!' And on three separate occasions he refers to this particular passage: in 'El recuerdo', in *Niño y grande,* and in a piece to be read at a prize-giving ceremony at a musical academy in Barcelona. [155] Other than this passage there is no evidence, yet Guyau's argument that true morality was based not on force but on 'life at its most intensive and extensive', must have appealed to Miró.

* * *

[152] 'Ofrenda', *Diario de Alicante,* 21 May 1908. Text in Ramos, *Vida,* p. 132.
[153] 'Evocación de Gabriel Miró', *Sigüenza,* May 1945, pp. 5-6.
[154] 'Cosas viejas y sabidas', *Diario de Barcelona,* 2 Aug. 1913, p. 10462.
[155] *Correspondencia de Alicante,* 24 Aug. 1909; *OC,* p. 457; 'Páginas inéditas', *Clavileño,* No. 26 (March/April 1954), 61-62. Cf. Guyau, op. cit. (Paris, 1905), pp. 12-13.

References to writers on the arts are few and unimportant. Winckelmann is quoted in *La mujer de Ojeda* (p. 66), perhaps a legacy of Miró's contact with his painter-uncle Lorenzo Casanova, for the source has not been found in the library. Much later a reference to Viollet-le-Duc in 'La paz de la catedral' reveals once again Miró's debt to Menéndez Pelayo. He writes: 'Las catedrales góticas pueden significar y ser todos los escondidos conceptos de los poetas y de los católicos románticos, y todo lo fausto evocador de Víctor Hugo, sin menoscabo del organismo preciso, razonado, metódico y laico que Viollet-le-Duc descubre y proclama en el arte gótico' (*Glosas*, pp. 62-3). Not only is the comment on Viollet-le-Duc from Menéndez ('En la arquitectura gótica todo es metódico, razonado, claro, ordenado y preciso', is a quotation from Viollet-le-Duc that Menéndez provides), but the rest of the sentence also is entirely based on information from the *Ideas estéticas*.[156]

Lastly, Miró quotes, in the same article, 'La paz de la catedral', from Emile Bayard. It is worth copying Bayard's original and setting it alongside what Miró offers as a continuous quotation from Bayard's own words, as an example of the lengths to which Miró would go in adapting another author to his own needs:

Bayard	*Miró*
La pensée des siècles dort dans ces pierres, dans ces meubles, en un mot dans ces choses qui survivent aux générations, comme autant de témoins de leurs moeurs et de leurs aspirations idéales.	'El pensamiento de los siglos duerme en esas piedras que definen un estilo.
Aussi bien, les caprices de la mode sont éphémères, tandis que l'immuable Beau, qui ne peut s'improviser est éternel, et c'est la marque d'une éternité que nous saluons dans les styles, l'essor d'une épuration, d'une synthèse, nées de l'effort humain, à travers ses tatonnements jusqu'à la trouvaille.	En los estilos saludamos una depuración, un sello de eternidad, el «hallazgo» después de los afanes de los hombres.

(p. 1)

L'architecture, pour naître et se développer, veut le concours d'un peuple, d'une race, d'une civilisa-	La Arquitectura necesita de un pueblo, de una raza, de una civilización, para alcanzar un estilo.'

[156] *Ideas estéticas*, first edition, Vol. V (Madrid, 1891), pp. 508-16.

tion, et des efforts persistants pendant des siècles: à ce prix, l'architecture conquiert un style.

(p. 3)

(Emile Bayard, *L'Art de reconnaître*
les styles: Architecture-Ameuble-   (*Glosas*, p. 63)
ment, Paris, n.d.)

The syntax is freely altered, lengthy excisions are made, and, in the
first sentence, words are supplied that correspond only in the loosest
possible way to the thought of the original. The passage in itself is
not important, but it is an excellent example of one of Miró's techniques. Not only did he adapt Bayard in this way, but when he came
to write his 'Estudio histórico del templo de San Vicente, de Ávila', he
quoted the same adapted passage, again attributing it to Bayard. This
was part of a larger-scale reshuffling of the article 'La paz de la catedral' to form an introduction to the new essay.

* * *

In his library Miró had a small number of books on psychology and
popular science. To these there correspond a few references and quotations. Fabre, for instance, whom Maeterlinck called 'a marvellous
poet in the strictest sense', is mentioned in a piece published in 1912:
Sigüenza 'aún no había leído a Fabre ni el «Antonio Azorín»' (*Glosas*,
p. 50). Miró had five volumes of Fabre in his library, but in 1912 probably only possessed *La Vie des insectes*.

Another scientific writer mentioned is Flammarion. The presence
of his *Dios en la naturaleza* and *Los mundos imaginarios* in Miró's library, alongside a volume by Kardec, is surely the legacy of an early
interest in spiritism. In *La novela de mi amigo* Federico is taken to a
spiritist meeting and there is much talk of reincarnation (*OC*, pp. 124-
5). The topic was, of course, enormously popular at all levels of society, as well as being a particular interest of writers belonging to the
movement away from science and positivism. But Miró's reference to
Flammarion appears only in 1930, a late memory of a youthful interest
(*Glosas*, p. 110), and, doubtless, of the society of those days, for Alicante at the turn of the century had its own local periodical entirely
devoted to Spiritism. [157] Elsewhere Miró quotes from the French phy-

[157] Albert Berenguer, *Bibliografía*.

siologist, Albert Dastre, author of *La Vie et la mort,* a work included in Miró's library in a Spanish version (*OC,* pp. 642-3), and he mentions Hansen and Neisser, two workers responsible for the discovery of the leprosy bacillus, names that Miró must have picked up through his interest in leprosy from *Del vivir* onwards (*OC,* p. 948).

Psychology was another subject that interested Miró, probably around the age of thirty. Théodule Ribot, three of whose works Miró possessed, all bound for him, is quoted in *El humo dormido* (*OC,* p. 673) and mentioned a second time in the first version (*EC,* VIII, 274). E. L. King, in the notes to his edition (p. 171), suggests a passage from *Les Maladies de la personnalité* as the source for Miró's quotation. However, the words Miró offers are so remote from the original that it seems that Miró 'quoted' from memory, not even consulting the original — perhaps he had read it earlier and could now no longer put his hand to the passage. Indeed the original thought of Ribot has probably been moulded by its stay in Miró's mind, so that presenting it as a quotation is more of a recognition of a debt to a starting-point than the production of outside evidence.

Curiously, Miró had earlier behaved similarly with the work of Alfred Binet, another distinguished French psychologist. In his library he had Binet's *Etudes de psychologie expérimentale: Le fétichisme dans l'amour, etc.* In *Las cerezas del cementerio* he mentions that Binet has pointed out that an object connected with a woman can suggest the image of that woman. This appears to be, once again, rather vaguely abstracted, resembling most a passage from Binet's work (p. 69) where, in explaining fetishism, he states that, in normal love, objects and the image of the loved one remain 'soudée'. Once again Miró probably did not refer to the original; indeed the necessity for accurate quotation was not uppermost in his mind, for he ends his reference with the words: '(...) según dijo Binet —y aunque no lo hubiese dicho—' (*OC,* p. 364). He referred again to Binet and his fetishism in the first version of the short story 'El reloj' (*EC,* IX, 305).

Lastly, a writer on psychology of less importance was Jules Payot, whose *L'Education de la volonté* was an enormously successful popular handbook early in the century, being connected with the contemporary interest in 'abulia' — Miró had it in his library bound in the same style as the work of Binet and Ribot, and in an article he refers to it jokingly: 'Y yo acudí ante mi mesa, creyendo con el buen Payot, que nada más sentándome y mojando la pluma, y sintiéndome poseído de la voluntad para el trabajo, me acudirían las ideas como palomas dóciles y enseñadas. Y nada.' [158]

---

[158] 'Pláticas: Nosotros', *Diario de Barcelona,* 10 Dec. 1911, p. 17901.

7. WRITERS ON CHRISTIANITY AND CHRISTIAN HISTORY

Inevitably, given the theme, Miró's *Figuras de la Pasión del Señor* draw even more heavily on written sources than his other work. Naturally the interests grouped around this ambitious project are represented by a further set of writers, those dealing with Christianity and its history. The dedication to the *Figuras* reads : 'A mi madre, que me ha contado muchas veces la Pasión del Señor.' At school with the Jesuits in Orihuela, too, he learned to know and meditate on the Bible. As a grown man he began to study, with increasing seriousness, the history and geography of the Middle-East at the time of Christ. All this material was passed through his imagination in order to reconstruct, to recreate, the figures around Christ. He reports using more than twenty volumes to complete three 'Figuras'. [159]

Thanks to his work in Barcelona on the ill-fated Catholic Encyclopaedia that he edited from 1914 to 1915, Miró had come to know local scholars and was able to use their libraries. In 1928, Ernesto Giménez Caballero, interviewing Miró about the way in which the *Figuras* were rooted in his childhood and the landscape of Alicante, asked : 'Pero, a pesar de esta tendencia biológica, ¿no hubo en su vida un hecho cultural decisivo que la encauzara?' Miró replied : 'Desde luego : mi permanencia en Barcelona con los capuchinos y nuestra común tarea en el ensayo de un Diccionario sagrado, al frente del cual estuve como técnico.' [160] And in *Años y leguas* Miró pictures Sigüenza searching for the site of the Garden of Eden : 'Lo buscó en la biblioteca del Institut d'Estudis Catalans, en la del convento de Capuchinos de Nuestra Señora de Pompeya, en la de Mosen Clascar' (*OC,* p. 1183). This is one of the few glimpses we catch of Miró at work in other libraries, for Sigüenza undoubtedly follows here in his creator's footsteps. Clascar, for instance, was a personal friend — Miró had three works by him with dedications. But all the time Miró's own library was growing. It is worth recording Giménez Caballero's impression on seeing it in 1928 : 'La librería de Miró era un auténtico taller. Un foco de constructivismo. Nadie quizá en España, con el «seminario» de poesía bíblica atesorado por Miró en su propia casa. Al pronto, más de un sabio orientalista que de un poeta se hubiera dicho su laboratorio.'

Miró not only tranformed all this material imaginatively : he also attempted physically to capture in himself the sensations of those des-

---

[159] Ramos, *Vida,* p. 202.
[160] 'Gabriel Miró', *El Sol,* 20 April 1928, p. 1.

cribed. Juan Gil-Albert, though not entirely reliable since he is writing in 1931 and purports to record Miró's own words, quotes the following: 'Yo necesito ver las cosas antes de escribirlas; necesito levantarlas, tocarlas. He tenido verdaderos días de obsesión hasta que conseguí apresar las figuras de Judas o de Poncio Pilato, y horas enteras me forzaba físicamente hasta acercarme, hasta sentir en mí mismo el suplicio de la inmovilidad en la cruz.' [161] Miró needed to perceive directly, so that the second-hand material he was forced to use by the remoteness in time and place of his subject-matter made it necessary for him to subject all the material to the powers that had been trained in Orihuela by the Ignatian spiritual exercises.

To grasp the personalities of those he described he could draw on what he had learned from writing fiction, while, most important of all, his recreation of the Palestinian landscape passed through the direct experience of his own countryside. Reading the *Figuras* one constantly comes across words and phrases that are used repeatedly in describing Alicante. The single word 'bancal', so heavily laden with suggestion when used by Miró, will serve as an example of the process whereby Miró not only imagined Palestine in terms of Alicante, but also applied to the expression of what he saw in the imagination the same literary tools that he had developed earlier to describe his own landscape. Critics pointed this out very soon, and in the lecture at Gijón, Miró referred to two of them, Unamuno and Georges Pillement, adding simply: 'Es verdad.' [162]

At first sight it may appear paradoxical to insist both on the dependence of Miró on previous writing and on his need to perceive directly, but in fact the apparent paradox explains precisely why Miró so frequently adapted texts that he quoted (we shall shortly see extreme examples of such adaptation). A text was raw material, just as the landscape of Alicante was: both were preliminaries from which Miró could set in action a process of visualisation that enabled him almost to live the Passion. The sources are not used to help the reader 'see' Palestine, but to help Miró see it, a vision that he then presents to the reader.

Yet all this work of imaginative transformation depended on the laboriously culled information. To study the processes whereby Miró created the *Figuras* from his sources would be a daunting task in itself; all that can be done here is to collect together the preliminary information from which such a study would have to start. Naturally enough Miró makes no references in the *Figuras* to the scholars whose work

[161] *Gabriel Miró*, p. 38.
[162] Ramos, *Literatura*, p. 314.

he used. One is forced therefore to examine the library and the references scattered through the lesser work connected with the *Figuras* in order to find the indispensable starting-point for such a study. The evidence seen so far all suggests that the library would be an excellent guide to Miró's sources in creating the *Figuras*. Yet in this particular field there are suggestions — some of them mentioned above — that he used other libraries. Do the references he makes to writers on Christianity offer any further evidence as to what the sources of the *Figuras* might be?

Flavius Josephus was naturally a prime source for Miró. He owned several editions of works by Josephus and refers several times to him. The first reference does not appear until 1912: in *Los pies y los zapatos de Enriqueta* the 'humanista', a forerunner of Don Magín, uses, like his successor, scholarship to astonish the simple faithful. He informs the village priest that Adam engendered Seth at the age of two hundred and thirty. Flavius Josephus said so (*OC*, p. 234). Whether by coincidence or not, there is still a bookmark at the page in the *Antiquities of the Jews* where the information is given. Further references occur in the first version of 'Pilato', in the *Figuras* itself, and in the articles 'Pentecostés', 'La momia de Jacob', and 'La conciencia mesiánica en Jesús'. [163] None of these references and quotations is of particular interest except as an index of Miró's use of Josephus. In the last case he specifically speaks of rereading Josephus in order to prepare the article.

Miró frequently refers to particular saints. A number of these were writers, but it would be meaningless to follow up each of these since they are usually mentioned as saints rather than as writers. Among the more important of these are St. Clement (*OC*, p. 727), St. Gregory (*OC*, p. 680), and St. Jerome (*OC*, pp. 725 and 799); Miró did not own the work of any of them. Two, however, seem to have been read directly by Miró; St. John Climacus and St. Augustine. The *Escala espiritual* of St. John Climacus is included in *BAE*, XI, the third volume of the works of Luis de Granada. Here Miró probably found material for a reference to the Saint in 'El poeta eterno' (*Amigos*, pp. 153-60). St. Augustine is quoted on four occasions: [164] Miró possessed copies both of the *Confessions* and of the *City of God*.

Miró makes use of the work of several other writers of the early church. Tertullian's disgust at the 'indignidades del matrimonio' is linked in *Nuestro padre San Daniel* with that of his nineteenth-century

---

[163] *Diario de Barcelona*, 19 March 1913, p. 3941; *OC*, 1295; *Glosas*, p. 59; *La Publicidad*, 29 Oct. 1919, p. 1; *OC*, p. 1225.
[164] *OC*, pp. 457, 727, 995, and 1225.

equivalent, Padre Bellod (*OC*, p. 790): one of the ways in which Miró sets Oleza into a wider perspective and thus comments on more than just Oleza. In *El óbispo leproso* Origen is mentioned (*OC*, p. 937), and an anecdote from Eusebius quoted, presumably from Miró's own copy (*OC*, p. 1017). Later in the novel Pablo reads the account by Prudentius of the martyrdom of the virgin Engratis, and ten lines of a Spanish translation are quoted. The passage, in the novel, is taken from the *Actas de los Mártires* which Padre Bellod insists on showing Pablo, even though he forbids him to read of the martyrdoms of virgins. We only read the passage when Pablo returns secretly to read the forbidden pages. [165] The use of the *Actas* and of Prudentius is a fine example of the novelistic use of quotation at its best. The sadism of the savage description offered by Prudentius conveys with great precision both Bellod's mentality and the awakening of Pablo's interest in sex while under the stern authority of his father, whose outlook is directly associated with that of Bellod. Miró had no copy of the *Actas de los mártires* in his library, but it looks as if, on this occasion at least, he must have had access to one, especially since he had no copy of Prudentius either. [166]

Few mediaeval Christian writers appear in Miró's work. There are two references to Thomas à Kempis (*OC*, pp. 657 and 1059), whose *Imitation of Christ* is included in *BAE*, XI, and one puzzling mention of Jacobus de Voragine, author of the *Golden Legend* (*OC*, p. 728). Miró possessed a copy of this famous work in Spanish, but it seems unlikely that he used it on this occasion. First, the author's name is given as 'Jacques de Voragine', and secondly, the information attributed to him does not all appear in the *Golden Legend*. [167] This is not the only puzzling attribution of this sort, for in 'Cuaresma', published in 1930, Miró adds at the end of a paragraph dealing with events in the crusade against the Albigensians: '(Pluquet: «Dict. des Heres.» P. Benoit)' (*Glosas*, p. 102). The first part of this is a reference to the eighteenth-century *Mémoires...: ou dictionnaire des hérésies* of François Pluquet of which Miró had a copy. In fact a good deal of the material immediately preceding the attribution is derived from the article 'Albigeois' in Pluquet's work, though as much again has come from the

---

[165] *OC*, pp. 1029-31: cf. *Perestephanon Liber*, IV, 115-38.

[166] The *Actas de los Mártires* also appears in the library of the Carlist Círculo de Labradores, alongside the '*Historia y estampas de los trajes de las Ordenes religiosas*, del abate Tirón ...', a work published in Barcelona in 1846-48, and 'el *Arte de pensar o Lógica administrativa*, por el doctor sorbónico don Antonio Arnaldo', a volume in Miró's own library, though its proper title is *Lógica admirable*, as well as works by Campomanes and Juan Carrillo, mentioned earlier (*OC*, p. 1028).

[167] See King, *Humo*, p. 201.

work of Millot, only acknowledged a page later, when further material of his is used as, we have seen earlier (pp. 143-5). But 'Benoit' seems to have nothing to do with Pluquet. Miró's rather arbitrary way of acknowledging his sources sometimes raises more problems than it solves.

After Pluquet, all the remaining writers mentioned by Miró are nineteenth-century figures. Almost all are scholars, and all except Johann Sepp and a number of briefly mentioned Assyriologists are to be found in the library. Indeed it is amongst these writers that the relationship between reference and library is most obvious and direct. But, as has been mentioned, there is evidence that Miró, at least in Barcelona, used libraries other than his own to write the *Figuras* and similiar work. One has therefore to strike a balance between the circumstantial evidence suggesting the use of outside libraries and the internal evidence suggesting an almost exclusive use of Miró's own books. Two points are perhaps worth making. In the first place, the *Figuras*, of course, do not include references to the sources; all the references now under consideration appear in factual or discursive writing, or in *El humo dormido*, or in newspaper articles uncollected by Miró, or in *Nuestro padre San Daniel*. All this work comes after the *Figuras*. Add to this the fact that a number of Miró's books on Christian history were not acquired until after the *Figuras* were published, and that he had only started to read seriously in this area around 1912. The explanation suggests itself that perhaps in the early days in Barcelona, and especially around the time of the Encyclopaedia, Miró tended to supplement his own books with the use of libraries rather more than he did once the *Figuras* had been completed.

In the second place, we have seen before how Miró's use of his sources was affected by their accessibility. In this case it may be that we have these particular references and quotations precisely because they were easily accessible at the time of writing. Only a careful study of the sources of the *Figuras* themselves could show exactly where the balance should be struck. What is clear is that the library forms an admirable starting-point for such a study.

The earliest of the nineteenth-century writers, and the only non-scholarly one, is Anna Katharina Emmerich, the German stigmatic and mystic. The book which records her meditations, entitled in Spanish *La dolorosa Pasión de Nuestro Señor Jesucristo,* is included in Miró's library. It was produced by the Romantic poet Clemens Brentano and is his record of what she told him. It is not clear how much Brentano contributed to the book either in the way of suggestions to Anna Emmerich while talking with her, or in the form of later elaboration of what she had said, but evidently Miró was not concerned about the question of authenticity. He naturally compared his own *Figuras* with her vision of the Passion, and very likely received a good deal of stimulation from them. Unamuno had a few years before drawn the same comparison when he spoke of Miró's 'fuerza de visión que a las veces recuerda la de la Beata Catalina Emmerich'. [168]

Miró deals with her work from a literary point of view, revealing at the same time something of his own view of what he had attempted in the *Figuras:*

> De improviso, he recordado una obra de título y asunto seme-
> jantes a la mía, de una mujer venerable, de sencillez compleja
> — como todo lo profundamente sencillo — : 'La Dolorosa Pa-
> sión', según las meditaciones de Sor Ana Catalina Emmerich.
> Todas sus páginas tienen la misma prolijidad, exactitud arbitra-
> ria, alucinatoria; es decir: a su arbitrio de iluminada reveren-
> cia. Lente magnífica para mirar, demasiado cerca, pueril, confuso
> y transido, el corazón de Sor Ana Catalina que no evoca, sino
> que registra sus imágenes de dolor.
>
> (Ramos, Literatura, p. 302)

Miró's earliest references to Christian scholars appear in the article entitled 'La potestad de un juez', in which he defends himself against the accusation of blasphemy brought against him by the judge who, in 1917, had imprisoned the editor of *El Noroeste* of Gijón for publishing an extract of the *Figuras*. One of these scholars is M.-J.-H. Ollivier, author of *La Passion* (Paris, 1902), a book Miró had bound in Barce-lona and which he quotes — accurately — in this article (p. 222). In his own defence Miró also referred to 'el doctor Sepp, teólogo alemán — es alemán y todo'. [169] As the quotation shows he was not only appropriate because of the reputation of Germanic learning, but also in the context of the conflict within Spain between Germanophiles on the right, such as would support the incarceration of the editor of *El Noroeste,* and supporters of the allies, including Miró, on the liberal side. A little later Miró used Sepp again, this time quoting in *El humo dormido* a passage, translated into Spanish, from a French version of Sepp's life Christ, *La Vie de N.-S. Jésus-Christ.* [170] This is the same work Miró used in 'La potestad de un juez', where he gives its title in a footnote. The title-page gives the author's name as 'le docteur Sepp', thus accounting for the absence in Miró of the Christian name Johann. This is the only nineteenth-century scholar Miró mentions who does

---

[168] Miró, *Niño y grande* (Madrid, 1922), p. 206.
[169] 'La potestad de un juez', *Diario de Alicante,* 10 May 1917.
[170] *OC,* p. 726: cf. Sepp, op. cit. (Paris, 1861), III, 171-2.

not appear in the library, but clearly Miró read this life of Christ, a reply to the Straussian school, and it must be added to the list of works that might be sources for the *Figuras.*

Another writer who appears in *El humo dormido,* and an important one, is Renan. E. L. King, who has studied Miró's biography in detail, writes: 'We may suppose that Miró's spiritual development roughly paralleled Renan's and that he felt about religion and his past much the same as Renan did' (*Humo,* p. 166). King has also drawn attention to Miró's habit of comparing himself with Jesus,[171] and it is interesting to note that the same observation has been made about Renan.[172] There are, of course, important differences also. Miró was born fifty-six years after Renan and neither Biblical scholarship nor ideas in general had stood still. Renan started from a position of admiration for science; Miró starts from the reaction, at the end of the century, against that very scientism. Unfortunately neither Miró's library nor his solitary allusion to Renan help one very much to understand their relationship. Miró possessed, early, a copy of *Los apóstoles.* He also owned a copy of *Souvenirs d'enfance et de jeunesse,* undated, but almost certainly of 1912. These are the only volumes in his library dated before the *Figuras,* and before *El humo dormido,* in which he alludes to the *Souvenirs.* Once settled in Madrid, Miró acquired six more titles and had them splendidly bound. Is it possible that he did not read the *Vie de Jésus* until the twenties? Whatever the facts may have been, he clearly attached great importance to Renan in the twenties, while the passage in *El humo dormido* speaks for his admiration for the *Souvenirs* in 1918. Renan is mentioned at the very start of Miró's book, which uses the image of the city of Is to establish the tone of the work and to indicate to the reader the kind of record he is about to face: 'No han de tenerse estas páginas fragmentarias por un propósito de memorias; pero leyéndolas pueden oírse, de cuando en cuando, las campanas de la ciudad de Is, cuya conseja evocó Renán, la ciudad más o menos poblada y ruda que todos llevamos sumergida dentro de nosotros mismos' (*OC,* p. 665). The reference, placed at the head of the work, indicates a keen sympathy for Renan's outlook, even if the question of influence cannot be resolved. Renán's own words in his introduction clarify something of what Miró was aiming at in *El humo dormido:*

> Il me semble souvent que j'ai au fond du coeur une ville d'Is qui sonne encore des cloches obstinées à convoquer aux offices sacrés des fidèles qui n'entendent plus.

[171] *Humo,* p. 170; 'Gabriel Miró introduced to the French', p. 332.
[172] Wardman, *Ernest Renan,* p. 73.

S'imaginer que les menus details sur sa propre vie valent la peine
d'être fixés, c'est donner la preuve d'une bien mesquine vanité.
On écrit de telles choses pour transmettre aux autres la théorie
de l'univers qu'on porte en soi.

Tout est vrai dans ce petit volume, mais non de ce genre de
vérité qui est requis pour une *Biographie universelle.*

These three extracts apply directly to the aims of Miró's work: to
recover the sound of the submerged bells, to transmit the theory of
the universe that one carries in oneself, and to express autobiographical
truths without resorting to completeness of anecdote or chronological
fidelity.

Another writer on religion to appear in *El humo dormido* is Ernest
Hello, a conservative catholic and a strong opponent of Renan. Miró
owned his *Fisionomías de santos,* translated by Maragall, and in view
of Miró's especial admiration for Maragall, it is interesting to see how
Miró deals with such a text. He presents it as if it were a straightforward quotation:

Miró	*Hello*
'El rayo que le hiere — dice Hello — manifiesta el carácter de San Pablo. San Agustín es atraído por un libro; los Magos, por una estrella; San Pablo, por un rayo... No perseguirá más a Jesús de Nazareth. Pero, entonces, ¿qué hará? Hombre de acción, hombre de todas las acciones, reclama una vocación práctica.' *(OC,* p. 726)	El carácter del rayo que le hirió revela el carácter de San Pablo. [5 lines omitted]. San Agustín es atraído por un libro; los Magos por una estrella; San Pablo por un rayo. [1 page]. Pero San Pablo es de tal modo hombre de acción, hombre de todas las acciones, que en seguida, *hic et nunc (aquí y ahora),* reclama una vocación práctica, exterior. No perseguirá más a Jesús de Nazareth; pero entonces, ¿qué hará? (Barcelona, 1904, pp. 33-4)

The order is changed, omissions are made, phrases and sentences are
shortened, a word changed, and a past tense made present. The
final result is more Miró than Maragall, not to speak of the forgotten
Hello: an excellent example of how material, not merely literary,
but of all kinds, is filtered through Miró's mind and moulded to his
own way of expression.

Another scholar mentioned in *El humo dormido (OC,* p. 731) is a
little better treated. Miró quotes from Fernand Cabrol, *La oración*

de la Iglesia. On this occasion the quotation is still altered somewhat, though less so than in the previous case. [173] Later it reappears exactly as in *El humo dormido* in the article 'La conciencia mesiánica en Jesús' (*OC*, p. 1225).

A similar case is that of the French classical scholar and secretary of the Academy, Gaston Boissier. Miró possessed three works by this highly successful writer; all three are marked in various places. In Miró's 1922 series of articles on Dante he quotes Boissier from *El fin del paganismo.* [174] The changes are again typical — a perfect tense changed to a present, shortening, and substitution of more emphatic verbs for verbs that have little more than a syntactic function. For 'han ocupado un puesto importante en' Miró uses 'se hincaron en'; for 'sería fácil seguir su huella' he writes 'su huella resalta'.

We have seen earlier (p. 108) how Miró used Boissier unacknowledged in an article of 1925 drawing a conclusion that the original (again *El fin del paganismo*), hardly warranted. Another book by Boissier in Miró's library, *Nouvelles promenades archéologiques,* presents a similar example of how Miró used his sources. In his copy Miró has left a sheet of paper reading: 'Para el capítulo «tocan a muerto» —véase págs. 82 y 83 de «Nouvelles promenades archéologiques».' A paragraph in 'Tocan a muerto' is indeed based on Boissier; Miró writes: 'El cristianismo incorporó a su liturgia funeraria el festín pagano de los ritos de la muerte. La *cena novendialis;* la comida *in memoriam* en torno de la tumba, es un arroz con pollastre en la comarca levantina' (*OC*, p. 1079). The basis for this in Boissier is: 'Le christianisme trouva ces usages si enracinés qu'il n'osa pas d'abord les détruire, et jusqu'à saint Ambroise on vint boire et manger sur la tombe des martyrs à l'époque de leur fête.' Miró again in passing his material through the creative process makes an assumption unwarranted by anything in the original. Boissier is referred to by name later in *Años y leguas* in connection with Horace, [175] who is also the occasion for an allusion to another French scholar, Bertrand Capmartin de Chaupy, author of *Découverte de la maison de campagne d'Horace.* [176]

'La potestad de un juez', *El humo dormido,* and 'Dante', these are the three occasions so far for the appearance of the names of foreign scholars working in this field. On another occasion, in the article 'La conciencia mesiánica en Jesús', Miró goes so far as to indicate the sources of his essay: 'Yo, aquí, escogeré cuatro autores de distinto acento de fervor: Stapfer, Chollet, Harnack y Le Camus' (*OC*, p. 1225). Of

---

[173] King, *Humo,* p. 203.
[174] *Glosas,* p. 75: cf. Boissier, op. cit. (Madrid, 1908), II, 27.
[175] *OC,* p. 1157: cf. Boissier, op. cit., p. 25.
[176] *OC,* p. 1138: cf. Boissier, op. cit., p. 2.

these only Stapfer is mentioned elsewhere, but all four are important works for Miró. His Harnack, in particular, is very battered.

But most important as a revelation of how Miró worked is the *conferencia*, the only one of his life, given in Gijón in 1925 on 'Lo viejo y lo santo en manos de ahora'. The lecture is a defence and explanation of his practice in writing the *Figuras*, and, amongst much valuable material, provides us with hints as to his more important sources. First to be mentioned should be Cabrol, who has already appeared in *El humo dormido*. In the Gijón lecture a quotation of his is given, again shortened, but otherwise untouched. [177] Enough examples have now been given of Miró's somewhat cavalier treatment of the quotations he used, but a final one from the Gijón lecture is worth examining, since it occurs in a factual, explanatory text, where there is no compelling reason for altering material to assimilate it to the style of its context. The passage in question is severely shortened, reasonable enough in a lecture, where the speaker may wish to pick out the essential points from his source. But Miró, even in these circumstances, polishes, and even rewrites his original, a technique that amounts in places to misrepresentation. The passage quoted is from the protestant Edmond Stapfer's *La Palestine au temps de Jésus-Christ*:

Miró	Stapfer
'Las enseñanzas rabínicas de la época de Jesús —escribe Edmond Stapfer— se resumían en estos dos términos: Practicad la Ley y esperad al Mesías. Unicamente practicando la Ley entraremos en el Reino de los Cielos. No se preguntaban entonces: Esto que hice ¿es bueno? ¿es malo? Sino: ¿Está permitido? ¿Está vedado? La religión no era sino una *gnosis* jurídica. Jesús rechaza la casuística farisáica. La deuda contraída con Dios no puede remitirse o satisfacerse por fórmulas legalistas, sino con actos de fe y de amor, porque Dios es el Padre. El reino de los cielos de Jesús no es el de sus contemporáneos. Jesús lo espiritualiza y lo coloca en el corazón de sus	L'enseignement rabbinique de ses contemporains [1 line] se résumait, nous venons de le rappeler, en ces deux mots: Pratiquez toute la Loi et attendez le Messie, roi de la terre. [7 lines]. A quelles conditions entre-t-on dans le Royaume de Dieu? se demandaient ses contemporains. Ils répondaient: en pratiquant la Loi [3 lines]. On ne se demandait plus: ceci est-il bien? ceci est-il mal? mais: ceci est-il permis? ceci est-il défendu? La religion était devenue une science, une gnosis. [10 lines] il a rejeté toute la casuistique pharisienne; il a montré que la dette contractée envers Dieu est inexorable et qu'il n'y a d'espoir que si Dieu remet toute cette dette et sans condition

[177] Ramos, *Literatura*, p. 306: cf. Cabrol, *La oración de la Iglesia* (Barcelona, 1909), p. 240.

discípulos... Le arranca los signos de fausto, las esperanzas políticas.

(Ramos, *Literatura*, p. 311)

aucune. Or, il la remet, car il est 'le Père'. [1 page]. Quant au Royaume de Dieu lui-même, il le spiritualise, il le place dans le coeur de ses disciples.

(Paris, n.d., pp. 468-70)

There is no indication in Miró's text as we have it as to where the quotation ends. Possibly 'discípulos' is the last word. But both before and after the quotation Miró draws on ideas provided by Stapfer — the quotation is merely the high point of a passage derived from his work. In the quotation itself the usual stylistic changes appear, but in this case what is important is the way in which Miró adapts Stapfer's theology to his own view of the significance of Christ. He leads up to this by a series of alterations that change Stapfer's emphasis. Stapfer presents the Pharisaic attitude of Jesus's time as a degeneration; he writes: 'On ne se demandait plus... .' Miró removes the Pharisees' attitude from this particular historical context: 'No se preguntaban entonces: (...).' Later Miró writes: 'La religión no era sino (...)' for Stapfer's 'La religion était devenue...' What for Stapfer is an historical conflict is for Miró a timeless one and the same one that is exemplified in so much of his work and especially in the Oleza novels.

A far more serious shift follows. In the sentence beginning: 'La deuda contraída con Dios', Miró starts by dropping the phrase 'il a montré' — again the statement is made less historical, more timeless — and from this he goes on to a statement that is radically different from Stapfer's but which accords very well with the ethic of the Oleza novels. Stapfer states the orthodox, traditional position with regard to the reconciliation of God and man: man's debt to God can only be cancelled by God — He does cancel it because He is the Father. Miró, on the other hand, purporting to translate Stapfer, presents Christ as telling us that the debt cannot be cancelled by obeying legalistic prescriptions but only by 'acts of faith and love'. That is, man can save himself. On this point Miró's version is not merely radically different from, but in total opposition to Stapfer's. Stapfer sees Christ as objecting, not to legalism *per se,* but to the Pharisaic notion that man, by obedience to the law, can save himself. From an orthodox point of view, Miró has fallen into the essential Pharisaic error of believing that man can redeem himself without the grace of God.

There could scarcely be better evidence as to the nature of Miró's departure from orthodoxy. This error in a crucial point of soteriology shows clearly how much he was in agreement with liberal theologians of the nineteenth century in seeing Christ as the bringer of a new ethic rather than of the reconciliation of God and man. The notions of atonement and redemption are simply not important to him and this is why he is able to misrepresent Stapfer to his audience.

But there is a further complication. Miró in quoting Stapfer not only translated incorrectly, but also omitted part of Stapfer's argument. The most significant change made in this way is to remove references to Jesus preaching justification by faith. The omission, of course, makes Stapfer's insistence on man's inability to save himself appear even more emphatic, and it makes it particularly curious that Miró should then have moved in the other direction in translating. But it suggests an explanation other than theological ignorance. Perhaps Miró was attempting to make a Protestant text acceptable to a Catholic audience: perhaps he knew enough theology to remove references to justification by faith, but in the process revealed his own prejudices.

Whatever the answer, the relevance to the Oleza novels is obvious. Don Magín is a Christ-like figure who acts from love rather than in accordance with the law. It is this replacement of the law by love that Miró sees as Christ's purpose, rather than the redemption of man.

Another scholar of whose work Miró made use was Maria Benedictus Schwalm, whose *La Vie privée du peuple juif* he mentions in the Gijón lecture. He does not quote, but draws upon eight pages from Schwalm to build up one of his own. [178] Miró had this work bound in Barcelona and it is marked — it was almost certainly an important source for the *Figuras.*

Finally, two more names appear in the Gijón lecture: 'De las descripciones de Víctor Guerin, De Sanley y otros palestinólogos, se infiere que la botánica y la geología de la Judea, de la Galilea y de Samaria tienen semejanzas con las variadas regiones de mi país.'[179] 'De Sanley' is evidently a misprint for De Saulcy, more fully know as Félicien Caignart de Saulcy, author of an *Histoire d'Hérode* that Miró owned and which he evidently, from the markings in it, used to prepare projected *Figuras.* Of Victor Guérin, Miró possessed three works. Here he is thinking of the *Description ... de la Palestine,* a work used again later, in the article 'El turismo y la perdiz' where Miró quotes from the part dealing with Galilee. [180]

In the same year in which Miró published 'El turismo y la perdiz', 1930, there appeared two articles entitled 'Cuaresma'. In the first of these the last two pages are composed of material drawn almost en-

---

[178] Ramos, *Literatura,* pp. 309-10: cf. Schwalm, op. cit. (Paris, 1910), pp. 169-76.
[179] Ramos, *Literatura,* p. 314.
[180] *Glosas,* p. 109: cf. Guérin, op. cit., Pt. III, *Galilée* (Paris, 1880), I, 213-214.

tirely from three works in Miró's library. First comes a paragraph drawn from Duchesne's *Origines du culte chrétien,* then two paragraphs from Kellner's *El año eclesiástico,* and finally three paragraphs from Guéranger's multi-volume *L'Année liturgique.* [181] There is scarcely a sentence in these two pages, which offer a short history of the celebration of Lent, that cannot be found in these three books. In this case Miró follows his sources fairly faithfully, merely selecting and omitting as is necessary to his purpose. However, both Guéranger and Duchesne were late acquisitions, bound in Madrid, so that they could not have been used for the *Figuras.*

In *Nuestro padre San Daniel* Miró is at pains to show that Don Magín is open to modern Biblical scholarship. To do this he has Magín discuss the various flood myths and later he shows him studying a map of Assyria. A series of names of eminent Assyriologists appears: George Smith and François Lenormant in connection with the flood (*OC,* pp. 801-2), and these two again, as well as Eberhard Schrader, J. Menant, and Rodwell, in the library of the bishop's palace, where Don Magín is studying (*OC,* pp. 859-60). Another orientalist, Sir Henry Rawlinson, makes an appearance in *Años y leguas,* though here some error has crept in, since Sir Henry was President of the Asiatic Society from 1878 to 1881, and not in 1836, as Miró suggests (*OC,* p. 1184). It is doubtless as a result of this interest in Assyriology that Miró quotes, also in *Años y leguas* (*OC,* p. 1128), from 'los Anales de un Rey asirio'.

* * *

In 1927 Miró published the final version of *Del vivir.* It included the following words:

> Los leprosos no se arrastraban por las rúas; no clamaban ni se amontonaban ni hervían como gusanos. Habitaban las más retraídas calles; en la última del pueblo, en la más honda, se ha-bían espesado.
>
> (*OC,* p. 10)

A year later he published the final version of *Años y leguas,* and, in the chapter 'Sigüenza y Sigüenza', he quotes his own words, referring to the Sigüenza of more than twenty years before:

> 'Los leprosos no se arrastraban por las callejas, no clamaban, no hervían como gusanos; habitaban en las más retraídas; y

---

[181] *Glosas,* pp. 98-100: cf. Duchesne, op. cit. (Paris, 1925), pp. 254-61; Kellner, op. cit. (Barcelona, 1910), p. 138; Guéranger, op. cit., V (Paris, 1925), pp. 4-11.

13

en la última del pueblo, en la más honda, se habían espe-
sado ...'

(OC, p. 1135)

The passage, first published in 1904, remained untouched in the revisions of *Del vivir* of 1918 and 1927, yet in *Años y leguas* Miró deals with his own prose as he had dealt with others'. The urge to seek constantly a more perfect expression never deserts Miró whether he is working on book, article, or lecture, on fiction, criticism, or 'recreation'.

The quotations take us back to *Del vivir* and the early years of the century, the starting-point for exploring the literary background of Gabriel Miró through his critics, his library, and his reading. This exploration has involved assumptions about the nature of Miró's work, and the next chapter, on *Del vivir*, attempts at one and the same time to justify those assumptions and to show how the exploration may help towards a better understanding of Miró. The argument is perfectly circular, but it presents, I hope, a picture of Gabriel Miró that coheres in a plausible fashion.

IV

MIRÓ AT WORK: *DEL VIVIR*

Gabriel Miró published *Del vivir* in 1904. As E. L. King writes:
'He was suddenly ready to speak for the person that he truly was in the
volume *Del Vivir*' (*Humo,* p. 34). The volume, as King carefully
describes it, was written in 1902 and 1903 and became the earliest of
Miró's work to be retained in his *Obras completas.* This alone gives it
great importance among Miró's work: it corresponds to the end of a
period of rapid development, of searching that is reflected in library
and reading. But it has a further importance. Because Miró retained
it he revised it, so that the version available today, based on the last
revision published in 1927, is considerably more polished than that of
1904. An intermediate revision was also published, in 1918, different
in many ways in its guiding principles from the 1927 revision, so that
Miró offers us the opportunity to compare his practice at the start of
his career, shortly after the *Figuras,* and shortly after *El obispo leproso,* three crucial moments in his writing life. Thanks to the
painstaking work of Pedro Caravia (never yet, as far as one is aware,
utilised in the study of Miró), variants are listed at the end of each
volume of the *Edición conmemorativa* of Miró's work — in the case
of *Del vivir* in Volume I. It is thus possible not only to see how Miró
wrote *Del vivir* in those important years, but to see to some extent
how he regarded his early work and in what respects he disagreed
with his earlier writing. The changes are almost all of detail, but they
add up to a considerable tautening of the work — Miró removes
sentences and phrases that labour a point already made, he gets rid
of unnecessary linking expressions, he changes occasional words to
achieve a meaning that is less harsh, less assertive, or less simplifying,
and he takes away most of the italicised dialect spellings of the first
version. The only change on a large scale is the removal, mentioned
before, of a long footnote in Chapter X, dealing with 'amor', that is a

direct reflection of Miró's contemporary fascination by ideas: social, philosophical, and psychological.

A study of *Del vivir,* for all these reasons, is a useful peg for a summary. The critical atmosphere in which Miró worked and which set up the problems concerning Miró that need answers, and Miró's reading and use of his reading in his work: these suggest a certain kind of writer. The question now is whether Miró's work and these details about his literary background form a coherent whole. Furthermore, to set one of Miró's texts alongside this background offers a valuable perspective. For instance, it is clear that Miró made great use of material quarried from books in the composition of his work. But a glance at *Del vivir* completes this observation, puts it back into balance, for it is equally clear how much Miró depends directly on the observation of reality. So much so, that the reader is constantly uneasy as to whether he is in the field of fiction or that of travel and autobiography. The reader constantly puzzles as to whether a fact or an anecdote is true, in the sense of not being fiction. There is a feeling that an imagined 'fact' would be a betrayal of the reader's trust, and a consequent slipping into the acceptance of *Del vivir* as a record of a journey, even though Miró uses narrative conventions from fiction and Sigüenza behaves as a fictional character. But when, for instance, Sigüenza is shown a book about leprosy in the district he is visiting, the sense of unease reappears. Surely Miró must have seen this book, surely the book exists — we refer constantly to the author, not just to the 'yo' of the narration, but to Gabriel Miró, the man behind it all. Even in a typical realist novel the reader does not make this demand, for the writer is allowed to describe the detail of a room that he has imaginatively reconstructed from many rooms: a novelistic room that is more of a room than any real room (to borrow from Ortega). But *Del vivir* evidently does not allow for even so limited a use of the imagination. Miró uses reality (allowing the hares that the term raises to race away unpursued), in a peculiarly direct way. *Del vivir* makes this very obvious, but it is present in the construction of all Miró's fiction: the characters, places, and anecdotes of the Oleza novels are examples. Miró takes chunks of the real world and reorders them into a whole that imposes his vision on them. But this is not to say that he is more realist than the realists. For the realist the operation of imaginatively transforming real rooms into a new room that captures the essence of the real rooms is his object in writing. For Miró the fact that he uses his material directly indicates that it is the ordering of it that is important.

Naturally, the record of Miró's experience of reality that forms the raw material of his work is valuable in itself. The details of the valley around Parcent and the village itself are often magnificently conveyed. Jesús Sampelayo and Sadi de Buen in their *La lepra y el problema de la lepra en España* (Madrid, 1923), writing on 'Trastornos mentales de la lepra' offer confirmation of Miró's accurate recording: 'Este complejo carácter y este fondo mental de los leprosos, aun mejor que en tratados de medicina, que todos ellos le dedican poco o ningún espacio, lo hemos encontrado maravillosamente descrito en la novela «Del vivir», de Gabriel Miró' (p. 102). Miró's intense faithfulness to the evidence of all his senses and his insight into spiritual reality are constantly apparent.

Yet Miró does not hesitate to alter the facts on occasion. He wrote *Del vivir* in 1902 and 1903, yet in the 1904 and 1918 editions he dates the two parts in 1903 and 1904 and clearly implies that he visited Parcent for the first and second time in those years : yet again the sort of thing that makes the reader uneasy, but evidence that for Miró reality is raw material only.

But though the experience of visiting Parcent provided Miró with the basic material for *Del vivir,* his reading remains an important source, and it is made very plain in the course of the book. In the main body of the text are more than a dozen quotations, while the 1904 footnote includes a further six. Altogether two dozen different writers are quoted or referred to. Those who appear in the footnote are used quite straightforwardly as part of the discussion : Lull, León Hebreo, Luis de Granada, Moreto, Feijoo, Plutarch, Grotius, Rousseau, de Staël, Fourier, Zola, Goethe, Schopenhauer, and Tolstoi. In the narrative itself quotations have more varied functions. In a few cases they are authoritative pronouncements that show how behaviour in the book is in agreement with what men of eminence have observed (*OC,* pp. 10 and 29), although in the latter case the maxim (Epictetus : do not talk about your own deeds too much), is modified by the narrator's comment that 'esto no encaja por Sigüenza y el médico (...) sino por los otros que también querían hablar de sus andanzas'. Alternatively, a quotation can explain and sum up a situation (*OC,* pp. 46, 51, and 56/57 [Juan Manuel and St. Teresa]). A reference can work in the same way. Sigüenza's guide is 'este otro Sancho'. Sigüenza thus immediately becomes a new Don Quixote (*OC,* p. 32). Or sometimes a reference can be merely illustrative (*OC,* pp. 27 and 40). All these quotations and allusions are introduced directly by the narrator to help in his task of conveying what is happening. Other quotations are presented as expressions of the thoughts of characters (*OC,* pp. 22, 45, 59, and 61). And once a character himself quotes. The innkeeper addresses Sigüenza : '— Vámonos, vámonos, señor de *Sigüensa* — repetía —. Pues «nada hay tan importuno como el hambre», que dijo Homero en su *Odisea*' (*OC,* p. 24).

The remark is somewhat incongruous in the mouth of the rough landlord. Curiously, in the 1904 and 1918 versions, the dash after 'repetía' is missing, and the words 'el divino' appear before Homer; originally it was the narrator who quoted, not the landlord. Presumably this is a rather unsuccessful attempt in 1927 to reduce authorial comment.

Almost all these quotations and references have been dealt with earlier: it is only necessary here to draw the evidence together. Just as Miró uses reality very directly, so he initially used quotations from other writers as if they were nuggets inserted into his own text. The positioning, the context of these quotations often makes them useful within the work, but they inevitably introduce a certain rigidity. It is as if Miró were not certain that he had achieved the effect he wanted, and therefore added a quotation to make all clear. A resonance of authority is added at the cost of Miró's own subtlety. In the later revisions he several times removed sentences and phrases that were over-explanatory — this suggests the same unsureness as a young writer that led to the excessive use of quotation. Though Miró had mastered the technique of recording what his senses told him, he had still not managed to deal in a fully novelistic way with the moral ideas that fascinated him.

If Miró in *Del vivir* records, orders, and speculates, the title reflects these aspects of the work. It is 'from life': its scenes are taken directly from the living reality that Miró has observed. It is 'from the life' (there is an echo of the artist's expression 'Del natural', earlier used as a title by Miró): that is, it is an artistic ordering of what is observed — Miró's time spent in his uncle's studio is evident in this. And it is 'about life', or rather 'about living'; it deals with the problems of pain and suffering and the 'falta de amor'. These three aspects must be taken together if the feeling of uneasiness on reading *Del vivir* is to be allayed. What sort of a work are we dealing with? Description, or fiction? Is it a unity, or a collection of 'apuntes'? Is Miró a 'paisajista', or an 'estilista'? And what is the status of Sigüenza? Is he a character or the author's mask? A glance at Vicente Ramos's collection of theories on the subject shows the puzzlement it has caused (*Mundo*, pp. 137-40). Ramos himself settles for Juan Chabás's 'Sigüenza es Sigüenza y Miró'. But surely the knot of theory can be simply cut by viewing Sigüenza as a fictional character. Doubtless he is in many ways very close to Miró, but many novelistic characters more or less embody at least parts of their author. For Miró, Sigüenza was a convenient means of self-analysis; for the reader he remains a character. The function of Sigüenza is that he forms the last link in a conventional chain leading from Miró to the narrator to the hero, a chain that allows context and perspective to be brought to bear on the hero's thoughts and actions. It seems to me that by paying close attention to the narrative technique of *Del vivir,* it is possible both to escape the confusing discussions over genre, and to approach Miró's meaning more closely.

Miró learned from his reading of the Spanish classics. From Cervantes and the picaresque novel he learned that plot is not the only means of articulating a work of fiction. In *Del vivir* a surface unity is provided by a hero who moves from episode to episode, and a deeper thematic unity lies beneath: the technique of *Don Quixote* and of the picaresque. The narration itself, however, is not in terms of the first person, as in the picaresque, nor through so impressive a chain of dubious authorities as in *Don Quixote.* Instead a conventionally omniscient narrator observes and tells the story. In the final version this narrator appears rarely. He speaks of 'un santo que mi mujer tiene en una estampa' (*OC,* p. 30), uses the expression 'dejémoslo' (*OC,* p. 30), and later comments on Sigüenza: 'Yo sé que en su interior tildábase de sandio y se desesperaba' (*OC,* p. 39). A little further on he seems to have lost his direct knowledge of affairs when he uses the expression 'cuentan que le interrumpió Sigüenza' (*OC,* p. 49). In the versions of 1904 and 1918 there were further first-person references that Miró removed in 1927. Evidently he then felt it better that the narrator should not intrude, even if he left the reference to 'mi mujer', and the 'yo sé' that implies the identity of the feelings of Miró and Sigüenza at this point. The passages removed were more obviously redundant: a 'yo no sé si (...)' (*DVi,* p. 117), or the comment: 'Yo apunto la historia', when the doctor tells Sigüenza an anecdote (*DVi,* p. 173). Two other passages cut out forced the narrator more strongly into the foreground: 'Pero yo no voy a pararme en esta y en todas cuantas futilezas preocupen a Sigüenza. Y me restituyo al zaguán donde aquél estaba mudo y admirativo' (*DVi,* p. 130). For all Miró's new and personal technique, he has still not broken with nineteenth-century narrative convention. In Chapter X, after a passage on the 'paisaje', the narrator exclaims '¡Paisaje mío!' (*DVi,* p. 183), an addition that, as Miró obviously realised later, intruded the personality of the narrator confusingly into the narrative. From all these changes emerges clearly an author concerned to establish a narrator, but in 1904 not yet very precise in his handling of the conventions of story-telling. Again, this is part of the explanatory over-statement noticed in the use of quotation.

When the narrator is not using the first person he still frequently comments on the action, and a good number of these comments, too, are removed in the 1927 version. A crippled boy watches other boys playing: 'Admiraba el ruido de pisadas y las huellas de pies; él hacía ruido de palo, de cosa; él pendía de muletas; y no jugaba ni braceaba; no hablaba ni reía con tono fuerte' (*OC,* pp. 26-7). In the first version

Miró had written: 'Admiraba con tristeza de celos el ruido (...)' This kind of narrator's comment is common in *Del vivir*, but Miró on many occasions in 1927 removed it. A few examples will suffice; the 1904 text is given, with the words removed in 1927 in brackets: '¡Oh, Sigüenza la odió con ferocidad! (¡El que antes se enterneciera con los solitarios del remanso! Mas, fue odio que se apagó luego.)' (*OC*, p. 5; *DVi*, p. 16), '¿Qué no era nada subir hasta renquear por aquella sierra quemante, resbaladiza? (Ya olvidaba que *estaba puesto* y que horas atrás gallardeóse.)' (32/106), '¡Cómo! «¿Otra piedra debo arrojarle; otra?» (Y se revolvió iracundo al descenderle esta idea al pecho.)' (33/109), 'El paisaje ha respirado la fragancia de sus entrañas generosas. Está quieto bajo la inundación de oro. («¡Amadme, comprendedme!» —pide.)' (57/193). These examples make clear the polishing process that *Del vivir* underwent and the enormous advances in narrative technique that Miró had made by 1927, the year in which he wrote: 'Creo que en «El obispo leproso» se afirma más mi concepto de la novela: decir las cosas por insinuación.' In revising Miró alters or cuts, he never adds, and of the more important changes a significant number are concerned with narrative rather than descriptive matters.

To set this in perspective let us look at all the corrections of a sample section. In the first two chapters Pedro Caravia notes over one hundred alterations. Almost exactly half of these were made in 1918, but of these, three-fifths were rejected in 1927 and the original reading restored, while a further quarter were altered a second time in 1927. Only eight corrections made in 1918 remain in the final version. Instead 1927 saw fifty-odd entirely new corrections. Clearly the two sets of corrections were made according to different principles. Miró must have had the 1918 edition to hand when he carried out the 1927 alterations, so that the rejection of the majority of the earlier emendations was a conscious affair. The principles Miró used are not entirely clear-cut, but a good deal emerges. In 1918 Miró removed almost none of the explanatory narrative passages mentioned above. This sort of cut had to wait until 1927. Indeed, in 1918, Miró cut out very little, most changes involving exchanging one word for another; and most of these exchanges seem to attempt to remove some of the more unusual words and expressions: 'negral verdor' is removed, 'sus cruces (...) linean sobre el azul' becomes 'tiemblan sobre el azul', 'greñas verdosas' change into 'árboles viejos', 'hedor a quemazón de casco' becomes 'hedor a casco quemado', and so on (*EC*, I, 255). Sometimes there is a tendency to more everyday syntax: 'Era en el valle de Jirona' is modified to 'Era el valle del Jirona' (*EC*, I, 255). All these examples were restored to the original reading in 1927; Miró seems to have become then more interested in polishing the narrative style, while respecting the original manner of expression. However, the use of *s* for *c* and *z*, and *-ao* for *-ado* in words italicised to render dialect pronunciation was spared in 1918, but usually rejected in 1927, leaving only particular dialect words here and there. Similarly, the regional diminutive *-ico/-ica* is removed on two occasions in 1927. Taken together, the 1927 corrections, with their much higher incidence of deletions as opposed to changes, produced a much tauter, more controlled and unified text, while in 1918 the new version mostly removed a certain number of idiosyncrasies.

Miró was, then, concerned with the narrative context of *Del vivir*, and this concern offers a way out of the puzzles over genre that perplex the reader. Yet the final section, addressed to the reader, offers a further problem. What is the status of this addition to the main text? Once again the reader has the feeling that if it were not in a sense factually accurate he would have been betrayed. Indeed the narrator addresses the reader in a matter-of-fact way: 'Aquí lo escribo porque son cosas que supe después de hacer las anteriores páginas' (57/195). [1] And later: 'El Sr. D. Hermenegildo Poquet no es figura de artificio, colocada aquí por antojo; no lo finjo' (61/205). Yet these are conventional devices in the nineteenth-century novel. Furthermore, these additional pages offer to a certain extent answers to the dismal conclusions of the main text. Sigüenza appears a changed man in some respects; and he meets at last the one man who does love the lepers. The coincidence between reality and the needs of the work only serves to increase the ambiguity of the status of these last pages.

What sort of a book, then, is *Del vivir*? In the first place, clearly, it is about the suffering of the lepers of this area of Alicante, and, above all, about their mental suffering. Sampelayo and de Buen testify to Miró's understanding of this. The lepers are cut off from society by society; they are taught to keep themselves alone. The innkeeper says, with the air of one totally confident of the social order: 'Ellos mismos se aíslan. Muy pocos tienen menester de *aviso*. Y aun éstos, con dos o tres veces que uno se aparte de ellos, les sobra para comprender que deben huir de los sanos antes que los sanos no les huyan' (10/33). Repeatedly Miró uses sexual parallels to illustrate this exclusion. Their plight is that of the eunuch (11/36). An anecdote concerns a leper-woman assaulted and then abandoned 'al darse la mujer a la dicha' (16/52), the victim of selfish 'amor'. Another leper-woman, through the dignity of her retiral from human society, turns her exclusion into a kind of chastity. The curious Sigüenza attempts to see her, to penetrate

[1] From here on, all quotations are from the 1904 edition. References are given to *OC* and to *DVi*, thus: 10/33 means *OC*, p. 10, *DVi*, p. 33.

her privacy: 'Ella era la Diana de la fealdad. Contemplarla era sa-
crílego' (39/128). She, too, though she accepts it with dignity, is excluded, and suffers as a woman in enforced chastity: '¡Y el goce se
alejaba como otro caminante muy cruel que sólo oía la risa y la voz de
los cuerpos bellos, fuertes, sin lepra!' (42/138). The figure of the 'caminante' links these two leper-women, one dignified and withdrawn,
the other full of hatred and envy, and links both with the theme of
sexual deprivation that for Miró illustrates the cruelty with which society strips lepers of the pleasures of human company. In between the
two passages quoted above, Miró offers the contrast of a vulgar and
petty 'tertulia', the rejecting society.

The suffering of the lepers is presented in the context of nature:
the lepers, like all men, are an integral part of the natural world. Sigüenza, for instance, at the end of the 'tertulia', wanders out and reflects on the 'Diana de la fealdad': 'Acaso, ahora, la sacudía el mandato al goce de la noche ardorosa, sensual, tocada con terciopelo prendi-
do de diamantes de estrellas' (42/138). Yet she is cut off from the possibility of pleasure. For Sigüenza the world around us issues an imperative to compassion and enjoyment; the agony of the leper is to know
that the longing that nature arouses will inevitably be unsatisfied. This
context of an active nature of which the deprived leper is a part is
given great prominence throughout *Del vivir,* showing the complexity,
variety, and closeness of man's relationship to his surroundings. Man
is seen as an integral part of the world. This is reflected, for instance,
in the way in which the senses mingle as participants in nature: 'Frecuentemente tropieza la mirada en un vallado' (4/12-13). The landscape
is totally active; much more than any statement of the narrator or
of Sigüenza, the language conveys this. Again and again, verbs of
action are used: 'Cegaban, dando sol, las puertas' (3/10), 'El paisaje
luce primores' (3/10), 'Los [casales] ve emerger de los sembrados,
asomar entre greñas verdosas, altear limpiamente en la montaña' (4/
12), 'La viña, la viña invadíalo todo, derramándose en lagos anchurosos'
(4/12). The senses of the observer take in this constantly active world
and feel themselves a part of it. The relationship is a two-way one:
at times the senses act on the observed world — the eye stumbles on
a 'vallado' — and at others the eye strives to report exactly what falls
on it without attempting to translate these sensations into some reality
presumed to underlie them. In so doing the eye admits the independent
life of the shapes and colours of the landscape. Abstract nouns replace
mere qualifying adjectives: 'negral verdor', 'una muy viciosa y aroman-
te espesura de dondiegos', 'un vallado de verdor espeso' (4/11-13). Colours and shapes become active enough to provoke verbs: 'verdean li-
ños infinitos de lujuriantes y caprichosas moreras' (3/11), 'sus piecezue-

los amarilleaban bajo la limpia agua' (4/13), 'rojea fuertemente la tierra' (5/15), 'sus cruces (...) linean sobre el azul' (4/11) — Miró's painterly training is very evident here. Moral and emotional qualities are perceived in the landscape: the 'espesura de dondiegos' is 'muy viciosa'. All these examples are from the first few pages alone — they are part of the regular practice of Miró's writing, not occasional flourishes.

Many critics have observed what goes with this language — the humanisation of nature. A favourite example is: 'Por unas bardas se descolgaban brazos de parra mustiada; brazos que se retorcían de desesperación y ansia como de cuerpo que busca el goce de la libertad y anchura' (5/17). Or with non-living things: 'la bocina que otorgaba el paro del trabajo' (7/22). This is not simply humanisation, but an aspect of the assumption that man is only one element of the natural world. For the reverse of humanisation appears also: 'En el cauce blanco y pedregoso se enjambraban hombres' (6/20). Men in swarms like insects, or else, as here, mere things no different in status from any other element of the landscape: 'Poníanse los hombres diagonales al suelo' (7/21). The pictorial treatment attacks the homocentric sense of the world that most of us share. When we observe a landscape, a man draws the eye in a quite different way from a tree, a rock, or a bird. Only the recording of the direct sense-perception can avoid this trick that the mind immediately plays with the information it receives, and thus show man's true situation.

The suffering of the lepers is, then, constantly in this context of a suffering, feeling, active world, of which man is an integral part. The problem of pain and suffering with which Miró is to grapple is a cosmic one — man's pain is not his own personal problem but a consequence of his being subordinated to natural forces.

The most extended passage dealing with the landscape in this way has been somewhat modified and shortened in the 1927 edition. It is therefore worth looking at the first version at some length. Sigüenza is up in the *sierra*:

> La blanca rambla, dos veces se la ve rasgar el llano. Miraba Sigüenza esas blancas máculas —dos trozos de papel caídos sobre el viñal—. Y la rambla se le antojó un ser apesarado con la punición eterna de arrastrarse seca en estío, cubierta de aguas gruesas, sucias, en días invernales por la campaña solitaria.
>
> Cosas, lugares, paisajes, miran, expresan grandemente. Acaso ese mirar y esa expresión irradian del alma que los contempla... Mas, no; tienen la suya soberana. Los paisajes, aunque sean pomposos, espléndidos en extremo, muestran siempre así... como una mueca ¡mueca, no! un gesto, un suavísimo

gesto de tristeza... ¡Campos y serranía, tan poderosos, tan in-
mensos, y la mano del labriego los desune, los cambia, los
sujeta; y el arado los desgarra con herida lenta y sutilísima;
el azadón los despedaza; los rompe el barreno... Y ellos, sin
voluntad, generosos, resignados... ¡siendo tan grandes! Los
oscurece la noche y quedan quietísimos: las frondas en sus
abrazos, las aguas en su correr forzado por el abierto suelo...
Y los alumbra la mañana y continúan pasivos; con los mismos
enlaces de ramas, con la misma distribución de verdores, igua-
les cruzamientos de arroyos y sequedades pedregosas... Viven
bellamente la calma.

Lluvias o recios vientos los rompen, los asuelan. Y ellos
grandes, quietos, resignados, esperando, esperando siempre. No
se ven amados del hombre; no es comprendida su soledad...
¿Cómo, las almas no se dejan inundar de las dulzuras de los
campos y serranía? Por eso, porque no las sienten, es su tristeza. Esperan el amor del hombre. ¿Por qué no amarlos; por
qué no agradecer tiernamente sus bellezas? Ellos se afligen
con el mudo padecer de la hermosa a quien no se admirase;
del artista, solo, incomprendido por indiferencia aniquiladora...

La pompa infinita de la viña llamó la mirada de Sigüenza.

(31/101-103).

The two long paragraphs, sandwiched between two reflections of
Sigüenza's, seem also to belong to his stream of thought. All the
characteristics of Miró's writing noted above are present: the verbs
of action for nature, the abstract nouns investing qualities with inde-
pendence, description in terms of immediate sense-perception ('blancas
máculas'), the perception of emotional and ethical feeling in the landscape (specifically 'la suya soberana', not the Romantic 'landscape is a
state of the soul'), and the personification of nature. The 'rambla'
drags its way burdened with eternal punishment through the solitary
countryside. Not only is this the world of which the leper and man
are integral parts, but there is constantly a direct parallel with the
leper's suffering. The vocabulary presents it: 'máculas', 'arrastrarse',
'cubierta de aguas gruesas, sucias'. The themes of an eternal damna-
tion without possible relief and of extreme solitude are also ones that
are associated with the lepers.

This landscape is hurt and destroyed by man; it remains unloved
and not understood. Man fails to respond to nature's imperative, fails
to understand his own relationship with the natural world. Only the
artist responds to suffering nature and he too is ignored by his fellow-
men. Sigüenza, of course, is an artist-figure, sharing his author's view

of the Artist as some kind of priest. Artist, leper, and nature share a common exclusion from society. [2]

The making one of nature and man appears not only through the language and as part of the ideas that shape Sigüenza, but it is also used in the narration of the work. Again and again a natural sound or sight is inserted into the narrative. In the episode of the tramp and the leper-woman an insect sounds a counterpoint to the anecdote. When it falls silent the tramp hears the slight sounds made by the leper-woman. Later the insect is pictured as sounding again in furious jealousy. He is alone. And the couple 'pensaron, un momento, en aquel insecto como se piensa en un hombre odioso' (16/52).

Often the sound of a fountain breaks in or a scent distracts. At the height of the tension between the leper Batiste and the men sent to uproot his tobacco plants, 'un pájaro cantó primorosamente' (36/118). Occasionally these inserted glimpses of nature flirt with the symbolic. As Sigüenza and the doctor ride back to Parcent the doctor tells sombre anecdotes of the district. He points out a tree where a father lay in wait for, and shot, his son. 'Distante, distante, rojeaban las llamas retorcidas y bulliciosas de una rastrojera que ardía.' He tells the story of a leper-woman's long and lonely decline after her friends rejected her: 'La rastrojera humeaba blanca y espesamente.' They reach Parcent where a happy, noisy group of boys 'saltaban una hoguera alta y crepitante... Del haz de fuego y del humo que subía retorciéndose brotaba desgranado el oro de las chispas' (53-54/173-176).

The suffering of the lepers is but a special case, an extreme case of the suffering of the universe that afflicts all men. The quotation from the Book of Job that stands at the head of *Del vivir* is faithfully quoted from Felipe Scio's translation of the Bible. But one word is added: 'Humanidad'. Job, instead of crying out to God, cries out to humanity: 'Clamo a ti y no me oyes: estoy presente y no me miras' (Job xxx. 20). Job presides over *Del vivir*, for Satan 'smote Job with sore boils from the sole of his foot unto his crown' (Job ii. 7), and in Miró's version a note by Scio suggests that some interpreters believe this to be leprosy. Later in *Del vivir* the eyes of a leper 'clamaban como Job', using the words of Job xix. 21: '¡Apiadaos de mí, apiadaos de mí, siquiera vosotros mis amigos, porque la mano del Señor me ha tocado!' (22/70). The whole of Job xix is an excellent example of the parallel between the plight of Job and the plight of the lepers — solitude, rejection by all, and the hatred even of servants and relatives are their common lot: 'I am an alien in their sight' (Job xix. 15). The

---

[2] In the 1927 edition Miró removed the four sentences beginning 'Por eso (...)', including the reference to the artist as a superior figure.

quotation from Epictetus '¡Oh Dios, llueve sobre mi calamidades!' (45/ 149) also relates to Job, through its derivation via Quevedo.

Job and the lepers cry out to 'Humanidad' in *Del vivir*. The typical answer is the unconsciously cruel, self-regarding one of the innkeeper, the man who teaches the lepers to avoid healthy men by shunning them a few times himself. His outlook and standards are those of village society in general. He enjoys teasing Batiste, a leper, about politics. Sigüenza never ceases to marvel that his comforts and satisfactions make him no more compassionate to the deprived. For he is fat and well-fed, while his house harbours a baby almost dying of starvation. When he pities, it is conventional; of a man who has lost all six sons, he says: '¡Con la falta que tiene de uno talludo para faenar en el campo! y así, o ha de estarse solo o pagarse un jornal' (12/38). What strikes him first is a commercial difficulty — reflecting Miró's loathing of 'los comerciantes'. Like the worthies of Ondara later on in the book, the innkeeper's values are self-centred and material.

There are many examples of such self-centred 'falta de amor' towards others. Women send the old men of the house out of doors to be rid of them. If they return, they are faced with 'Salga, abuelo, salga, que *la mucha casa* no es bueno' (26/82). Or, if the man is so senile that he cannot move, the women carry him outside ('Sí, *él, él* se distrae viendo jugar.'), and return, 'en sus rostros dulzuras de alivio, júbilo discreto, recatado. ¡Iban a faenar, a vivir, sin la muda inspección de aquel cadáver con los ojos abiertos!' (27/86). In each case the women disguise their own wishes as concern for the good of others.

The first main episode that Sigüenza meets is a catalogue of the appalling paradoxes that pain produces. A leper-mother, not allowed to feed her baby, hopes that it will be saved from starvation by the death of another baby. It is the grandmother who has forbidden the mother to feed her baby, although this is an apparently pointless precaution. In this situation the mother and grandmother pray, with the thought that the death of another may help them (18/57). When the other child does die, the mother blesses the Lord (20/63).

This woman is, of all the lepers, the most bitter about her sickness. She states most powerfully the problem of why she should be the one to suffer. She is offered by the grandmother the conventional reply: 'Habían de conformarse con la voluntad del Señor... ¡El Señor proveería!' (17/55). This draws a retort which is regretted as blasphemous. She finds no consolation, but merely hopes for men 'llenos de amor' to come with help. The Church, in fact, is consistently pictured as of no use to those suffering. Early on Sigüenza notes groups of women in Parcent praying and exclaims: '¡Es muy católico este pueblo!' (10/31) — the word 'católico' was changed to 'devoto' in later editions. The innkeeper replies: 'A estas horas acostumbran el *reso*. ¡Si no saben qué *haser*!... Y como se oyen unas a otras... pues les entran ganas' (10/ 32). Their prayer 'no es muy de iglesia', but instead is an expression of that majority society that excludes those who are different. Christian faith is seen as a part of the self-regarding outlook, its beliefs reduced to sentimental clichés, as in the 'cromo de la Virgen del Carmen' stuck above Sigüenza's bed at the inn: the faces 'traían a la memoria de Sigüenza los rostros impasibles de los figurines de sastrería' (14/16). Priests scarcely appear in *Del vivir*; when a seminarist is described he is repellent: 'Sus ojos eran negros, de un negro sucio como de tizne, y sus manos carnosas pedían la esteva o la podadera. Sudaba. Vociferaba brutalmente' (26/84). When he is called away from a game for a funeral, 'acabó enviando una ultrajosa maldición a la inocente madre de la campana, y a ésta y al cura y al muerto' (27/88). In the 1927 edition Miró slightly softened this portrait: the word 'ultrajosa' was removed, as was, a little earlier, the seminarist's thought on hearing the bell: '¡Dónde aflicción más insufridera!' (27/87). Similarly, the voice of the women praying is no longer 'gazmoñera', but 'plañidera' (10/31). The young Miró clearly felt strongly that the institution of the Church failed to carry out the Christian precepts that he admired so much. Hence the total absence of Christian love from Parcent. Where a leper is consoled by resigning himself to God's will, it is portrayed as an aspect of his beaten-down, broken spirit, and Miró immediately adds a quotation from Aeschylus's *Prometheus Bound* (sometimes compared with Job as a study of the problem of suffering). Prometheus explains why mortals have ceased to regard death with terror: '*Hice habitar entre ellos la ciega esperanza*' (46/150).

Man, then, lacks charity in his personal dealings with other men. This 'falta de amor' is incorporated into human society, including the Church, which has been captured by that society for its own ends. Miró offers examples of the cruelty of the organisation of society. In order to protect the tobacco monopoly, it is illegal for private individuals to grow it. A special force of men exists to see that this law is obeyed: 'Caminaban arrancando plantas de tabaco, porque así lo quieren algunos hombres que han creado el delito de cultivarlas y tenerlas' (28/92). One group of the poor pursue another for a crime that has been arbitrarily made so by a group of wealthy men. Again Miró was using reality very directly: this was a live issue at the time, with agitation for the repeal of an 1887 law in order to alleviate rural poverty. Miró sees clearly the mixture of social and personal forces that work together in this situation. Evils in a social system start from individuals — the wealthy who exploit and the exploited who are only in part helpless:

Sigüenza contempló a los de la ronda. Estaban abrasados, estenuados por buscar unas matas. Lo hacían forzados de un jornal miserable. ¡Los pobres!

Pero, los pobres, ¿por qué mostraban encendida la mirada, deseosa de la planta, y al verla se regocijaban y la arrancaban hasta brutalmente?

¿No era esto malquerer, dañar con voluntad inmensa, con voluntad horra de toda fuerza del hambre, libre de todo mandato odioso?

(35/115-16)

Some pages later Sigüenza witnesses a fable that draws together this portrait of society. He visits a farm and sees how a newly-purchased cock is rejected by the farmyard animals. The whole passage is full of personifications that refer this animal society to a human copy. Men are not only shown, as before, to be a part of their universe, but in a more traditional way, to behave like animals. The established leader of farmyard society, an aristocrat, fights and defeats the 'advenedizo', an 'hidalgo'. After the defeat, the hens, previously afraid or murmuring hypocritically, treat the defeated newcomer with scorn. But soon they are content to forget about him; their society has been momentarily threatened, but the outsider has been excluded and their confidence in themselves renewed; they can set about feeding. Miró conveys remarkably the way in which the successful overcoming of a threat merely serves to reinforce the intolerance and self-centredness of their society over against one who does not belong, though the members of that society had become fearful and hypocritical with the arrival of the threat. Much more sinister are the turkeys, 'hundidas las cabezas en la negra sotana de sus plumas'. The suggestion that they are the priests of this society is carried forward by their actions: they do not fight, but watch intently, throwing all their support on the side of the established leader. When the hens and cock forget the defeated intruder, they persist in pursuing him, until the call of food is too strong. When the outsider attempts to feed, a white turkey, like 'una aya inglesa', informs and the black turkeys 'lo acometieron con sus picos costrosos de salvado'. At night a riot ejects the newcomer from the hen-house and, 'a la entrada del sombrajo se apostaron los pavos, inmóviles, inexorables, siniestros como enlutados hombres y como hombres tenaces en su aborrecer, hasta sacrificar su descanso para dañar a sus hermanos...' (47-48/153-158). The priest-like turkeys end as ironic guardians at the gates of Paradise.

In the footnote removed after the first edition, Miró reflects on this lack of charity among men. He distinguishes between 'amor a todos' and 'amor a Dios, a la mujer, a la Ciencia, a la Belleza', and goes on: 'Engañosa o hipócritamente se piensa que como estos amores se siente o pueda sentirse aquél y que es natural ternura, origen y nacimiento de la caridad y de cuantas virtudes nos llevan a favorecer a nuestro prójimo' (*DVi*, pp. 184-5). This, Miró tells us, is a confusion not to be found amongst 'moralistas y sutilísimos *filógrafos*'. Since Christ understood the poverty of human affections, He commanded us to love every man. It was for this commandment that He was crucified (presumably, for Miró, another example of the social rejection of the outsider). Fray Luis de Granada, Miró continues, says that this is a difficult commandment, and points to man's likeness to God and to the fact that we are all 'hechos una misma cosa' (185), in order to help men obey it. We must *work* at loving our neighbour and see him not 'como a extraño, sino como imagen de Dios' (186).

Even in the most exalted love between man and woman, Miró goes on, there is a 'mezcla de egoísmo', and he cites Moreto in evidence: 'Quien ama con fe más pura, / Pretende de su pasión / Aliviar la pena dura' (186), followed by León Hebreo: 'El fin singular del amor es la delectación del amante en la cosa amada' (187). Perhaps the lover even seeks the selfish good of being loved. Perhaps Werther would not have died if his love had been free from selfishness. Miró concludes: 'Pues si en este particular amor tropezamos con la impureza de la busca febril del propio goce, ¡qué mucho, entonces, que se deslice el egoísmo (aunque de otro linaje) en el *amor práctico,* en la lástima por el mal ageno!' (188). In evidence of this Miró quotes *Del vivir* itself (four paragraphs in Chapter IX beginning: '¿No sentís piedad (...)?' — 51/ 167-8): pity for others is fed by fear of the same fate for ourselves. To love is to prefer, so that 'amor a todos' can only be achieved by the head. If it is suggested that the Spartans achieved a society where all men loved each other (Miró offers as an example of such love the old Spartan husband allowing his wife to have children by a younger man for the good of the race), then Miró answers that the Spartans loved not each other, but Lycurgus, their lawgiver. After his death, the introduction of money destroyed his work. And in any case, even the Spartans dealt cruelly with their enemies. In any future Utopia, Miró insists, love will not be its motivation.

The terminology is confusing. Miró in effect argues that 'amor a todos' cannot be achieved through 'amor': the reader must constantly be aware which 'amor' he has in mind. The terminology becomes particularly slippery in the passage on the Spartans: '¿No podríamos alcanzar otra Esparta sin aledaños, tan grande como el mundo, donde los hombres enseñados por Cristo se amasen universalmente, unos a otros? Debemos creer que no' (190). The difficulty is in 'amasen'. If Christ commanded 'amor a todos' and this *'lógrase con la cabeza',* then the argument that men will never love each other is no obstacle to a society of 'amor a todos'. On the other hand to compare Christ with Lycurgus implies that Christ's command, like that of Lycurgus, fails. In that case, why does Miró praise the wisdom of Christ in imposing love as a commandment?

But such difficulties in the argument are not very important here: it is plain where Miró's heart lies. What is important is how these ideas and the portrait of a suffering world work in the book itself. As Miró confesses on behalf of Sigüenza: 'Pero esta nota ¿era indispensable, necesaria? No, no lo era. Así lo reconoce. ¡A qué citar a nadie como autoridad y testimonio de que no amamos a todos, de que aparentamos afecciones insentidas, si nuestra alma triste y constantemente nos lo dice!' (192). The showing of insincere affection is newly introduced and is at the heart of Miró's dilemma. Love is by definition sincere, so that the suggestion that we should love by an effort of mind and will is repellent. Charitable action has to spring from this effort, but it must not be accompanied by 'afecciones insentidas'. This is the real reason for Miró's insistence on the complete separation of 'love' and 'charitable action' ('amor a todos'). [3]

As Sigüenza progresses through the book he offers the kind of ideas that have been discussed. But he is a character in a work of fiction and as such his statements and his actions are constantly modified by the context. Miró captures well the relationship of Sigüenza to the local inhabitants: they treat him with a respect that conceals their mixed feelings of puzzlement, amusement, and scorn for a useless observer. They constantly stare at him, and he is well aware that he does not belong. He is shy and sensitive to others. When he stops to watch ducks some washerwomen laugh at him and he at once moves on, causing, himself, through his sensitivity to others, 'en la región del dolor, la primera tristeza gustada por Sigüenza' (4/14). This self-defending timidity leads to what the narrator calls 'la palabrería del forastero' (49/159): he tries to please. It leads also to the fact that his emotions are wildly dependent on how people think of him; when his ass brays loudly in a village, he hates it (5/16). When both are out of sight, he loves it again. Why is this traveller 'hombre apartadizo'? Not merely to enjoy the landscape, for as he swings between self-doubt and an elusive self-confidence we see the contrasted but related states of mind of such an insecure nature. He sees himself as the lonely, mis-

[3] In passing, we learn that for Miró love is the 'elemento primero de la Estética'. How much better a starting-point for understanding Miró's aesthetic is this notion of love as its first element, than the 'embelleced la verdad' that is at the heart of the usual assessment.

understood artist; but he is also desperately dependent on what others
think of him. He is the lover of solitude; but he is also obsessively
concerned with himself: 'Estaba dominado aquella tarde de un feroz
egoísmo' (46/151), we read when Sigüenza refuses to chat to a farmer
whom he knows would be made happy by a listener. He is self-asser-
tive in his fantasies, but self-doubting as soon as reality destroys them.
He gives himself the noblest of intentions, but breaks down into self-
disgust when he fails.

Sigüenza is, of course, full of such illusions and fantasies. Here
is an example of the interplay of self-deception and crushing reality.
Sigüenza attempts to see a particularly ugly leper-woman:

> ... La vió Sigüenza desde lejos. Representóse su fealdad,
> que distinguirla no podía, porque él estaba en los primeros
> bancales de la lozana huerta.
> ...'Si yo me acercase, si yo me acercase..., ¡cuánto no me
> diría de su vida de inmunda! Los males desbastan el espíritu,
> lo agrandan y hermosean... Y esta mujer, al mostrarme la hon-
> dura de su pena, recibiría consuelo... ¡Si yo me acercase...!'

But he doesn't move, out of fear: 'Se preguntó. ¿Será lástima, respeto?
No, miedo, un miedo inefable' (38/125-6). Since he cannot actually
see her, he imagines her ugliness. He imagines his curiosity satisfied,
and to justify this low motive he adds a piece of conventional idealis-
tic wisdom to which he has earned no title: suffering polishes the
spirit. He finds a further justification — he will be helping her. But
the whole structure of fantasy collapses with a desperate, unsuccessful
attempt to disguise fear as pity.

On a much larger scale, Sigüenza is constantly behaving in this way.
He imagines ('finjióse', 3/9) that Parcent is 'un lugarejo hórrido', and
is disappointed to find that some people there are happy, revealing even
lower motives than mere curiosity. But perhaps the character of Sigüenza is best seen in the episode of the scorpion in Chapter VI. He
sets off with his usual mixed motives; he looks forward to '¡Un día
de monte, de silencio augusto y deleitoso!' (30/97), but also to seeing
the search for illicit tobacco. As he rides up the hillside he feels sorry
for his ass and for the guide, who is on foot. But he does not get off.
His conscience troubles him:

> Y para divertirla le dijo al rústico, muy admirativamente:
> —¡Cuidado si es usted fuerte! Eso, eso es subir, eso...
> ¿Y cómo puede resistir tanto? La verdad... yo, estaría aca-
> bando, y en cambio, usted... usted...
> —Está uno puesto —contestó jadeante el peón. Y gallar-
> deóse.

The scene of two liars playing out a game with each other is distinctly Cervantine.

After this Sigüenza rests and watches the landscape in the passage already studied (above, pp. 191-2) where he discerns nature's sadness at being unloved. The guide lies on his back with his hat over his face, while the ass grazes. Quotation can only hint at the wealth of suggestion of the next few pages, in which Miró goes to the heart of Sigüenza's personality. A deliciously sketched scene, in which Sigüenza offers to pay the guide handsomely and is hated for it, leads to this hatred being diverted onto a scorpion. The guide goes off to look for something with which to kill the scorpion: '¿Qué pensaba, qué apercibía aquel arriero? se interrogó Sigüenza ganoso de conocer el tormento, bien que prometiéndose enternecerse cuando se llegara su cumplimiento y hasta interceder piadosamente por la víctima.' His conscience worries him again. Why does he not chase the scorpion away?

> Y apeteciendo un motivo que le distragese de su discurso (ya punzador), miró al jumento. El jumento estaba, como si fuera hecho de argamasa, inmóvil; lánguido, el cuello; abatidas, las orejas. ¿A qué santo esa aflicción? —protestó Sigüenza con los nervios crispados. ¿Qué remordimientos le atenazaban? ¿Qué lucha le consumía? ¡Ah, hipócrita, indignado de ser asno, porque el asno es animal muy serio, que jamás usa de falacias y ficciones. ¡Mustiarse! ¡Mirar con amargor el valle! ¿De quién se dolía?

Not only does Sigüenza see in perspective his self-deceptions at this particular moment, but also his thoughts of a little while ago as he studied the landscape. It takes an ass to show his own fantasies for what they are: self-indulgence.

But he remains unable to act. He throws a stone, so half-heartedly that it does not reach the scorpion.

> ¡Qué sufrimiento tan agudo y necio! Y todo venía de ennoblecer los seres y cosas más ínfimos y humildes y concederles consideraciones de humanos, o lo que tal vez era más cierto y aflictivo, de bastardearse él, de envilecerse, no sofocando esos chispazos de crueldad que en todas las almas se producen.

Of course, in his more elated moments the treatment of animals as persons was a part of an ideal vision. But now the guide returns and Sigüenza can do nothing to save the scorpion. In any case, 'bicho más sandio y cachazudo no vió en su vida. Pudo escapar perfectamente. Debió escapar'. The progress from 'pudo' to 'debió' catches nicely the growing reassertion of self-interest on Sigüenza's part. Finally: 'Bueno; ahora veríamos.' All that remains is to watch. As the scorpion dies an agonising death, the guide comments: 'Parece que se estira, que se pone de pie, como una persona, ¿verdad?', emphasising the reverse change from men to beasts in the onlookers (33-4/108-12). This then, is Sigüenza's personality; ideals and cruelty, pride and self-disgust, solitude and self-indulgence, illusions and the self-inflicted wounds of illusions stripped away, all these spring inter-dependent from the one shy, insecure personality. A flatterer, a liar, a coward, a dreamer, an 'abúlico', suppressing his conscience, needing to be liked and understood, blaming others for his own faults, Sigüenza yet draws our sympathy as we see ourselves in him. For Miró it is a cruel self-examination, befitting an admirer of St. Teresa.

The clash between Sigüenza's ideals and his actions echoes throughout *Del vivir*. He condemns men for coming to study the lepers but doing nothing to help: exactly what he does with the scorpion. When the landlord is condemned for his selfish attitude to lepers, it is Sigüenza who does the condemning, thus exposing not only the innkeeper's selfishness, but his own. This kind of device is what one expects in a work of fiction, in a novel. The operation of a network of links, juxtapositions, contrasts, and perspectives, is everywhere evident. Sigüenza chooses solitude; the lepers have it forced upon them. The lepers are prevented from responding to nature's imperative; the villagers fail to perceive it; Sigüenza perceives it, feels its attraction, and fails to act. Or, a somewhat different example, when the women have to bring the crippled old man back into the house when the game is over, 'Sigüenza creyó que las dos mujeres mostraban desabrimiento y tristeza' (28/89). We are left wondering whether they did look sad, or whether Sigüenza's desire to see the 'falta de amor' he condemns is deluding him again.

At the end of the main part of *Del vivir* Sigüenza is about to leave. The innkeeper is laughing happily. Sigüenza notes the splendid morning: 'Es día para amarse.' But contrary to Sigüenza's supposition, the innkeeper is not happy because of life's goodness, but because of the discomfiture of a political boss: 'Ahora, está ahí', he explains, 'y se despulsa porque usted le salude y se pare a hablarle, para darnos después qué sentir... y usted ni le ha *mirao* tan siquiera. Yo lo he visto, y yo sé cómo estará por dentro... ¿Dise usted que si me río? ¡Pues no me he de reír!' (55/180).

Sigüenza reflects: 'He aquí (...) hombre que puede, que debe amar y nada más que amar a sus hermanos, a los brutos, a las cosas, a todo, a todo... Y ved que cría y anida odios bellacos.' In explanation he quotes Kant from the *Groundwork of the Metaphysic of Morals*. Kant distinguishes between a love that is inclination, that cannot be commanded, that is pathological, that resides in a tender sympathy; and a love that is a duty, that may have as its object someone or something repugnant, that is practical, that depends on the will and on ethical principles: the same distinction that Miró is soon to make in his footnote. [4] For Sigüenza this distinction explains the behaviour of the innkeeper. If inclination and charitable action are independent, then it is not surprising that Nature's imperative to love does not result in 'amor a todos'. The reader has already seen how this Nature-inspired love is a fickle thing, depending on the right surroundings; the poor ass suffered from its fickleness. And, as the narrator pointed out early on, 'si es en un ocaso tranquilo (...) se piensa en amar mucho, en amarlo todo' (6/20). For the distinction is of course also relevant to Sigüenza himself. No sooner has he pronounced Kant's words to himself than 'un pensamiento trivial, pueril, invadió a Sigüenza, deslizándose entre la metafísica del filósofo de Koenigsberg. ¿Hablaría o no al sujeto de patillas blancas, de alpargatas rudas y bastón tenido delicadamente?' (56/181). Inevitably Sigüenza fails to live up to the principles he has just stated; he ignores the 'cacique'. His inclinations override his duty. The only difference between Sigüenza and the innkeeper or the women with the crippled old man, is that Sigüenza knows his duty, while the others have convinced themselves that duty and inclination coincide; to put the old man outside is for his sake, not theirs. Sigüenza is both a walking contradiction of his own ideas, and a walking explanation of why they do not work.

The reader has now been offered all the material he needs. If he persists in seeing Sigüenza as a simple reporter or agrees with him that it is indeed sad that men do not love each other, without reflecting that such a notion without corresponding action is self-indulgence, then he too becomes a Sigüenza.

For the remainder of the main part of the text Miró recapitulates the major themes. As Sigüenza leaves he passes several of the characters he has seen. He goes out into the countryside that is 'como alma a quien no se comprende', and offers the parallel with the lepers: '¡Sus almas están solas!' He turns to himself, the other outsider, and admits: 'Amor no le llevó, sino la sed de ver.' He looks again and it is as if the landscape 'le trajese la visión de toda la tierra'. And this earth lacks love. When all is well, 'amor, entonces, place, conmueve,

[4] Immediately before the passage quoted, Kant writes: 'It is doubtless in this sense that we should understand the passages from Scripture in which we are commanded to love our neighbour and even our enemy' — another idea taken over into Miró's footnote.

regocija... pero luego se apaga, se torna en la acritud y sequedad de un deber'. Juan Manuel and St. Teresa are quoted in evidence, and then Miró offers one of his images from nature intruding into the narrative: an olive-tree, its trunk split into two, imitates with its branches 'dos viejos luchadores, acometiéndose ferozmente'. Men, sprung from one stock, fighting; two forms of love, struggling against each other. The despair of Sigüenza at all that should be in harmony, yet is divided, including even Sigüenza's own ambivalent personality, is expressed here (56-7/183-6).

Again Sigüenza looks back at Parcent and sees the farm where the two cocks fought, and sees the turkeys 'que odiaban y perseguían como los hombres'. Nature again intrudes as the guide stamps on an antnest. Sigüenza reflects that: 'Esos seres, modelos de sociables, también se acaban, se aniquilan en guerras estupendas...' (57/191-2). His misery at human conflict leads him for the first time to see cruelty even in that Nature that commands love. His last illusion, set in perspective by the ass up in the *sierra,* is destroyed.

If this thematic summary is repetitious, it is still important to show that this kind of thematic structure rules *Del vivir.* The care with which the last chapter completes and recapitulates what has gone before makes it clear that this is no simple travelogue. The sense of an ending is very much present.

By contrast, the additional pages added a year later offer a second ending. In presenting his portrait of a suffering world and the mechanism of the human mind that prevents us from helping others, Miró excluded any character who had overcome this mechanism. In these last pages he presents such a character, so that while the main text answers the question: Why do men allow suffering?, the new answer transcends the earlier pessimism and shows a possible escape. Sigüenza returns to Parcent a little more than a year later. This time he is a somewhat changed man: 'No siente predisposición de hablar de la lujuria de aquellos viñedos, de la suavidad y gracia de sus colinas, del reposo y soledad de los caseríos' (57-8/195-6). But he is still the innocent, for he swallows the arguments presented by the notables of Ondara against the building of a *Leprosería.* These men are confusers of inclination and duty on a grand scale, for their real fear is that the sales of oranges to England will fall, while their overt argument is that a *Leprosería* is not in the best interests of the lepers themselves.

Sigüenza is set right by Don Hermenegildo, the one man who reconciles love and duty. Appropriately, Sigüenza's arrival in Parcent this time is marked not by causing distress to ducks at the hands of small boys, but by saving a dragonfly, by his presence, from another small boy. The atmosphere of the narrative is completely changed, and detaíls are changed as if in a mirror image of the first visit. The church reappears as a benevolent institution — one priest has become a leper himself 'dando alivio a la desolación de sus espíritus' (61/207). When a leper dies Hermenegildo consoles him, sometimes accompanied by a priest, at other times by 'los hermanos del mal'. The consolation consists of descriptions of heaven, but now there is no suggestion of blind hope.

Sigüenza visits Batiste with Hermenegildo, as he had earlier with the innkeeper. This time Batiste makes a joke about his ills and explains them to Sigüenza. But Sigüenza is afraid of the leper: 'Entonces se comprende todo lo grandioso y extraordinario que es el ánimo de D. Hermenegildo' (62/210). Visiting another leper, Hermenegildo specifically mentions solitude: she is not alone if he is around. Under the influence of this man whose will is not paralysed by self-doubt, Sigüenza sees Parcent and its pain differently. Perhaps the vision that we are given in the main part of *Del vivir* is but yet another of Sigüenza's illusions, the illusion of a man who came to see suffering, and where he did not find it, created it.

Del vivir is not a masterpiece. It is Miró's first work in his own manner, and the extraordinary skill and assurance of parts are marred by an overemphatic narrative method that narrows the range of the events recounted and sometimes pushes them into sentimentality. Yet the typical excellences are there, and the very over-emphasis makes it easier to see what Miró was attempting, so that the book, especially in its unrevised version, offers considerable insight into what was more subtly achieved in the masterpieces that were to come.

Criticism has not yet seen Miró whole. Some of his qualities have been recognised. Many others have been neglected: his Cervantine grasp of the tricks played by the mind, his faithfulness to unmediated sense-perceptions, his vision of the world as one, both materially and spiritually, his psychological penetration and his narrative irony, his rooting of art in love for what is honestly observed, his new and precise use of language to recreate and to create meaning, his obsession with goodness and the acceptance of life, and with cruelty, suffering, and negation, his slowly-won ability to build immensely complex structures by linking series of scenes and episodes through images and a wealth of continuing and unifying themes, his grasp of the meaningful shaping and ordering of material. Miró's work belongs both to his own time and to the great Spanish tradition with which he linked himself so closely through his reading. Only when all his qualities are seen steadily and whole and in this context, will it be possible to set the critical record straight and to judge the value of his work.

APPENDIX

A CLASSIFIED LIST OF THE BOOKS IN THE LIBRARY OF GABRIEL MIRÓ

The method of classification used in this list has been explained elsewhere (see above, pp. 40-2). The complete classification, arranged in rough chronological order, is as follows:

1. Books from Miró's childhood.
   (a) First type of binding: leather spine marked 'G. MIRÓ'.
   (b) Others.
2. *Biblioteca de Autores Españoles*.
3. Second type of binding: cloth spine marked 'G. MIRÓ' or 'G. M.'.
4. Third type of binding: leather spine marked 'G. M.'.
5. Books published bound before 1914.
6. Books left unbound, published before 1914.
7. Books privately bound, but apparently not for Miró.
8. Fourth type of binding: by Subirana of Barcelona.
9. Books published bound from 1914 to 1918.
10. Fifth type of binding: by Raso of Madrid.
11. Books published bound from 1919 to 1927.
12. Books left unbound, published 1914 to 1927.
13. Books published 1928 to 1930.
14. Books inscribed by their authors, translators, or editors.
15. Books listed by Clemencia Miró, but now missing.

The list includes all the books found in the library (except two dated after 1930), the books in Dr. Emilio Luengo's bookcases that are self-evidently Miró's, and the books in Clemencia Miró's list that are now missing. Names of authors and titles of books both follow the title-page, though forms of address before names have generally been omitted and titles of books have sometimes been shortened. When necessary the names of works included in a book but not mentioned on the title-page have been added in brackets. Among eighteenth-century books and earlier, those in parchment covers have been listed as bound, those in paper covers as unbound. Books by Miró himself have been omitted, and all books not appearing in Clemencia Miró's list of the library have been marked with an asterisk.

The method of classification that I have adopted must, from a bibliographer's point of view, appear wilfully unorthodox. But the interest of Miró's library is principally literary — its bibliographical importance seems to me fairly small — and this list is therefore designed above all to clarify as objectively as possible the development of Miró's literary interests and of his writing. This does not, of course, mean that accuracy or consistency have been sacrificed, but that, with regard to classification as well as to the amount of information supplied, I have evolved rules especially for the purpose in hand.

There remains the problem (see above, p. 39) of the discrepancies between the books found in the library and Clemencia Miró's list. When one compares Clemencia's list in detail with the present library one finds that sixteen titles listed by her are now missing. On the other hand, there are about forty titles in Miró's bookcases that are not listed by Clemencia Miró, and a further forty that are also clearly Miró's, though not listed by Clemencia, can be found in other bookcases in the room. In addition, some of the books are out of order. Otherwise list and library coincide.

Unfortunately we do not know when the list was compiled. This is the more important in view of the note at the end of the list, stating that some of Miró's books went into Dr. Emilio Luengo's library, and that others were given to friends. Is it possible that the sixteen books listed but now missing include some given away to friends, that Clemencia remembered them and therefore included them in the list in order to improve its completeness? She would certainly have been familiar with her father's library for a long time before his death, and might well have known where in the shelf-order to list the missing books. Or must we assume that these sixteen books have been lost since the list was compiled and that the 'algunos libros' given away were never listed?

If we turn to the books in Dr. Luengo's library, the latter suggestion seems the more likely one, since among these books — including for this purpose all the bookcases that are not Miró's — are, as we have mentioned, about forty titles that are obviously Miró's though Clemencia has not listed them as such. If, in compiling her list, she ignored these books on which she could easily check, it seems unlikely that she would have included in the list books that had been given away. A few books listed by Clemencia do appear among Dr. Luengo's, but this hardly affects the main argument: probably they have simply been misplaced since the list was compiled, the unlisted ones being already outside Miró's bookcases at the time of compilation. It looks as if Clemencia must have drawn up the list simply on the basis of what she found in Miró's bookcases, ignoring the books that though obviously his were elsewhere in the room, and, *a fortiori,* those that had been given away.

An unknown number of books has probably, then, disappeared. We can make a guess that the number is not very great, for if the 'muchos libros' that went into Dr. Luengo's library amount to about forty, then the 'algunos' given away must be a small number. Further books may have disappeared in that there may be books in Dr. Luengo's library that were once Miró's though they cannot now be distinguished from it. The nature of Dr. Luengo's collection —largely formed after Miró's death — suggests that there are few such books. But what remains more puzzling is the presence on Miró's own shelves of forty titles that are not listed by Clemencia even though most of them are unequivocally his. It his hard to imagine why so many books, spread apparently at random over the shelves, should have been left out of a list compiled in shelf order.

1. BOOKS FROM MIRÓ'S CHILDHOOD

(a) First type of binding: leather spine marked 'G. MIRÓ'
*Larra, Mariano José de, *Obras completas,* Barcelona, 1886
*Le Bon, Gustavo, *La civilización de los árabes,* Barcelona, 1886
Las plantas que curan y las plantas que matan, Barcelona, 1887
*Rengade, J., *La vida normal y la salud,* Barcelona, 1886
*Saavedra, Ángel de, *Obras completas,* Vol. II, Barcelona, 1885 (*El moro expósito, Poesías sueltas*)
*[Saavedra, Ángel de], [*Obras*], Vol. II, no t.p. (*Romances históricos, Leyendas, Teatro, Prosas*)
*Wood, J. G., *Los precursores del arte y de la industria,* Barcelona, 1886

(b) Others
*Castelar, Emilio, *Nerón,* 3 vols., Barcelona, 1891-3
*Cervantes, *Novelas ejemplares,* 2 vols., Barcelona, 1886
*Gonzenbach, E. V., *Viaje por el Nilo,* Barcelona, 1890
*Hugo, Víctor, *Dramas,* Barcelona, 1887
*Lamartine, A. de, *Jocelyn,* Barcelona, 1883
*Montalvo, Juan, *Capítulos que se le olvidaron a Cervantes,* Barcelona, 1898
*Montemayor, Jorge de, *La Diana*; Gaspar Gil Polo, *La Diana enamorada,* Barcelona, 1886
*Oloriz, Juan Crisóstomo de, *Molestias del trato humano,* Barcelona, 1887
*Rojas, Fernando de, *La Celestina,* Barcelona, 1886
*Schiller, C. F., *Dramas,* Barcelona, 1882
*Tasso, T., *La Jerusalén libertada,* Barcelona, 1884
*Zabaleta, Juan de, *El día de fiesta,* Barcelona, 1885

2. «BIBLIOTECA DE AUTORES ESPAÑOLES»

Volumes I-LXXI, Madrid, 1858-1902

3. SECOND TYPE OF BINDING: CLOTH SPINE MARKED 'G. MIRÓ' OR 'G. M.'

Agustín, San, *La ciudad de Dios,* 4 vols., Madrid, 1893

*Alarcón, Pedro Antonio de, *El sombrero de tres picos,* Madrid, 1898

Albert, Carlos, *El amor libre,* Madrid, 1900

Apuleyo, Lucio, *La metamorfosis; o, El asno de oro, Las floridas, El demonio de Sócrates,* Madrid, 1890

Aristófanes, *Comedias,* 3 vols., Madrid, 1880 (I), 1885 (II-III)

Bécquer, Gustavo A., *Obras,* 3 vols., Madrid, 1885

Bossuet, Jacobo Benigno, *Oraciones fúnebres,* Madrid, 1892

Byron, *Poemas dramáticos: Caín — Sardanápalo — Manfredo,* Madrid, 1886

Campoamor, Ramón de, *Poética,* Madrid, 1883

Castelar, Emilio, *Un viaje a París,* Madrid, 1878

    (Bound with: Luis Taboada, *París y sus cercanías,* Madrid, 1880)

Cervantes Saavedra, Miguel de, *Trabajos de Persiles y Sigismunda* [*La jitanilla, Rinconete y Cortadillo*], Madrid/Barcelona, 1859

*Chateaubriand, *Atala, René, El último Abencerraje, Viaje al Mont-Blanch, Pensamientos, reflexiones y máximas,* Barcelona, 1895

Cicerón, Marco Tulio, *Obras completas,* Vols. I-XV, XVII, Madrid, 1880-1901 (Bound in 15 volumes)

(Clarín), Leopoldo Alas, *El gallo de Sócrates,* Barcelona, 1901

Clarín (Leopoldo Alas), *Su único hijo,* Madrid, 1890

Condillac, *Traité des sensations, Première partie,* Paris, 1885

*Daudet, Alfonso, *Las cartas de mi molino,* Barcelona, 1899

*Daudet, Alfonso, *Cuentos amorosos y patrióticos,* Valencia, n.d.

*Daudet, Alfonso, *Jack,* 2 vols., Barcelona, 1901

*Daudet, Alfonso, *El nabab,* 2 vols., Barcelona, 1900

*Dickens, Carlos, *El endemoniado,* Valencia, n.d.

Diógenes Laercio, *Vidas, opiniones y sentencias de los filósofos más ilustres;* Quevedo, *Nombre, origen, intento, recomendación y descendencia de la doctrina estoica,* 2 vols., Madrid, 1887

Eschylo, *Las siete tragedias,* Madrid, 1899

Espronceda, José de, *Obras poéticas y escritos en prosa,* Madrid, 1884

Eurípides, *Tragedias,* Madrid, 1865

*Flaubert, Gustavo, *Salammbó,* Barcelona, 1901

Floro, Lucio Anneo, *Compendio de las hazañas romanas,* Madrid, 1885

Gelio, Aulo, *Noches áticas;* Publio Syro, *Sentencias,* 2 vols., Madrid, 1893

Giner, Francisco, *Estudios filosóficos y religiosos,* Madrid, 1876

                    Estudios de literatura y arte, Madrid, 1876

    (Bound as one volume)

Goethe, *Fausto,* 2 vols., Madrid, 1886

Goethe, *Werther,* Valencia, 1894

González Garbín, A., *Lecciones histórico-críticas de literatura clásica latina,* Granada, 1896

Gracián, Baltasar, *El héroe, El discreto,* Madrid, 1900

Heine, Enrique, *Poemas y fantasías,* Madrid, 1900

Herodoto, *Los nueve libros,* 2 vols., Madrid, 1898

Homero, *La Ilíada,* 3 vols., Madrid, 1898-9

Homero, *La Odisea, La batracomiomaquia,* 2 vols., Madrid, 1886

Ibn-Gebirol, *La fuente de la vida,* Madrid, n.d.

Juvenal y Persio, *Sátiras,* Madrid, 1892

*Lamartine, Alfonso de, *Graziella,* Valencia, n.d.

Le Sage, *Historia de Gil Blas de Santillana,* 2 vols., Madrid/Barcelona, 1860

Lucano, Marco Anneo, *La Farsalia,* 2 vols., Madrid, 1888

Luciano, *Obras completas,* 4 vols., Madrid, 1882-90

Lucrecio Caro, Tito, *Naturaleza de las cosas,* Madrid, 1893

Mantegazza, Pablo, *Fisiología del amor,* Madrid, 1899

Masía y Lucas, Hugolino, *Los ritos orientales,* Madrid, 1883

*Maupassant, Guy de, *La mancebía,* Valencia, n.d.

Menéndez y Pelayo, Marcelino, *Historia de las ideas estéticas en España,* 9 vols., Madrid, 1884-91 (The first two volumes are of the second edition; the remainder are of the first.)

Merejkowsky, Dmitri de, *La muerte de los dioses,* Madrid, n.d.

*Mesonero Romanos, *Artículos escogidos de las Escenas matritenses,* 2 vols., Madrid, 1879 (Bound as one volume)

Nietzsche, *El crepúsculo de los ídolos,* Madrid, 1900

Nietzsche, Federico, *El origen de la tragedia,* Madrid, n.d.
El anticristo, Madrid, n.d.
(Bound as one volume)

Obras de los moralistas griegos, Madrid, 1888 (Marcus Aurelius, Theophrastus, Epictetus, Cebes)

Ovidio Nasón, Publio, *Las heroidas,* Madrid, 1884

Ovidio Nasón, Publio, *Las metamorfosis,* 2 vols., Madrid, 1887

*Pereda, José M. de, *La Montálvez,* Madrid, 1891

Píndaro, *Odas,* Madrid, 1893

Platón, *Diálogos polémicos,* 2 vols., Madrid, 1885
(Bound as one volume)

Platón, *La república,* 2 vols., Madrid, 1886

Plutarco, *Las vidas paralelas,* 5 vols., Madrid, 1900-1

Poetas bucólicos griegos, Madrid, 1888 (Theocritus, Bion, Moschus)

Poetas líricos griegos, Madrid, 1884 (Anacreon, Sappho, Simonides, etc.)

Quevedo Villegas, Francisco de, *Obras políticas, históricas y críticas,* 2 vols., Madrid, 1893

Quevedo Villegas, Francisco de, *Obras satíricas y festivas,* Madrid, 1893

Quevedo Villegas, Francisco de, *Política de Dios y gobierno de Cristo*, Madrid, 1894

Renan, Ernesto, *Los apóstoles*, 2 vols., Barcelona, 1901

La Santa Biblia, tr. Felipe Scio de San Miguel, 5 vols., Madrid, 1852 (I), 1869 (II-V)

Schopenhauer, A., *Sobre la voluntad en la naturaleza*, Madrid, 1900

*Scott, Walter, *Ivanhoe; o, El cruzado*, Madrid/Barcelona, 1857

*Scott, Walter, *Quintin Durward*, Madrid/Barcelona, 1857

*Scott, Walter, *Rob-Roy*, Madrid/Barcelona, 1858

Sénancour, *Obermann*, Paris, 1901

Séneca, Lucio Anneo, *Epístolas morales*, Madrid, 1884

Séneca, Lucio Anneo, *Tratados filosóficos*, 2 vols., Madrid, 1884

Shakespeare, William, *Obras*, Vol. I,   *Poemas y sonetos*, Madrid, 1877
  Vol. II,   *El mercader de Venecia*, Madrid, 1872
  Vol. III,   *Julieta y Romeo*, Madrid, 1872

*Sienkiewicz, E., *Hania*, Barcelona, 1901

*Sienkiewicz, *Más allá del misterio (Sin dogma)*, no t.p.

*Sienkiewicz, *Las tres novias del pintor*, Barcelona, 1900

Staël, Mme de, *De l'Allemagne*, Paris, n.d.

Terencio Africano, P., *Las seis comedias*, Madrid, 1890

Tíbulo, *Elegías*, Madrid, 1874

Tolstoï, León, *El matrimonio*, Barcelona, 1896
  La sonata a Kreutzer, Barcelona, 1896
  Amo y criado, Barcelona, 1899
  (Bound in one volume with: Amadeo de Bast, *Madame de Pompadour en Compiègne*, Barcelona, 1899)

Tolstoy, León, *Resurrección*, 3 vols., Barcelona, 1900
  (Bound as one volume)

Tucídides, *Historia de la guerra del Peloponeso*, 2 vols., Madrid, 1889

Valera, Juan, *Algo de todo*, Seville, 1883

Valera, Juan, *Doña Luz*, Madrid, 1891

Valera, Juan, *Estudios críticos sobre literatura, política y costumbres de nuestros días*, 3 vols., Seville/Madrid, 1884

Valera, Juan, *Genio y figura*, Madrid, 1897

*Valera, Juan, *Juanita la larga*, Madrid, 1899

Virgilio Marón, Publio, *Eneida*, 2 vols., Madrid, 1901 (I), 1890 (II)

Xenofonte, *La cyropedia; o, Historia de Cyro el mayor*, Madrid, 1882

Jenofonte, *Las helénicas; o, Historia griega*, Madrid, 1888

Xenofonte, *Historia de la entrada de Cyro el Menor en el Asia*, Madrid, 1882

Zola, Emilio, *Germinal*, 2 vols., Madrid, n.d.

4. THIRD TYPE OF BINDING : LEATHER SPINE MARKED 'G. M.'

Alcover y Maspons, Joan, *Cap al tard,* Barcelona, 1909
Arréat, Lucien, *Journal d'un philosophe,* Paris, 1887
Binet, Alfred, *Etudes de psychologie expérimentale,* Paris, 1891
Cervantes Saavedra, Miguel de, *Teatro completo,* 3 vols., Madrid, 1896-7
(Clarín), Leopoldo Alas, *Cuentos morales,* Madrid, 1896
Clarín (Leopoldo Alas), *Ensayos y revistas,* Madrid, 1892
Costa y Llobera, M., *Poesies,* Barcelona, 1907
Darwin, Carlos R., *El origen del hombre,* no t.p.
Dastre, A., *La vida y la muerte,* Madrid, 1906
Dostoyevsky, Fedor, *Los hermanos Karamazov,* Paris, n.d.
Dubufe, Guillaume, *La Valeur de l'art,* Paris, 1908
Flaubert, Gustave, *L'Education sentimentale,* Paris, 1905
France, Anatole, *La isla de los pingüinos,* Madrid, 1912
France, Anatole, *El olmo del paseo,* Madrid, 1905
France, Anatole, *Opiniones de Jerónimo Coignard,* Madrid, 1907
Frilley, Jorge, *La India y la literatura sanscrita,* Paris, n.d.
Goethe, *Les Affinités électives,* Paris, n.d.
Goethe, *Werther, Hermann et Dorothée,* Paris, n.d.
Guyau, M., *Esquisse d'une morale sans obligation ni sanction,* Paris,
  1905
Haeckel, Ernesto, *Las maravillas de la vida,* Valencia, n.d.
Hoffmann, *Contes posthumes,* Paris, 1856
Hugo, Victor, *Littérature et philosophie melées,* Paris, n.d.
Ibsen, Enrique, *Los espectros, Hedda Gabler, El maestro Solness,* Va-
  lencia, n.d. (The last title appears on the t.p. but not in the book.)
*Josefo, Flavio, *Historia de las guerras de los judíos,* 2 vols., Madrid,
  1891
Josèphe, Flavius, *Oeuvres complètes,* Vols. I, III, VII, Paris, 1900 (I),
  1904 (III), 1902 (VII) (Vols. III and VII bound as one)
Kant,M., *Crítica del juicio,* 2 vols., Madrid, 1914
La Bruyère, *Les Caractères,* Paris, n.d.
Lamarck, Juan, *Filosofía zoológica,* Valencia, n.d.
Maeterlinck, Mauricio, *El tesoro de los humildes,* Valencia, n.d.
Michelet, J., *L'Amour,* Paris, 1870
Montesquieu, *De l'esprit des lois,* 2 vols., Paris, n.d.
Nietzsche, Federico, *La gaya ciencia,* Madrid, n.d.
Paulhan, Fr., *Les Phénomènes affectifs,* Paris, 1901
Payot, Jules, *L'Education de la volonté,* Paris, 1906
Ribot, Th., *La Logique des sentiments,* Paris, 1905
Ribot, Th., *Les Maladies de la personnalité,* Paris, 1906
Ribot, Th., *Les Maladies de la volonté,* Paris, 1906
Ruskin, John, *Las piedras de Venecia,* 2 vols., Valencia, n.d. (Bound
  as one volume)
Schopenhauer, Arturo, *La libertad,* Valencia, n.d.

Stendhal, *De l'amour,* no t.p.
Stendhal, *El rojo y el negro,* Paris, n.d.
Stendhal, *Souvenirs d'égotisme,* Paris, 1892
Stendhal, *Vie de Rossini,* Paris, 1892
Stendhal, *Vies de Haydn, de Mozart et de Métastase,* Paris, 1887
Sudermann, Hermann, *El deseo, La mujer gris,* 2 vols., Valencia, n.d.
  (Bound as one volume)
Taine, H., *La inteligencia,* 2 vols., Madrid, 1904
*Tchekhov, Antón, *Vanka,* Valencia, n.d.
Tertuliano, Quinto Septimio Florente, *Apología contra los gentiles,* Madrid, 1889
Verdaguer, Jacinto, *La Atlántida,* Barcelona, 1902
Wilde, Oscar, *Théatre,* Vol. II, *L'Evantail de Lady Windermere, Une Femme sans importance,* Paris, 1910

5. BOOKS PUBLISHED BOUND BEFORE 1914

Abelardo y Eloisa, *Verdaderas cartas,* Barcelona, 1875
Baedeker, Karl, *Palestine et Syrie,* Leipzig/Paris, 1912
*Balzac, H. de, *El contrato de matrimonio, Un debut en la vida,* Barcelona, n.d.
*Balzac, *Una hija de Eva, Memorias de dos jóvenes casadas,* Barcelona, n.d.
Barcia, Roque, *Primer diccionario general etimológico de la lengua española,* 5 vols., Barcelona, n.d. (I-II), Madrid, 1881-3 (III-V)
Cabrol, Fernando, *La oración de la Iglesia,* Barcelona, 1909
Cervantes Saavedra, Miguel de, *El ingenioso hidalgo Don Quijote de la Mancha,* 2 vols., Barcelona, n.d.
Church, Alfredo J., *Historia de Cartago,* Madrid, 1889
Dante Alighieri, *La divina comedia,* 2 vols., Barcelona, 1884
Duruy, Víctor, *Historia de los griegos,* Vols. II-III, Barcelona, 1890-1
Eça de Queiroz, *La reliquia,* Barcelona, 1902
Emmerich, Ana Catalina, *La dolorosa pasión de Nuestro Señor Jesucristo,* Madrid, 1906
Flaubert, Gustave, *La Tentation de Saint-Antoine,* London/Paris, n.d.
Flaubert, Gustave, *Trois contes,* Paris, n.d.
Hedenstjerna, A. von, *El señor de Halleborg,* Barcelona, 1910
Hedenstjerna, A. von, *El señor de Halleborg,* Barcelona, n.d.
Hello, Ernesto, *Fisionomías de santos,* Barcelona, 1904
Hosmer, James K., *Historia de los Judíos,* Madrid, 1893
Joly, Enrique, *Psicología de los santos,* Barcelona, 1911
Kampen, Alberto van, *Justus Perthes' Atlas Antiquus,* Gotha, n.d.
Kannengieser, Alfonso, *Obras,* Vol. V, *Judíos y católicos en Austria-Hungría,* Barcelona, 1900
Kellner, K. A. Enrique, *El año eclesiástico y las fiestas de los santos,* Barcelona, 1910

APPENDIX

Lafuente, Modesto, continued by Juan Valera, *Historia general de España,* 6 vols., Barcelona, 1877-82
Lavedán, Enrique, *Su majestad,* Barcelona, 1911
Le Camus, E., *Vie de N. S. Jésus-Christ,* Brussels/Paris, 1897
Lenormant, François, *Atlas d'histoire ancienne de l'orient,* Paris, n.d.
León, Luis de, *Poesías completas,* no t.p.
Mislin, El abad, *La tierra santa,* Barcelona/Madrid, 1863
Nicolay, Fernando, *Historia de las creencias,* 3 vols., Barcelona, 1904
Ragozin, Zénaïda A., *Historia de Caldea,* Madrid, 1889
Rawlinson, Jorge, *Historia del antiguo Egipto,* Madrid, 1889
Renan, Ernest, *Souvenirs d'enfance et de jeunesse,* Paris, n.d.
Robiou, Félix, *Lectures historiques: L'Orient,* Paris, 1893
Siélain, R., *Atlas de poche des plantes des champs, des prairies et des bois,* Series I-II, IV, Paris, 1910 (I), 1907 (II), 1911 (IV)
Sienkiewicz, Enrique, *Quo vadis?,* 2 vols., Barcelona, 1901
Yepes, Diego de, *Vida de Santa Teresa,* 2 vols., Barcelona, 1887

6. BOOKS LEFT UNBOUND, PUBLISHED BEFORE 1914

Alfieri, Vittorio, *Tragedie,* 6 vols., Florence, 1829
Augustin, Saint, *Les Confessions,* Paris, n.d.
Barnabé d'Alsace, Le père, *Le Prétoire de Pilate et la forteresse Antonia,* Paris, 1902
Carner, Josep, *Els fruits saborosos,* Barcelona, 1906
Fabre, J.-H., *Les Merveilles de l'instinct chez les insectes,* Paris, 1913
Fabre, J.-H., *Les Ravageurs,* Paris, n.d.
Fabre, J.-H., *La Vie des insectes,* Paris, n.d.
Ganivet, Ángel, *Cartas finlandesas,* Madrid, 1905
Guérin, Paul, *Vie des Saints,* Vols. VI, XII-XIV, Paris, 1866 (VI), 1869 (XII-XIV)
Guérin, V., *Description géographique, historique et archéologique de la Palestine: Troisième partie: Galilée,* 2 vols., Paris, 1880
Harnack, Adolphe, *L'Essence du cristianisme,* Paris, 1907
Huysmans, J.-K., *A vau-l'eau,* Paris, 1911
Martín, Manuel Joseph, *Historia trágica y verdadera de Herodes el Grande,* Madrid, 1780
Martín, Manuel Joseph, *Historia verdadera del falso y perverso profeta Mahoma,* Madrid, 1781
Martínez Ruiz, J., *Antonio Azorín,* Madrid, n.d.
Martínez Ruiz, J., *La evolución de la crítica,* Madrid, 1899
*Pérez Bueno, L., *Artistas levantinos,* Madrid, 1899
Rabelais, F., *Les Cinq Livres,* Vol. I, Paris, n.d.
*Rabelais, Francisco, *Gargantua,* Madrid, 1910
Rogers, Mary Eliza, *La Vie domestique en Palestine,* Paris, 1865
Santos Alonso, Hilario, *Historia verdadera, y espantosa del diluvio universal del mundo,* Cordoba, n.d.

Schoebel, Charles, *L'Histoire des Rois Mages*, Paris, 1878
Tractat de Scipió y Anibal, La destrucció de Jerusalém, ed R. Miquel y
Planas, Barcelona, 1910
Wölfflin, H., *L'Art classique*, Paris, 1911
Xenius, *La ben plantada*, Barcelona, 1911

7. BOOKS PRIVATELY BOUND, BUT APPARENTLY NOT FOR MIRÓ

Adricomio Delpho, Christiano, *Breve descripción de la ciudad de Je-
rusalem*, Madrid, 1799
Allan Kardec, *Le Ciel et l'enfer*, Paris, 1865
Ambrosio, San, *Tratado de las vírgenes*, Madrid, 1914
Antenor, Viages de, 'tr.' E. F. Lantier, 3 vols., Madrid, 1802
Aristóteles, *La poética*, Madrid, 1778
Arnaldo, Antonio, *Arte de pensar: o, Lógica admirable*, Madrid, 1759
Arnod y Suard, Los señores, *Variedades literarias*, 2 vols., Madrid, 1779
Balmes, Jaime, *El criterio*, Barcelona, 1880
        Cartas, no t.p.
        (Bound as one volume)
Balmes, Jaime, *Curso de filosofía elemental: Lógica*, Barcelona, 1866
        *Curso de filosofía elemental: Metafísica,*Barcelona, 1863
        Curso de filosofía elemental: Etica, Barcelona, 1863
        Curso de filosofía elemental: Historia de la filosofía, Bar-
        celona, 1863
        (Bound as one volume)
Balmes, Jaime, *Escritos póstumos*, Barcelona, 1868
Barbey d'Aurevilly, J., *Ce qui ne meurt pas*, 2 vols., Paris, 1888
Barthélemy, L'abbé, *Voyage du jeune Anacharsis en Grèce*, 8 vols., Paris,
1830 (Bound in 4 volumes)
Bentham, Jeremías, *Tratados de legislación civil y penal*, Vols. I-II, IV-
VIII, Bordeaux, 1829
Béranger, *Oeuvres complètes*, Brussels, 1830
Berault-Bercastel, El abad, *Historia eclesiástica*, Vols. VIII-IX, Madrid,
1805
Boileau-Despréaux, *Satires et oeuvres diverses*, London, 1777
Boissier, Gaston, *Cicéron et ses amis*, Paris, 1921
Buffon, *Historia natural, general y particular*, Vol. I, Madrid, 1785
Chateaubriand, *Oeuvres complètes*, Vols. VIII-X,*Itinéraire de Paris à
Jérusalem et de Jérusalem à Paris*, Paris, 1826
Codorníu, Antonio, *Examen de las que quieren ser monjas*, Gerona, 1825
Condillac, *La Logique*, Paris, 1789
Condillac, *La Logique*, Paris, 1835
[Croiset, Jean], *Año christiano*, tr. Castellot, Vol. III, Madrid, 1789
Crónica general de España, 52 vols., Madrid, 1865-71 (Bound in 12 vol-
umes)
Curtius, Ernesto, *Historia de Grecia*, 8 vols., Madrid, 1887-8

Dante Alighieri, *La Divine Comèdie, La Vie nouvelle,* Paris, 1862

Delgado, Jacinto María, *Adiciones a la historia del ingenioso hidalgo Don Quixote de la Mancha,* Madrid, n.d.

Feyjóo, Benito Geronymo, *Cartas eruditas,* Vols. I, III-V, Madrid, 1742 (I), 1750 (III), 1774 (IV), 1761 (V)

Feyjóo, Benito Geronymo, *Theatro crítico universal,* Vols. II-IV, VI-IX, Madrid, 1732 (II), 1737 (III), 1737 (IV), 1750 (VI), 1736 (VII), 1777 (VIII), 1740 (IX)

Flammarion, Camilo, *Dios en la naturaleza,* Madrid, 1873

Flammarion, Camilo, *Los mundos imaginarios,* Madrid, 1873

Florian, *Fables,* Paris, 1792

Francisco de Sales, San, *Introducción a la vida devota,* Madrid, 1850
Declaración mística del Cántico de los Cánticos, Madrid, 1849
(Published as one volume)

Garcilaso de la Vega, *Obras,* Madrid, 1817

Gómez Hermosilla, Josef, *Arte de hablar en prosa y en verso,* 2 vols., Madrid, 1826

Góngora, Luis de, *Todas las obras,* no t.p. [Madrid, 1654]

Gracián, Lorenzo, *Obras,* 2 vols., Barcelona, 1700 (I), n.d. (II)

Hipócrates, *Aforismos,* Valencia, 1845

Hope, Th., *Histoire de l'architecture,* 2 vols., Paris, 1839

Horacio, *Poesías,* 4 vols., Madrid, 1844 (Bound in 2 volumes)

Hugo, Víctor, *Los miserables,* 5 vols., Madrid, 1869-70

Joseph, Flavius, *Oeuvres complètes,* Paris, 1838

La Fontaine, *Fables, suivies d'Adonis, poème,* 2 vols., Paris, 1817 (I), 1799 (II)

Le Bon, Gustavo, *La evolución de la materia,* Madrid, 1907

Lenormant, François, *Manuel d'histoire ancienne de l'orient,* 3 vols., Paris, 1869

La leyenda de oro, 4 vols., Madrid/Barcelona, 1853

Martín, El abate, *Historia de la tierra santa,* 2 vols., Barcelona, 1840

Maura, Juan, *Sta. Teresa de Jesús y la crítica racionalista,* Palma, 1883
(Bound with:
Antonio J. González, *Santificación del día de fiesta,* n.p., n.d.
A. J. González, *Concepto del trabajo,* Murcia, n.d.
Ángel Pulido, *Estudios médicos,* Madrid, 1889
José M. Sarget, *Siluetas de ideas,* n.p., n.d.)

Menéndez y Pelayo, M., *Estudios de crítica literaria,* Series I-II, no t.p. (I), Madrid, 1895 (II)

Menéndez y Pelayo, Marcelino, *Historia de los heterodoxos españoles,* Vol. II, Madrid, 1917

Michelet, J., *Introduction à l'histoire universelle,* Paris, 1879

[Millot, C. F. X.], *Histoire littéraire des troubadours,* 3 vols., Paris, 1774

Montaigne, *Ensayos,* 2 vols., Paris, 1899

Montesquieu, *Grandeur et décadence des Romains, Lettres persanes, Politique des Romains, Dialogue de Sylla et d'Eucrate,* Paris, 1851

O., D. P. M. de, *Nueva descripción de la Tierra Santa formada según el itinerario del viage executado en el año de 1806 por J. A. de Chateaubriand,* Madrid, 1817

Overberg, Bernard, *Histoire de l'ancien et du nouveau testament,* Paris, 1854

Ovidio Nasón, P., *El arte de amar;* Torcuato Taso, *Aminta,* Madrid, 1820

Pascal, *Cartas provinciales,* Madrid, 1879

[Pluquet, F. A. A.], *Mémoires pour servir à l'histoire des egaremens de l'esprit humain par rapport à la réligion Chrétienne; ou, Dictionnaire des hérésies,* 2 vols., Paris, 1776

Quevedo y Villegas, Francisco, *Obras posthumas y vida de Don Francisco de Quevedo y Villegas, Parte tercera,* Madrid, 1724

Ríos, Vicente de los, *Análisis del Quijote;* Martín Fernández de Navarrete, *Vida de Miguel de Cervantes,* Barcelona, 1834; José Mor de Fuentes, *Elogio de Miguel de Cervantes,* Barcelona, 1835 (Published as one volume)

Rousseau, J.-J., *Emile,* Paris, 1860

Rousseau, J.-J., *Julie; ou, La Nouvelle Héloïse,* 5 vols., Paris, n.d. (Bound in 2 volumes)

Rousseau, J.-J., *Oeuvres complètes,* Vol. I, *Les Confessions,* Vol. II, *Suite des confessions, Rêveries, Botanique,* Paris, 1856

Saintine, *Historia de la hermosa cordelera, El mutilado,* Barcelona, 1844

Sánchez Calvo, Estanislao, *Los nombres de los dioses,* Madrid, 1884

Sans Monge, Joseph, *El sabio ignorante; o, Descripción de los defectos de los sabios,* 2 vols., Barcelona, 1763

Santos, Francisco, *Día y noche de Madrid,* Madrid, 1766

Sarmiento, M., *Demonstración crítico- apologética de el Theatro crítico universal,* 2 vols., Madrid, 1751

Saulcy, F. de, *Histoire d'Hérode,* Paris, 1867

Sempere y Guarinos, Juan, *Historia del luxo,* 2 vols., Madrid, 1788

*Sigüenza, Pedro de, *Tratado de cláusulas instrumentales,* Barcelona, 1705

Tacite, *Les Annales, I-III,* Paris, 1861

Thompson, Jayme, *Las estaciones del año,* Madrid, 1801

Tomás de Aquino, Santo, *Opúsculos,* Seville, 1862

Torres Villarroel, Diego de, *Vida,* Madrid, 1792

Torres Villarroel, Diego de, *Vida,* Madrid, 1799

Valera, Juan, *Pasarse de listo,* Madrid, n.d.

*Valera, Juan, *Pepita Jiménez,* Madrid, 1890

Vigouroux, F., *La Bible et les découvertes modernes en Palestine, en Egypte et en Assyrie,* 4 vols., Paris, 1879 (I-III), 1882 (IV)

[Voltaire], *La Enriada,* tr. Virués, no t.p.

Yriarte, Tomás de, *La música,* Madrid, 1779

8. FOURTH TYPE OF BINDING : BY SUBIRANA OF BARCELONA

Bayard, Emile, *L'Art de reconnaître les styles: Architecture — Ameublement*, Paris, n.d.
Binet-Sanglé, *La Folie de Jésus*, 2 vols., Paris, 1911 (I), 1910 (II)
Boissier, Gaston, *El fin del paganismo*, 2 vols., Madrid, 1908
Chollet, J.-A., *La Psychologie du Christ*, 2 vols., Paris, 1903 (Bound as one volume)
Eusèbe, *Histoire ecclésiastique*, 3 vols., Paris, 1905-13
Evangiles apocryphes, 2 vols., Paris, 1911-14
Friedlieb, J. H., *Archéologie de la Passion*, Paris, 1897
George, Henry, *La ciencia de la economía política*, Madrid, 1914
Marx, J., *Compendio de historia de la Iglesia*, Barcelona, 1914
Maspero, G., *Historia antigua de los pueblos de Oriente*, Madrid, 1913
Ollivier, M.-J., *La Passion*, Paris, 1902
Reinach, Théodore, *Histoire des Israélites*, Paris, 1910
Rosadi, Juan, *El proceso de Jesús*, Barcelona, 1904
Schwalm, M.-B.,*La Vie privée du peuple juif*, Paris, 1910
Stapfer, E., *La Palestine au temps de Jésus-Christ*, Paris, n.d.
Suetonio Tranquilo, Cayo, *Los doce Césares*, Madrid, 1902.

9. BOOKS PUBLISHED BOUND FROM 1914 TO 1918

Annunzio, Gabriel d', *La hija de Iorio*, Madrid, 1917
Ariosto, Ludovico, *Orlando furioso*, 2 vols., Barcelona, 1916-17
Baedeker, Karl, *Egypte et Soudan*, Leipzig/Paris, 1914
Cossío, M. B., *El entierro del Conde de Orgaz*, Madrid, 1914
Cossío, M. B., *Lo que se sabe de la vida del Greco*, Madrid, 1914
Edersheim, Alfred, *Jesus the Messiah*, London, 1916
France, Anatole, *Pierre Nozière*, Paris, n. d.
Garcilaso y Boscán, *Obras poéticas*, Madrid, 1917
Guiraud, Paul, *Historia griega: Vida pública y privada de los griegos*, Madrid, 1915
Guiraud, Paul, *Historia romana: Vida pública y privada de los romanos*, Madrid, 1917
Loti, Pierre, *Jérusalem*, Paris, n.d.
El Nuevo Testamento, tr. Félix Torres Amat, Bilbao, 1916
Oficio de la Semana Santa y Pascua de resurrección en latín y castellano, tr. José María Quadrado, Barcelona, 1915
Pijoán, J., *Historia del arte*, 3 vols., Barcelona, 1914-16
Royo, Eduardo, *Autenticidad de la 'Mística ciudad de Dios', y biografía de su autora*, Barcelona, 1914
Serra i Boldú, Valeri, *Calendari folklòric d'Urgell*, Barcelona, n.d.
Suarès, André, *Don Quijote en Francia*, Madrid, 1916
*Turguenef, *Lluvia de primavera*, Madrid, n.d.
Valbuena, Bernardo de, *El Bernardo del Carpio*, 2 vols., Barcelona, 1914

10. Fifth type of binding: by Raso of Madrid

Boissier, Gaston, *Nouvelles promenades archéologiques,* Paris, n.d.
Couchoud, P.-L., *Le Mystère de Jésus,* Paris, 1924
Delaporte, L., *La Mésopotamie,* Paris, 1923
Duchesne, L., *Origines du culte chrétien,* Paris, 1925
Flaubert, Gustave, *Correspondance,* Series I-IV, Paris, 1887-93
Goguel, Maurice, *Jésus de Nazareth: Mythe ou histoire?,* Paris, 1925
Guéranger, Prosper, *L'Année liturgique,* 15 vols., Paris, 1920-6
Guérin, V., *Description de l'île de Patmos et de l'île de Samos,* Paris, 1856
Guérin, V., *Ile de Rhodes,* Paris, 1880
Huart, Clément, *La Perse antique,* Paris, 1925
Karppe, S., *Etude sur les origines et la nature du Zohar,* Paris, 1901
Lamartine, *Oeuvres complètes,* Vols. VII-VIII, *Souvenirs, impressions, pensées et paysages pendant un voyage en Orient,* Paris, 1845
Marrast, Augustin, *La Vie Byzantine au VIe siècle,* Paris, 1881
Moret, A., and G. Davy, *Des clans aux empires,* Paris, 1923
Pater, Walter, *Platon et le platonisme,* Paris, 1923
Pater, Walter, *La Renaissance,* Paris, 1917
Platon, *Le Banquet,* Paris, 1926
Platon, *Phédon,* Paris, 1926
Platon, *Phèdre,* Paris, 1926
Ragozin, Zénaida A., *Historia de Asiria,* Madrid, 1890
Renan, Ernest, *Les Apôtres,* Paris, 1921
Renan, Ernest, *Les Evangiles,* Paris, 1926
Renan, Ernest, *Histoire du peuple d'Israël,* 5 vols., Paris, 1926-8
Renan, Ernest, *Marc-Aurèle,* Paris, 1925
Renan, Ernest, *Saint Paul,* Paris, 1918
Renan, Ernest, *Vie de Jésus,* Paris, 1925
Ridder, A. de, and W. Deonna, *L'Art en Grèce,* Paris, 1924
Vendryes, J., *Le Langage,* Paris, 1921
Vigouroux, F., *Dictionnaire de la Bible,* 10 vols., Paris, 1912 (I-VIII), 1922 (IX-X)

11. Books published bound from 1919 to 1927

Alfonso X el Sabio, ed. Antonio G. Solalinde, 2 vols., Madrid, 1922
Borrow, J., *La Biblia en España,* 3 vols., Madrid, n.d.
*Brontë, Emily, *Cumbres borrascosas,* Madrid, 1921
Dostoiewski, Fedor, *Un adolescente,* 2 vols., Madrid, 1922
Dostoievski, *El doble,* Madrid, 1920
Dostoiewski, Fedor, *Los hermanos Karamazov,* 4 vols., Madrid, 1927
Girard, P., ed., *Los trágicos griegos,* Madrid, 1919
Hourticq, Louis, *El arte en Francia,* Madrid, 1922

Kipling, Rudyard, *Kim,* Madrid, 1921
Kipling, Rudyard, *La litera fantástica,* Madrid, 1921
Mann, Tomás, *La muerte en Venecia, Tristán,* Madrid/Barcelona, 1920
Menéndez Pidal, Ramón, *Estudios literarios,* Madrid, 1920
*Naval y Ayerve, Francisco, *Tratado compendioso de arqueología y bellas artes,* Madrid, 1920
Philippe, Charles-Louis, *La madre y el niño,* Madrid, 1920
Real Academia Española, *Diccionario de la lengua española,* Madrid, 1925
*Reinach, Salomon, *Apollo,* Paris, 1922
Stapley, Mildred, *Tejidos y bordados populares españoles,* Madrid, 1924
*Turguénev, I., *Anuchka, Un incendio en el mar, Pequeños poemas en prosa, El brigadier,* Madrid, n.d.
Turró, R., *Filosofía crítica,* Madrid, 1919
Wells, H. G., *Esquema de la historia,* 2 vols., Madrid, 1925
Wells, H. G., *El país de los ciegos y otras narraciones,* Madrid, 1919
Wilde, Oscar, *Un marido ideal, La importancia de llamarse Ernesto,* Madrid, 1923
Wilde, Oscar, *Una mujer sin importancia, El abanico de Lady Windermere,* Madrid, 1923
Wilde, Oscar, *El príncipe feliz y otros cuentos,* Madrid, 1920
Wilde, Oscar, *El retrato de Dorian Gray,* 2 vols., Madrid, 1919

12. BOOKS LEFT UNBOUND, PUBLISHED 1914 TO 1927

Adès, Albert, and Albert Josipovici, *Le Livre de Goha le simple,* Paris, 1919
Alembert, D', *Discurso preliminar de la Enciclopedia,* Madrid, 1920
El arte en España, 19 vols., Barcelona, n.d. (First 19 volumes of this series published from 1914-1934)
Azorín, *La voluntad,* Madrid, 1919
Balzac, H. de, *Un asunto tenebroso,* 2 vols., Madrid, 1921
Balzac, H. de, *Eugenia Grandet,* Madrid, 1920
Balzac, H. de, *La piel de zapa,* Madrid, 1923
Berkeley, Jorge, *Tres diálogos entre Hilas y Filonús,* Madrid, 1923
Betí Bonfill, Manuel, *El pintor cuatrocentista Valentín Montoliu,* Castellón, 1927
Biron, Réginald, *Table générale de l'Année Liturgique du R. P. Dom Prosper Guéranger,* Tours, 1924
Caminero, Francisco Javier, *El libro de Job,* Madrid, n.d.
César, C. Julio, *La guerra de las Galias,* Madrid/Barcelona, 1919
Darwin, C., *El origen de las especies,* 3 vols., Madrid, 1921
Diderot, *La paradoja del comediante,* Madrid, 1920
Un doigt de la lune: conte d'amour hindou, Paris, 1919
Dozy, R., *Historia de los musulmanes en España,* 4 vols., Madrid/Barcelona, 1920

*Eça de Queiroz, *Una campaña alegre,* Madrid, n.d.
*Eça de Queiroz, *San Onofre,* Madrid, n.d.
Eckermann, Juan Pedro, *Conversaciones con Goethe,* 3 vols., Madrid, 1920
Fabre, J. H., *Los destructores,* Madrid/Barcelona, 1920
Fabre, J. H., *La vida de los insectos,* Madrid/Barcelona, 1920
Ganivet, Ángel, *Epistolario,* Madrid, 1919
Gautier, Teófilo, *Viaje por España,* 2 vols., Madrid, 1920
Gide, André, *Les Nourritures terrestres,* Paris, 1924
Gómez-Moreno, Manuel, *Catálogo monumental de España: Provincia de León,* 2 vols., Madrid, 1925-6
Gómez-Moreno, Manuel, *Catálogo monumental de España: Provincia de Zamora,* 2 vols., Madrid, 1927
Góngora, *Versos,* Córdoba, 1927
Gudiol y Cunill, Joseph, *En bach de Roda,* Vich, 1915
Gudiol, Joseph, *El bisbetó,* n.p., n.d.(*Lectura popular,* no. 239)
Gudiol y Cunill, Joseph, *L'indumentària litúrgica,* Vich, 1918
Gudiol y Cunill, Joseph, *El museu arqueológich-artistich episcopal de Vich en 1919,* Vich, 1920
Guasp, Gonzalo, *Espronceda,* Madrid, n.d.
Hebbel, Christian Friedrich, *Herodes y Mariene,* Madrid, 1923
Heine, Enrique, *Cuadros de viaje,* Vols. I-III, Madrid, 1920-1
Hume, David, *Tratado de la naturaleza humana,* 3 vols., Madrid, 1923
Jörgensen, Johannes, *Santa Catalina de Siena,* Madrid, 1924
José de Ciria y Escalante, Madrid, 1924
Joyce, James, *El artista adolescente,* Madrid, 1926
Larbaud, Valéry, *Amants, heureux amants...,* Paris, 1923
La Rochefoucauld, *Memorias,* Madrid, 1919
Loti, Pierre, *El desierto,* Barcelona, 1925
Luengo, Emilio, *Agua y fiebre tifoidea,* n.p., 1927
Luengo, E., et al., *Conferencias en relación con la ingeniería sanitaria dadas sucesivamente por los señores Bello, Pittaluga, Luengo y González Quijano,* n.p., n.d.
Madariaga, Salvador de, *Semblanzas literarias contemporáneas,* Barcelona, 1924
*Mamin Sibiriak, *Los millones,* Madrid, 1921
*Marichalar, Antonio, *Girola,* n.p., 1926
Mélida, José Ramón, *Catálogo monumental de España: Provincia de Cáceres,* 3 vols., Madrid, 1924
*Merimée, Próspero, *Crónica del reinado de Carlos IX,* Madrid, 1920
Monlaur, Reynés, *Jerusalén,* Barcelona, 1925
O'Neill, Eugenio, *El emperador Jones, Antes del desayuno,* Madrid, n.d.
Orueta y Duarte, Ricardo de, *La vida y obra de Pedro de Mena y Medrano,* Madrid, 1914
*Pittaluga, Gustavo, *La guerra entre el Adriático y los Alpes,* Madrid, 1917
Shakespeare, W., *Las alegres comadres de Windsor,* Madrid, 1923

Shakespeare, W., *La comedia de las equivocaciones*, Madrid, 1924
Shakespeare, W., *Enrique VIII*, Madrid, 1923
Shakespeare, W., *Hamlet*, Madrid, 1922
Shakespeare, W., *Julio César*, Madrid, 1921
Shakespeare, W., *Macbeth*, Madrid, 1920
Shakespeare, W., *Noche de Epifanía*, Madrid, 1924
Shakespeare, W., *El rey Juan*, Madrid, 1924
Shakespeare, W., *Ricardo II*, Madrid, 1923
Shakespeare, W., *Ricardo III*, Madrid, 1921
Shakespeare, W., *La tempestad*, Madrid, 1924
Stendhal, *La vida de Enrique Brulard*, Madrid, n.d.
Tagore, Rabindranath, *Morada de paz*, Madrid, 1919
Taine, H., *Notas sobre Inglaterra*, 2 vols., Madrid, 1920
Valera, Juan, *Dafnis y Cloe*, Madrid, 1927
Valera, Juan, *Las ilusiones del doctor Faustino*, 2 vols., Madrid, 1926
Valera, Juan, *Morsamor*, Madrid, 1926
Valera, Juan, *Pepita Jiménez*, Madrid, 1925
*Vega Inclán, El marqués de la, *La casa de Cervantes*, Valladolid, 1918
*Vega Inclán, El marqués de la, *Yuste y la Sierra de Gredos*, Madrid, 1919
Virgilio Marón, Publio, *Eglogas y Geórgicas*, Madrid, 1924
Voltaire, *Historia del imperio de Rusia bajo Pedro el Grande*, 2 vols., Madrid, 1921
Wells, H.-G., *La Merveilleuse Visite*, Paris, n.d.

13. BOOKS PUBLISHED 1928 TO 1930

Annunzio, Gabriel d', *Sueño de una mañana de primavera, La ciudad muerta*, Madrid, n.d.
*Artigas, Miguel, *Semblanza de Góngora*, Madrid, 1928
Azorín, *Old Spain, Brandy, mucho Brandy, Comedia del Arte*, Madrid, 1929
*Baeza, Ricardo, *Clasicismo y romanticismo*, Madrid, n.d.
Balart, Federico, *Dolores*, Barcelona, 1929
Balart, Federico, *Horizontes*, Barcelona, 1929
Bell, Clive, *Civilización*, Madrid, 1929
Bourget, Paul, *El demonio de mediodía*, 2 vols., Madrid, 1930
Castro, Américo, *Santa Teresa y otros ensayos*, Santander, 1929
Clarín, *Doña Berta, Cuervo, Superchería*, Madrid, n.d.
Cossío, Manuel B., *De su jornada*, Madrid, 1929
Driesch, Hans, *El acto moral*, Madrid, 1929
Driesch, Hans, *El hombre y el universo*, Madrid, n.d.
Escholier, Raimundo, *La vida gloriosa de Víctor Hugo*, 2 vols., Paris, 1930
Fleg, Edmond, *Moïse*, Paris, 1928
Frank, Waldo, *Primer mensaje a la América Hispana*, Madrid, 1930

Frank, Waldo, *Redescubrimiento de América,* Madrid, 1929
Garcilaso de la Vega, El Inca, *Antología de los comentarios reales,* Madrid, 1929
Gide, André, *Corydon,* Madrid, 1929
Giraudoux, Jean, *Siegfried,* Madrid, 1930
Golferichs, Macario, *La Alhambra,* Barcelona, 1929
Harris, Frank, *Vida y confesiones de Oscar Wilde,* 2 vols., Madrid, 1928
Herriot, Eduardo, *La vida de Beethoven,* Madrid, n.d.
Hessen, J., *Teoría del conocimiento,* Madrid, 1929
Hoyland, J. S., *Breve historia de la civilización,* Madrid, 1930
Huici, S., and V. Juaristi, *El santuario de San Miguel de Excelsis (Navarra) y su retablo esmaltado,* Madrid, 1929
Husserl, Edmundo, *Investigaciones lógicas,* 4 vols., Madrid, 1929
Katz, David, *El mundo de las sensaciones táctiles,* Madrid, 1930
Krische, Pablo, *El enigma del matriarcado,* Madrid, 1930
Lakhovsky, Jorge, *El secreto de la vida,* Madrid, 1929
Ludwig, Emil, *Le Fils de l'homme,* Paris, 1928
Ludwig, Emil, *Julio, 1914,* Barcelona, 1929
Ludwig, Emil, *El Kaiser Guillermo II,* Barcelona, 1929
Ludwig, Emil, *Napoleón,* Barcelona, 1929
Luengo, Emilio, *El paludismo en las zonas mineras, Los anquilostomiasis en las minas españolas,* Madrid, 1928
Madariaga, Salvador de, *Ingleses, franceses, españoles,* Madrid/Barcelona, 1929
Magre, Maurice, *Magiciens et illuminés,* Paris, 1930
Maurois, André, *Ariel; o, La vida de Shelley,* Madrid, 1930
Maurois, André, *Lord Byron,* Madrid, n.d.
Mayer, Augusto L., *El estilo gótico en España,* Madrid, 1929
Meinhold, Hans, *Sábado y domingo,* Madrid, 1929
Mommsen, Th., *Histoire romaine,* 7 vols., Paris, n.d.
Nola, Ruperto de, *Libro de guisados,* Madrid, 1929
Notovich, N., *La vida desconocida de Jesucristo,* Barcelona, n.d.
Ortega y Gasset, José, *El espectador, VIII,* Madrid, 1929
Ortega y Gasset, *Kant,* Madrid, 1929
Paleologo, Mauricio, *Cavour,* Madrid, 1930
*Pastor, José Francisco, ed., *Las apologías de la lengua castellana en el siglo de oro,* Madrid, 1929
Pereyra, Carlos, *Las huellas de los conquistadores,* Madrid, 1929
*Pereyra, Carlos, *La obra de España en América,* Madrid, 1930
Pérez Galdós, Benito, *Memorias,* Madrid, 1930
Pfandl, Ludwig, *Introducción al estudio del siglo de oro,* Barcelona, 1929
Pi y Margall, F., *Las nacionalidades,* Madrid, 1929
Rathenau, Walther, *Crítica de la época,* Barcelona, n.d.
Rolland, Romain, *Beethoven,* 2 vols., Paris/Madrid, 1929
Saenger, Samuel, *Stuart Mill,* Madrid, 1930
Sarasola, Luis de, *San Francisco de Asís,* Madrid, 1929

Scheler, Max, *El puesto del hombre en el cosmos,* Madrid, 1929
Siebeck, Hermann, *Aristóteles,* Madrid, 1930
Smith, Sydney, *Early History of Assyria,* London, 1928
Stevenson, Robert Louis, *Aventuras de un mayorazgo escocés,* Madrid, 1929
Suarès, André, *Variables,* Paris, 1929
Urabayen, Leoncio, *La casa navarra,* Madrid, 1929
Valera y Menéndez Palayo, *Epistolario,* Madrid, 1930
Villa-Urrutia, El marqués de, *El general Serrano,* Madrid, 1929
Wassermann, Jakob, *Cristóbal Colón,* Madrid, 1930
Wilde, Oscar, *La balada de la cárcel de Reading,* Madrid, 1929
Wilde, Oscar, *Epistola: In carcere et vinculis (De profundis),* Madrid, 1929
Wilde, Oscar, *Epistolario inédito,* Madrid, 1929
Wilde, Oscar, *Palabras, ideas, crítica,* Madrid, 1929
Zweig, Stefan, *Tres maestros,* Madrid, 1929

14. BOOKS INSCRIBED BY THEIR AUTHORS, TRANSLATORS, OR EDITORS

Alberti, Rafael, *Marinero en tierra,* Madrid, 1925
Alonso, D., ed., *Góngora: Soledades,* Madrid, 1927
Alonso, Dámaso, *Temas gongorinos,* Madrid, 1927 (From *Revista de filología española,* 14 (1927))
Alvarez del Vayo, Julio, *Rusia a los doce años,* Madrid, 1929
Azorín, *Blanco en azul,* Madrid, 1929
Azorín, *Castilla,* Madrid, 1912
Azorín, *Las confesiones de un pequeño filósofo,* Madrid, 1909
Azorín, *Félix Vargas,* Madrid, 1928
Azorín, *Lecturas españolas,* Madrid, 1912
Azorín, *Superrealismo,* Madrid, 1929
Bacarisse, Mauricio, *Mitos,* Madrid, n.d.
Batlle, Y. Carmen de, *Cuentos españoles de autores contemporáneos,* Paris, 1930
Bergamín, José, *El cohete y la estrella,* Madrid, 1923
*Bergamín, José, *Tres escenas en ángulo recto,* Madrid, 1925
*Bernácer, Germán, *Sociedad y felicidad,* Madrid, 1916
Blanco Fombona, Horacio, *Panoramas mejicanos,* Madrid, 1929
Carayon, Marcel, *Lope de Véga,* Paris, 1929
Carco, Francis, *Printemps d'Espagne,* Paris, 1929
Carner, Josep, *Verger de les galanies,* Barcelona, 1911
    Les monjoies, Barcelona, 1912
    Auques i ventalls, Barcelona, 1914
    La paraula en el vent, Barcelona, n.d.
    (Bound as one volume)
Chabás y Martí, J., *Espejos,* Madrid, 1921
Chabás, Juan, *Puerto de sombra,* Madrid, n.d.

Chacón Enríquez, Juan, *Eduardo Rosales,* Madrid, 1926
Clascar, Frederic, *Evangeliari,* Barcelona, 1913
Clascar, Frederic, *El Gènesi,* Barcelona, 1915
Clascar, Frederic, *Vindicació documental d'unes notes al Gènesi,* Barcelona, 1915
Conde, Carmen, *Brocal,* Madrid, 1928-9
Cornet, Bartolomé, *Versos,* Mexico, 1909
Correa-Calderón, *Índice de utopías gallegas,* Madrid, 1929
Diego, Gerardo, ed., *Antología poética en honor de Góngora,* Madrid, 1927
Diego, Gerardo, *Versos humanos,* Madrid, 1925
Díez-Canedo, Enrique, *Epigramas americanos,* Madrid, 1928
Domenchina, Juan José, *La corporeidad de lo abstracto,* Madrid, 1929
Espina, Antonio, *Luis Candelas,* Madrid, 1929
Esplugues, Miquel d', *Semblances,* Barcelona, 1916
Estrada, Genaro, *Crucero,* Mexico, 1928
Floretes de Sant Francesch, Barcelona, 1909 (Translated and presented by Joseph Carner)
Frédérix, Pierre, *Goya,* Paris, 1928
Gallegos, Rómulo, *Doña Bárbara,* Barcelona, 1929
Gallegos, Rómulo, *La trepadora,* Barcelona, 1930
Gallinal, Gustavo, *Crítica y arte,* Montevideo, 1920
*García Martí, Victoriano, *El sentimiento de lo eterno,* Madrid, 1929
Garrido Merino, Edgardo, *El barco inmóvil,* Madrid, 1928
Gaziel, *Hores viatgeres,* Barcelona, 1926
*Gil-Albert, Juan, *Como pudieron ser,* Valencia, 1929
*Gómez de la Serna, Ramón, *La sagrada cripta de Pombo,* Vol. II, Madrid, n.d.
González, Fernando, *Viaje a pie,* Paris, 1929
*González Blanco, Andrés, *Los contemporáneos: Primera serie,* Vol. I, Paris, n.d.
Grau, Jacinto, *El Conde Alarcos,* Madrid, 1917
Grau, Jacinto, *En Ildaria...,* Madrid, 1917
Grau, Jacinto, *El hijo pródigo,* Madrid, 1918
*Grau, Jacinto, *El señor de Pigmalion,* Madrid, 1921
Guarner, Luis, ed., *Antología lírica de Jacinto Verdaguer,* Madrid, n.d.
Gudiol y Cunill, Joseph, *El mobiliari litúrgich,* Vich, 1920
Guillén, Jorge, *Cántico,* Madrid, 1928
Guzmán, Martín Luis, *La sombra del caudillo,* Madrid/Barcelona, 1929
Hebbel, *Judit,* Barcelona, 1918 (Translated and presented by Ramón M. Tenreiro)
Iglesias Figueroa, Fernando, *Toledo,* Madrid, 1928
Jarnés, Benjamín, *El convidado de papel,* Madrid, 1928
Jarnés, Benjamín, *Locura y muerte de nadie,* Madrid, 1929
Jarnés, Benjamín, *El profesor inútil,* Madrid, 1926
Jarnés, Benjamín, *Sor Patrocinio,* Madrid, 1929
Jiménez, Juan Ramón, *Eternidades,* Madrid, 1918

Jiménez, Juan Ramón, *Piedra y cielo,* Madrid, 1919

Jiménez, Juan Ramón, *Poesías escojidas,* New York, 1917

Johnson, Ben, *Volpone; o, El zorro,* Madrid, 1929 (Translated and presented by Luis Araquistain)

Lafora, Gonzalo R., *Don Juan, Los milagros y otros ensayos,* Madrid, 1927

*Laguía Lliteras, Juan, *Humos de señorío,* Barcelona, 1918

Larbaud, Valéry, *Enfantines,* Paris, 1918

Larbaud, Valéry, *Fermina Márquez,* Paris, n.d.

Ledesma Miranda, *Antes del mediodía,* Madrid, 1930

León, Ricardo, *Alcalá de los Zegríes,* Málaga, 1910

León, Ricardo, *Casta de hidalgos,* n.p., 1908

León, Ricardo, *Los centauros,* Madrid, 1912

Loon, Hendrik W. van, *Historia de la humanidad,* Barcelona, 1930 (Translated and presented by Juan Gutiérrez Gili)

López-Picó, J. M., *Espectacles i mitología,* Barcelona, 1914

Maragall, J., *Artículos (1893-1903),* Barcelona, 1904

Marichalar, Antonio, *Riesgo y ventura del Duque de Osuna,* Madrid, 1930

Martínez Sotomayor, José, *La rueca de aire,* Mexico, 1930

Massó-Ventós, Josep, *Arca d'ivori,* Barcelona, 1912

Mazorriaga, Emeterio, *Platón el divino,* Vol. I, Madrid, 1918

Menéndez Pidal, R., *Flor nueva de romances viejos,* Madrid, 1928

Mínguez, Joan, *Dies verges,* Barcelona, 1929

*Morales, Tomás, *Poemas de la gloria, del amor y del mar,* Madrid, 1908

Morales, Tomás, *Las rosas de Hércules,* 2 vols., Madrid, 1919-22

*Nadal, Alfonso, *Místico amor humano,* Barcelona, 1925

Nervo, Amado, *Juana de Asbaje,* Madrid, 1910

Ors, Eugenio d', *Cuando ya esté tranquilo,* Madrid, 1930

Ors, Eugeni d', *Glosari 1906,* Barcelona, 1907

Ossorio, Ángel, *Derecho y estado,* Madrid, 1928

Ossorio, Ángel, *La justicia poder,* Madrid, 1927

*Pedroni, José B., *La gota de agua,* Buenos Aires, 1923

Pí Suñer, Augusto, *Los mecanismos de correlación fisiológica, adaptación interna y unificación de funciones,* Barcelona, 1920

Pí Suñer, Augusto, *La unidad funcional,* Barcelona, n.d.

Pittaluga, Gustavo, *La intuición de la verdad y otros ensayos,* Madrid, 1926

Pittaluga, Gustavo, *Una teoría biológica del vicio,* Madrid, 1925

Pittaluga, Gustavo, *El vicio, la voluntad, la ironía,* Madrid, n.d.

Poema de mío Cid, Madrid, 1926 (Modernised and presented by Pedro Salinas)

*Prado, Pedro, *Alsino,* Santiago de Chile, 1920

*Quesada, Alonso, *La umbría,* Madrid, 1922

Reyes, Alfonso, *El plano oblicuo,* Madrid, 1920

Ríos Urruti, Fernando de los, *La filosofía del derecho en Don Francisco Giner,* Madrid, 1916

Rodezno, Conde de, *Carlos VII,* Madrid, 1929

Rodó, José Enrique, *Motivos de Proteo,* Montevideo, 1909

Romero y Murube, Joaquín, *Sombra apasionada,* Seville, 1929

Ruiz Manent, José Ma., *Balmes, la libertad y la constitución,* Madrid, 1929

Ruyra, Joaquim, *Marines y boscatges,* Barcelona, 1907

Sainz y Rodríguez, P., *Don Bartolomé José Gallardo y la crítica literaria de su tiempo,* New York/Paris, 1921 (From *Revue Hispanique,* 51 [1921])

Salaverría, José María, *Nuevos retratos,* Madrid, 1930

Salinas, Pedro, *Presagios,* Madrid, 1923

Salinas, Pedro, *Seguro azar,* Madrid, 1929

Salinas, Pedro, *Víspera del gozo,* Madrid, 1926

Sayé, Luis, *Profilaxis de la tuberculosis,* Barcelona, 1924

Suarès, André, *Poète tragique,* Paris, 1921

Suarès, André, *Sur la vie,* 2 vols., Paris, 1925

Suriñach Senties, R., *Petites proses,* Barcelona, n.d.

Tenreiro, Ramón María, *La esclava del señor,* Madrid, 1927

Torón, Saulo, *El caracol encantado,* Madrid, 1926

Torre, Claudio de la, *El canto diverso,* Madrid, 1918

Torre, Claudio de la, *En la vida del señor Alegre,* Madrid, 1924

Torre, Claudio de la, *La huella perdida,* Madrid, 1920

Torres Bodet, Jaime, *La educación sentimental,* Madrid, n.d.

Turró, R., *Filosofia critica,* Barcelona, 1918

Turró, R., *Orígenes del conocimiento,* Barcelona, n.d.

Unamuno, Miguel de, *La sfinge senza Edipo,* Milan, 1925
    (Translated and presented by Piero Pillepich)

Urbina, Luis G., *Puestas de sol,* Paris/Mexico, 1910

Valle Arizpe, Artemio de, *Ejemplo,* Madrid, 1919

Valle-Inclán, Ramón del, *El resplandor de la hoguera,* Madrid, 1909

Valle-Inclán, Ramón del, *Romance de lobos,* Madrid, 1908

Vegue y Goldoni, Ángel, *Temas de arte y de literatura,* Madrid, 1928

15. Books listed by Clemencia Miró, but now missing

Delgado, Félix, *Paisajes y otras visiones*

Diccionario valenciano

Ercilla, *La Araucana;* Balbuena, *El Bernardo,* 1 vol.

La España del siglo XIX, 3 vols.

Eurípides, *Tragedias*

Freud, *Obras completas,* 12 vols.

Gracián, *Morales de Plutarco,* 1761

Josué, Eduardo, *Libro de regla o cartulario de la antigua abadía de Santillana del Mar*

Llopis Villamil, *Cartas de conspiradores*
Lomas, F. G., *Diccionario latino-español*
Lytton, *Los últimos días de Pompeya*
Maura, Gabriel, *Carlos II y su corte*, 2 vols.
Moore, *El epicuro*, 2 vols.
Romey, *Historia de España*, Vols. II-IV
Sófocles, *Tragedias*
Vallejo, Juan de, *Memorial de la vida de Fray Francisco Jiménez de Cisneros*

BIBLIOGRAPHY

For the writings of Gabriel Miró the fundamental bibliography is that by Clemencia Miró in *El lugar hallado,* ed. Joaquín Fuster, Polop de la Marina, 1952. It is brought up to 1970 and partly incorporated in Ramos, *Mundo,* pp. 459-73.

For writings on Gabriel Miró see the bibliography by Clemencia Miró and Juan Guerrero Ruiz in *Cuadernos de literatura contemporánea,* Nos. 5-6 (1942), 245-282. This is also continued to 1970 and incorporated in Ramos, *Mundo,* pp. 473-509.

The following bibliography lists works cited.

1. BOOKS BY GABRIEL MIRÓ

a) *Obras completas, Edición conmemorativa,* 12 vols., Barcelona, 1932-1949. The authoritative text, accompanied by lists of variants and bibliographies of the works included, and prefaces by Azorín (Vol. I), Unamuno (II), Marañón (III), Augusto Pí Suñer (IV), Ricardo Baeza (V-VI), Salinas (VII), Oscar Esplá (VIII), Dámaso Alonso (IX), Madariaga (X), Gerardo Diego (XI), Duque de Maura (XII).

The volumes are arranged as follows:

I   *Del vivir, La novela de mi amigo*
II   *Las cerezas del cementerio*
III   *Dentro del cercado, La palma rota, Los pies y los zapatos de Enriqueta*
IV   *El abuelo del rey, Nómada*
V-VI *Figuras de la Pasión del Señor*
VII   *Libro de Sigüenza*
VIII *El humo dormido, El ángel, el molino, el caracol del faro*
IX   *Niño y grande, Corpus y otros cuentos*
X   *Nuestro padre San Daniel*
XI   *El obispo leproso*
XII   *Años y leguas*

However, since this edition is rare, references in the text are usually to:

b) *Obras completas,* fourth edition, one volume, Madrid, 1961
c) *Glosas de Sigüenza,* Buenos Aires, 1952 (a collection of articles edited by Clemencia Miró)
d) Other separately published items :
    La mujer de Ojeda, Alicante, 1901. Includes a preface by Luis Pérez Bueno
    Hilván de escenas, Alicante, 1903
    Del vivir, Alicante, 1904
    El hijo santo (Los contemporáneos, No. 24), Madrid, 11 June 1909
    Amores de Antón Hernando (Los contemporáneos, No. 48), Madrid, 26 Nov. 1909
    Del huerto provinciano, Nómada, Barcelona, 1912
    Los amigos, los amantes y la muerte, Barcelona [1915]
    Dentro del cercado, La palma rota, Barcelona [1916]
    Niño y grande, Madrid, 1922. Includes comments on the *Figuras* by Antonio Maura, Azorín, and Unamuno.
    Del huerto provinciano, Nómada, Barcelona, 1930

2. ARTICLES BY GABRIEL MIRÓ

'Domingo Carratalá', in *De mi barrio,* ed. E. Mendaro del Alcázar, Alicante, 1901, pp. 46-9

'Cartas vulgares', *El Ibero,* 16 Jan. 1902, pp. 43-5

'Del natural', *El Ibero,* 16 March, 1 and 16 April, 1 and 16 May 1902, pp. 99, 117, 140, 161, and 169

'Vulgaridades', *El Ibero,* 1 and 16 June, 1 and 16 July, 1 Aug. 1902, pp. 188, 209, 231, 248, and 270

'A don Benito Pérez Galdós : El maestro', *La República de las letras,* 22 July 1907

'Las cerezas del cementerio : Fragmento de una carta del libro que, con dicho título, se publicará pronto', *Heraldo de Madrid,* 5 Aug. 1907

'Historia que no se cuenta', *Revista Latina,* 1, No. 2 (30 Oct. 1907), 19-22 (an early version of *El hijo santo*)

'Cuartillas de Miró', *Heraldo de Madrid,* 16 Feb. 1908 (text in Ramos, *Vida,* pp. 120-3)

'En un pueblo', *Revista Latina,* 2, No. 5 (29 Feb. 1908), 27-31

'Ofrenda', *Diario de Alicante,* 21 May 1908 (text in Ramos, *Vida,* pp. 128-32)

'Del huerto provinciano : Galeote de su fama', *Los Lunes de el Imparcial,* 15 Feb. 1909

'Del salón de retratos : F. Figueras Pacheco', *Gérmenes,* 15 March 1909 (copy only seen)

'El recuerdo', *Correspondencia de Alicante,* 24 Aug. 1909 (copy only seen)

'La coronación del maestro', *Diario de Alicante*, 13 Nov. 1909 (copy only seen)

'Altamira en su huerto provinciano', *Prometeo*, 3, No. 15 (1910), 14-18

'Oradores en el huerto provinciano', *Diario de Alicante*, 24 Nov. 1910 (signed 'Tomé Cecial' — copy only seen)

'Las últimas vestales', *Diario de Alicante*, 7 Jan. 1911

'Oradores en el «huerto provinciano»', *Diario de Alicante*, 16 Jan. 1911 (signed 'T. C.')

'El mantenedor', *Diario de Alicante*, 2 Aug. 1911

'Pláticas: La paz lugareña', *Diario de Barcelona*, 8 Sept. 1911, pp. 12500-1

'Figuras de antaño', *Diario de Barcelona*, 1 Oct. 1911, pp. 13752-4

'Pláticas: Literatura feminista. — «Yolanda», *Diario de Barcelona*, 8 Oct. 1911, pp. 14140-1

'Pláticas: Nosotros. — La sonrisa del Sultán', *Diario de Barcelona*, 10 Dec. 1911, pp. 17900-2

'Pláticas: Los estudiantes. — En las Audiencias y en la vida', *Diario de Barcelona*, 13 Dec. 1911, pp. 18052-3

'Pláticas: El amor de las ciudades', *Diario de Barcelona*, 18 Jan. 1912, pp. 871-2

'Pláticas: El alto asiento.—Cajas de fósforos vacías', *Diario de Barcelona*, 9 May 1912, pp. 7390-1

'Pláticas: De los comerciantes', *Diario de Barcelona*, 23 Oct. 1912, pp. 15642-3

'Pláticas: De las corridas de toros', *Diario de Barcelona*, 28 Nov. 1912, pp. 17452-3

'Un libro', *Diario de Barcelona*, 11 Jan. 1913, pp. 472-3

'Comentado', *Diario de Barcelona*, 21 Feb. 1913, pp. 2558-9

'Figuras de la Pasión del Señor: Pilato', *Diario de Barcelona*, 19 March 1913, pp. 3941-3

'Asuntos crematísticos', *Diario de Barcelona*, 13 June 1913, pp. 8202-3

'Cosas viejas y sabidas', *Diario de Barcelona*, 2 Aug. 1913, pp. 10462-4

'Jornadas de Sigüenza: La hermosa señora', *La Vanguardia*, 20 Dec. 1913, pp. 8-9

'Jornadas de Sigüenza: En la ciudad grande', *La Vanguardia*, 27 Feb. 1914, p. 9

'Jornadas de Sigüenza: Nosotros', *La Vanguardia*, 13 March 1914, pp. 8-9

'Jornadas y comentarios de Sigüenza: De la lectura de «La Bien Plantada»', *La Vanguardia*, 19 April 1914, pp. 12-13

'Páginas inéditas', *Clavileño*, No. 26 (March/April 1954), 61-2 (First pub. in *Música*, 5 April 1915, pp. 51-2)

'La potestad de un juez', *Diario de Alicante*, 10 May 1917

'Los dejos de los días: Pan y queso', *La Publicidad*, 3 July 1919, p. 3 (signed 'Félix Olivar')

'Los dejos de los días: La momia de Jacob', *La Publicidad*, 29 Oct. 1919, p. 1

'Los dejos de los días: Almas medianas', *La Publicidad,* 2 Nov. 1919, p. 1

'Nuevas jornadas de Sigüenza: I — Lector: La nariz', *La Publicidad,* 1 Sept. 1920, p. 1

'Estudio histórico del templo de San Vicente de Ávila', *Clavileño,* No. 16 (July/Aug. 1952), 65-72

'Estudio histórico de la iglesia y convento de Santo Tomás de Ávila', *Clavileño,* No. 17 (Sep./Oct. 1952), 66-71

'Lo viejo y lo santo en manos de ahora', in Vicente Ramos, *Literatura alicantina,* Barcelona, 1966, pp. 300-17

'¿Por qué no escribe usted para el teatro?: Don Gabriel Miró', *ABC,* 16 June 1927, pp. 10-11

3. BOOKS AND ARTICLES BY OTHERS

(Works cited because Miró quotes from them, or because they are in his library, are omitted.)

Aguado, José María, in 'Boletín de literatura', *La ciencia tomista,* 19 (1927), 243-5

Alberich, José, *Los ingleses y otros temas de Pío Baroja,* Madrid, 1966

Albert Berenguer, Isidro, *Bibliografía de la prensa periodística de Alicante y su provincia,* Alicante, 1958

Alcover, R., 'El gallinero literario: El premio Fastenrath', *El Siglo Futuro,* 25 Jan. 1927, p. 1

Alonso, Dámaso, *La lengua poética de Góngora,* Madrid, 1950

Astrana Marín, Luis, 'El estilo leproso', *El Imparcial,* 27 Feb. 1927, pp. 5-6

Astrana Marín, Luis, 'Más sobre el estilo leproso', *El Imparcial,* 6 March 1927, p. 5

Astrana Marín, Luis, 'El homosexualismo en nuestras letras', *El Imparcial,* 13 March 1927, p. 5

Azorín, *Obras completas,* Vol. VI, Madrid, 1948

Baeza, Ricardo, 'Gabriel Miró, prosista', *El Sol,* 9 April 1927, p. 1

Baeza, Ricardo, 'Prosa de Gabriel Miró', *El Sol,* 14 April 1927, p. 1

Baeza, Ricardo, 'La prosa pura y Gabriel Miró', *El Sol,* 16 April 1927, p. 1

Baquero Goyanes, Mariano, '*Las cerezas del cementerio,* de Gabriel Miró', in E. Alarcos, et al., *El comentario de textos,* Madrid, 1973

Baquero Goyanes, Mariano, *Perspectivismo y contraste,* Madrid, 1963

Baroja, Pío, *Desde la última vuelta del camino,* Vol. V, *La intuición y el estilo,* Madrid, 1948

Becker, Alfred W., *El hombre y su circunstancia en las obras de Gabriel Miró,* Madrid, 1958

Berkowitz, H. Chonon, *La biblioteca de Benito Pérez Galdós,* Las Palmas, 1951

Bernácer, Germán, 'Evocación de Gabriel Miró', *Sigüenza* (Alicante), May 1945, pp. 5-6

Bernácer, Julio, 'Estampa mironiana', in *El clamor de la verdad*, Orihuela, 2 Oct. 1932, p. 8

Bernácer, Julio, 'Gabriel Miró o la pureza artística', *Eco*, May 1934

Brown, G. G., *The Twentieth Century* (*A Literary History of Spain*, Vol. VI), London, 1972

Candamo, Bernardo G. de, 'La novela de mi amigo', *El faro*, 18 Oct. 1908, p. 450

Cansinos-Assens, R., *La nueva literatura*, 2 vols., Madrid, n.d.

Casalduero, Joaquín, *Estudios de literatura española*, Madrid, 1962

Casares, Julio, *Crítica efímera*, Madrid, 1962

Castro, C. de, 'El panteísmo de Gabriel Miró', *Heraldo de Madrid*, 5 Aug. 1907

Cejador y Frauca, Julio, 'Valle-Inclán y Gabriel Miró', *Nuevo mundo*, 25 April 1919

Cejador y Frauca, Julio, *Historia de la lengua y literatura castellana*, Vol. XII, Madrid, 1920

Chabás y Martí, Juan, 'Crítica concéntrica: Gabriel Miró', *Alfar*, No. 38 (March 1924), pp. 7-14

Chabás y Martí, Juan, 'Un libro nuevo', *La Libertad*, 10 Dec. 1926, pp. 6-7

Dehennin, Elsa, *La Résurgence de Góngora*, Paris, 1962

Diego, Gerardo, 'Gabriel Miró', *Cuadernos de literatura contemporánea*, Nos. 5-6 (1942), 200-8

Díez-Canedo, Enrique, 'Gabriel Miró: «El humo dormido»', *La Ilustración Española y Americana*, 8 May 1920, p. 272

Díez de Tejada, Vicente, 'Crónica: Señales de los tiempos', *El Liberal*, 16 April 1916, p. 1

Entrambasaguas, Joaquín de, 'Gabriel Miró', in *Las mejores novelas contemporáneas*, ed. Entrambasaguas, Vol. IV, Barcelona, 1959, pp. 595-726

Esplá, Oscar, *Evocación de Gabriel Miró*, Alicante, 1961

Fernández Almagro, Melchor, 'Una novela de Gabriel Miró', *La Epoca*, 18 Dec. 1926, p. 3

Fernández-Galiano, Manuel, 'El mundo helénico de Gabriel Miró', *Ínsula*, No. 53 (15 May 1950), p. 1

Figueras Pacheco, Francisco, 'La mujer de Ojeda', *El Ibero*, 16 Nov. 1901

Gil-Albert, Juan, *Gabriel Miró*, Valencia, 1931

Giménez Caballero, Ernesto, 'El obispo de Miró', *El Sol*, 21 Dec. 1926, p. 2

Giménez Caballero, Ernesto, 'Gabriel Miró', *El Sol*, 20 April 1928, p. 1

González-Blanco, Andrés, *Los contemporáneos*, Series I, Vol. 2, Paris [1907]

González-Blanco, Andrés, *Historia de la novela en España desde el romanticismo a nuestros días*, Madrid, 1909

González Olmedilla, J., '«El obispo leproso», novela de Gabriel Miró' *Heraldo de Madrid,* 18 and 25 Jan. 1927, pp. 4 and 4

González-Ruano, César, 'Un sillón vacío en la Academia: Gabriel Miró no se presenta candidato', *Diario de Alicante,* 28 Dec. 1929

González Ruiz, Nicolás, 'Las ideas y el estilo de Gabriel Miró', *El Debate,* 4 March 1927, p. 8

Guardiola Ortiz, José, *Biografía íntima de Gabriel Miró,* Alicante, 1935

Guillén, Jorge, *Language and poetry,* Cambridge, Mass., 1961

Gullón, Ricardo, *La invención del 98 y otros ensayos,* Madrid, 1969

Hoyos, Antonio de, 'Un gran creador de filosofía y estética', *Revista Latina,* 30 Oct. 1907, pp. 33-6

Huidobro, Vicente, *Obras completas,* 2 vols., Santiago de Chile, 1964

Jarnés, Benjamín, 'De Sigüenza a Belén', *La Gaceta literaria,* 15 Jan. 1927

King, E. L., 'Gabriel Miró y «el mundo según es»', *Papeles de Son Armadans,* 21 (May 1961), 121-42

King., E. L., 'Gabriel Miró introduced to the French', *Hispanic Review,* 29 (1961), 324-32

King, E. L., ed., G. Miró, *El humo dormido,* New York, 1967

Lott, Robert E., *Language and psychology in 'Pepita Jiménez',* Urbana, 1970

Maeztu, Ramiro de, *Las letras y la vida en la España de entreguerras,* Madrid, 1958

Maragall, Joan, *Obres completes,* Barcelona, 1947

Marquerie, A., and Melchor Fernández Almagro, 'Valle-Inclán, Azorín, Baroja, Miró, Gómez de la Serna: ¿Han influído en el estilo de nuestros escritores jóvenes?', *A B C,* 11 Nov. 1945

Marquina, Rafael, 'Homenaje a Gabriel Miró', *Heraldo de Madrid,* 18 Jan. 1927, p. 4

Mendaro del Alcázar, E., ed., *De mi barrio,* Alicante, 1901

Mingot, J., 'La mujer de Ojeda' (Cutting from Alicante?, 1901? newspaper, at Biblioteca Gabriel Miró, Alicante)

Montero Alonso, José, 'La fiesta del libro', *La Libertad,* 8 Oct. 1930, p. 8

Morize, André, *Problems and methods of literary history,* Boston, 1922

Mudarra y Párraga, Prudencio, *Lecciones de literatura general y literatura española,* Seville, 1895

Navarro y Ledesma, F., 'Hilván de escenas, por Gabriel Miró', *Lectura,* 3 (1903), 363-4

Nora, Eugenio G. de, *La novela española contemporánea,* Vol. I, second ed., Madrid, 1963

Nuez, Sebastián de la, 'Cartas de Gabriel Miró a Alonso Quesada', *Papeles de Son Armadans,* 47 (1967), 72-105

Ortega y Gasset, José, 'Un libro: «El obispo leproso»: Novela, por Gabriel Miró', *El Sol,* 9 Jan. 1927, p. 3.

Ortega y Gasset, José, *Obras completas,* Vol. III, sixth ed., Madrid, 1966

Palau y Dulcet, A., *Manual del librero hispanoamericano,* Barcelona, 1923-27, and 1948-

Pina, Francisco, 'Orihuela y Gabriel Miró' (Cutting dated 28 May 1932, seen at Biblioteca Gabriel Miró, Alicante)

Precioso, Artemio, '«El obispo leproso» por Gabriel Miró', *El Liberal,* 18 Jan. 1927, p. 1

Pujol, Juan, 'Al otro lado del desierto', *Heraldo de Madrid,* 17 June 1911

Ramos, Vicente, *Vida y obra de Gabriel Miró,* Madrid, 1955

Ramos, Vicente, *El mundo de Gabriel Miró,* second edition, Madrid, 1970

Ripoll, Enrique María, *Memoria: Liga de contribuyentes de Alicante y su provincia,* Alicante, 1895

Rivas Cherif, C., 'Autobiografía sin comentarios y notas al margen de una conversación con Gabriel Miró', *Heraldo de Madrid,* 18 Jan. 1927, p. 4

Robin, Marcel, 'Lettres espagnoles', *Mercure de France,* 16 Sept. 1912, pp. 430-4

Roig, Rosendo, 'Diálogo con el padre de Gabriel Miró', *Hechos y dichos,* April 1965, pp. 383-5

Romano, Julio, 'Pío Baroja nos habla del escritor Hermann Hesse', *Madrid,* 20 Nov. 1946, p. 3

Ruiz-Castillo, J., '«Hilván de escenas», por Gabriel Miró, Alicante, 1903', *Helios,* 10 (1903), 372

Sainz Rodríguez, Pedro, 'El momento de Miró', *El Liberal,* 5 April 1927, p. 1

Salinas, Pedro (Reports of his lecture given to the Lyceum-Club, Madrid), *El Sol, A B C,* 14 Nov. 1931

Sampelayo, Jesús H., and Sadi de Buen, *La lepra y el problema de la lepra en España,* Madrid, 1923

Sobejano, Gonzalo, *Nietzsche en España,* Madrid, 1967

Suriñach Sentíes, R., 'L'hoste: En Gabriel Miró a Barcelona', *La veu de Catalunya,* 22 Nov. 1913, p. 1

Tenreiro, Ramón María, 'Las cerezas del cementerio, por Gabriel Miró', *Lectura,* Nov. 1911, pp. 324-7

Tenreiro, Ramón María, 'El abuelo del rey', *Diario de Alicante,* 1 Oct. 1915

Tenreiro, Ramón María, 'Libro de Sigüenza, por Gabriel Miró', *Lectura,* 3 (1918), 70-1

Tenreiro, Ramón María, 'Gabriel Miró: El obispo leproso', *Revista de Occidente,* Jan. 1927, pp. 114-23

Torrente Ballester, Gonzalo, *Panorama de la literatura española contemporánea,* second ed., 2 vols., Madrid, 1961

'Vargas, Luis de' (Andrés González-Blanco), 'La vida literaria: Gabriel Miró: Del vivir', *La República de las Letras,* 8 July 1905, pp. 7-8

Wardman, H. W., *Ernest Renan,* London, 1964

Woodward, L. J., 'Les images et leur fonction dans «Nuestro Padre San Daniel» de G. Miró', *Bulletin Hispanique,* 56 (1954), 110-32

Xenius, 'Del novecentista Gabriel Miró', *Diario de Alicante,* 8 April 1911

UNSIGNED NEWSPAPER ARTICLES:

'Gabriel Miró Ferrer', *Heraldo de Madrid,* 22 Jan. 1908, p. 1

'Banquete a Miró, *El Mundo,* 16 Feb. 1908, p. 3

'La novela de mi amigo', *El Liberal,* 14 Oct. 1908, p. 2

'Día tras día', *La Tribuna,* 13 Feb. 1913

'Miró juzgado por los escritores', *Heraldo de Madrid,* 18 Jan. 1927, p. 4

'Gabriel Miró, propuesto para candidato', *El Sol,* 24 Feb. 1927, p. 1

'El obispo leproso, novela', *La Vanguardia,* 26 Feb. 1927, p. 1

'Gabriel Miró: El gran escritor falleció anoche', *La Noche* (Barcelona), 28 May 1930, p. 13

'Anoche, a las nueve y media, falleció el insigne literato Gabriel Miró', *A B C,* 28 May 1930

'Gabriel Miró, nuestro ilustre y querido colaborador falleció ayer en Madrid', *El Sol,* 28 May 1930

'Anoche falleció el insigne escritor Gabriel Miró', *La Libertad,* 28 May 1930, p. 3

'En la muerte de Miró', *El Debate,* 29 May 1930, p. 1

'La prensa', *La Libertad,* 30 May 1930, p. 1

'Mesa revuelta', *El Siglo Futuro,* 31 May 1930, p. 2

INDEX

Italicised page-numbers are used to indicate references to Miró's works where the title of the work itself is not mentioned.

17

COLECCION TAMESIS

SERIE A - MONOGRAFIAS

The Comedias of Calderón. A facsimile edition prepared by D. W. Cruickshank and J. E. Varey, with textual and critical studies. 19 vols. (Published in collaboration with Gregg International Publishers Limited.)

CRITICAL GUIDES TO SPANISH TEXTS

(Publicadas en colaboración con Grant and Cutler Limited)

J. E. VAREY: *Pérez Galdós: Doña Perfecta.*
JENNIFER LOWE: *Cervantes: Two novelas ejemplares.*
VERITY SMITH: *Valle-Inclán: Tirano Banderas.*
D. L. SHAW: *Gallegos: Doña Bárbara.*
P. HALKHOREE: *Calderón de la Barca: El alcalde de Zalamea.*
A. TERRY: *Antonio Machado: Campos de Castilla.*
R. A. CARDWELL: *Blasco Ibáñez: La barraca.*
J. W. SAGE: *Lope de Vega: El caballero de Olmedo.*
J. D. RUTHERFORD: *Leopoldo Alas: La Regenta.*
C. A. JONES: *Sarmiento: Facundo.*
D. Henn: *Cela: La colmena.*
N. G. Round: *Unamuno: Abel Sánchez.*